Shadows of Doubt

Shadows of Doubt

Language and Truth in Post-Reformation Catholic Culture

STEFANIA TUTINO

OXFORD
UNIVERSITY PRESS

OXFORD
UNIVERSITY PRESS

Oxford University Press is a department of the University of Oxford.
It furthers the University's objective of excellence in research, scholarship,
and education by publishing worldwide.

Oxford   New York
Auckland   Cape Town   Dar es Salaam   Hong Kong   Karachi
Kuala Lumpur   Madrid   Melbourne   Mexico City   Nairobi
New Delhi   Shanghai   Taipei   Toronto

With offices in
Argentina   Austria   Brazil   Chile   Czech Republic   France   Greece
Guatemala   Hungary   Italy   Japan   Poland   Portugal   Singapore
South Korea   Switzerland   Thailand   Turkey   Ukraine   Vietnam

Oxford is a registered trademark of Oxford University Press
in the UK and certain other countries.

Published in the United States of America by
Oxford University Press
198 Madison Avenue, New York, NY 10016

© Oxford University Press 2014

Library of Congress Cataloging-in-Publication Data
Tutino, Stefania.
Shadows of doubt : language and truth in post-reformation Catholic culture / Stefania Tutino.
pages cm
Includes bibliographical references and index.
ISBN 978–0–19–932498–9 (hardcover : alk. paper) — ISBN 978–0–19–932499–6 (ebook)
1. Catholic Church—History—Modern period, 1500–   2. Truth—Religious aspects—Christianity.
3. Language and languages—Religious aspects—Catholic Church.   I. Title.
BX1330.T88 2014
282.09'03—dc23
2013015744

1 3 5 7 9 8 6 4 2
Printed in the United States of America
on acid-free paper

*Siamo molto superficiali, io e voi. Non andiamo ben addentro allo scherzo, che è più
profondo e radicale, cari miei. E consiste in questo: che l'essere agisce necessariamente per
forme, che sono le apparenze ch'esso si crea, e a cui noi diamo valore di realtà. Un valore
che cangia, naturalmente, secondo l'essere in quella forma e in quell'atto ci appare. E ci deve
sembrare per forza che gli altri hanno sbagliato; che una data forma, un dato atto non è
questo e non è così. Ma inevitabilmente, poco dopo, se ci spostiamo d'un punto, ci accorgiamo
che abbiamo sbagliato anche noi, e che non è questo e non è così; sicché alla fine siamo
costretti a riconoscere che non sarà mai né questo né così in nessun modo stabile e sicuro;
ma ora in un modo ora in un altro, che tutti a un certo punto ci parranno sbagliati, o tutti
veri, che è lo stesso; perché una realtà non ci fu data e non c'è, ma dobbiamo farcela noi, se
vogliamo essere: e non sarà mai una per tutti, una per sempre, ma di continuo e infinitamente
mutabile. La facoltà d'illuderci che la realtà d'oggi sia la sola vera, se da un canto ci sostiene,
dall'altro ci precipita in un vuoto senza fine, perché la realtà d'oggi è destinata a scoprire
l'illusione domani. E la vita non conclude. Non può concludere. Se domani conclude, è finita.*

Luigi Pirandello, Uno, nessuno e centomila

CONTENTS

ACKNOWLEDGMENTS

I could not have written this book, indeed I could not do my job, without being able to count on the competence, generosity, and kindness of the staff of the libraries and archives where I work. I am especially grateful to Mons. Alejandro Cifres, Fabrizio De Sibi, and Daniel Ponziani at the Archivio della Congregazione per la Dottrina della Fede; Prof. Martín Morales, Cristina Berna, Lorenzo Mancini, and Irene Pedretti at the Archivio della Pontificia Università Gregoriana; Mauro Brunello, Francesco Stacca, and Salvatore Vassallo at the Archivum Romanum Societatis Iesu; Giovanni Castaldo and Carlo Piacentini at the Archivio Segreto Vaticano; the staff of the manuscript room and early printed books room at the Biblioteca Apostolica Vaticana; Giuseppe Finocchiaro at the Biblioteca Vallicelliana.

Also, while working on this book I have enjoyed the support, criticism, and suggestions of many friends and colleagues. Among them, I would like to mention Hilary Bernstein, Alison Bjerke, Anna Boschetti, Tom Carlson, Tom Cogswell, Simon Ditchfield, Lori Anne Ferrell, Michael Geiss, Margaret Jacob, Carol Lansing, Marc Lerner, Anthony Milton, Adriano Prosperi, Debora Shuger, Jon Snyder, Ann Taves, Nicholas Terpstra, Alexandra Walsham, Colleen Windham-Hughes, Ronald Witt. I am grateful to Alessandro Vascon for providing the cover image.

I would like to thank the editorial staff at Oxford University Press, especially Charlotte Steinhardt and Cynthia Read, who even in difficult times never failed to offer advice and encouragement. This book has benefited from the insightful and engaged criticism provided by the anonymous readers: even though I did not follow all of the suggestions they gave me, their comments were immensely helpful in refining my thinking. Of course, I take full responsibility for the final shape that this book has taken.

I had the opportunity to discuss parts of the second and third chapters, respectively, at the 2010 Mellon workshop on early modern studies at the University of California, Riverside, and at the 2011 History of Political Ideas Seminar at the Institute of Historical Research, University of London. I am grateful to the conveners (Richard Bourke, Randy Head, Jeanette Kohl, and Avi Lifschitz) and to the participants for their stimulating feedback. A version of the first chapter was published as "Nothing but the truth? Hermeneutics and morality in the doctrines of equivocation and mental reservation in early modern Europe," in *Renaissance Quarterly* 64, no. 1 (2011), pp. 115–155 (© 2011 by The University of Chicago Press).

As the reader will see, by focusing on the relationship between truth and language this book seeks to identify and make sense of connections between the past world of early modern Catholic intellectuals and the present intellectual and cultural context. I should add here that this book connects the past and the present at a different and distinctively personal level. I grew up in Sicily, in a small town that, like many others in my region, perfectly embodies a long and deep-seated tradition of economic depression and utter disrespect for any kind of civic and social rule. Despite the fact that my immediate family and my neighbors had many desires that could not be satisfied and many needs that could not be met, one thing that we had in great abundance was the ability to tell good stories. We all told stories, as I remember, in which we were simultaneously characters and narrators. We told stories to help each other make sense of things or to make things more bearable or because if you just managed to say it in another way, then things would become actually different. We told story *per passarci il tempo*—a typically Sicilian grammatical idiosyncrasy that can be translated simultaneously as "so that we can pass the time" and "so that we can surpass, or overtake, time." When I was young, it did not occur to me that the manifold and complex ways in which this Sicilian expression connects narrative and time deserved much thought—to be honest, nothing about that place and those people seemed to me worthy of much thought at that time. Only later did I begin to reflect seriously on the nexus of language, reality, and temporality while reading the work of the thinkers who have informed much of my own intellectual perspective and whose presence looms large in this book. In a way, this book is my attempt to find some sort of continuity between what I knew then and what I know now and to make sense of what I was then and of what I have become. I want to dedicate it to my town, a great place to be from: Divieto, frazione di Villafranca Tirrena, provincia di Messina.

LIST OF ABBREVIATIONS

ACDF   Archivio della Congregazione per la Dottrina della Fede, Rome
APUG   Archivio della Pontificia Università Gregoriana, Rome
ARSI   Archivum Romanum Societatis Iesu, Rome
ASV   Archivio Segreto Vaticano, Rome
BAV   Biblioteca Apostolica Vaticana, Rome
BOD   Bodleian Library, Oxford
PL   *Patrologia Latina*, 221 vols. (ed., J. P. Migne, Paris 1844–1865)
VAL   Biblioteca Vallicelliana, Rome

Unless otherwise noted, all the translations are my own. Whenever I quoted from manuscripts or from certain specific kinds of printed primary sources, I modernized the punctuation when I thought it could facilitate reading, but apart from that I reproduced the citations as I found them in the original. Also, unless otherwise noted, the scriptural quotations in English are from the King James Version of the Bible; those in Latin are from the *Vulgata*.

Shadows of Doubt

Introduction

Looking out from the Edge of the Cliff: History,
Language, and Truth

This book is simultaneously a work of history and a work on history. This is to say that this book presents not only my attempt to give a fresh account of certain debates, themes, and doctrines usually associated with a supposedly culturally sterile and intellectually decadent "Counter-Reformation" but also the fruit of my reflections on how I see my own work as a historian. This latter aspect is perhaps less visible in the overall structure of my book, and yet this book was actually conceived as I began to grapple with the theoretical and methodological premises of my work. In the spirit of historical and historiographical self-awareness, I offer a brief account of the genesis of my methodological reflections, and I hope that the reader will forgive a short detour to my own intellectual biography.

I was not yet born when Hayden White published *Metahistory* (1973) and when Michel de Certeau published *L'écriture de l'histoire* (1975). When the first edition of Paul Ricoeur's *Temps et récit* appeared (1983–1985), I was in elementary school. In 1990 I was in junior high school when Saul Friedlander organized a conference at UCLA, which represented a fundamental moment in the dramatic debate over the ethical, not just epistemological, consequences of the so-called linguistic turn in historiography.[1] In my college and graduate school years, I came out of Foucault's work, which I have always taken in its most structuralist sense, mostly unscathed (this might have been a mistake, perhaps a forgivable one). Instead, I was influenced (without entirely being aware of it until much later) by two different forces. One, which I breathed daily at the Scuola Normale Superiore in Pisa, where I studied, was that of Arnaldo Momigliano and his muscular attitude toward historical documents and historical reality. The other, which I embraced in part as a form of teenager-like rebellion against my alma mater, was that of the poststructuralist hermeneutics of Gadamer and, looming hazily in the background, of Heidegger. In a sense, I became a historian

1

because I have always been captivated by the centrality of the question of temporality, and I have always struggled with making sense of how the existential condition of being-in-time affected my own attitude toward the past.

This brief account should have shown that in my intellectually formative years I never experienced the tension between historical representation and the reality of the past with the urgency of somebody fighting on the front line. Rather, with the tendency to dramatize and simplify that is typical of young people, I looked at those frontline combatants, people like Ginzburg and Momigliano on the one side and White, Derrida, and Barthes on the other, almost in the same way as I look at Hector and Achilles: heroes of a time in which Troy was still standing and in need of being conquered. By the time I came of age as a historian, it seemed to me that the debate over the epistemological and ethical implications of the linguistic turn had grown out of its most dramatic and violent phase. Thanks to the works of scholars as different in their approaches as Roger Chartier, Pierre Bourdieu, Gabrielle Spiegel, Lynn Hunt, and Allan Megill (just to pick a few people out of a much longer list that certainly deserves a more accurate treatment than I am giving it now), I could detect a sort of cease-fire, in which it became possible to bury the dead and reckon with the outcome of the battle.

The fact that I lived my adult life in what I perceived as a time of relative peace rather than war meant that for many years I did not give much thought to the tension between narrative and truth. Rather, I treated it as an endemic, chronic, rarely painful, and ultimately benign cyst in the body: I knew it was there, but more often than not I could safely ignore its presence. This book is the result of my decision to stop ignoring the cyst and to start thinking about it instead. In other words, this book was conceived when I decided to really grapple with the fact that, on the one hand, I am fully aware of the narrative dimension of history and of the peculiar condition of loss that affects our being-in-time and has distinctive effects on historians insofar as they are human beings steeped in time and engaged in looking at and through time. On the other hand, however, I find myself holding on with deep conviction and almost unshakable faith to the belief that the product of my narrative enterprise as a historian aims at finding some truth (here I mean truth without qualifications, inverted comas, or other ironic linguistic markers). I believe that the product of my historical work seeks to offer a true narrative of the past, being fully aware of the tension between the epistemological import of the adjective "true," the poetic dimension of the noun "narrative," and the epistemological as well as ethical implications of using the indefinite article "a." I (and, I suspect, many other historians of my generation) know full well that we stand like Felix the Cat on the edge of the cliff, as Michel de Certeau said while speaking about Foucault's work,[2] but I also know that I can still look out from the edge because my belief in the truth-value of history functions as a powerful break that will keep my car from falling into the sea beyond.

Once I realized the centrality and the complexity of the tension between a force pushing me toward the cliff and a different force that at the same time prevents me from falling, I decided that I wanted to make this tension a core feature of my work as a practicing historian of post-Reformation Catholicism. I am aware that other historians have engaged with different aspects of the same question and have tried to use the methodological and epistemological insight provided by the tension between narrative and reality as tools for a properly historical, rather than simply theoretical, investigation. In this respect, the works of, among others, Elizabeth Clark, Constantin Fasolt, Gabrielle Spiegel, and especially Susan Schreiner have paved the way for the kind of investigation that I am proposing in this book, which is intended as a contribution to this line of scholarship.[3]

The premise of the historical argument I make in this book is that the tension between the linguistic and the extralinguistic world, which is at the core of what we call the linguistic turn in historiography and is presupposed as a starting point for the reflections of postmodern philosophy, is a fundamental and constitutive element of our current intellectual horizon. Taking seriously the hermeneutical, moral, and epistemological anxieties of postmodernity allows me to connect historically with early modernity by means of a newly found sensitivity to the fractures and discontinuities between language, reality, and truth. This, in turn, allows me to see features of early modernity that have always been present in it but that before have not been visible because the intellectual horizon of traditional historians of post-Reformation Catholicism, generally speaking, did not allow those features to come to the fore. The result of my looking at early modern Catholicism with fresh eyes and with a pair of self-aware and self-conscious postmodernist glasses, so to speak, is that I can see early modern Catholicism not simply as a world of solid certainties to be opposed to the Protestant falsehoods but also as a world in which the stable Truth of theology existed alongside with, indeed contributed to originate, a number of far less stable truths concerning the world of men. In this perspective, then, post-Reformation Catholic culture was concerned not only with articulating, affirming, or in certain cases negating absolute truths but also with exploring the complex tension between certainty and uncertainty. Scholarship on post-Reformation Catholicism has for the most part ignored this shadowy aspect, which occupies a precarious, delicate, and in some sense liminal position between the two opposite poles of dogmatism and skepticism while remaining equally distinct from both. My book seeks to recover it and to bring it to light; through this fascinating lens, I argue, we will be able to reconsider the significance of several authors, texts, and themes that have usually been denigrated as minor by-products of the "Counter-Reformation." By t, post-Reformation Catholic culture emerges from my investigation as t laboratory for many of the issues that we face today: it was a world of fractures and fractured truths that we, equipped with a heightened sensitivity to discrepancies and discontinuities, are now well suited to understand.

My book does not want to be an exercise in what Kant thought was understanding Plato better than himself, in the sense that I do not wish to obliterate the past by means of the present. Rather, I use the present in order to illuminate parts of the past that would otherwise remain and that, in fact, have so far mostly remained hidden in the dark. Or to paraphrase John Lewis Gaddis, I am aware that in choosing our present theoretical concerns to map the past I am in some measure oppressing it. At the same time, however, I am also liberating it "from the prospect of being forgotten," thus making the past, in this specific case early modern Catholic culture, free to be relevant to the present.[4] In this book, therefore, I seek, not to erase, but to think through the distance between the current theoretical frameworks and the early modern intellectual and theological context.[5] In their elaborations on the relationship between truth and language, current postmodern intellectuals articulate the complex, multiform, and fractured nature of the relationship between human subjectivity and the objective reality of the world outside. Early modern Catholic intellectuals and theologians, by contrast, could neither perceive nor articulate such fundamental fractures in the relationship between truth and language, given the centrality of the Truth of theology in post-Reformation Catholic culture. This Truth, in fact, was independent from and at the same time made sense of the linguistic and nonlinguistic truth of men. While the distance between the early modern and the postmodern world is undeniable, nevertheless I argue that some early modern Catholic theologians started to harbor some doubts on the firmness and tightness of the bond connecting language, human truth, and divine Truth, and thus they started to perceive the fragility of the system. These initial, embryonic, hermeneutical and epistemological doubts coexisted with and to a certain extent were originated by the need to assert and defend the absolute theological Truth. From this perspective, these embryonic doubts connect the distant early modern world of strong convictions to our current world of weakened and complicated certainties. Late modern and postmodern critical theory is an insightful means to bring to the fore the implications of such doubts, both in the early modern intellectual and theological context and in the longer history of Western thought. In sum, the doctrines, discussions, and elaborations that this book examines are the early modern symptoms of a postmodern disease—or the early modern initial signs of a postmodern recovered health. Either way, postmodernity can provide not just the prognosis but also a very acute diagnosis.

Essentially, in this book I try to identify, articulate, and make sense of connections between the past and the present. One could define the specific intersection between the traces of the past and the intellectual tools provided to me here and now as a case of hermeneutical fusion of horizons, à la Gadamer. One could also attribute the connections I present to the peculiar quality of historical narrative, a specific kind of poetic creation that "stands for" the reality of the dead past as an indelible reference for the sake of the present reader, à la Ricoeur. Moreover, if Lyotard was right and postmodernism is what modernity forecloses at its inception before the modern can actually begin,[6] the fact that early modernity and postmodernity resonate with one another should not be surprising. Indeed, this resonance will not surprise anybody familiar with that particular form of dialogue between the historian and the past, a dialogue in which, as Marc Bloch wrote, even the "clearest and most accommodating" historical documents will "speak only when they are properly questioned."[7] While reflecting on the changes he saw in the historical scholarship of his own time, Carlo Sigonio remarked, somewhat gloomily, "*alia tempora nunc, alii mores.*"[8] We can say the same now: times are different and historians' questions are changing. Historians, in turn, must listen to the new answers provided by the "accommodating documents" while, at the same time, recognizing and respecting their foreignness, the silence of what no longer is, as Michel de Certeau put it. Or to borrow from Caroline Bynum, "we must never forget to watch ourselves knowing the otherness of the past, but this is not the same as merely watching ourselves."[9]

In concluding this section on the general framework informing my book, I should probably restate openly that I have no pretense to follow, provide, or articulate a specific theoretical model. In fact, while the reader will certainly see in this book the presence, both explicit and implicit, of those theorists who have influenced me the most, she will not find a comprehensive and philosophically stringent theory of history. Rather, to say it with Burckhardt, this book simply records what I, living in this present age, find worthy of note in the early modern age.[10] Thus, I hope that the reader will find it an honest and sincere attempt to look at a time past on the part of a historian who is aware of being steeped in and caged by a specific cultural, intellectual, and social present.

In terms of structure, my book is framed as a collection of case studies centered on the relationship of language, the truth of men, and the Truth of theology. Most of these case studies concern little-known figures in the history of early modern Catholicism. While we can appreciate the militant aspects of post-Tridentine Catholicism by studying people like Robert Bellarmine or Cesare Baronio, the solid pillars of the intellectual and theological structure of the Church of Rome, if we want to see the shadowy side of early modernity we need to dive into the demimonde of post-Reformation Catholicism.

We need to examine the thinkers whom few scholars mention and fewer read, the unexpressed possibilities, the roads not taken. It is precisely by looking at the margins that we can see the seeds of doubt being planted and starting to germinate. This is not to say that the solid intellectual and theological pillars of post-Reformation Catholicism were completely free from any epistemological and theological tension, and in fact in this book readers will see some instances in which the same seeds of doubt germinated in the work of prominent theologians engaged in high-profile debates. Indeed, the question of the nature of papal authority, which was central to the theological, political, and ecclesiological identity of the post-Tridentine Catholic Church, was subject to a great deal of controversy, not only in political and theological terms but also from the point of view of language and interpretation.[11] I believe, however, that by highlighting minor thinkers who have so far received little attention and by putting them alongside the better known and more distinguished figures, we will gain a more accurate sense of the complex and multidimensional nature of post-Reformation Catholic culture.

Moreover, the case studies I examine in this book pertain to different topics in the field of early modern Catholic culture. Each of these topics has its own specialized literature and has often been examined by current scholarship in isolation from the others. Nevertheless, it is important to remember that disciplinary boundaries are very different now from what they were in the early modern world, where moral theology, historiography, and rhetoric were all parts of the same intellectual universe. I have thus decided to sacrifice a measure of thematic coherence in order to give readers a taste of what has now become an unfamiliar intellectual system.

Finally, I should add that the topics I selected for this book are not, of course, meant to provide an exhaustive treatment of how the hermeneutical and epistemological doubts I examine emerged in the entire post-Reformation Catholic culture, since there are many other contexts in which one could have followed this theme. For instance, one of the most interesting features of post-Reformation Catholic culture is its global, not simply European, dimension. In this respect, the Jesuit and Catholic missionaries who sought to spread the Gospel around the world encountered a number of linguistic and theological problems when they needed to translate the Truth of Catholicism into a different language and into a different cultural context. European Catholics were, in turn, influenced by the cultural context they tried to Christianize; thus this two-way process of cultural translation produced fascinating results, theologically, hermeneutically, and epistemologically.[12] However, taking these global questions into account seemed outside the scope of this work and outside the expertise of its author, both limited to the center rather than expanding into the periphery of the Catholic world.

The first chapter provides a reconsideration of the relationship between language and truth in early modern theological thought by illuminating the hermeneutical anxieties emerging from the doctrines of equivocation and mental reservation. Felipe Fernández-Armesto's book on the history of truth contains a brief section dedicated to the doctrine of equivocation in early modern Europe. In that section Fernández-Armesto remarked that today equivocation "has disappeared from the witness-stand" because "equivocation was a necessary resource against interrogation in a world of strong convictions, when deponents were not in any serious doubt about the truth or falsehood of what they said."[13] This passage summarizes most of the current view on equivocation and mental reservations: doctrines that expressed the elasticity (or lack thereof) of certain moral and theological convictions in a world in which strong convictions were fighting one another, assuming the correspondence between language and reality as a certainty. Against this common view, I argue instead that the doctrine of equivocation did in fact betray a fundamental doubt about the capability of language to reflect reality truly and truthfully.

The second chapter examines the relationship between truth and language in early modern history writing, especially in that genre of post-Humanist historiography known as *ars historiae*. Traditional scholarship has judged the *artes historiae* mainly as trite collections of equally trite tropes and precepts.[14] In this chapter I question this traditional view. I focus on Agostino Mascardi, an ex-Jesuit intellectual and author of a five-volume treatise entitled *Dell'arte historica* and published in 1636. Mascardi's reflections are very different from the methodological developments both of the French school of historical jurisprudence exemplified by Jean Bodin's *Methodus*, and of the seventeenth-century antiquarians already described by Arnaldo Momigliano. This, however, does not mean that Mascardi's "narrativist" approach collapsed facts into fiction. Rather, Mascardi elaborated a novel theory of history in which the documentary and empirical dimension of historical research was both distinct from and complementary to the narrative and poetic dimension of history writing. Thus, my examination of Mascardi's work in its intellectual context reveals that Mascardi's *ars historiae* offered fundamental insight into crucial questions for the development of historiography, such as the relationship between narrative and fact, the truth-value of history, and the tension between documents, explanation, and interpretation.

The third chapter focuses on ecclesiastical history and on the debate among Catholic intellectuals on the advantages and limitations of using historical documents to uncover the Truth of the Catholic Church. I start with an examination of the relationship between theology and philology in Cesare Baronio. While virtually all scholars working on Baronio have seen the cardinal's documentary prowess and his ideological commitment as two forces that pulled him in

opposite directions, I argue that for Baronio the Truth of dogma was the necessary condition for, not a limitation to, his documentary criticism. After exploring the implications of Baronio's view of the indissoluble link between historical
truth and theological Truth, I show how other Catholic intellectuals challenged
Baronio precisely because they started to harbor some doubts on the coherence and stability of his system of linking human traces and theological dogmas.
Among these intellectuals, this chapter focuses in particular on Paolo Beni, who,
like Mascardi, was an ex-Jesuit theologian and literary critic active at the end of
the sixteenth century and the beginning of the seventeenth. On several occasions during the course of his career Beni criticized Baronio's work—a rather
controversial move in post-Reformation Rome, which contributed to putting
Beni at odds with the Catholic hierarchy of his time. Beni's criticism of Baronio
stemmed from his deep-rooted hermeneutical and theological doubt on the
very possibility of writing a "human" history of a divine institution. My analysis
of Beni's arguments and of the controversy that they originated brings to light
the important implications of Beni's position for the development of ecclesiastical historiography and, more generally, for the question of how to conceptualize
the relationship of traces, documents, and theology.

Chapter 4 analyzes another critical moment of tension between language and
reality by focusing on some aspects of the teaching of rhetoric in post-Reformation
Rome. Thanks to the seminal works of John O'Malley and Marc Fumaroli, historians are now quite familiar with the importance of rhetoric in early modern
theological and political culture, and influential work has recently been done on
the relationship between rhetoric and homiletics in early modern Catholicism.
This chapter focuses in particular on two Jesuit professors of rhetoric, Pedro Juan
Perpiñán and Famiano Strada. Perpiñán taught rhetoric at the Roman College
between 1561 and 1565. Together with such people as Marc-Antoine Muret and
Francesco Benci, Perpiñán was an integral part of the intellectual circle that in
the second half of the sixteenth century revisited Ciceronianism and adapted
it to the new challenges faced by the post-Reformation Catholic Church. In
addition, Perpiñán was one of the main figures involved in the systematization
of Jesuit education prior to the finalization of the *Ratio Studiorum*, and he was
also in charge of revising the first edition of Cipriano Soares's *De arte rhetorica
libri tres*, which became the main textbook of rhetoric in all Jesuit schools and
as such an international bestseller. Famiano Strada was professor of rhetoric
at the Roman College between 1600 and 1614. One of the most sophisticated
intellectuals of his time, Strada was also a historian (the author of a two-volume
history of the Dutch revolt entitled *De bello Belgico*, published between 1632
and 1647) and a theorist of history (a section of his *Prolusiones academicae*, published in 1617, was a dialogue, entitled "Muretus," devoted to the question of
the relationship between history and truth). Scholars of early modern Catholic

culture do not doubt that both Perpiñán and Strada had a pivotal role in setting the tone for the Jesuit (and Catholic) elaboration on rhetoric, but they usually interpret Perpiñán and Strada mainly as masters of style. By contrast, I argue that Perpiñán and Strada made rhetoric the linchpin of a novel hermeneutical theory centered on language as the medium that connects humans with their world, thus providing a powerful new way of articulating the fragility of the bond linking language, human reality, and theological certainties.

The fifth and final chapter examines the early modern debate on the hermeneutical aspects of the oath, which Giorgio Agamben suggestively defined as the "sacrament of language."[15] According to Agamben, oaths should be considered the most sacred form of language because they are composed of words that are meant to "become" reality. From this perspective, an oath is not simply an example of performative language at its most effective, but it is indeed the closest human approximation to the creative power of the divine Word: a word that makes things in the very moment it is uttered. Agamben's "philosophical archaeology" of the oath is both a response to and a critique of the religio-juridical historical interpretation of oaths given by Paolo Prodi, according to whom an oath is a "sacrament of power," that is, the basis for political pacts in western Europe.[16] In this chapter I bridge Agamben's linguistic perspective and Prodi's religio-juridical history: I argue that by focusing on the early modern elaborations on the oath as the sacrament of language we can get a historically and philosophically significant sense of an important evolution in the ways in which Western civilization articulated the ties linking language, thought, and reality. In my reading, the oath becomes almost a synecdoche of the human experience of language and of the historical and philosophical effort to find meaningful ways to connect one's words to one's world.

Telling the Truth: Equivocation
and Mental Reservation Between
Morality and Hermeneutics

The doctrines of equivocation and mental reservation represent an ideal starting point for my investigation into the intricate and complex ways in which language and truth were linked in post-Reformation Catholic thought. Examining the distinctive theological and intellectual contexts in which these doctrines were elaborated and the debates which they contributed to originate can open up a valuable window, from which we can see that a fundamental uncertainty over the capability of language to reflect human reality truthfully and truly started to creep in among early modern Catholic thinkers.

This hermeneutical aspect of equivocation and mental reservation has virtually been ignored by traditional scholarship, whose interpretation of these doctrines tends to lean on two basic assumptions. First, most scholars link the Jesuits tightly with these doctrines. Even when the origin of these doctrines is rightly traced back to the Dominican theologian Domingo de Soto and to the canonist Martín de Azpilcueta—better known as Doctor Navarrus, from the region where he was born—many of the scholars working on this topic have focused on the Jesuits as their most original interpreters and most aggressive practitioners or have neglected to show in detail the differences between those early theorists of equivocation and the later Jesuit elaborations.[1] Second, equivocation and mental reservation are usually considered a part of moral theology. Scholars who study equivocation, as well as polemicists who write against it, all seem to agree that this doctrine is a distinctive mode of understanding the relationship between intention and action—to borrow the words of Pascal, whose influence in the scholarly and popular perception of these doctrines should not be underestimated.[2] In this perspective, therefore, equivocation and mental reservation are usually considered and analyzed as a distinctive and more or less ethically acceptable way to allow a certain course of action by bending moral norms traditionally perceived as rigid in the name of a different and higher moral principle.[3]

Of course, there is more than some truth in both of these assumptions: equivocation and mental reservation were indeed theorized and put into practice mostly by Jesuits in early modern Europe, and they became a relevant part of the Jesuits' (and of Catholic) moral theology. However, these elements are only a component, albeit an important one, of the significance of these doctrines. Thus, this chapter offers a different and complementary interpretation by taking into account other elements of the history of these doctrines. In order to do this, we need, first of all, to substitute the traditional backward-looking Pascalian vantage point with a more forward-looking perspective, so to speak. When one notes that the first substantial engagement with and the fullest elaboration of the doctrines of equivocation and mental reservation need to be attributed to Soto and Navarrus, one should also note that those theologians discussed these doctrines with a specific theological and intellectual context in mind, which needs to be explained in detail if we want to gain a historically accurate and intellectually correct view of the genesis of these doctrines. After explaining the intellectual and theological context of the genesis of equivocation and mental reservation, we will clearly see that these doctrines, as conceived by Soto and Navarrus, had less to do with questions of morality than with questions of hermeneutics. In other words, Soto's and Navarrus's elaborations were intended, not to loosen up or modify the rigidity of certain moral norms, but rather to explore the limitations and potentialities of human language and the relationship between words and things.

Once we are able to appreciate the hermeneutical significance of Soto's and Navarrus's elaborations, we will be better able to appreciate the theological and theoretical shift that important Jesuit (and also non-Jesuit) theologians made between the end of the sixteenth and the beginning of the seventeenth century, when they slowly modified the debate on equivocation and mental reservation from a debate over the nature of language to a debate over the moral value of human intentions. Of course, this shift will have important intellectual, theological, and political consequences that can be fully appreciated only by following the developments of these doctrines until the end of the seventeenth century, when the rigorist and antiprobabilist wave crashed against equivocation and mental reservation, wiped the slate clean of their moral undertones, and opened the way for a further hermeneutical reflection.

Let us start where everybody starts—with Augustine. For Augustine, as is abundantly well known, the definition of lying included two elements; that is, *duplex cor* and *intentio fallendi*.[4] According to Augustine's definition, a lie is an utterance that does not accord with the intention of the speaker (*duplex cor*) when the speaker in question is aware of the said lack of accord (*intentio fallendi*).

If the speaker uttered something objectively false—for instance, that the city of Los Angeles was in New England— which she nevertheless thought to be true, she would not be lying, for her mind and mouth would be in perfect accord. By the same token, if a speaker said that Los Angeles was in California, while believing that it was in fact in New England, she would indeed lie, even if her statement expressed a fact.[5]

Augustine's reflections on lying had a lasting impact in the history of Christian thought, and in particular, they left two fundamental legacies. First of all, Augustine's position distinctively excluded any conceptualization of lying as a question of interpretation. For Augustine, language (both truthful and deceitful) was less an act of communication between a speaker and a hearer than the expression of the link (or lack thereof) between the speaker's thought and the speaker's tongue. Indeed, Augustine did not engage profoundly with the question of the hearer's role as an interpreter of the speaker's statement. In fact, the *intentio fallendi* is still measured on the internal relationship between the speaker's intention and utterance, not on the effects or results of the speaker's utterance upon the hearer. This relative lack of consideration for the interpretative aspect of language in Augustine comes from his distinctive theological notion that human language is a gift of God's grace given to humans to express their thoughts. Even though human language is by its very nature relatively unstable and unreliable, nevertheless it can, if properly used, allow us to participate in the essence of God, "the radiant truth-teller," as Paul Griffiths put it.[6] In other words, for Augustine human language is an imperfect form of incarnation, modeled upon the incarnation of Jesus Christ, the *Logos* of the Father. Just as the *verbum Dei*, that is, the unity of God the Father and God the Son, is perfectly realized through the incarnation of the *Logos*, so in human language the mind of the speaker is imperfectly incarnated in the spoken words. Thus, in a sense, this analogy between human language and the *Logos* of God makes speaking not so much a form of communication as a form of adoration or an act of devotion.[7] In this respect, then, the interpretative aspect of language is not relevant to the act of accepting God's gift of speaking, just as the devotional value of, say, kneeling in front of the Cross does not depend on how such kneeling is perceived by the person sitting next to us in a church.

From another perspective, as Hans-Georg Gadamer has suggested, the Augustinian position on language represented a fundamental shift with respect to the Greek notion of separation between the word and the thing or between the inner and the outer world. In contrast to the Greek insistence on separation, for Augustine human language reflects the mystery of the unity between the Father and the Son expressed in the *Logos*, and thus it is precisely through language that the outside world finds a new connection with the inside world.[8] Once again, then, while the Augustinian notion of language has the hermeneutical benefit

over the Greek philosophical tradition of granting a distinctive ontological validity to human language, it still does not address language as dialogue. To put it
differently, Augustine's notion of language as an imperfect reflection of the incarnation of the *Logos* excludes the interpretation of language as a coming to an
understanding, which in a Gadamerian perspective is the true form of coming
into being of human words.[9]

From this first consideration, we can gather the second important legacy of
the Augustinian notion of lying: when someone lies—that is, says something
different from what she has in mind—she always sins, no matter what the circumstances or the effect of the lie might be. Since language is an act of devotion
in that it mirrors the incarnation of the *Logos*, whenever one breaks the bond
between intention and utterance, one ruptures one's relationship with God,
thereby sinning. And since, for Augustine, sin should always be condemned, no
lie can ever be condoned.

The Augustinian position, then, locks up, so to speak, the question of lying
with a double padlock: first, it restricts the definition of lying to the lack of
accordance between the speaker's tongue and thoughts, thus excluding the
hearer from the equation; second, it attaches firmly the act of lying in this
speaker-restricted sense to the moral category of sin. Such a double padlock
would remain mostly intact throughout early modern times; even Aquinas
admitted that lying, insofar as it meant saying something contrary to one's
mind, was always to be considered a sin, even though he distinguished between
different degrees of sinfulness based on the extent to which different kinds of lie
oppose the virtue of charity.[10]

The Hermeneutical Reflection

The Augustinian padlock started to be attacked significantly for the first time
in Spain during the middle of the sixteenth century, when the Spanish Church
saw one of its most turbulent periods. As the Spanish Inquisition, led by Juan
de Tavera, was consolidating its power over the Spanish Church, a number of
important juridical and theological problems came to the fore. Briefly put, the
main jurisdictional tension that emerged between the Inquisition and the rest
of the Spanish Church involved the limitations of the area of competence of the
Inquisition in matters of heresy. More specifically, this tension became manifest
in matters of so-called occult heresy, which involved crimes of heresy for which
there was no witness and that were disclosed to the priest in a sacramental confession. The juridical tension, in turn, highlighted a difficult theological problem
linked to the precept of the so-called *correctio fraterna*, or fraternal correction.
In a nutshell, the question referred to the exegesis of Matthew 18:15, which in

the King James Bible reads: "if thy brother shall trespass against thee, go and tell him his fault between thee and him alone: if he shall hear thee, thou hast gained thy brother." This evangelical precept seemed to impose a private correction for private sins before a public denunciation and prosecution of the crime—but how far could one stretch the limitations of this private correction? As Aquinas explained in *quaestio* 33 of his *IIa IIae*, the evangelical precept was clear enough, but there were many cases in which the opposite practice seemed to be put in place. For instance, usually members of religious orders were asked to publicly confess and were publicly chastised within their own order before making any attempt to correct the sin privately.[11] Thus, as Aquinas seemed to hint at, surely there was some obligation to correct the sinner privately, but there could also be cases in which this obligation could and should be ignored.

By the middle of the sixteenth century this theological knot became a dramatic institutional crisis for the Spanish Church. As the Inquisition claimed more and more space to intervene in matters of occult crimes, some influential clergymen and theologians viewed this intervention as an act of usurpation against the evangelical precept of the fraternal correction. Indeed, the most famous (or infamous) Spanish trial of the sixteenth century, the trial against Bartolomé Carranza de Miranda, archbishop of Toledo, involved precisely the question of *correctio fraterna*. In fact, Carranza was put on trial by the Spanish, later the Roman, Inquisition for, among other things, having "fraternally corrected" the heretical opinions of the Italian gentleman Carlo de Seso in a sacramental confession without denouncing the suspected Italian heretic to the Inquisition.[12]

The Carranza trial was just the sharpest tip of a giant iceberg of theological and juridical debates over the extent to which a sin known in confession should be disclosed by the confessor: was the authority of the Inquisition more powerful than the precept of keeping the confessional seal? Was the Inquisition's intervention in the secret relationship between confessor and sinner an act of police or a means to a more effective correction? Under certain circumstances a confessor could absolve a sinner *in foro conscientiae*—that is, before the tribunal of the conscience rather than before the external tribunal of the Inquisition (in this case)—but which exceptions could and should be made to the rule? And, this being the question that most interests us, if a confessor was questioned by an inquisitor about a sin he had heard in confession, what should he say, and what could he not reveal?[13]

Spanish theologians debated this issue widely and profoundly in the 1540s and 1550s. There were those who, like Bernardino de Arévalo, supported a very limited reading of the evangelical precept expressed in Matthew 18:15 and argued that a person could fraternally correct only those sins committed against himself or herself and, in very limited circumstances, against other people. In no case, however, could a sin against God, such as the sin of heresy, ever be corrected privately. There were theologians who, like Navarrus (one of Carranza's lawyers in the Roman trial), defended the practice of *correctio fraterna* against what they saw as an act of police on the part of the Spanish Inquisition, which was aimed not so much at correcting but at defaming the sinner.[14] There were also theologians who, like Domingo de Soto, assumed a very influential and relatively Inquisition-friendly middle ground. In his important work on the subject, *De ratione tegendi et detegendi secretum*, published in Salamanca in 1541, Soto argued that while, in principle, the confessional seal could not be broken and thus in general a fraternal correction needed to precede a public denunciation of a sinner, nevertheless in the cases of sins *"perniciosa rei publicae aut proximo"* (destructive for the commonwealth or for your neighbor), which included crimes of heresy, the precept of postponing the public denunciation to the fraternal correction did not apply.[15]

Now, those theologians like Soto and Navarrus, who acknowledged in small (in the case of Soto) or large (in the case of Navarrus) measure the necessity of keeping the confessional secret, found themselves between the proverbial rock and hard place when they needed to address the question of what, in practice, a confessor needed to do in case he was asked to reveal crimes that he was not supposed to reveal. On the one hand, the confessor had the moral imperative of keeping the confessional seal intact; on the other hand, when pressed to reveal what he had heard in confession, he would find himself squeezed against the other moral imperative of not lying. So what was the confessor to do? It is precisely in this context that Soto and Navarrus turned their attention to the potentialities and limitations of language by elaborating on the doctrines of equivocation and mental reservation. In fact, the differences between their views of language are a manifestation of the different force with which they defended the necessity of keeping secrets.

The first time in which Soto engaged with the doctrines of equivocation and mental reservation was in his *De ratione tegendi et detegendi secretum*. The text is divided into three parts: the first two are devoted, respectively, to the necessity of keeping secrets and to the relationship between the precept of the *correctio fraterna* and the juridical space of the Inquisition. In the third part Soto discussed some practical aspects and dilemmas arising from an interrogation in which somebody was asked to reveal secrets.[16] Soto devoted a short section of this part to investigate whether one asked to reveal secret crimes could legitimately use *"verborum ambiguitas & amphibologia"*—that is, verbal ambiguity and amphibology. Soto began by declaring that there are two absolutely rigid moral norms that constrain any elaboration on this issue. The first is that nobody is allowed to lie. The second is that in certain cases—for instance, that of a confessor asked to break the confessional seal (for certain specific sins)—nobody is allowed to reveal any secrets heard.

Because neither of the previously mentioned moral principles can ever be bent, Soto turned his attention to the third element of the equation: language. For Soto, both the limitations and the potentialities of language as a means of communication between two people can allow a priest to get out of his conundrum, because "in order to keep the secret of the confession, it is always allowed to the priest, when he is being interrogated over something he learned in confession, to reply that he does not know, and there is no need for other verbal tricks, because in this case one can answer in that manner without lying."[17] The reason this was possible, Soto argued, is that when I use the verb *scire* to say that I "know," I imply that I as myself have learned something. Now, when a priest learns of a sin in confession, "even if he knows [the sin] as an individual, he nevertheless knows it in the forum and tribunal of God, which God wanted to be so secret that the sins confessed there were certainly considered as forgotten, as if they never happened." Therefore, "when a priest, as God, says 'I absolve you', he promises to consider the sins as if he never heard them; thus in the external forum the priest can say that he never knew of them."[18]

Following this, Soto went deeper into his analysis of the verb *scire*: "even though we commonly say that we know what we believe on the basis of appropriate testimonies, nevertheless we properly say that we know what we comprehend with the firm reason of our mind (these are Augustine's words, in the first book of his *Retractationes*, chapter 14) and thus we cannot properly know for sure what we know from somebody's testimony." As Aristotle argues, *scientia* (i.e., knowledge of something) is "the certain and evident apprehension of the truth."[19]

It is important to note at this point that this form of verbal ambiguity depends, not on the moral quality of the motives for concealing the secret, but on the meaning of the verb *scire*, and this is why the confessor asked unlawfully to break the confessional seal is not the only one entitled to take advantage of the verbal ambiguity. In fact, Soto specified, not only people who are unjustly questioned but "even a man who is rightfully interrogated does not commit any wrong if he responds not to know what he knows from second-hand knowledge."[20] This does not mean that everybody should take advantage of the built-in ambiguity of the verb *scire*, for "*citra necessitatem*" (without necessity), Soto argued, everybody should speak as plainly as possible. However, if one chose to take advantage of the verbal ambiguity without necessity, one would not be telling a lie, even though by deceiving the audience one would still commit a sin, because the obligations of social life demand that we speak as clearly as possible.[21]

By the same token, when, for instance, somebody is unjustly questioned over something that should be rightly kept secret, if the question is posed in such a way as to exclude the use of the expressions "*scio*" or "*nescio*," the person under interrogation must disclose the truth. If a "most mischievous man" said to me: "tell me whatever you know about this, even if it is secret and cannot be rightly revealed," I could not reply simply "I do not know," "*nescio*," for this expression would not make sense as a response to the aforementioned question. Therefore, as Soto noted, using this expression in this context should be considered a lie.[22] While I could say without lying that I do not know something that I do if the knowledge of the thing is not certain, the fact that my certain knowledge of something would be used for evil purposes does not allow me to change the meaning of the expressions "*scio*" and "*nescio*." Likewise, if somebody asked me, either lawfully or unlawfully, whether I committed a crime, I could not answer "*nescio*" without telling a lie, for I must know what I did (or didn't) do.

As Soto explained, because of the morally delicate implications of this case, some theologians argued that in case of an unjust interrogation one could, without lying, say that one did not commit that crime, mentally meaning that one did not commit it insofar as the interrogator was asking unlawfully. For Soto, however, this was not acceptable: while the verb *scire* has some built-in room for semantic ambiguity, the verb *facere* does not, for either one "does" something or one does not.[23] By the same token, an adulterous woman asked by her husband whether or not she committed adultery (or a man asked by a tyrant under pain of death to reveal a secret in such a way as to exclude the possibility for the man to answer "*nescio*") could not resort to the potential ambiguities of language in order to avoid lying, no matter whether the motives for not revealing the secret were morally commendable (in the case of the man) or morally despicable (in the case of the woman). In fact, Soto concluded, in both cases and in all similar ones, if one wants to avoid both lying and revealing the secret, the only remaining option is death.[24]

From this analysis of Soto's *De ratione* I single out two elements. The first one is the distinctively dialogical nature of the kind of conversation Soto imagined as the starting point for his elaboration. The setting of the juridical interrogation, with its back-and-forth answers and questions between the judge performing the interrogation and the man obliged to answer, introduces an important hermeneutical point that Soto wanted to make about language, a point that differentiates Soto's analysis from Augustine's. Borrowing from Gadamer's insistence on dialogue (as opposed to the "form of statements that demand to be set down in writing") as the proper mode of communication and as a description of the very essence of the hermeneutical task, one could say that Soto's description of the various stages of an interrogation mirrors the "process of question and answer, giving and taking, talking at cross purposes and seeing each other's point" that "performs the communication of meaning."[25] In other words, the juridical setting of Soto's imaginary examples points to an important shift in the concept of language with respect to the Augustinian model: in Soto we can clearly see that language has become a means to communicate meaning through dialogue between a speaker and a hearer rather than simply a form of adoration of God through an internal correspondence (or lack thereof) between the hearer's thought and tongue.

The second element to be singled out is the fact that Soto's elaboration on language is morally neutral. While Soto started his discussion with the morally charged example of the confessor asked to break the confessional seal, his reflections on the built-in ambiguous meaning of the verb *scire* transcended questions of both morality and motive, so much so that, as Soto argued, even men justly questioned can take advantage of the specific semantic ambiguity of the expressions "*scio*" or "*nescio*," just as those rightly entitled to keep their secrets are obliged to reveal them in case the question was posed in such a way as to preclude the use of those expressions.

Both those elements are confirmed and, indeed, stressed, in Soto's later reflections on equivocation in *De iustitia et iure*.[26] In this work, Soto engaged with the question of equivocation in the sixth *quaestio* of the fifth book, which is devoted to exploring the rights and duties of a defendant. The section on equivocation is in the second article, and it starts with a discussion of secrets and of the circumstances in which one is morally obliged to keep them. The first case examined is that of a confessor asked to break the confessional seal, and in that context Soto declared that a confessor, as well as anybody who is interrogated unlawfully, can make use of certain forms of verbal ambiguity.[27] Soto admitted that it would be desirable if in those cases one could use that "*antiquus doctorum clypeus*" (the ancient shield of the scholars): simply cutting the conversation by saying "I deny the proposed questions in the way in which they are proposed." However, because the judge would not be satisfied with this statement and would push further, in the question-and-answer mode of conversation, the man under interrogation needed to take advantage, once again, of language. In this context, Soto made the by now usual distinction between things that one has heard of and things that one is accused of having done. In the first case, one can easily say "*nescio*" without lying, for "since words are the signs of concepts, that expression '*nescio*' can be taken without lie in the sense of 'I do not know in such a way as to be able to tell you,'" since to properly know something means to have full knowledge of the thing in question.[28]

Because of the same semantic argument, however, one cannot say the same of the verb *facere*, because "'to do' does not have the same connection as 'to know' with what it is that I might say."[29] Because of the semantic limitations, the moral quality of the prospective equivocator's motives has no bearing. Soto addressed this question in a rather implicit but controversial way when he affirmed that because of the more limited semantic area of the verb *facere*, an adulterous woman could not affirm not to have "committed" adultery, with the intention of saying that she did not do it "that day," without lying. Thus, Soto concluded, the adulterous woman and other "unhappy people" like her could do nothing but "withstand death, as martyrs, rather than transgressing the natural and divine law by lying," just as the "unhappy girl who is threatened by a tyrant with death unless she consented to his base desires has no other remedy but to succumb to the sword."[30] In this passage, then, for Soto there is no difference between an adulterous woman and an innocent girl trying to save her virginity: both of them have to die "as martyrs," because neither one can take advantage of the built-in ambiguities of language. Indeed, even Navarrus who, as we will see shortly, had a much more elastic view of equivocation, would express his amazement at Soto's putting at the same level the case of the virgin and that of the adulterous woman.[31]

Thus, Soto examined the question of falsehood not simply under the moral category of sin but under the hermeneutical question of the communication of meaning between a speaker and a hearer. In this respect, in his work we can see a fundamental shift in the ways in which Christian tradition engaged with the question of language and lying. Soto did so, I argue, because he was prompted by the double moral imperatives of telling the truth and not breaking the confessional seal, but this initial moral conundrum stirred him to explore in some measure the semantic possibilities and limitations inherent in language. The result of Soto's elaboration on equivocation, as with his opinion on the authority of the Inquisition to investigate occult crimes, was a moderate endorsement of a limited space for semantic ambiguities, which resonates with his equally moderate endorsement of a limited room for fraternal correction as opposed to public denunciation to the Inquisition. Navarrus, who, like Soto, was engaged in the same theological debates, assumed a more radical position on both fraternal correction and equivocation.

As is well known, Navarrus was more aware than many other theologians of his time of the potential dangers represented by the Inquisition's attempts to control the internal forum of the conscience, usually reserved for the confessor. Both in his works as a moral theologian (especially in the famous and influential *Enchiridion*, or *Manual* for confessors) and in his juridical role as one of Carranza's lawyers, Navarrus had insisted on the need to limit the range of the inquisitorial procedures and had defended vigorously the space of the conscience, as it opened up between the confessor and the penitent, from what he saw as police-type aggression.[32] In his battle, Navarrus found a powerful ally in the Society of Jesus, especially during the 1580s. Jesuit confessors, in fact, enjoyed the papal privilege of being able to absolve crimes of heresy *in foro conscientiae*, and the Spanish Inquisition threatened precisely this privilege. Many controversies, some of them involving high-profile members of the Spanish clergy, arose over the question of the absolution of crimes of heresy and, more generally, over the question of how to regulate the sacred and mysterious space of the confessional. For instance, in 1586 the inquisitors of Valladolid had four Jesuit fathers, including Antonio Marcén, the superior for the province of Castile, arrested for not having denounced to the Inquisition a case of heresy and *sollicitatio ad turpia* within the Society itself. The case in question took place in the Jesuit College of Monterey, in Galicia, where a Jesuit father by the name of Sebastian de Briviesca allegedly solicited a group of women and taught them some doctrines close to those of the *Alumbrados*. One of the women involved confessed the fact to another Jesuit father, Diego Hernández, who then informed Marcén; the Jesuit superior ordered Hernández to absolve the woman without denouncing either her or Briviesca to the Inquisition, thus keeping the entire affair secret. Hernández, however, troubled by his scruples, decided to ignore his superior's orders and informed the Inquisition, which then proceeded to the arrests. The ensuing trial was an incredibly tense affair, which at times pitted the Inquisitor General of Spain Gaspar de Quiroga, Pope Sixtus V, and Philip II against one another. The trial ended with a small local victory for the Society, for in 1588 the pope ordered Quiroga to end the trial and free the Jesuits. Even though Sixtus V was famously hostile to the Society, he nevertheless understood that such a public internal controversy could potentially be extremely dangerous for Spanish Catholicism and could upset the relationship between the papacy and Philip II.[33] At a Roman level, however, the Society paid a steep price, for Sixtus V in 1587 suspended the privilege that the Jesuits enjoyed of absolving heretics *in foro conscientiae*.[34]

This episode clearly shows that in the second half of the 1580s Spanish (and Roman) Jesuits were immensely invested in understanding and mastering the rules of the complex game played in the confessional, where a confessor needed to find a theological, juridical, and even linguistic balance between the duty to keep the secrets of the sinner and the necessity to correct the sins. Thus, it is not a coincidence that Navarrus's *Commentarius in cap. Humanae Aures* (first published in Rome in 1584), in which he expressed his more radical views on equivocation and mental reservation, was written at the request of the Jesuits in Valladolid, who submitted to Navarrus the case of conscience on which Navarrus's commentary is based.[35] The case in question referred to a man who had said to a woman, "I take you as my wife," without having any intention to do so. When he was asked under oath by a judge whether or not he said those words, the man replied that he did not, "*subintelligendo mente*" (mentally reserving) that he did not say them with the intention of actually taking the woman as his wife. This being the case, Navarrus asked, could the man be said to have lied in front of God? Even if it was licit for him to lie, did he commit perjury in front of God? And finally, assuming he neither lied nor committed perjury, did the man commit any other kind of sin?[36]

In answering the first two questions (I return to the third shortly) Navarrus set up the core of his theory. Navarrus started with Augustine's definition of lying as a lack of accord between what the speaker thinks and what the speaker says. However, what does it really mean to "say"? Here Navarrus launched into a very interesting exploration of the nature of language: as Aristotle and the other "*Dialectici*" argued, an *oratio*, a statement, need not just be vocal; it can be written or mental, such as when one tells something to herself. So why can't those different forms appear mixed in the same statement? Or in Navarrus's words, "one same reasoning can be composed of different parts, some of which are vocal, others written, others silent and mental," and even though the different parts can be false when taken individually, "the entire proposition can be true."[37] For instance, even though the man in question said vocally that he did not promise to take the woman as his wife, since he had mentally added that this was not his intention, the entire proposition encompassing the mental and vocal parts is not false, and thus the man did not lie. In Navarrus's reading, then, one's mental language and one's vocal language are all legitimate parts of language that can be combined however the speaker wishes.

This means, first of all, that Navarrus expanded the potentiality for ambiguity in human language. While Soto had already admitted the built-in semantic ambiguities in certain words, Navarrus expands those ambiguities by assuming that "saying inwardly" is a type of language that can be combined with "saying outwardly," another type of language. In other words, the act of communication through language, according to Navarrus, is performed through a series of different forms of "saying," and saying inwardly is just as legitimate as saying outwardly. Whenever those two ways of saying are disconnected from one another, that is, whenever a speaker says inwardly something different than she expresses vocally, the speaker hides a part of her statement, which, if it were joined with the other, vocal, one, would make the entire statement true. The result of this is that the internal statement functions as a hidden corrective that makes the entire proposition truthful from the point of view of the speaker, since in Augustinian terms the speaker's entire statement reflects what she really thinks. But what are the consequences of this hidden statement on the communication of meaning between the speaker and the hearer? There are two sides to this question: one is the hermeneutical issue, which refers to the effects of mental reservation on the interpretative aspect of the conversation. The other is the moral issue, which refers to the question of whether or not the results of mental reservation (i.e., the hearer's deception) could and should be judged from a moral perspective.

I think that in order to answer both questions we can try to read Navarrus's theory through Ludwig Wittgenstein's notion of language-games and, more specifically, Wittgenstein's notion that pretending—that is, outwardly showing something that does not correspond to our inward feeling—is a language-game like any other.[38] In fact, according to Navarrus, from a hermeneutical perspective the fact that the speaker has at her disposal the language-game of pretending (i.e., of combining inward and outward saying at will) does not deny the possibility of communication between a speaker and a hearer. Instead, assuming that pretending is a language-game like any other means that in order to communicate meaning, one needs to be trained to understand that specific language-game. Indeed, Navarrus explained that not only did the allegedly deceitful man not lie because he was in perfect accord within himself but also he could not even be said to have failed to communicate his real intention. It was the judge who listened to the man's statement and took it at face value, also the woman who believed the man's promise of marriage at face value, who made an interpretative mistake. The judge in charge of interrogating the man, in fact, should have been interested in knowing whether a marriage was actually contracted, and therefore he should have asked whether the man had the intention of marrying the woman. But since the judge asked only about the words pronounced, he could not expect the man, under trial for a marriage question, not to use mental reservation to defend himself.[39] Besides, in cases of matrimony it is notorious, Navarrus wrote, that what people say cannot be taken at face value, that one should "believe the person who swears [to intend to marry somebody] if it seems verisimilar to learned, prudent and morally sound people" or when "the circumstances of people, time and place" warrant such faith. For instance, if the man "is much more wealthy or noble than the woman," it is plausible that his expressed intention to marry her is not a genuine reflection of his inward intention.[40]

In other words, when two people communicate, they can legitimately use the language-game of pretending (or using mental reservation). In order for meaning to be correctly communicated, one needs to master this language-game of pretending, which requires a distinctive and, in a sense, superior skill with respect to mastering the language-game of truth telling, for "a child has much to learn before it can pretend." Moreover, one can never reach a perfect knowledge of lying: "I might recognize a genuine loving look, distinguish it from a pretended one. . . but I may be quite incapable of describing the difference."[41] Transposing Wittgenstein's reflections onto Navarrus's example, a judge could certainly interrogate a man over his matrimonial status, but he should constantly fine-tune his own intention and meaning to correspond with the intention and meaning of the man under interrogation, by means of a complex interplay of vocally expressed sentences and inward intentions. The outcome of this interplay is not certain: the judge, blinded by his own mistaken ends, might never ask the right questions, or he might never properly understand the answers.

Therefore, if in Soto's model of dialogical conversation language represented a fixed limit, in Navarrus's model, language or, rather, languages are many, and their interaction is far from fixed. Indeed, the difference between Soto's and Navarrus's arguments is, in my view, closely mirrored in the difference between Gadamer's and Wittgenstein's notions of language as game. For Gadamer, language is a game that plays itself, in the sense that language is where meaning comes into being through the dialectic participation of the protagonists of the conversation,[42] just as for Soto language has intrinsic potentialities and limitations that regulate the way in which the protagonists of a conversation can play the game of talking with one another. For Wittgenstein, communication is achieved through a complex variety of language-games—for instance, the game of pretending and the game of truth telling—and the meaning of a conversation is, so to speak, buried in these complexities,[43] just as, for Navarrus, mixed propositions are an example of the complex interplay between saying inwardly and saying outwardly. Thus, in a sense, in saying something that sounds false to the hearer, the speaker has decided to use the language-game of pretending, and the hearer has not been able to understand or follow the rules of that specific game. Understanding one another, then, becomes a complex hermeneutical task whose achievement and completion are not guaranteed, since they depend on a number of factors or on the interplay between different language-games.

A Wittgenstein-infused reading of Navarrus can elucidate also the moral implications of his theory. For Wittgenstein, while it is true that one needs a motive to lie (whereas the language-game of telling the truth does not need a motive), it is equally true that the motive is not the justification for the existence of the language-game of pretending.[44] For Navarrus, likewise, one needs a motive to use mental reservation and that motive could be morally reproachable or morally commendable, but the different moral quality of the motive has no bearing on the question of the justification of the existence of mixed propositions, since the existence of those propositions or the existence of the language-game of pretending is an intrinsic characteristic of human language.

Navarrus treated the relationship between morality and mental reservation in the third part of his commentary, where he dealt with whether or not the man in question, while not being guilty of lying or perjury, did in fact commit other sins. This is the part of the text where Navarrus introduced the distinction between *dolus* and *mendacium*—a distinction that was, for reasons which by now should be clear, largely foreign to Augustinian theology. While *mendacium* is the sin of lying (i.e. asserting something different from what one thinks), *dolus* is the moral judgment over the cause (and the effects) of the use of mixed propositions. It is true that using a mixed proposition is not the same as lying, and it is also true, as Navarrus had previously argued, that there are a number of ways in which one can make sure that the conversation between a hearer and a speaker is a means to communicate meaning. For instance, if the judge asks the right question for the right purpose, he can avoid having to take things at face value, or if a man's promise is weighed against a number of other factors, it can be understood aside from its verbal meaning. Nevertheless, there are cases in which communication fails and a woman does indeed believe a man's promise to marry is real or a judge takes the man's words at face value. In those cases the hearers have been deceived, even though the speaker has not lied. How, then, do we judge that deception?

Navarrus explained that deception itself can be either good or bad: if, say, the man had deceived his prospective wife for good reason, because, for instance, he wanted to remain unmarried so as to be able to join a religious order, he deceived the woman "*bono dolo, & ex iusta causa,*" thereby not sinning and, indeed, committing a morally commendable act. If, on the other hand, he deceived the woman only because he wanted to consummate the marriage without taking on the marital responsibility, then he deceived her *dolo malo* and sinned both for dissimulating in an evil sense and for the *stuprum*—that is, for the illegitimate sexual act. After introducing this distinction, Navarrus continued by praising a number of occasions in which one might rightly employ mental reservation, both in everyday life (as in the case in which we are asked to lend money we do not have) and in politics (as in the cases of princes who need to dissimulate in order to be more effective in their government).[45]

As Perez Zagorin has written, in this section Navarrus "laid down a basic distinction between good and bad dissimulation." The "criterion" to distinguish good from bad is represented by "the limits of just cause."[46] Indeed, most scholarship on dissimulation has explored the distinction between good and bad dissimulation and the notion of just cause as an important and novel contribution to moral theology. The point that I want to make here is that these moral aspects of Navarrus's doctrine should not overshadow its hermeneutical implications. In other words, while using mental reservation can be either good or bad, mental reservation exists as an intrinsic part of human language, regardless of the good or bad use that one can make of it. In a sense, one can say that the real, radical, and upsetting aspect of Navarrus's theory is not so much that it made the moral criterion of just cause into a relatively controversial measure of the rightness (or lack thereof) of one's dissimulation. Rather, Navarrus proposed a theory in which human language is not a tightly regulated venue where meaning is communicated between people, but a complex set of different types of communication, a situation that makes coming to an understanding highly problematic. In this perspective, Navarrus's theory did not introduce a measure of moral flexibility but a measure of hermeneutical uncertainty. What one says, what one thinks, and any combination of the two are all legitimate language-games one could play at will. In these forms of communication interpretation is crucial, complex, and uncertain, aside from and beyond the rigidity of moral norms. It is not a coincidence, in fact, that while the example of the good confessor asked to break the confessional seal features prominently at the beginning of Navarrus's commentary, the text deals primarily with another, a much less morally clear-cut kind of example: that of a man who did not fulfill his promise to marry a young woman.

The Moral Turn

Navarrus's theory produced two effects. First, it introduced a powerful and radical theory of language, which Navarrus saw as composed of different kinds of language-games, to use Wittgenstein's terms. This meant that saying inwardly and saying outwardly could be combined at will, and the disjunction between those two—that is, saying in words something different from what one thinks inwardly—was just another kind of language-game. Second, Navarrus showed how one could use mental reservation—that is, this distinctive kind of language-game—for just cause and in a commendable way. In so doing, he showed the immense potentialities of theorizing and putting into practice the good dissimulation in a number of contexts, from the dilemma of the confessor asked to break the seal to the case of the prince who could use a degree of good dissimulation to run his political affairs.

Many influential theologians, especially Jesuits, immediately took up both aspects of Navarrus's theory. In the second half of the sixteenth century the Jesuits shared Navarrus's concerns regarding the limits of the Inquisition in matters of heresy and were greatly invested in the battle to maintain their privilege of absolving heretics *in foro conscientiae*. At the end of the sixteenth and the beginning of the seventeenth century, however, they started to see both the defensive potential of dissimulation in those contexts in which Jesuits and Catholics lived under heretical sovereigns, thus under the increasingly harsh threat of persecution, and the aggressive potential of dissimulation as a way to strengthen their apostolical and political influences.[47] They also understood that Navarrus's defense of good dissimulation came with a distinctive theory of language, which, as I have argued, implied that mixed propositions were an intrinsic aspect of human language. While some of those theologians were willing to embrace Navarrus's defense of good dissimulation, virtually all of them reacted strongly against his hermeneutical position.

Catholic theologians were well aware of the potential dangers of Navarrus's theory of language: many of them, in fact, rejected Navarrus's mental reservation in favor of Soto's more conservative theory of equivocation. For instance, not only the Augustinian Pedro de Aragón but also the Jesuit theologians Juan Azor and Paul Laymann clearly specified that even if one were unjustly questioned, he could avoid lying only by using words that were ambiguous in the common use of the language.[48] The most interesting indicator of the anxiety that Catholic theologians felt towards Navarrus's theory of language, however, can be found not in those who completely rejected Navarrus's mental reservation but in those who embraced it and yet could not stomach the ways in which Navarrus framed mixed propositions. In a nutshell, while those theologians accepted that mental reservation was a legitimate way to express true, not deceitful, meaning, they denied that the existence of Navarrus's mixed propositions was a natural feature of language and insisted instead on the centrality of one's just (or unjust) cause for dissimulating.

For instance, the Jesuit Gregory of Valencia began his discussion of equivocation by specifying that when one talks about the precept of telling the truth, one must distinguish between the "negative" and the "affirmative" form of that precept—that is, between the precept of not lying and the precept of always telling the truth. Furthermore, he distinguished between *communis conversatio* (everyday conversation) and conversations held under special circumstances, such as the case of a man unjustly interrogated.[49] Thus, he declared that in those specific circumstances a man could use both ambiguous speech and forms of mental reservation. The reason for this was that "when one is interrogated unlawfully he can use words to express meaning in the same way as if he was not interrogated at all," for the judge in this case is illegitimate. Thus, if the man uttered a statement that sounded false to the illegitimate questioner, he could not be accused of lying: he simply refused to utter the "one determined truth" that he was being asked about and chose instead to say "another, different truth, since he is not bound to utter the truth which the judge requests from him unjustly."[50] For instance, if I were asked whether I committed a homicide I did commit and if I were to reply, "I did not do it," referring to another crime (e.g., a robbery), I would not contravene the precept of not lying, for my mouth and my mind would be in accord. Nor would I contravene the precept of always telling the truth, because I would have vocally said (not just mentally added) *one* truth—that is, that I am not a thief, even if I was asked the truth about the homicide. Because the person asking me about the homicide is not a legitimate interrogator, I do not have any obligation to take the specific question into account.

For Gregory, however, this was valid only in those special circumstances that made the interrogation invalid. In common conversation, in fact, to say something true but unrelated to the question asked would not save anybody from committing a sin against truthfulness. While the sinner in question would not have committed a proper *mendacium*, "a sin against the negative precept of truth" (since even without the special circumstances the mind and mouth of the speaker would still be in accord), he would have certainly "sinned against the affirmative precept of truth," since he failed to say the "right" truth.[51]

In his elaboration, then, Gregory refused to embrace the theory of mixed propositions as a natural feature of language, and for this reason he introduced the argument of different truths, whose specificity is determined by the circumstances of the question asked. Thus, for Gregory there is no uncertainty of interpretation, nor are there different language-games at play. Vocal statements must always be true, even though in certain cases the circumstances can modify how specific the truth of one's statement must be with respect to the conversation being held.

The same insistence on the circumstances as the key factor in determining the truthfulness of statements and the same reluctance to accept Navarrus's theory of language can be found in the Dominican theologian Domingo Bañez. For Bañez, as for Gregory of Valencia, there is no such a thing as a mixed proposition. A proposition is one entity; that is, it consists only of the part vocally expressed. However, the truthfulness of a proposition is the result of the combination of the meaning of the words and "of the circumstances of times, places, and people" in which the words are uttered. Thus, in the case of a man unjustly asked whether he committed a crime that he indeed committed, the man's reply, "I did not do it," means that given "the circumstances of the people" involved in the interrogation—that is, given the fact that the person asking the question is illegitimate—for the sake of that precise interrogation, he truly (and truthfully) did not commit the crime.[52]

Gregory of Valencia and Bañez changed, slightly but significantly, Navarrus's defense of mental reservation in that they denied that mixed propositions were a natural feature of language, and in parallel they stressed the importance of the circumstances of one's motives to use equivocation and mental reservation. In the case of Bañez, for instance, the just cause or right circumstances for one's decision to use mental reservation influence the properly linguistic aspects of a statement, since the same statement could be truthful or not precisely according to the specific circumstances. In a sense, one could say that those theologians corrected the Wittgenstein-like multiplicity of language-games they saw in Navarrus by stressing context and background as necessary factors in determining the meaning of a sentence.[53] The upshot, for those later theologians, was to eliminate the radical hermeneutical uncertainty inherent in Navarrus's theory of mixed propositions and to focus instead on the context of the vocal propositions so as to be able to apply a moral criterion of justification to the context itself.

These initial modifications to Navarrus's doctrine were to be developed more and more at the end of the sixteenth and the beginning of the seventeenth century, when equivocation and mental reservation ceased simply to be matters for theological discussion and instead became proper techniques to defend oneself from heretical persecutions or to make more effective the apostolic task of converting people and countries to the Catholic truth. As such, those doctrines were increasingly tied to the Society of Jesus, arguably the most aggressive religious order of post-Tridentine Catholicism in the fight against the heretics. In parallel, equivocation and mental reservation became the object of an intense public propaganda and were attacked as examples of the devious and politically seditious way of proceeding of the Jesuit missionaries.

The case of England was probably the one in which both the use of and the attack against equivocation and mental reservation came to the fore in the most polemically and politically explosive manner.[54] Late Elizabethan and early Jacobean England was quite unlike sixteenth-century Spain. While in Spain Soto, Navarrus, the Jesuits, and the Inquisition were engaged in an internal confessional conflict, England was one of the territories most hotly contested between Catholics and Protestants. While in Soto's and Navarrus's elaborations the verbal and mental dialogue was conducted by two Catholic protagonists, in the English elaborations on equivocation the prospective (or actual) equivoca- tors were Catholic priests or Catholic people asked by heretical judges about the whereabouts of other Catholic missionaries. In fact, the cause célèbre regarding equivocation in England, that of the Jesuit missionary Robert Southwell, cen- tered precisely on the question of what means were necessary to survive per- secution and to keep the Jesuit mission alive. Southwell arrived in England in 1586, and in the following years he worked clandestinely to foster Catholicism. In 1592, however, he was betrayed by his former patron, Anne Bellamy, and arrested. During his trial (which ended in 1595 with Southwell's condemnation to death) she testified that Southwell had suggested that she practice equivoca- tion: if the Elizabethan agents had come and asked whether Southwell was in her father's house (assuming that Southwell was indeed there), she could have equivocated by denying it vocally and mentally reserving a part of the proposi- tion, thus saving herself from a lie and Southwell from imprisonment. When questioned about Anne's statement, Southwell defended the legitimacy of the practice of equivocation: if France were to invade England and French soldiers were to ask where Queen Elizabeth was, what would a loyal English subject do? Would she betray her sovereign or sin by lying, when in fact she could be both loyal and truthful by equivocating?[55]

In the last decades of the sixteenth century and especially after Southwell's trial, the doctrine of equivocation was targeted in Protestant propaganda as one of the clearest examples of the deceitful means used by the Jesuits to infiltrate England and to overthrow the state. For example, in 1589 George Abbot, in the preface to his *Quaestiones sex*, had already condemned the Jesuit mission- aries' "frauds, impostures and deceits. . . because they open the door not only to lying, but also to perjury."[56] In 1606 Thomas Morton dedicated a large part of *A full satisfaction* to attacking the doctrine of equivocation, which he defined as a "new-bred Hydra, and uglie Monster," which not only conflicted with the basic Christian prohibition against lying but also introduced sedition and politi- cal rebellion into the English realm.[57] The same insistence on equivocation as a new Jesuitical trick for fostering anti-Christian political sedition can be seen in the very title of the treatise that Henry Mason wrote against equivocation in 1624: *The new art of lying*.[58] The doctrine of equivocation played also a small but polemically significant part in the Gunpowder Plot. A manuscript copy of the *Treatise of equivocation,* written as an explicit defense of Southwell by the Jesuit Henry Garnet, the superior of the English mission, was found in possession of Thomas Tresham, one of the conspirators. In 1606 Garnet was arrested for his alleged participation in the plot, and Sir Edward Coke questioned him at length on equivocation. At the end of the trial Garnet was condemned to death and executed.[59]

The question of equivocation in early modern England, however, not only opposed the Catholic victims to the Protestant persecutors but also touched a sensitive nerve within the Catholic community itself. Just as Catholics could equivocate to save a missionary's life from the Protestant persecution, they could in fact also equivocate to save their own life and goods. This second form of equivocation, in both its verbal form and its "behavioral equivalents"—that is, various forms of dissimulation and outer conformity—could weaken rather than strengthen the strong "recusant" character that people like Cardinal William Allen and the Jesuit Robert Persons, two of the leaders of the English Catholic community and of the Jesuit mission, wanted the English Catholics to maintain against the Protestants.[60]

The question of what a Catholic could and should do if he wanted to remain loyal to his faith at the same time he remained loyal to his government—and possibly alive and in possession of his goods or lands—surfaced in many contexts and was articulated in a number of ways in early modern England. The scruples of Catholic consciences ranged from whether or not a Catholic host could prepare a meal for a heretic friend or neighbor[61] to whether or not a husband could be allowed to conform and attend Protestant services, thus saving the family estate by acting as a church papist while the wife remained a recusant and was left to hold the domestic fort in the confessional battle.[62] Such vexing problems provoked a series of relatively public and potentially dangerous controversies within the Catholic camp. One of the most dramatic of those controversies centered on Thomas Bell, a Catholic seminary priest and missionary. In a manuscript work entitled "A comfortable advertisement to afflicted Catholics," Bell argued that recusancy was a work of supererogation and, as such, it could not be imposed on ordinary men and women, for whom attending Protestant services should be allowed since such attendance, far from being a sort of theological badge of identity, was simply a means to show one's political loyalty. Bell's tolerance toward these kinds of dissimulatory behaviors was fiercely attacked by the Jesuit missionaries and especially by Henry Garnet, who, as we have seen, defended vigorously Southwell's pious equivocation. In 1592 Bell left the Catholic camp and converted to Protestantism, just as William Allen was issuing an open letter to English Catholics in which he recognized the difficult situation of the laity but also vigorously condemned Bell's opinions.[63]

All these examples, which indeed could be multiplied, should serve to demonstrate that because of the pressure of the confessional fight, because of the pressure of the polemical wave of anti-Jesuitism and antiequivocation that was mounted on the part of the Protestant establishment, and because of the delicate and potentially destructive implications that verbal and nonverbal forms of dissimulation could have on the already fragile political and theological equilibrium of the English Catholic community, it became even more crucial for Catholic authors who supported equivocation to stress the justness of the cause. That is why the defenses of the practice of equivocation written by English Jesuits in those years started to emphasize more and more the question of just cause, following Gregory of Valencia and Bañez, at the expense of Navarrus's theory of language, which was in this perspective morally neutral.

For instance, when Henry Garnet defended the legitimacy of mental reservation in his *Treatise of equivocation*, he referred to Aristotle's notion of vocal and mental propositions without mentioning Navarrus.[64] Immediately afterwards, he mentioned "2 great Devines, which will more declare that which hath bene sayed."[65] One of those two "great Devines" was Gregory of Valencia, who argued that "in case that a man be not lawfully asked. . . it is as lawfull for a man to use wordes for to signifye what sense he will as if he were asked by no manner of person, or of no determinate thinge, as for example, if he were alone or before others, and for recreation sake or for other end should talke with hym selve."[66] The other was Domingo Bañez, who "defendeth such speeches from a lye, whan according to the circumstances of place, tyme, and persons, some particles may in a proposition be understood and supplyed, which, if they were expressed, woulde make a manifest truth. In such case it is all one whether those particles bee expressed or concealed."[67] The reason why Garnet privileged those theologians' reading instead of Navarrus's is that he was interested in underscording that "the use of these kyndes of concealing of trewth contayneth no falsehood or lye (which alwayes were a synne) but is altogither lawfull *in places and seasons*."[68] In other words, mixed propositions are not a natural and neutral feature of language; rather, one can "create" and take advantage of mixed propositions only in specific places and seasons; in those alone could mental reservation thus be used without lying or committing any other sin (and saving a missionary's life from the heretics' fury was, for Garnet, a most right place and a most right season to use mental reservation even when interrogated under oath).

Robert Persons dedicated the entire second part of his *Treatise tending to mitigation* to a complex and lengthy defense of the doctrine of equivocation from the attacks of Thomas Morton.[69] Persons's text had many different polemical agendas. First, it was supposed to defend the doctrines of equivocation and mental reservation from the accusation of being a Jesuitical novelty aimed at promoting political sedition, and thus it needed to present equivocation and mental reservation as doctrines over which there was a general agreement among Catholic theologians, provided that those doctrines were used appropriately. Second, Persons needed to promote the right use of the doctrine of equivocation as a means to strengthen the Catholic mission in a time in which priests and missionaries were forced to live underground and depended on the protection of the laity for survival, just as in the case of Southwell. Third, Persons needed to discourage the indiscriminate use of equivocation and mental reservation, for those doctrines could be used not only by Catholic missionaries in their fight against the heretics but also by Catholic laymen and laywomen who could pretend to be Protestant and thus avoid fines and punishment.[70]

Thus, unlike Garnet, Persons needed to quote Navarrus (and Soto) in order to prove that the doctrine of equivocation was not a Jesuitical invention but a part of traditional Catholic theology. As Persons argued, mental reservation "for the space of these last 400 yeares. . . hath byn receaved for true, and lawfull doctrine in our schooles, and consequently practised also throughout Christendome, when iust occasion was offered, without breach, or discredit of publique faith."[71]

However, since setting appropriate limitations on just cause was necessary for Persons both to defend rightful equivocation and to discourage cowardly equivocation, he chose Gregory of Valencia and Bañez over Navarrus. When discussing the justification for equivocation, in fact, Persons started by mentioning Navarrus and his commentary, in which, according to Persons, Navarrus "proveth that the said defendant being so pressed uniustly to answere, when he hath no other way lefte to defend himselfe, may truly, and without any lye at all, say, *he did it not*, with the foresaid reservation of mynd, *that he did it not in some such sense*, as in his owne meaning, and in the eares of Almighty God, is true; though the uniust Iudge taking it in another sense, be deceaved therby, which falleth out iustly unto him, for that he proceedeth iniustly against law."[72] Notice at this point that Persons conveniently glossed over the fact that the defendant in question was on trial for matters concerning an unfulfilled promise of marriage or, for that matter, that Navarrus specifically argued that the existence of mixed propositions did not depend on the justness of one's motives. In fact, when Persons discussed Navarrus's proofs to justify his position, the English Jesuit avoided any mention of the theory of mixed propositions but simply declared that "the said Doctor proveth this his assertion by many arguments taken both out of Scriptures, Canon law, and reason it selfe."[73] After this brief introduction of Navarrus, Persons continued by stating that "all publicke Readers of Devinity" allowed the use of mental reservation and, for brevity's sake, he only mentioned two: the first was Gregory of Valencia and the second was Domingo Bañez.[74]

Thus, by the beginning of the seventeenth century we can identify a series of small but important modifications in the way Catholic theologians treated the doctrines of equivocation and mental reservation with respect to Soto's and

Navarrus's elaborations. Those modifications were prompted by the theoretical concerns initiated by Navarrus's morally neutral theory of language and by the historical context, in which the fight against heretics was a prominent point in the agenda of the post-Tridentine Church. The result of these contextual and theoretical moves was that, first of all, mental reservation was not, as in Navarrus's theory, linked with a distinctive view of language but instead became more and more an issue of moral theology. Second, by the beginning of the seventeenth century the doctrines of equivocation and mental reservation were tightly linked with the Society of Jesus, whose members were quite invested in elaborating, defending, and practicing the best mechanisms of defense and offense in the fight against the heretics.

We can see some preliminary results of these processes in the way the Jesuit Leonardus Lessius treated equivocation and mental reservation in *De iustitia et iure*, first published in 1605, a theological treatise written in Latin rather than a pamphlet written in a vernacular language. Unlike Persons and Garnet, Lessius was not fighting on the front lines of the antiheretical battle. On the other hand, Lessius lived and taught in Louvain, a very delicate location in terms of confessional conflict. Thus, his work reflects both the academic theological milieu of the discussion of equivocation and some of the antiheretical concerns typical of a confessionally contested land.[75]

Lessius discussed equivocation, not in the sections of his work dedicated to the rights and duties of the defendant (as Soto, Gregory of Valencia, and Bañez had), but in a section of the chapter on oaths specifically concerning whether or not one could swear "in another sense with respect to another person's understanding."[76] Recall that in the analysis of Persons's and Garnet's texts, the use of equivocation or mental reservation to avoid lying under oath when such an oath was requested by a heretical judge had been substituted for the question of the confessor's duties and rights as the typical case study for these doctrines. Moreover, when Lessius offered his own justification of mental reservation, even though he specified that using mental reservation without a legitimate reason was not properly a form of lie, he nevertheless strongly stressed that just cause was the criterion for the legitimate use of mental reservation, and indeed he enlarged the range of the possible just causes by including utility (*utilitas*) together with necessity (*necessitas*).[77]

If Lessius's position on mental reservation still maintained a certain distinction between *mendacium* and unjust dissimulation, another famous and influential Jesuit theologian, Théophile Raynaud, had no scruple about completely abandoning Navarrus and embracing the just-cause theory both morally and hermeneutically. Raynaud was a prolific, influential, and controversial French Jesuit. His written production is abundant and eclectic. To mention a few of his works, in 1630 he wrote a book entitled *De martyrio per pestem*, in which he argued that those who contracted the plague while helping to cure ill people and who died because of it should be considered true martyrs; in 1637 he wrote a *Discussio erroris popularis*, in which he criticized the practice of taking communion for the sake of the dead; in 1653 he published a work entitled *Erotemata de malis ac bonis libris*, which criticized the procedure of the Congregation of the Index in censoring books. Between the mid-1640s and the end of the 1650s the Congregation of the Index censored all of these works and indeed almost all Raynaud produced (the book I am about to analyze is the exception).[78]

In 1627 Raynaud wrote a book entitled *Splendor veritatis* under the pseudonym Emonerius. It was a defense of Lessius's and Persons's endorsements of mental reservation against the criticism of John Barnes.[79] Barnes, an English Benedictine located in France, was the author of *Dissertatio contra aequivocatores*, a lengthy and complex attack accusing Lessius and Persons of having invented a new, evil, and unfounded theological justification for lying. Barnes quoted Lessius's passage on the fact that a right reason, including *utilitas* or *necessitas*, could absolve whoever used mental reservation from lying. For Barnes, Lessius's justifications made what was a lie into a non-lie, and what was a perjury into a non-perjury: "with an awesome metamorphosis he [Lessius] transformed black into white, darkness into light, falsity into verity."[80]

Barnes condemned Lessius's use of the just cause, which according to Barnes Lessius had stretched so much as to render it a criterion for distinguishing truth and lies, not just bad and good dissimulation. Raynaud, for his part, mounted a theoretically and theologically thorough defense of the criterion of the just cause, both as a justification for good dissimulation and as a justification for the language of mental reservation. For this reason, he openly and forcefully attacked Navarrus's opinion on mixed propositions and his entire theory of language, on the basis of which mixed propositions were justified.

The greatest problem with Navarrus's theory of mixed propositions, Raynaud wrote, was that "it assumes basically *gratis* that a mixed proposition out of vocal and mental terms can legitimately exist, even though this is precisely what is under controversy."[81] The reason for the controversy is that the vocal and mental parts are heterogeneous, for the vocal proposition is expressed through signs (*signa*), which do not apply to the mental proposition, which is only expressed inwardly. Thus, if Navarro wanted to prove his theory, he should have "proved and declared that that mixture of proposition from a vocal and a mental part, or from a sign and a non-sign, holds together properly."[82] What Raynaud rejected from Navarrus's theory of language is precisely the fact that for Navarrus mixed propositions exist as intrinsic features of language. By contrast, Raynaud saw "inward saying" and "outward saying" as heterogeneous, and thus he thought that in order to mix and match heterogeneous entities one needed a good reason. For Navarrus, no reason was necessary, since the possibility of mixing and matching was an intrinsic aspect of language. Raynaud, of course, also realized that Navarrus's theory of mixed propositions was a theoretically sound manner in which to justify mental reservation and, consequently, to defend good dissimulation. Thus, his solution was to correct Navarrus's theory of mixed propositions by supplying the good reason: "That divided expression of a concept . . . is not illicit *when there is a just cause and a more urgent law than truthfulness.*"[83] In other words, the just cause defines not only whether the *dolus* is *bonus* or *malus* but indeed whether one lies or not. Or put differently, language does not possess the intrinsic capability of being mixed; rather, it acquires such capability whenever a just cause intervenes.

Raynaud's modification, then, did not stem from the need to clarify the distinction between just or unjust causes but from the need to eliminate any uncertainty in the degree of adaptation between words and things and to avoid the difficulties in communicating meaning that could have resulted from an indiscriminate use of the language-game of pretending. As Raynaud explicitly claimed, since many words can have many meanings, and indeed "every word . . . is ambiguous and full of different meanings, an incredible anxiety would occur every time a word must be uttered, and it would be necessary to try to remove the ambiguity of words with gestures or other signs. These scruples are addressed once we reject a general condemnation of ambiguous words, and we allow their use for a just cause."[84]

New Questions and Old Beginnings

Raynaud's forceful endorsement of the moral, rather than the linguistic, nature of mixed propositions closed the cycle, so to speak. It was a product of a process that lasted almost a century, in which the hermeneutical "incredible anxiety" that Navarrus's theory of language had provoked was eliminated and mental reservation became a part, albeit a controversial one, of moral theology. In fact, as the seventeenth century progressed, the doctrines of equivocation and mental reservation came under attack from both the periphery and the center of the Catholic world precisely as a manifestation of probabilism and indeed of laxism—that is, of systems of moral theology that in cases of moral uncertainty allow a certain course of action on the basis of the solid (in the case of probabilism) or even slight (in the case of laxism) probability that the course of action in question is not unlawful.

We can see the initial signs of uneasiness of the Catholic world towards mental reservation already in the 1620s. Barnes's book had come out in 1625 in both Latin and French editions, and even before its publication the Congregation of the Index had an eye on it. The reason for this attention was that Barnes's book was not simply a piece of polemical writing against equivocation and was not even simply a manifestation of the conflict between English Jesuits and English Benedictines, which in the first decades of the seventeenth century was quite dramatic. Barnes lived in France, and his book was endorsed by the theologians of the Sorbonne as "most salutary and useful against the frauds, deceits, lies, and perjuries which under guise of equivocation have inundated the Christian world in these unhappy times."[85] This involvement of the Parisian theologians pointed to a larger and dangerous conflict between certain sectors of the French Church, the Society of Jesus, and the Roman Curia, whose relations were very delicate from the start of the seventeenth century and especially in the aftermath of the murder of Henri of Navarre and were to become dramatically tense after the publication of Jansenius's *Augustinus* in 1640.

In 1620s, then, the Congregation of the Index was monitoring the French situation very closely. Indeed, in July 1624 it examined the text of Barnes's *Dissertatio* and "ordered the book to be prohibited." However, the members of the Index were also very aware of the potential conflict that Lessius's doctrine of equivocation could instigate, precisely because in Lessius's formulation the doctrine of equivocation was framed as a part of moral theology. This is why after prohibiting Barnes's book they "ordered to admonish gently the Father General of the Jesuits to suggest that Lessius remove from his work *De iustitia et iure* that word 'utility' in chap. 42, disputation 9," where *utilitas* and *necessitas* were used as the criteria for allowing dissimulation under oath.[86] Evidently, the members of the Index saw clearly how Lessius's mention of "utility" as a valid moral criterion smelled too much of probabilism and laxism, and as such it could become problematic especially in the French theological landscape, in which both the Jesuits' political papalism and their distinctive understanding of moral theology were looked at with suspicion and, in certain quarters, with outright hostility.

It should be said that the antiprobabilism and antilaxism moment had not arrived yet, and even assuming that Lessius was actually warned by the general (of which warning, in any case, I found no record), he and his Jesuit superiors did not feel compelled to change anything in his work. In fact, the passage noted by the censors in the first editions of *De iustitia et iure* remained identical in subsequent editions, and the 1653 edition of Lessius's treatise contained as an appendix Raynaud's *Splendor veritatis*, which was even more explicitly Lessian than Lessius's own work.[87]

Soon enough, however, times would be changing, and the rigorist wave would invest the Roman Curia and sweep away equivocation and mental reservation, together with probabilism and laxism. Out of the sixty-five laxist propositions condemned by Innocent XI and the Holy Office in 1679, two concerned the doctrine of equivocation. The twenty-sixth concerned the right to use mental reservation under oath, and the twenty-seventh concerned the justification of such use because of a just cause; that is, because of necessity or utility both of the body and of the soul.[88] Indeed, while Raynaud's *Splendor veritatis*, unlike his other works, had managed to avoid a censure from the Index in the 1640s and 1650s, in 1681 the treatise could not escape the explicit antiequivocation stance that the papacy had taken, and it was prohibited.

We have the copy of the censures that three members of the Congregation of the Index made on the text. The first two censures were very similar and raised three main objections: first, that Raynaud had used very harsh words against Barnes, who was a Catholic man and as such deserved a measure of respect; second, that Raynaud deserved to be punished for having written under a pseudonym; and third, that since the doctrine contained in the book was explicitly against Innocent's pronouncement, it undoubtedly deserved to be condemned.[89] The third censure, written by a Theatine cardinal, erudite scholar, and future saint, Giuseppe Maria Tomasi (1649–1713),[90] is slightly different. Tomasi started by stating that there were two issues to be examined. As for the first, the perceived excessive verbal violence against Barnes, Tomasi declared that since Barnes too had used strong words, Raynaud's mistake should be considered "venial" and not to be condemned.[91] As to the second and more important issue, doctrine, Tomasi was perplexed. It is true that equivocation was officially condemned, but it is equally true that Raynaud wrote the *Splendor veritatis* "more than fifty years before the condemnation," and, therefore, it seemed that he "should be excused," since a retroactive prohibition did not sound fair. Moreover, "he was not unique in his opinion, and indeed he followed not ignoble writers," especially Navarrus, "not a vulgar author." In this situation, Tomasi concluded, "I do not see how the book of this author should be prohibited, while the others should not."[92]

Tomasi's opinion was evidently discarded. The Roman Curia of his time was interested in fighting against probabilism and laxism (both seen as intrinsically Jesuit doctrines); therefore, embarking on a long and dangerous theological exegesis involving Navarrus was not on the agenda. However, as I have argued throughout this chapter, Tomasi was not entirely correct in seeing Raynaud's and Navarrus's doctrines as identical. Indeed, they were different precisely because Navarrus saw mixed propositions as a feature of language at the disposal of everybody, regardless of the justness of one's reason to use them. For Raynaud, on the contrary, mixed propositions existed only if whoever wanted to use them had a right reason to do so. From this perspective and *pace* Tomasi, Rome had been coherent in focusing on Raynaud and leaving Navarrus alone.

The condemnation of Raynaud in 1681, paradoxically, represents the ultimate success of the Jesuits' theological attempts to appropriate and modify the doctrines of equivocation and mental reservation. By making those doctrines a part of moral theology, the Jesuits tried to erase the hermeneutical anxiety inherent in Navarrus's theory of language, and they were so successful that when laxism was condemned, equivocation and mental reservation were condemned also. The hermeneutical and indeed epistemological uncertainty, however, started to resurface shortly thereafter.

In 1701 the influential theologian and professor of the Roman College José Alfaro was asked to write a memo on equivocation and mental reservation to be given to the Jesuit superior for the French province.[93] Alfaro praised the attempts made by the French superior to have his Jesuits avoid talking or writing on equivocation and mental reservation, but he also warned that rejecting these doctrines *tout court* could have originated a difficult conundrum. On the one hand, rejecting any form of equivocation would make it difficult to maintain the confessional seal, which instead needed to be protected. On the other hand, it was necessary to remember that because of Innocent's condemnation, *"restrictio pure mentalis,"* pure mental restriction, could not be allowed under any circumstance, no matter how just the cause for using it was. What was then the solution for anybody who wanted to avoid the Scylla of jeopardizing the confessional seal and the Charybdis of contravening the explicit prohibition of a pontiff? According to Alfaro, "sometimes it is licit, indeed necessary", to use "a restriction which is called real"; that is, when the uttered words actually allow an ambiguous interpretation. As an example, Alfaro quoted the intrinsic semantic ambiguity of the verb *scire*, which a confessor might take advantage of when refusing to reveal sins "he learned of in confession," which was Soto's starting point.[94] The cycle of hermeneutical uncertainty was starting all over again.

Equivocation, however, was not the only issue on which such uncertainty resurfaced, as we will see if we take a closer look at Alfaro himself, who had reintroduced Soto's linguistic ambiguity as an antidote to the morally problematic doctrine of mental reservation. In addition to being a relatively famous theologian and professor of the Roman College, Alfaro was a great supporter of Tirso González de Santalla (the general of the Jesuits between 1687 and 1705) in his battle to eradicate probabilism from the moral theology of the Society of Jesus.[95] On this subject, Alfaro wrote a short treatise, entitled *Observationes*, aimed at defending González's antiprobabilistic *Tractatus succinctus de recto usu opinionum probabilium*, published in 1691 and vigorously attacked by the more philoprobabilistic faction of the Society of Jesus.[96] In particular, in 1693 a German Jesuit, Christophorus Rassler, had published a work entitled *Controversia Theologica Tripartita Academicae Disputationi subiecta de recto usu opinionum probabilium*, in which he explicitly and virulently opposed the general's positions in matters of moral theology. In his *Observationes* Alfaro attacked Rassler's work so thoroughly that the hierarchy of the Society of Jesus, moved by Alfaro's arguments, decided to prohibit Rassler's book and to eliminate all the extant copies.[97]

Since the debate in which Alfaro entered concerned whether one could, without sinning, act on the basis of a less probable and less safe opinion and discard a more probable and safer one, most of Alfaro's treatise is concerned with the moral and theological consequences of acting according to a probable opinion rather than with the hermeneutical and epistemological question of how to arrive at a probable opinion. Nevertheless, in one of his chapters Alfaro had to discuss Rassler's epistemological argument that acting on the basis of a probable opinion was not sinful provided that one arrived at said opinion "*omnibus rite ac sine passione perpensis*"; that is, "after having pondered everything properly and without passion."[98] Rassler's statement, Alfaro wrote, was unacceptable for many reasons. First, affirming that to act on the basis of a probable opinion was never sinful meant affirming that an erroneous conscience was in all cases excused from sin, which Aquinas had already denied in *Ia IIae*, questions 8 and especially 19. Moreover, Alfaro added, even assuming that it is indeed safe to act on a probable opinion provided that one arrives at such opinion in good conscience, how can anybody ever be certain of his or her good conscience? In fact, more often than not people are deceived in that respect, since they think they ponder questions in good conscience but in reality they do so "temerariously and imprudently and deceived by some kind of passion." Indeed, Alfaro continued, the Jews, the pagans, and the heretics are all in good conscience in their hatred of the Christians, and yet they most certainly sin in their mistaken beliefs.[99]

But finally, even if this were true and people could legitimately and without sin act on the basis of an opinion that they in good conscience think they have explored properly, how can one be certain that something has been properly explored? This certainty, Alfaro wrote, is something that nobody can and should ever be sure of attaining. Rather, "one should and must fear to have failed in his consideration of virtue and truth" and always assume to have been "clouded" by his own interest or some kind of "*perturbatio*" of his soul. In other words, for Alfaro the moral certainty of being free of sin in acting is mirrored by the epistemological and hermeneutical certainty of being correct in thinking, knowing, understanding. Both certainties run against the *perpetua solicitudo et anxietas* that all the holy and saintly men rightly had and that every man and woman, according to Alfaro, needed to acknowledge and hold on to.[100] When people have to decide on something controversial, they often think they have reached a correct understanding of that controversy because they believe they have "searched out the truth without passion and negligence, but by pondering everything properly." That "clarity [*evidentia*] and security" that they think they have acquired, Alfaro concluded, is often "futile and imaginary and pernicious."[101]

Alfaro ended this chapter with a series of quotations from the Bible, Augustine, and St. Gregory, all on the theme of the danger that men and women incur when they exhibit an excessive certainty about the salvation their souls.[102] Alfaro's own preoccupation, however, concerned the excessive certainty of not simply the status of one's soul but also the status of one's knowledge and, more generally, men's ability to understand and represent truly and truthfully the world outside. We found a version of the same uncertainty at the beginning of the elaboration of the doctrines of equivocation and mental reservation. As I argued at the beginning of this chapter, Soto's and Navarro's intuitions regarding the uncertain and complex ways in which words and things are related made possible a radical reflection on the potentialities and limitations of language as a venue to express an extralinguistic reality. Aware of the radical implications of these doctrines in terms of language, theologians like Bañez, Gregory of Valencia, Persons, Lessius, and Raynaud sought to eliminate the hermeneutical uncertainty underlying these doctrines and to substitute for it moral criteria that justified both the theoretical foundations of these doctrines and their practical application. It is interesting, in this respect, that for Alfaro moral probabilism, which was the rubric under which at that time those doctrines were discussed, justified, and applied, was not a way to articulate a sort of moral uncertainty, as opposed to moral rigidity. Rather, probabilism was the expression of an excessive certainty and confidence in the capability of humans to both know and act. Thus, when Alfaro wanted to attack moral probabilism, he opposed to it, not the clarity of moral certainty, but the obscurity of moral and epistemological uncertainty, just as when he wanted to caution his French confreres against mental reservation, he opposed to it the linguistic and hermeneutical ambiguity of Soto's doctrine of equivocation. In other words, at the very moment in which Alfaro attacked a way of knowing and acting on the probable rather than the true, he proposed as an antidote, not certainty, not truth, but a radical epistemological and moral uncertainty, which was the proper marker of the human condition and which was reflected in the ambiguities and complexities of human language.

In conclusion, even at the end, so to speak, of the early modern elaboration of these doctrines, we still find the same hermeneutical and epistemological uncertainty we found at the beginning. In a sense, we are still in this same cycle—that is, we are still grappling with the complexities concerning moral, hermeneutical, and epistemological certainty (or lack thereof), which is a fundamental component of our late modern and postmodern sensibility. The doctrines of equivocation and mental reservation show how these complexities were reflected in the elaboration on language, and my analysis of the development of the Catholic views on them reveals a sort of fundamental embryonic doubt about the capability of language to reflect reality truly and truthfully, not just in a morally commendable manner. In this respect, the Catholic debate over these doctrines is a perfect way to introduce the question of the relationship between reality *lato sensu* and its linguistic representation as it began to emerge and to be articulated in post-Reformation Catholic culture. Let us now move to other areas in which we can discern aspects of the same tension between language and truth.

Writing the truth: Agostino Mascardi and Post-Reformation Historiography by Way of Paul Ricoeur

Cicero's definition of history as *lux veritatis* had become a sort of stale commonplace in post-Humanist historiography, and especially in the genre known as *ars historiae*. Most of the *artes historiae* written between the end of the sixteenth and the beginning of the seventeenth century were characterized by a stylistically unappealing verbosity and by a general lack of attention to historical methodology. These features contributed to identify this kind of production as something completely out of step with the more "modern" and "scientific" developments of historical scholarship and therefore as an expression of the decadence experienced by historical studies between the glorious Humanist moment and the birth of modern historiography. This is more or less the standard view of the *artes historiae* found in traditional scholarship.[1] In this chapter I seek to question this traditional view and to propose a different interpretation of this genre. I focus on Agostino Mascardi, an ex-Jesuit historian, literary critic, and theorist of history, who in 1636 published one of the last and most influential examples of *ars historiae*, a five-volume treatise entitled *Dell'arte historica*.

Mascardi's methodology is indeed very different from that of the French school of historical jurisprudence, and it is also very distant from the critical and documentary sophistication that, as Arnaldo Momigliano showed, seventeenth-century antiquarians started to develop. This, however, does not mean that Mascardi's "narrativist" approach should be considered an unoriginal exemplar of a historiographically insignificant genre.[2] Rather, Mascardi elaborated a novel theory of history, in which the documentary and empirical dimension of historical research was both distinct from and complementary to the narrative and poetic dimension of history writing.

Mascardi's view of history is a perfect expression of the shadowy side, so to speak, of post-Reformation historiography. While it is certainly true that the fight between Protestants and Catholics enhanced and refined the historical method by contributing to elaborate and to refine the tools for searching the truth,[3] I argue that the Reformation forged also the tools needed to question, dissect, and complicate the concept of truth. We already saw a specific manifestation of this latter aspect when we examined the hermeneutical implications of the doctrines of equivocation and mental reservation, and now we will see another manifestation of the same aspect in Agostino Mascardi's work. Mascardi's insistence on the representational character of historical narrative aimed neither at denying the truth of history nor at collapsing the truth of history into the fiction of the story. Instead, Mascardi conceived and articulated the truth of history as a slippery, complex, multilayered component of the story of humans as historical creatures. Reconsidering Mascardi's work in its historical context and putting it alongside with, not in opposition to, the more "scientific" developments in early modern historical research will therefore allow us to appreciate from a distinctive angle how post-Reformation culture grappled with the tension between truth and representation and between certainty and uncertainty in the realm of human affairs and, more specifically, in the question of what it means to represent the past truly and truthfully.

Agostino Mascardi: A freelance Intellectual in Rome

Agostino Mascardi was born in Sarzana in 1590, from a family of noble origins and of modest economic means.[4] While still very young, he moved to Rome and entered the Society of Jesus. The Roman College of the Jesuits was the setting of Mascardi's formative years and the source of important influences throughout his career: at the Roman College he studied with Famiano Strada (who for Mascardi remained a constant intellectual referent) and with Tarquinio Galluzzi (with whom Mascardi had a very controversial relationship for almost his entire life).[5] After his Roman studies, Mascardi taught rhetoric briefly in the Jesuit colleges of Parma and Piacenza. While in the Estense territory, however, Mascardi started to cultivate higher intellectual ambitions and to feel that his role as a Jesuit might have been too restrictive. In the 1610s, in fact, he was introduced to the inner circle of the Estense court, and in the meantime he began to devote himself to poetry, laudatory orations in honor of the family d'Este, and other nonreligious literary activities.

In 1617 Mascardi was officially expelled from the Society of Jesus; the specific causes of his expulsion remain mysterious. In a letter to Camillo Molza, one of his early patrons at the Estense court, Mascardi wrote that "the obstinacy of fortune obliged me to depose the habit which I have worn for eleven years." According to Mascardi, "the principal reason of such calamity has been my employment with the family d'Este," which his Jesuit superiors saw as a sign that Mascardi had decided to put his personal ambitions before the interests of the Jesuit order.[6] In the Jesuit Archive there is no hint of the specific cause of Mascardi's expulsion,[7] but there is a telling censure by Bandino Gualfreducci on Mascardi's *Iuvenilia* (a collection of Latin poems that Mascardi later published in the *Silvae*).[8] In his censure Gualfreducci stated that Mascardi's poems were not yet ready to be collected into a volume and printed. However, "as more things are added which are either more pious, or more moral, such as could be expected from a religious person, it will be possible to publish a part of a whole volume. In the meantime the author should undoubtedly revise and improve them."[9] While no direct connection between this document and Mascardi's expulsion can be made, from the censure we can see that aside from Mascardi's personal involvement with the Estense family, the tone of his literary production during his Jesuit years already seemed inappropriate to the Jesuit hierarchy, for it was not suitably pious or moral. It is not hard to see that Mascardi was champing at the bit during his time as a Jesuit: a larger intellectual world was waiting for him, in terms of both intellectual interests and personal patronage.

After his expulsion from the Jesuits, which coincided with the severing of the financial bonds that tied him to his family, Mascardi had no choice but to throw himself into the larger intellectual community of his time. Thanks to his familiarity with the Estense court and, most importantly, to the support he received from the Barberini family (especially after the election of Maffeo Barberini to the pontificate) and from Cardinal Maurizio di Savoia, Mascardi became a relatively prominent fixture in the Roman intellectual scene of his time. He was a member and later *principe* of the Accademia degli Umoristi and *sopraintendente* of the Accademia dei Desiosi, which started to be assemled by Cardinal Savoia in 1625 and was officially founded in 1626, and which became one of the most intellectually vivacious venues in early seventeenth-century Rome.[10] Among the people who routinely attended the meetings of the Umoristi and of the Desiosi, there were antiquarians, such as Cassiano dal Pozzo, and Catholic intellectuals, such as Giovanni Ciampoli and Virgilio Cesarini, who were early supporters of Galileo's scientific views. Indeed, during the Carnival festivities of 1625 Mascardi had the poet Giuliano Fabrici recite, in front of an audience that would become the bulk of the soon-to-be founded Accademia dei Desiosi, an oration entitled "Dell'ambitione del letterato," which repeated the same anti-Aristotelian arguments of Galileo's *Assayer*.[11]

Mario Biagioli has described Rome's cultural and patronage scene as "a volcanic archipelago subjected to rapid cycles of change."[12] The protagonists of the Accademie and of the cultural life in Rome depended, as far as their job security was concerned, largely on the patronage of the pope or of a cardinal or of a religious order. Because of the high turnover of popes and cardinals and of the frequent power struggles within the hierarchy of the religious orders, insecurity about one's position was high. Moreover, since the misfortune of one's patron could potentially end one's career, if an intellectual wanted to maintain his post he needed to keep his network of alliances broad and flexible, so as to be able to move swiftly between different centers of power. Also, it was important to avoid alienating people who could potentially become future patrons. As Mascardi had declared in the inaugural oration of the Accademia dei Desiosi, "the flexibility to adapt himself to the nature of other people is one of the most necessary skills for a courtier,"[13] a maxim which was evidently applicable also to the learned men in charge of educating courtiers. For Mascardi this was especially true: since his expulsion from the Society, he had lost the institutional safety that came with being a member of a religious order, and he was therefore obliged to fend for himself in the intellectual landscape of post-Tridentine Rome, which meant that his career was very much at the mercy of the wills of his patrons. The game Mascardi was playing was a difficult one, and indeed Mascardi experienced on several occasions the difficulty of keeping himself afoot.[14]

If one considers, for instance, Mascardi's intellectual production in the 1620s against the background of what is left of his personal correspondence, one can gain a vivid image of his great intellectual ambitions and, in parallel, of the fragility of his personal financial situation. The 1620s, especially after the election of Urban VIII, were the most productive years of Mascardi's career. In 1624 he published the *Pompe del Campidoglio*, in which he described the apparatus arranged in Rome to celebrate the election of Urban VIII as a figural representation of all the qualities of the pontiff (possibly as a sign of appreciation for the work, Urban VIII conferred upon Mascardi the title *cameriere d'onore*). In 1625 he published the *Prose vulgari*, a selection of orations and compositions in Italian, which included the inaugural oration delivered to celebrate the foundation of the Accademia dei Desiosi. In 1627 he published his *Discorsi morali su la Tavola di Cebete Tebano*, an eclectic and influential collection of short prose compositions devoted to discussing a number of literary and philosophical questions.[15] In 1628 Francesco Barberini recommended Mascardi for a teaching post at the *Sapienza* as a professor of rhetoric.

Notwithstanding this professional success, in Mascardi's letters to his friends and patrons from those years we can read over and over a servant's plea for money, favors, and protection and a servant's panic and terror when the said money, favors, and protection did not seem to arrive. For instance, between January and February 1626 Mascardi wrote three letters to Molza to communicate his fear of having lost the *"buona grazia"* of his patrons. In those letters Mascardi mentioned two things that made him especially anxious. A first source of worry was the fact that Massimiliano Montecuccoli, who as an agent for the

Estense family in Rome had often served as an intermediary between Mascardi and his Roman and Estense *padroni*, seemed to ignore his letters and requests. The other worrisome event concerned a shipment of salami, which Molza had promised to Mascardi and which had not yet arrived.[16] The fact that the missing charcuterie coincided with a period of relative neglect on the part of the Estense court might explain Mascardi's anxiety over the salami, and it is a good indication of the precarious and volatile nature of his condition, in which his physical sustenance and livelihood literally depended on his patrons' good grace.

Even when the substance of Mascardi's requests had less to do with personal sustenance and more with intellectual matters, the tone of his letters is still that of a servant begging, and the monetary cost associated with Mascardi's intellectual pursuits is always in the foreground. For instance, when Mascardi asked the Cardinal d'Este to intercede with the Congregation of the Index on his behalf so that the Congregation would allow him to read prohibited books, he specified that this favor would enable the cardinal "to promote my studies without any expense on your part."[17]

Of course there was an important element of formulaic self-fashioning in these letters: Mascardi knew that in Rome, the theater of the intellectual world, he had a part to play, and he knew the linguistic and behavioral rules governing his role. Nevertheless, behind the rhetorical self-fashioning there was a socially difficult reality. Mascardi's career was and remained volatile for much of his life, and the setbacks he experienced were real and dramatic. In a sense, because of the peculiar nature of the papal court and of the papal office, nobody was entirely safe in early modern Rome. Even Robert Bellarmine, one of the intellectual pillars of post-Tridentine Catholicism, experienced a difficult time in the late 1580s due to the hostility of Pope Sixtus V. Nevertheless, people like Bellarmine, the royalty of Rome's intellectual landscape, could count on a series of safety nets to break possible falls, including the protection of his own religious order.[18] Mascardi, on the other hand, did not have any safety net at his disposal, especially after his expulsion from the Society of Jesus.

The 1620s mark not only the apex of Mascardi's Roman career despite the financial instability he continued to face, but also the beginning of his involvement with history and historiography. By the mid-1620s Mascardi had decided to write a continuation of Guicciardini's *Storia d'Italia*, and for this reason he started to collect relevant primary sources. In 1627 he wrote to the Senate of the Republic of Genoa explaining his project and asking the members of the Senate "to tell me what you think and to pass on to me the appropriate information [regarding the events that happened in the government's reforms as well as in the establishment of the republic's freedom], with the certainty that I will serve you with the faith and affection which I owe you, except for the truth which my conscience, my reputation, and the aim of the public good prescribes to me."[19]

These two themes, that is, the "truth" that Mascardi's conscience prescribed and the "faith and affection" that Mascardi needed to show to actual and potential patrons, resurface more clearly in another letter that he wrote to duke of Modena in the same year. Mascardi informed the duke that a part of his projected history of Italy was supposed to touch on the war of Siena (a war fought between 1552 and 1555 in the context of the Italian wars between the emperor Charles V and the French kings Francis I and Henri II). Two members of the Estense family, Cardinal Ippolito d'Este and Alfonso d'Este, had a prominent role in the war of Siena as supporters of the French side against Cosimo de' Medici and the imperial faction, and in his historical work Mascardi planned to discuss and assess their roles. He told the duke that two considerations inspired his work: first, the duty that "his conscience and reputation" owed to truth and, second, "the true devotion" he felt for the "glory of the Estense princes." Thus, as if trying to reconcile these two forces pulling him in different directions, Mascardi first asked the duke whether he approved of Mascardi's use of Florentine sources, hostile to the Francophile positions of Ippolito and Alfonso. Then Mascardi asked whether the duke could give him access to the archives.[20]

The tension between Mascardi's desire to find out the truth of history through the use of the archives and his desire to celebrate the glory of his patrons, expressed in his request to the duke to vet his use of secondary material, is very indicative of the difficult position an intellectual in Mascardi's situation found himself in and of the additional difficulties that such a position presented in the specific case of historical research. Mascardi's letter here betrays a fundamental methodological and social predicament. Even though Mascardi did not articulate this issue, nevertheless he seemed aware of the fact that primary and secondary sources were not the same thing and that using either kind of source could have different consequences for the truthfulness of his account and for the security of his employment. At this stage he thought that he could combine them, but soon enough he would realize just how difficult this was, and he would pay a steep price for it.

As Mascardi started to collect materials for his history of Italy, he decided to "give a taste of the whole work" by sending to press a short historical account of the 1547 rebellion of the Count Gianluigi Fieschi in Genoa, against Andrea and Giannettino Doria. In the epistle to the reader, which contains some (admittedly scant) methodological considerations, Mascardi explicitly stated that "the object of my pen is the truth, which in my pages will appear uncontaminated, without being ruled by ill-regulated passions."[21] After this initial affirmation of the truthfulness of his account, in the traditional sense of an account written *sine ira et studio*, Mascardi explained that this work, and the larger history of Italy of which the Fieschi rebellion was but a small part, was unlike any other he had published before. His earlier work "was born by chance. . . in order to serve to a particular occasion" and as such it was almost a "divertissement"; this history, however, "is directed to the public good, brings with itself the need of instructing the readers, conserves the memory of valorous men, and is an authentic testimony of the past."[22]

At first glance, this list of the components of his history seems a trite collection of tropes common to the *ars historiae* genre: the theme of the *historia magistra vitae* and the insistence on truth as a general law of history are not a prelude to any sort of methodological discussion, but seem to be commonplaces of a certain manner of seeing history as a rhetorical exercise rather than as a method of research. While it is undeniable that Mascardi's *Congiura* has many components of a rhetorical exercise, it will be worth noticing a few elements that suggest that Mascardi's view of history was more complex than that.

For instance, again in his epistle to the reader, Mascardi introduced a few possible objections to his work that readers might have and anticipated some preliminary answers. The first objection concerned the relationship between the *Congiura* and the larger work of which it was a part: why did Mascardi think it appropriate to publish "such a small part of a whole volume"? Mascardi replied that his work was intended, not as a part of the whole, but as a stand-alone episode, which "in the body of history appears in a different form, since in the universal narrative I do not have to dissect so much every particular accident." The point of his history of the rebellion, Mascardi continued, was not to relate all events that happened in those years but "to write a complete action with its parts, so as to have occasion to try out all those issues that can arise in a long history. And I do not do this without following the examples of the ancients, and especially that of Sallust."[23] References to Sallust and his *Catilinae Coniuratio* that we usually find in post-Tridentine historical works and in the *ars historiae*-type of authors tended to have either a moralizing value (the precepts, or *sententiae*, that usually accompany the character of the villain or of the hero, in order to suggest to the reader the appropriate response of condemnation or of praise) or a stylistic connotation (especially on the question of harangues, which in Sallust's work were many and famous). While Mascardi's text contains both a number of Sallustian *sententiae* and an even larger number of Sallustian harangues,[24] it is noteworthy here that the first mention of Sallust concerns neither of those issues but rather the issue of the tension between history as a narrative of chronological events and history as a narrative of a unitary action in Aristotelian terms.[25]

A second objection that Mascardi foresaw concerned another Sallustian issue, which by Mascardi's time had become somewhat unfashionable—that is, whether or not harangues belonged to historical narratives. The sixteenth- and early seventeenth-century debate over the inclusion of harangues in works of history represents the evolution of Renaissance historiography and, in a sense, its demise. Traditional Renaissance theorists of history defended harangues for their rhetorical function of making the historical narrative more pleasant and more elegant, à la mode of ancient historiography. By the end of the sixteenth century, however, the practice of including harangues was very much frowned upon by the more "scientifically" and documentary-oriented historians as a leftover of a "rhetorical" understanding of history. Mascardi's *Congiura*, as I said, does present many of the tropes of history as a rhetorical exercise, and as such it contained a great number of harangues. Mascardi, however, was not uncritically reproducing the tradition. In fact, he was fully aware of the suspicion with which harangues were seen among certain historians, and that is why in his epistle to the reader he wrote: "Perhaps my harangues will be judged long and frequent. I would have much to say in my defense, but I will only say that I have myself considered the flaws [of my harangues], and I do not want to write my own defense before having heard the accusations against me."[26] Despite this initial refusal to confront his possible detractors, Mascardi felt the need to add some arguments in defense of his use of harangues, and he continued: "Since I wanted to give a taste of everything that can happen in history, it was necessary to consider the occurrences which could not otherwise be ignored, and in deliberating a most grave affair, when there are contrary opinions, it is not so easy to get out of trouble in six words, if one needs to weigh the different reasons."[27]

In this passage Mascardi defended his numerous harangues neither on the basis of stylistic or "rhetorical" reasons nor on the basis of the necessity of representing more effectively the moral lessons to be gained by the story of the rebellion (both features were indeed very prevalent in the actual way in which Mascardi wrote his book). Rather, he presented as an argument in defense of the harangues the fact that if one wants to see what happens in "history," considered here ambiguously as both historical events and history writing, one needs to be able to "weigh the different reasons," that is, to understand and to give an account of what lies behind the scene of an important affair. In this context, harangues appear as a heuristic tool that the historian has at his disposal to make sense of and explain for his readers the background of the historical events.[28] Once again, Mascardi did not explore the implications of what he wrote, but after this remark he closed his epistle to the reader declaring that he anxiously awaited the readers' opinion on his work, which he considered not so much a "sentence" pronounced by a judge as an occasion for feedback and improvement.[29]

After the dedicatory epistle, the first page of the narrative contained a sort of subtitle, printed in a different font with respect to the rest of the text, that reads: "This subject matter is treated by Foglietta, Sigonio, Campanaccio, Bonfandio, de Thou, and many private documents."[30] The narrative proper started after this phrase. This brief list of works consulted by Mascardi contained both primary sources, such as the "private documents" he collected, and secondary material from local historians, such as Umberto Foglietta, as well as from international and controversial (especially in post-Tridentine Rome) authors, such as Jacques-Auguste de Thou. This list is the only place in the *Congiura* where this information can be found, since the text contains no marginal notes and no other reference. As such, this is the only part in the text where Mascardi explicitly refers to the elements on which the truthfulness of his account is based.

In sum, the *Congiura* betrays the fact that at this point in Mascardi's elaboration there were a number of different and, in certain cases, opposite issues that he was considering and that in this text appeared in their contradictory and scattered nature. The question of the truth of a historical account both in the sense of a truthful narrative of events and in the sense of a narrative written without "passion"; the fact that historical narrative had an intimate relationship with chronology and historical time but was, at the same time, a self-contained "action" or story; the hermeneutical value of rhetorical tools such as the harangues: all these elements make the methodological premises of the *Congiura* incoherent and contradictory, but the text's incoherent and contradictory nature is an indication that Mascardi's work was a sort of cauldron in which many ingredients were simmering, still in an embryonic and unstructured state.

The *Congiura* had several effects on the rest of Mascardi's career, almost all of them negative. First of all, despite his attention to the needs of his patrons, Mascardi ended up getting in trouble with some of them for the content of the narrative. Mascardi's *Congiura* was a sort of ultrarepublican reading of Sallust's *Catilina*. Mascardi portrayed Gianluigi Fieschi, the instigator of the plot, as a second Catilina, who indeed fashioned himself explicitly on the Sallustian antihero. Mascardi described Fieschi as "a young man of a great vigor of mind and of turbulent thoughts," who constantly sought to find an outlet for his incredible ambition, "the ordinary evil of noblemen," as Mascardi glossed. This is almost literally the same description that Sallust gave to Catilina as a young nobleman *"magna vi et animi et corporis, sed ingenio malo pravoque."*[31] Indeed, Mascardi added that in order to gain some inspiration on his ill designs, Fieschi "on his friends' advice, started to read diligently the life of Nero, the rebellion of Catilina, and the small book on the prince by Machiavelli. These books progressively instilled in his soul cruelty, wickedness, and the love for his own interest over any human or divine consideration."[32]

The target of Fieschi's ambition was the government of Genoa, which Mascardi portrayed as a republican government protected by the wise rule of Andrea Doria, who had negotiated with Charles V the freedom for the city after the domination of the French king. In fact, aside from Fieschi, the other villain of Mascardi's story appears to be the French, guilty of having betrayed Doria and also of boycotting the newly reestablished republican government. Indeed, in Mascardi's narrative Cardinal Agostino Trivulzio, cardinal protector of France and bitter enemy of the Doria-imperial faction, pronounced a long harangue that incited Fieschi's hatred against the Dorias and thus strengthened his resolve to organize a plot against them.[33]

Mascardi dedicated the *Congiura* to the prince Ercole Trivulzio, Agostino's descendant, perhaps in the hope of making up for the less than flattering portrait of the cardinal in the Fieschi affair. Nevertheless, portraying an ecclesiastical man from a powerful family as one of the instigators of the rebellion did not sit well with the Trivulzio circle in Rome, and Mascardi was forced to defend himself in a public and annoying dispute.[34] Even more annoying for Mascardi was the cold reaction to his work on the part of his patrons in Rome, especially the Barberini circle and Cardinal Savoia, who were openly pro-French and thus did not appreciate Mascardi's anti-French take on the rebellion. From a letter written by Mascardi to Francesco Barberini after the publication of the *Congiura*, we can see that Mascardi was fully aware of the anti-French character of his work, and this is why he had sent the text to Cardinal Barberini prior to publication asking him to vet it. Accordingly, Mascardi wrote that "whenever you indicated that something was not to your liking I cancelled it, and, according to your will, my work remained buried for several months, and was finally published with your consent." Notwithstanding this precaution, Mascardi detected "some trace of bitterness" in Cardinal Barberini, fostered by his detractors who were spreading false rumors.[35] Barberini should rest assured of Mascardi's respect and veneration, and as far as the *Congiura* was concerned, he should remember that "the princes involved in the rebellion that I narrated have graciously embraced the truthfulness of my history as well as the honesty of the historian, and as a testimony of their good will toward the enterprise that I am carrying out, some of them have given me the appropriate information, and some others have kindly promised me they were going to do the same."[36]

The questions of the truthfulness of the historical account and of the honesty of the historian return, once again linked in a complex manner. The truthfulness of the account is connected to the question of the historian's use of the archives, while the honesty of the historian is connected to the question of the princes' permission to use the archives. From Mascardi's letter, in a sense, one can gather that access to primary documents and archival "information" is both the evidence of the fact that the events narrated in the *Congiura* happened as he wrote them and the prize Mascardi was awarded by the princes for his dispassionate attitude towards both the protagonists of past events and his present patrons.

Even though at the time of this letter Mascardi seemed to be still willing to "carry out his enterprise," that is, the continuation of Guicciardini's history, soon afterwards he interrupted his work. It is possible that the personal attacks that followed the publication of the *Congiura* made him change his mind. As we have seen, Mascardi thought that it was possible to write a truthful historical account, both in the sense of an account based on archival material and in the sense of a dispassionate account, and that as long as he achieved this double truthfulness, he would be safe from dangerous criticism and would continue to enjoy the support of his patrons. The aftermath of the publication of the *Congiura* proved him wrong, and as Bellini put it, history "checkmated" Mascardi. From this setback Mascardi might have learned that history was "not simply a stylistic gymnasium where the writer's rhetorical skills were put to the test, but that it was inextricably linked to the possibility of verifying the facts: access to the archives became what distinguished the narrative of history from silence."[37]

There is another, less generous, possible explanation for Mascardi's decision to interrupt his research on the history of Italy. Francesco Fulvio Frugoni, a seventeenth-century writer and literary critic, in his short biography of Mascardi wrote that in the preparatory phase of his history Mascardi had asked the Italian princes not simply for permission to access their archives but also for money to finance his studies. Since many of the princes responded positively to both requests, possibly hoping that a generous donation would ensure them a positive and laudatory treatment in the final version of the work, Mascardi "amassed in a few months a very large sum of *scudi*." Once Mascardi "achieved his aim" which was that of getting money in a moment of particular penury, he lost interest in the enterprise.[38]

I believe that there is no need to choose one option over the other, since the "checkmate" of history is in fact very tightly linked with the question of money. Indeed, I think that we should see the fragility and uncertainty that Mascardi experienced in his dealing with his patrons in connection with his understanding of the complexity and uncertainty of history as a means to recover the past. In other words, the tension between Mascardi's intellectual ambitions and his personal financial situation is linked to the tension between the truth of history in the sense of documentary evidence, and the truth of history in the sense of dispassionate account. This tension, in turn, stirred Mascardi to think more thoroughly about the representational character of the historical narrative and about the difficulty of recovering the past events that the historical narrative was supposed to truthfully represent. These elements were already present, in a sketchy and incoherent form, in the dedicatory epistle to the reader at the beginning of the *Congiura*, and by the publication of his 1636 treatise *Dell'arte historica* they had become the core of a coherent, novel, and profound elaboration on historical methodology.[39]

This is not to say that Mascardi's historiographical reflections originated directly from his autobiography, since, after all, Mascardi's works must be situated within a specific and specifically codified intellectual tradition in Renaissance and post-Reformation Europe. Nevertheless, the uncertainty of Mascardi's personal position is not a mere biographical datum. Rather, since Mascardi shared his fate with many other thinkers of his time who were concerned with the same intellectual preoccupations that he had, we should see Mascardi as a relatively common type in the intellectual demimonde of post-Tridentine Rome. Indeed, Mascardi and other people like him represented an important aspect of post-Tridentine Catholic culture. All too often post-Tridentine Catholicism is seen through the eyes of people like Bellarmine or Baronio, the cornerstones of its intellectual and theological structure. At the bottom of the structure, however, there were fragile grounds, not simply in the socioeconomic sense. People like Mascardi experienced post-Reformation Catholicism not as a world of solid certainties to be opposed to the Protestant falsehoods but rather as a world in which the stable Truth of theology coexisted with a great number of intellectual, social, and cultural uncertainties. Thus, by paying attention to the context in which Mascardi lived, we can not only identify the social and cultural factors that made Mascardi and his likes "minor" figures, but we can also understand better the significance of the intellectual tradition he belonged to.

Rhetoric, Time, and Narrative

After the backlash of the *Congiura*, Mascardi experienced another very turbulent period. As Francesco Barberini's affection toward him began to cool down, in 1627 Cardinal Maurizio di Savoia was forced to leave Rome because of the financial troubles he incurred with his liberal expenses. In this uncertain moment, Mascardi begged the grand dukes of Tuscany for help, and in 1630 he managed to obtain an academic post in Pisa and was simultaneously welcomed in the Roman court of Cardinal Carlo de' Medici. Mascardi accepted the invitation to join the court of Carlo de' Medici in Rome but declined the offer to teach in Pisa. In 1635 Cardinal Maurizio came back to Rome, and Mascardi tried, in a rather ungraceful manner, to transfer back to Maurizio's court while, at the same time, continuing to work for Carlo de' Medici. In 1636 he published *Dell'arte historica*, and just as he was starting to taste the success and fame that followed an enthusiastic initial reception of his work in Rome, Mascardi fell ill. Sick, old, and possibly fatigued by the cat-and-mouse game he must have felt he was playing with fortune, Mascardi decided to leave Rome and move back to his native Liguria. In 1640, four years after the publication of *Dell'arte historica*, Mascardi died in Sarzana.[40]

Dell'arte historica is a long, complex, profound, and at times insufferable work. It is divided into five treatises, which were supposed to follow, by and large, the different components of Cicero's laws of history in *De oratore* 2.62–64 and to explore or, in certain cases, argue against Cicero's rhetorical precepts for history writing. The actual distribution of topics within the five treatises, however, is far from coherent: precisely because Mascardi's views were not a pedestrian reelaboration of the Ciceronian tropes, the format that Mascardi chose for his work did not follow organically its content. In addition, the style of *Dell'arte historica* is uneven and difficult to follow; beautifully suggestive pages are buried among numerous rhetorical tirades and digressions into seventeenth-century literary polemics. A superficial reading of *Dell'arte historica* will certainly leave the impression of a largely unoriginal and unnecessarily difficult work that perfectly embodies the flaws of post-Humanist historiography, especially as they emerged in the genre of the *ars historiae*. However, an attentive reading of the work reveals that Mascardi's considerations on historiography were far from unoriginal and uninteresting.

Let me start by conceding that it is certainly true that the critical and methodological considerations contained in Mascardi's *Dell'arte historica* are embedded in an overall approach that privileges the narrative and rhetorical dimension of history. But what do we mean by rhetoric and narrative? Usually by these names we mean a synonym of fiction as opposed to fact or an excess of words used to cover up or substitute for the actual thing. This understanding of rhetoric and narrative, however, does not fit early modern understanding of rhetoric and narrative, and indeed it does not do justice to the richness and complexity that these concepts had inherited from their classical past and acquired in the early modern period.

First of all, as Carlo Ginzburg has demonstrated, rhetoric (especially in a specific Aristotelian tradition) had a deep connection to history and proof: Aristotle's discussion of traces (*semeia*) and of necessary signs (*tekmeria*) in his *Rhetoric*, Ginzburg argued, had much in common with historical methodology.[41] The kind of rhetoric that Mascardi was involved in was different from this Aristotelian strand. It was the product of the rhetorical school of the Jesuit Roman College, especially of the elaboration of Famiano Strada, whom Mascardi quoted often in his work and who was one of Mascardi's teachers during his years as a student of the College.[42] The Roman College and the Jesuit colleges in general had become, by the beginning of the seventeenth century, the main centers for the study of rhetoric in early modern Catholic Europe; indeed, the entire educational project of the Society of Jesus hinged on the study of rhetoric as one of the pinnacles of the *studia humanitatis*. The rhetoric that Strada and his colleagues taught took Cicero as its model. Generally speaking, the Jesuits' Ciceronianism was constituted as a sort of middle way between the strict imitators of Cicero and the Asianist anti-Ciceronians, and as such it became a fruitful way to integrate classical rhetoric with Christian preaching.[43] Because of this Ciceronian character, much of seventeenth-century Jesuit rhetoric was concerned, in its practical application, with *dispositio* and especially with *elocutio* rather than with the question of proof and evidence as it emerged from the Aristotelian tradition identified by Ginzburg. This, however, does not mean that Strada and his colleagues ignored the distinction between fact and fiction. Rather, Strada's and his colleagues' attention to narrative forms and narrative modes created the theoretical space to reflect more fully on the tension between rhetoric, truth, and history.

If we want to understand better the ways in which these intellectuals elaborated this tension, I think it fruitful to take Paul Ricoeur as our interpretative guide. As Ricoeur put it, the fact that one "writes" history "is not external to the conceiving and composing of history," but it is rather "constitutive of the historical mode of understanding. History is intrinsically historio-graphy."[44] The intrinsically narrative quality of history writing, in Ricoeur's argument, does not collapse history and fiction. Rather, for Ricoeur the historical narrative contains specific features that distinguish it from other modes of narrative and that allow history to retain its value of providing truth-finding knowledge. The Roman College and the Jesuit rhetorical school more generally, I argue, provided an important venue to discuss precisely what differentiated historical narrative from other kinds of narrative. It is in this cultural atmosphere that Mascardi elaborated his own theory of history.

Before getting to the heart of Mascardi's argument, let us briefly consider what Strada, who among other works wrote a popular historical account of the Dutch revolt,[45] had to say about history and rhetoric. In his *Prolusiones academicae*, published for the first time in 1617 and then reprinted several times over the course of the seventeenth century, Strada had argued at length about history insofar as it was both a discipline involving writing (in this respect history came from the same family as rhetoric and poetry) and a distinctive mode of gaining knowledge (in this second sense it was quite distinct from both rhetoric and poetry). A section of his *Prolusiones*, a dialogue entitled "Muretus," started with a criticism of Cicero, who had affirmed that history was nothing but a part of rhetoric, and indeed the entire dialogue was dedicated precisely to defining around history "fixed boundaries" that differentiated it from both poetry and rhetoric.[46] Those boundaries can be synthesized in one word: the truth, which should be the one and only law for historians. It is true that the "Muretus" was not much concerned with the technical tools for seeking the truth that were at a historian's disposal; nevertheless the text grappled with some of the theological and theoretical implications of the truth-value of history.

As an example of what the "Muretus" did and of what it did not do, I will only mention a long section of the dialogue devoted to the question of whether or not the historian could or should disclose a hidden truth that brought *infamia* to the historical character under discussion. In this section, the interlocutors of the dialogue discussed neither the ways in which a historian can learn about obscure facts nor the methodological procedures at a historian's disposal for weighing the reliability of the sources that mention the shameful act. Rather, taking for granted that the shameful act in question truly happened, they debated the larger theological implications of the need to conceal or reveal a secret, which as the text explicitly states, was a much discussed topic among the theologians of the time. In this manner, the interlocutors of Strada's dialogue discussed the theological definition and implication of *infamia* and weighed the need to expose a truth against the need to avoid bringing infamy to the memory of a historical character and the need to correct the audience by exposing and openly condemning the historical character's sin.[47] This part of the text is not simply evidence of Strada's "moralizing," counter-Reformation anti-Tacitist spirit (after all, the target of Strada's discussion on the historian's duty of revealing secrets was Tacitus, with his habit of revealing hidden motives and concealed truths), nor is it simply a proof of Strada's methodological ignorance. Rather, I think that this part is evidence of Strada's awareness of the complexity of the notion of truth, which both history and theology engaged with. Indeed, the question of under which conditions hidden truths were to be revealed or whether they could be revealed at all was central to the development of the doctrines of equivocation and mental reservation, other doctrines that, as I argued in the previous chapter, betray not simply a measure of moral anxiety but indeed a deep hermeneutical concern over the relationship between language and reality. From this perspective, Strada cannot be said to have failed to understand the peculiar truth-value of history with respect to the other forms of narrative. Rather, the kind of truth that he was interested in thinking through was less a question of methodological techniques proper to history than a larger theoretical problem involving the core of post-Reformation theological and intellectual elaborations.

Also, before publishing this text, Strada lectured for almost two decades on rhetoric and poetry. From his lecture notes and unpublished material we can see the same attention to the relationship between history and narrative and the centrality of the question of historical truth. In 1608, for instance, he lectured on Aristotle's *Poetics*. On the question of poetic imitation, Strada noted, explaining a familiar Platonic argument, that while poets fabricate simulacra of things and thereby create a sort of duplicate reality, historians deal with a different kind of imitation, one that represents real things without creating any simulacrum of them.[48] When a historian describes Hannibal, Strada explained, he is not fabricating a second Hannibal because he "does not seek to form a simulacrum similar to the real Hannibal, but strives to divert the reader from the historian and from his history and to turn to the things themselves that the reader examines, so that the reader might be present in those things rather than being absent and simply reading them." The poet, on the other hand, wants the reader to contemplate his simulacrum not insofar as it relates to the real thing but rather as a means unto itself.[49] This implies that for Strada history is a representation of reality whose job is to mediate between the reader's present and the past events, while poetry is a representation whose value is contained in the simulacrum itself.

When Strada revised his lecture notes, he made an important addition to this passage. After his explanation of history's method of representation, he added: "and this is why the author of the *Rhetorica ad Herennium*, while defining history in the first book, wrote that history is *res gesta* far from the memory of our reality: who does not see that he alludes to this, that history is not the *res* itself but the *narratio rei*?"[50] While the quote from the *Rhetorica ad Herennium* was usually discussed by the theorists of the *ars historiae* in the context of the question of whether history only concerned ancient times or whether one could write history of contemporary events, for Strada that definition was not about the time of history but about the relationship between historical narrative and historical facts. In other words, the "remoteness" of history is not to be found in the time elapsed between us and the events of the past but in the fact that the events of the past are not present but through the narrative. This historical narrative is therefore neither the *res gestae* themselves nor simply a "*mythistoria*," or historical fiction, such as the Arthurian saga.[51] Rather, for Strada historical narrative acts as a mediator between the reader or writer of history and the actual historical events that truly happened in the past. In sum, it is not so "curious" that Strada, "father of Baroque conceptism," was well aware, indeed the first proponent, of the "divorce of the couple history-oratory," as Sergio Bertelli argued.[52] Indeed, this is an indication that the differentiation between history and oratory was part and parcel of Strada's rhetorical tradition, and the reason for this is that Strada's rhetoric was not a sort of night where all the cows are black but rather a pasture in which different types of cows grazed as they were being branded, if you pardon my Baroque metaphor.

Agostino Mascardi, whose work, unlike that of Strada, was entirely dedicated to history, reflected much on narrative as the central component of history, with quite interesting results. Let us start from the fourth and fifth treatises of Mascardi's work, dedicated to the question of the "order" to be kept when writing history. Mascardi's reflections open up with a discussion of the relationship between poetry and history based on Aristotle's considerations in section 9 of the *Poetics*, which was the locus classicus for this kind of discussions. In particular, Mascardi started by attacking Lodovico Castelvetro's commentary on Aristotle, which presented history as subordinate to poetry because history deals with particular events as they actually happened, while poetry deals with human events as they ought to have happened and therefore with universal representations of particular events. "Castelvetro," Mascardi argued, "misunderstands the subject of history, which is not a small mistake: history is not, as he believes, the represented thing, but the representing thing, since it is a narrative, according to truth, of human actions that actually happened and that are worthy of being remembered, for this is the definition that Castelvetro himself brings. Thus, the represented thing will be the human actions, the representing thing will be the history that narrates them, so that history cannot be called the represented thing neither in comparison with poetry, nor with respect to itself and its subject."[53] Once Mascardi identified two levels in history, that is, the historical narrative on the one hand and the events represented by the narrative on the other, he grafted this double level of history onto time. In the process, he introduced a third temporal and narrative level, that of the reception of the work of history.

The question of history as a representation, Mascardi continued, brings up the question of the order of the historical narrative. The events that history represents are temporal events, which happened according to and indeed in chronological time. Mascardi was fully aware that situating events in chronological time was necessary for any historian to do, and he was fully aware of the recent developments in the study of chronology. Indeed, at the very beginning of his work Mascardi had argued that any historian needed to grasp "an exact knowledge of the time in which the things comprised within the span he deals with happened," so as to avoid anachronism, and recommended Scaliger as a modern authority on the subject.[54] Since history is a narrative of human events, it is therefore necessary that such narrative "follow, as much as possible, the order given by time, and the reason for this is most clear: because, if we believe that the proper enterprise of the historian is to represent the past events to the reader in such a vivid manner that the reader could see the events, it is certain that, since an event happened after another, so one event needs to be narrated after the other."[55] Thus for Mascardi history is a representation of past events for the benefit of the present reader: following the chronological order is not only necessary to narrate what happened but also to re-present—that is, to make present—the past events to the present reader, who will be brought into the past by means of the chronological order. Indeed, Mascardi continued, even when the historical narrative explains events causally, the causal relationship is permeated and "transcended" by chronological order, since "the natural order [of the causes. . . occasion and motives of an event] is inseparable from the chronological order."[56]

This, however, does not mean that historical narrative needs to imitate the chronological order of the events that it sets out to represent, because as Mascardi argued, "history sometimes can, indeed must, neglect the rigor of that order which accompanies the chronological succession, and anticipate and postpone the events in its narrative, so as to make it easier and more convenient for readers to acquire understanding and memory [*l'intelligenza e la memoria*] of those events."[57]

From these passages of Mascardi's work we can see that, first, he identified the level of the historical events represented by narrative, which happened in chronological order. He also identified the level of the readers of the work of history, for whom the past needs to be made present so as to enable them to acquire both "memory" and "understanding" of past events.[58] Finally, there is the historical narrative itself, which mediates between the chronological time of the event and the present time of reader. The time of this historical narrative, therefore, cannot be the same as the time of the historical event, nor can it be the same as the time in which the reader acquires memory and understanding of the past. It needs to be a peculiar time, which needs to be linked to chronological time but, at the same time, to the present time of the reader. In other words, using terms borrowed from narratology, according to Mascardi the historical narrative has the prerogative of emplotting the chronological events: by structuring the chronological time of the historical events into a story with agents, motives, causes, occasions, and the like, it creates a narrative that mediates between the events that happened in the past and the reader who, in the present, receives the historical narrative.[59] In this way, from the point of view of narrative structure, Mascardi's notion of historical narrative shows an awareness of the distinction between *récit* and *histoire* on the one hand and of the distinctive role of the reader's reception of the text as the fulfillment of the historical narrative on the other hand. Because Mascardi clearly grafted these distinctions onto time, we can say that his notion of historical narrative contains in embryo the three forms of mimesis that Ricoeur attributed to the narrative mode; that is, Mimesis$_1$ (the "preunderstanding of the world" that lies before the narrative or, in this case, the understanding of the historical events in their temporal nature), Mimesis$_2$ (the plot and time created by the historical narrative itself), and Mimesis$_3$ (the temporal and cognitive world of the reader, or what lies on the other side of the historical narrative).[60]

The fact that Mascardi emphasized both the intimate ties and, at the same time, the autonomy of the historical narrative with respect to the chronological order of the historical events signifies that he did not treat history as any other form of narrative. Thus, the peculiarity of historical narrative as opposed to fictional narrative for Mascardi was precisely the fact that the historical narrative had as its referent the reality of events that happened in the chronological time. In a sense, and pushing the Ricoeurian character of Mascardi's work a little further, one could say that Mascardi understood that historical events lie at one side of the historical narrative, which represents past events by standing for them and referring to them. On the other side of the text, as it were, there is the reader who, by receiving the work of history and thus acquiring both "memory" and "understanding" of the past events being represented, fulfills the purpose of history. Or to put it another way, Mascardi's peculiar notion of the time of the historical narrative mediates between the "lived time" of the reader, who in the present moment acquires "memory" and "understanding" of past events, and the "calendar time," the "ordinary time" of the chronological order of the past events.[61]

Having established that Mascardi's theory of history distinguishes, in an embryonic but clear manner, these three "times" from one another—that is, the time of the historical events, the time of the historical narrative, and the time of the reader's reception—let us see what he has to say about each of those times.

The Historical Events: The Past as Absence

History is a narrative of events that happened in the past. How can the historian find the building blocks of this narrative, that is, the traces of those past events? Mascardi mentioned two kinds of traces of the past that "save for posterity the actions of our progenitors." The first are the physical traces left by dead men and women as *memorie*, "testimonies," of notable things: "the paintings, the sculptures, the inscriptions, the arches, the columns and similar public testimonies [*memorie*] were a silent narrative of great and noble deeds, from which without touching a book the people learned and still learn the deeds of honorable men."[62] Even though Mascardi declared that the arches of Constantine and Septimius, the Trajan column, and other such relics were like "books of marble" that contained much information about the events and people of the past, nevertheless he did not think that they constituted the raw material of a proper historical narrative: "I did not propose this kind of testimonies [*memorie*] as the object of the *ars historica* which I am writing. When I talk about history in these pages, I mean commonly and without metaphysics that narrative which one usually makes of the events which occur, and which is preserved in books."[63]

Carlo Ginzburg exemplifies a widespread view among traditional and current scholars when he interprets Mascardi's distrust of those marble books as a typical expression of the disinterest on the part of a "narrative historian" toward the antiquarians who, right around Mascardi's time, were developing a methodological sophistication that, according to Momigliano, laid the foundations for the modern historical profession.[64] While there is certainly some element of that at play, I think that there was another reason why Mascardi distrusted those marble relics. As Mascardi repeated often in his treatise, the fragmentary state of those relics was a testament to the destruction of the past operated by time, "devourer of marble and bronze." And it was precisely time's destructive power that the "magic of history," as Mascardi put it, was supposed to counteract.[65] This reference to time as a devourer of marble points to a fundamental theme of Mascardi's view of history—that is, the theme of the past as an absence: the physical relics left over, in this sense, are less the pieces of a mosaic left for the historian to reconstruct than a powerful reminder of what is lost and can never be completely recovered.

The written equivalents to these marble books, the repository of the less fragmentary relics needed to construct a truthful historical narrative, were the archives and the books. Despite their less fragmentary state, however, the written testimony of the archives for Mascardi still cannot not provide a full and exact image of the past. Mascardi reminded the princes and the public authority (for Mascardi history was first of all political history) of the necessity of keeping an accurate and full account of their papers in their archive, "since whoever needs to write will not have a more secure capital to enrich posterity with solid precepts than the certainty of the knowledge, which should be kept in the archives of the commonwealths and principalities as in a shrine."[66] Nevertheless, he was fully aware that penetrating into the secret affairs of princes and commonwealths was more difficult than solving the enigma of the Sphynx, as he put it. Sometimes the public authorities actively destroyed documents that they did not want anybody to see, and even when a historian could find an archival document, he could not be certain that it contained true information, given that falsehoods and mistakes could easily creep into the records. For instance, when a historian examined an ambassador's report, even if the ambassador had transcribed faithfully the content of the report, he might have been given false or incomplete information by his own prince.[67]

In sum, the fragmentary state of the physical traces of the past is not completely canceled by the archival material: indeed, Mascardi explained in a beautiful passage, "among the stuff that gets passed over in places and in times, nothing is more corruptible than truth, and Saturn, that is, time, is said to be the father of truth because he devours and consumes her together with his other children, and therefore it is not surprising that truth in time incurs the same risk that the marbles themselves in the magnificent monuments are subject to." As a visual representation of the destructive power of Saturn, Mascardi suggested the image of an ancient statue left without an arm, a leg, or the head: in this case time has not only destroyed the statue, but rendered it unrecognizable, "a trunk without name."[68] This passage is fundamental for a number of reasons. By twisting the familiar trope of *veritas filia temporis*,[69] Mascardi saw time as a devourer not just of marbles but also of the written word. As a result, the traces that the historian needs to reconstruct the historical events do not provide a true and entire image of the past but serve almost as a reminder of the loss of what once was and now is no more. Surely, Mascardi added, the historian can do something with those traces: imitating Thucydides, who, according to his biographer Marcellinus, made sure to collect both the Athenians' and the Spartans' versions of the Peloponnesian wars, "the wise writer of history can, and indeed should, draw from contrasting versions all the light that he can, and with the scale of his pondered judgment he will be able to weigh exactly the motives of both sides, checking them carefully against the circumstances of that event, and then, as a well-informed judge in a debate, he will be able to pronounce his sentence frankly."[70] This ability of the historian to act as a judge of his sources (we will come back to the metaphor of the historian as judge), however, still does not ensure that the historical narrative will illuminate past events as they truthfully happened: "truth is by nature elusive and slippery,"[71] and when the truth concerns the past, it cannot be spared from the devouring power of time.

Now, it will be easy at this point to note what Mascardi did not provide in this treatise: a fuller discussion of various techniques that were at a historian's disposal to verify and "judge" the documents' authenticity, which jurists of the French historical school like Jean Bodin and seventeenth-century antiquarians were perfecting. But rather than accusing Mascardi for what he was not, let us investigate more fully what he was. The lack of "scientific" elements in Mascardi's work, in my view, is an indication that he did not share some of his contemporaries' faith in the power of history to objectively reconstruct the past as it really happened. Rather, he saw the traces of the past as the presence of an absence, the present signs of the past as the indication that whatever had been is no longer, as Michel de Certeau put it.[72] In this manner, for Mascardi the inherent untrustworthiness of documents cannot be completely overcome by a refinement of the technical skills in interpreting them, because such untrustworthiness is not simply the indication of a historiographical problem. Rather, it is the marker of the human condition, which is inherently historical and therefore exposed to the perils of forgetting and at the same time able to produce the "magic" of remembering.

There is a deep and most interesting tension in Mascardi's work on the meaning of history as history writing that mirrors the "insurmountable ambiguity" of the pharmakon given by the god Theuth, father of writing, to king Thamus in Plato's Phaedrus.[73] Historiography is simultaneously the operation that allows one to confront the unrecoverable character of the past, devoured mercilessly by time, and the means by which the historian can represent that dead past and make it present to the reader, who through the historian's writing will simultaneously acquire knowledge and memory of what once was and no longer is. In this sense, we should highlight the special place attributed by Mascardi to writing, both with respect to written documents as simultaneously the traces of the dead past and the proper tools of the historians and with respect to the historical narrative as a piece of writing that provides readers with both knowledge and memory of the otherwise dead past. Such special place that writing occupies in Mascardi's elaboration, in fact, is very indicative of the tight and tense relationship between truth and history in Mascardi's entire work.[74]

The epistemological tension that Mascardi's work highlights prevented him from believing that historical narrative could reconstruct the past as it really happened, but it also prevented him from going to the other extreme by assuming a skeptical attitude towards the truth-value of historical knowledge. Indeed, Mascardi strongly and clearly disagreed with those skeptics who took this lack of absolute certainty to mean that history could offer no true knowledge.[75] Historians might certainly make mistakes, willingly or unwillingly, and while the reader should know "the difference between error and deceit," he should also realize that neither error nor deceit can taint completely the validity of history.[76] Besides errors and deceit and at a more fundamental existential level, because of the "human caducity" the past as it truly happened has been devoured by time, which means that aside from the historian's good faith and technical ability, one can never be absolutely certain that the historian's narrative of past events reproduces faithfully those events: "The faith that one has in history is a human faith, that is, always joined with doubt, because in its very essence it does not move away from opinion. The reader is therefore insulting the historian when he requires from him the infallible certitude based on unquestionable authority. Let us leave to divine faith that undoubted truth owed to the god revealing it."[77] The historian thus faces the task of making sense of the past through a true narrative of events, which, because of the irrevocable loss inflicted by time, can never be reproduced with "infallible certitude" but which nevertheless must retain some truth-value. How can he accomplish that task?

The Historian's *Giudicio* and the Hermeneutics of the Verisimilar

The single most important skill that a historian needs in making sense of the past, for Mascardi, is *giudicio*, in the sense of both judgment and discernment. Indeed, understanding the manifold meanings of the word *giudicio* in Mascardi's work is the best way to understand more fully his hermeneutical and methodological view of history, as well as his view of humans as historical creatures.

We have already encountered one of Mascardi's uses of the word *giudicio*, in the sense of judgment or sentence pronounced by a judge, when Mascardi cautioned his historian to "weigh with the scale of a pondered judgment" the discordant versions of the same event so as to identify the most correct one.[78] In this first sense, according to Mascardi, the historian is in the position of the judge with respect to his documentary sources, which appear as discordant witnesses in need of being pondered, weighed, judged, and sentenced.[79] In Mascardi's work, however, there is a second sense in which the word *giudicio* is used. This second sense involves, not the sentences over discordant documentary witnesses to a historical event, but rather the understanding and interpretation of the causes of the historical event itself.

For Famiano Strada, just as for an entire school of early modern Jesuit intellectuals, the business of investigating the causes of historical events was a tricky one: "when one approaches a historian, he approaches him in order to understand the past, for the historian is a witness (*testis*) of the past, and therefore he plays badly the role of the judge since people require a testimony (*testimonium*), and not a judgment (*iudicium*) from him."[80] Behind this formulation there is Strada's (and his colleagues') anti-Tacitism, since Tacitus, with his proclivity to explain in ungenerous and immoral terms the reasons behind political choices, represented for this group of intellectuals the model of a specific kind of history, both conjectural and immoral, that needed to be avoided.

Mascardi shared, in part, Strada's moral concerns about Tacitus's historiography, and this is why he felt the need to specify that Tacitus had indeed been too malicious in his almost obsessive search for immoral causes.[81] Mascardi, however, also understood that emplotting the historical events in terms of causes, motives, and occasions was the backbone of a historical narrative that could instill both memory and knowledge in the reader's mind. Thus, for Mascardi the historian enjoyed a certain freedom to judge the causes of historical events, even though, he warned, "the job that the historian fulfills by judging is nevertheless dangerous, and just as he can use the freedom he has in pronouncing sentences on other people's acts, so he risks being judged by other people. Therefore, it is necessary for the historian to go about this with an aware and open eye, and not to pronounce sentences as easily as usually people do when they look at few things only. For, since the truth of the judgment depends on the exact knowledge of the circumstances accompanying the event, if the historian does not know or does not take into account some of those circumstances, he will pronounce most wrongful sentences. Thus, I would think it most useful for the historian to propose, rather than pronounce, his sentences with caution, unless he be so sure of the matter that in his heart he cannot harbor any doubts."[82] In this passage, *giudicio* crosses over two different semantic areas: the historian's *giudicio* should manifest itself not in "pronouncing sentences" but rather in "proposing sentences" over the events of the past, since the historian's aim should not be, as Tacitus's was, morally condemning people and motives but rather understanding what happened, so that the reader would acquire memory as well as knowledge of the historical events. In this sense, *giudicio* is less the skill of a judge than the skill of the interpreter who seeks to both explain and understand the historical events.[83]

This second meaning of *giudicio* does not borrow its metaphorical power from the courtroom; it has its root in Strada's and the Roman Jesuits' rhetoric. As Marc Fumaroli has brilliantly explained, one of the main innovations of Strada's and his colleagues' Ciceronianism is the position of privilege they assigned to *iudicium*, that is, "discernment," over both *memoria* (the characteristic usually highlighted by the pedantic imitators of Cicero) and *ingenium* (the characteristic usually highlighted by Asianist anti-Ciceronians). In this respect *iudicium*, an old rhetorical concept already used by Varro and Quintilian among others, became a sort of *trait d'union* and, at the same time, a middle way between those schools of rhetoric, and as such it became the backbone of the distinctive middle-of-the-road Ciceronianism of the Jesuits. In Fumaroli's reading of Strada's rhetorical theory, *iudicium* was the main feature of an orator not simply because it allowed him to maintain an equilibrium between unrestricted wit and dull memory but also because it allowed rhetoric to be connected to philosophy—that is, to connect the discipline whose main task was persuasion with the discipline in charge of assessing stable and immutable truths. According to Strada, human affairs were fickle, mutable, and subject to the *"temporum inconstantia"*: *iudicium*, therefore, allowed the orator to adapt firm and stable philosophical truths to the realm of inconsistent and mutable human affairs.[84]

It is noteworthy that in Strada's definition of *iudicium* as the cornerstone of rhetoric and as a mediator between the immutable truths of philosophy and the mutable truths of human affairs, the notion of time is theoretically fundamental. It is because human affairs are steeped in time that they are mutable, and it is precisely because the truths of philosophy are atemporal that they need to be mediated through the orator's *iudicium* if they are to be adapted to the realm of human affairs. For Mascardi, as we have seen, history is the area over which time exercises its devouring and destructive power, and at the same time, history is the only means to rescue human actions from that destruction. In this respect, just as for Strada the orator's *iudicium* is the mediator between the atemporal character of philosophical truths and the distinctively temporal human condition, so for Mascardi the historian's *giudicio* is the mediator between the absence of what once was and the present traces of that absence, re-presented by means of the historical narrative. Or to say it in a different way, the historian's *giudicio* is the linchpin of historical narrative insofar as historical narrative is, in Michel de Certeau's terminology, a "mixed discourse" that provides "a true content . . . in the form of a narration."[85]

Thus, for Mascardi the historian does not simply need to "judge" witnesses but needs to use "discernment" in understanding and explaining the documentary traces that, without the historian's *giudicio*, will simply stand as silent witness to the death of the past. In this respect, the historian's *giudicio* does not simply "fill in the gap" left by time, the devourer of marble and books, but indeed re-presents, makes present, gives sense to, what would be otherwise absent, dead, and meaningless. Or to say it once again with Michel de Certeau, the historian's *giudicio* produces the peculiar character of the historical narrative as a text *feuilleté*, "laminated," because it comprehends within its own structure both the documentary materials on which it is founded and its own explanation and understanding of the material.[86]

Mascardi is quite explicit about the fact that the historian's *giudicio* is necessary for the production of historical knowledge: "good discernment (*il buon giudicio*). . . is enough to make the historian understand how necessary it is to consider what in the historical narrative needs to be said and what needs to be passed over, what needs to be touched on in passing and what needs to be diligently explained."[87] More specifically, Mascardi argues that *giudicio* is the faculty that allows historians to make "conjectures" and that the historian's conjectures are a fundamental component of searching for the truth of human events, since documentary traces alone are not sufficient to present them: "all human affairs, whose manifest knowledge does not fall under the knowledge of feelings, have as their characteristic that their occult truth must be recovered with a studious examination. Most efficacious tools for that are conjectures, and if conjectures are judiciously (*giudiciosamente*) adapted to the circumstances of the affair, they never or very seldom deceive the narrator, indeed they firm up a universal verisimilar, with which they help to draw the particular truth."[88]

Thus, the conjectures are product of the historian's *giudicio*, and their main contribution to the historian's task of recovering the truth of past events is to provide the basis of the "universal verisimilar" onto which the particular truth needs to be attached. The question of the opposition of universal verisimilitude and particular truth has its origin in Aristotle's *Poetics*, in which Aristotle laid down his opinion on the difference between poetry and history (which was also the reason of the superiority of the former to the latter): poetry concerns universals in that it provides examples of how things ought to happen, while history concerns the particular truth of the individual events as they actually happened. Mascardi's peculiar view of historical narrative as a representation of true events (as opposed to the true events themselves), in which the documentary traces attest to the reality of the past which would otherwise remain dead unless the historian's representation made it present to the reader, puts pressure on this Aristotelian distinction, and Mascardi was fully aware that his theory implied a radical rethinking of such distinction. After the above-mentioned passage on the role of conjectures in making sense of the universal verisimilar as a way into, rather than as opposed to, the particular truth of history, Mascardi concluded: "therefore, whoever makes use of conjectures and applies them well to the circumstances of the affair he is dealing with, can make conclusions without fallacy of discourse, and thus he does not simply find the verisimilar, but indeed the true, as much as it can be found in human affairs, which are subject to a thousand accidents."[89]

Thus, for Mascardi the historian's *giudicio* and the documentary evidence are in a complex relationship. The historian's *giudicio* produces "conjectures," by means of which the historian can explain the causes of the historical events. The documentary evidence stands as a testament to the fact that these events truly happened but that at the same time they are no longer because they have been mercilessly devoured by time. In this respect, the relationship between the historian's discernment in explaining the past events and the documentary traces of the past events cannot be posed in terms of verisimilar versus true or in terms of subjective interpretation versus objective proof since, as Mascardi wrote, the kind of knowledge that one attains through the historian's conjecture is a necessary way to get to the understanding of human facts in general.[90] This peculiar blend of objective and subjective and of explanation and proof produces a peculiar kind of knowledge, which is both true and verisimilar. Mascardi was aware of the fact that his notion of truth and verisimilitude ran against Aristotle's definition of history in the *Poetics*, since it reframed the Aristotelian distinction between what truly happened (the realm of history) and what is being represented as necessary and verisimilar (the realm of poetry). This is why in his work Mascardi proposed a profound modification to the Aristotelian distinction between true and verisimilar.

Mascardi's most radical theoretical move is situated in the part of the text dealing with the question of the harangues, which for Mascardi, as he had already hinted at in the *Congiura*'s epistle to the reader, had a properly hermeneutical value, in that they were not a "rhetorical" embellishment but rather an exemplary product of that mix of *giudicio* and documentary evidence that was the only way to write a true and truthful history. Let us follow Mascardi's argument closely. He started by relating the most common objection on the part of the antiharangue historians: "the duty of the historian, my adversaries say, is to narrate truthfully the truth, in such a way that events can be seen in the narratives (*memorie*) without a gap between those two." The harangues, in this view, are an expression of that gap between the historical events as they happened and the historian's *memoria*; that is, narrative representation of them.[91] To this kind of argument, Mascardi first opposed a number of harangues written by historians whom nobody ever suspected of not being truthful in their narrative. Then he started to engage the problem in a more theoretical manner, by claiming that to link truth and language in a sort of necessary and unique relationship, as if there were only one linguistic mode in which the truth can be said or written, is a slippery slope. For instance, the Vulgate is a translation, which by definition uses different words than the original version. Yet the truth of the Vulgate is not up for discussion, since "the variety of the words with which events are narrated does not create a variety of events, and the very same events can be written with more or less elegance, or in a more succinct or more verbose manner, with ornament of rhetorical figures or with the straightforwardness of natural speech, without any mutation whatsoever as to the substance of the truth."[92]

Mascardi knew that behind the question of the relationship between truth and language there was the hermeneutical and epistemological question of

the relationship between the true and the verisimilar: those who wrote against
harangues in works of history believed firmly that history is the realm of truth
and harangues are in the realm of the verisimilar, and for this reason no connection could be legitimately made between those two. In order to attack this
principle, Mascardi modified substantially the terms of the question, and in the
process he constructed an original hermeneutics of the historical verisimilar.

For Mascardi, first of all, it was wrong to oppose *tout court* the true to the
verisimilar because "there are two kinds of verisimilar, as far as this question is
concerned: one concerns the falsehood, the other has the truth as its object."
When Virgil, Mascardi continued, imagined that Dido fell in love with Aeneas
and killed herself because of his rejection, he narrated a verisimilar episode,
since many women actually kill themselves out of desperation and love. And
yet since Dido did not actually meet Aeneas, this kind of verisimilar concerns a
false event, an event that never happened, and therefore it should be called "false
verisimilar." By contrast, the episode narrated by both Polybius and Livy concerning Scipio, who after defeating Carthage saw a beautiful woman and, instead
of treating her as a prize for the victory and raping her, gave her back to her
father (according to Polybius) or to her betrothed (according to Livy), is likewise verisimilar, since many young Romans were virtuous enough to put glory
before lust. This episode, however, contains also some truth, because Scipio
truly defeated Carthage, there were in fact many young women whom victorious
generals could rape and violate at their will, and finally Scipio truly had an education informed by the principles of virtue and glory.[93] This second kind of verisimilar, Mascardi continued, is called "true verisimilar." While poets make use of
both kinds of verisimilar, the historian "abhors the false verisimilar, and he never
uses it in his writing, since he has truth as his object, and the false similitude
is the enemy of truth. Sometimes the historian uses the true verisimilar as an
instrument to find the truth."[94] At the same time, Mascardi continued, since the
historical narrative is indeed a narrative, that is, a representation of true events,
and since the events that truly happened are subject to the uncertainty that gov-
erns all human events, in which the truth is always conjoined with doubt, unlike
the infallible truth of theology and philosophy, and finally, since the past events
are especially victim of the destruction operated by time, the result is that "the
true verisimilar, in the way in which the historian uses it, is equivocally called
verisimilar: since it does not extend outside of the truth which in civil matters
the human diligence prescribes, it can be simply called true."[95]

Thus, what we have here is a peculiar blend of truth and "true" verisimilitude: this blend, I emphasize, is not constructed in order to collapse facts into
fiction, for indeed Mascardi introduced this distinction between true and false
verisimilar precisely in order to distinguish the prerogative of the historical narrative from other forms of narrative, such as poetry, in which historical truth is

not at stake. At the same time, this blend of truth and true verisimilitude really reshuffles the question of the distinction between objective evidence and subjective interpretation or between the empirical side of history and the narrative moment of history. For Mascardi, as we have seen, historical documents, the traces left over by time, are quite distinct from the historical narrative, and yet, at the same time, without the historical narrative that emplots them, explains them, makes conjectures on them, the historical documents have no voice and do not speak to the reader, who is the ultimate beneficiary and at the same time the one who fulfills the purpose of the historical narrative.

In sum, Mascardi's peculiar hermeneutics of the verisimilar can be best understood as the core of a peculiar view of historical narrative as representation, in Ricoeur's sense of something that "stands for" the past. For Ricoeur, just as for Mascardi, the historical narrative is "indeed a present image of an absent thing; but the absent thing itself gets split into disappearance into and existence in the past." Saturn—that is, time—devours truth but at the same time leaves a trace of what happened, so that "no one can make it be that [past things] should not have been."[96] It is this peculiar double quality of the past, at once dead and alive, which for Mascardi the historian's *giudicio* needs to recover and to make present for the reader in the historical narrative. In this sense, the *giudicio* is the venue in which the historian's consciousness expresses itself as distinct from the object of study but at the same time as inseparable from the production of historical narrative. This peculiar character of historical narrative for Mascardi does not collapse the difference between history and fiction, but at the same time it does not conceal the aporias inherent in the task of the historian and, more generally, in the human condition, which for Mascardi was historical insofar as it was marked by being-in-time.

Evidence and *Evidentia*

In a recent and important essay, Carlo Ginzburg elaborated on the relationship between description and citation as a means to understand important features of the development of modern historiography. Roughly summarizing his rich argument, Ginzburg argued that the vividness of description (*enargeia* in Greek and *evidentia in narratione* in Latin) offers what ancient historians considered the effect of reality; citation, by contrast, is the effect of reality constituted by proof or evidence. "The difference between our concept of history and that of the ancients," Ginzburg writes, "could be summed up as follows: for the Greeks and Romans historical truth was based on *evidentia*... for us, on evidence."[97] The early modern period was the moment in which we can see the shift from the former concept of historical truth, which even if "it did not correspond to the reaction of the public" was nevertheless "a question of persuasion," to the latter concept of historical truth, founded on "an objective weighing of the facts."[98]

Arnaldo Momigliano famously argued that this shift came to fruition starting with the second half of the seventeenth century, thanks to the work of the antiquarians, who used nonliterary testimonies to reconstruct specific historical realities. Edward Gibbon, who merged the antiquarian tradition with the Enlightenment *histoire philosophique*, can thus be considered the father of modern historiography.[99] Ginzburg proposes to modify Momigliano's chronology and argues that the shift was already happening a century before, especially in two main areas. First, Ginzburg singled out the peculiar mix of rhetoric, history, and proof that was elaborated in the Aristotelian circles in Padua. The results of this mix can be seen, for instance, in the work of Francesco Robortello, who integrated antiquarian research into a framework characterized by Aristotle's rhetorical tradition that, in Ginzburg's argument, was linked tightly with the concept of proof. The other venue for this shift was ecclesiastical history. Indeed, Baronio's citations in the *Annales* represent, for Ginzburg, the textual signs of the tension between *evidentia* and evidence and the textual signs of the victory of the latter over the former: the vividness of narrative was superseded by the evidence indicated in the marginal notes.

In this essay Ginzburg mentioned Agostino Mascardi as an example of the losing side of this battle, as it were: Mascardi ignored Baronio and was very dismissive of the antiquarian research, while he paid great attention to vividness and other rhetorical features of historical writing. In sum, Mascardi was one of those people who discarded the "documentary proof (*evidence*)" for the sake of the "*enargeia (evidentia in narratione)*," even though by the time in which he composed his work, both antiquarians and ecclesiastical historians had already started the process of reversing this order and establishing documentary evidence as the foundation of historical truth,[100] which is the model that contemporary historians, generally speaking, still follow.

While I certainly agree with Ginzburg's main thesis, which is that the relationship between history, rhetoric, and proof, as it was theorized or practiced by people like Robortello on the one hand and Baronio on the other, is an important venue to investigate the birth of modern historiography, I want to contend that Agostino Mascardi has a place in this story and not simply as a representative of what was left behind. In other words, as I have been arguing throughout this chapter, Mascardi's understanding of the peculiar character of historical narrative is no less important in the development of the truth-value of history than Robortello's Aristotelian attention to proof. In this section I want to show that the very pages that Mascardi dedicated to the question of *enargeia*, or vividness, testify to the fact that Mascardi was fully aware that *evidentia* and *evidence* are different. The nature of this difference is not the same as it appears in Robortello, because Mascardi came from a different rhetorical tradition. At the same time, Mascardi's rhetorical tradition did bring something interesting to this discussion.

The parts of the text in which Mascardi engaged with the significance of *enargeia* in historical narrative are contained in the fifth treatise, devoted to some questions concerning the structure of the historical narrative, and more specifically in the section of that treatise concerning the relationship between oratory and history. The less original theorists of the *ars historiae* usually assigned an important role to the capability of the historian to "move the passions," as they would put it. Because the main aim of history, in this traditional Ciceronian reading, was that of being *magistra vitae* by providing a catalogue of useful examples of vice and virtue, it was necessary for historians to narrate those examples in a persuasive manner, so that the reader could be suitably stirred to follow virtue and avoid vice. In order for the historian's style to be persuasive, it was necessary that historical narrative borrow some of the orators' techniques.

By now it should not be surprising to see that Famiano Strada, who, as we saw, was deeply engaged in discussing the relationship between oratory and history and in assessing their respective autonomy, had categorically forbidden historians from using, as he put it in the "Muretus," the "*exaggerata verba atque flexamina*" proper to the orator.[101] Strada was aware that many theorists believed that historical narrative should contain some textual ways to guide the reader through the narrative. Indeed, time and again one would find the drawing of the index finger of a hand next to a particularly important passage, precisely in order to advise the reader to pay special attention to that passage. Why can't the historian also add his own interpretations, judgments, and annotations to "wake up the sleeping reader" and move him or her to virtue?[102] The specificity of historical narrative, however, as opposed to rhetoric and poetry, consists in the fact that it is a narrative of the *res gestae* and not a catalogue of the historian's personal opinions and taste. At this point in the text Strada mentioned the tradition, transmitted by Diodorus Siculus and other ancient historians, according to which history began in Egypt and the first historical records were the signs that the yearly rises of the Nile left on the Memphis columns. While for Strada this was not necessarily a truthful account of the origin of history, it was certainly an "*exemplar atque imago*" of what history should do: narrate the past events without any personal addition.[103]

When Mascardi discussed the same problem, he started by referring to this opinion of the "*elegantissimo* Strada," which he did not entirely share. Mascardi recognized that Strada had forbidden the historian to use the orator's techniques to move the audience because such techniques had no place in an account that needed to be truthful rather than persuasive. However, for Mascardi not all rhetorical artifices were in contrast with history's truthfulness. While it was true that orators used their eloquence in order to "triumph over the souls [of their audience]" and in so doing they often "obfuscated" truth, "the historian, by contrast, seeks, according to his duty, to represent the matters he treats accurately, but vividly, and therefore he manages to impress in the readers' mind the matters as they are. Thus, the historian's first aim is to express the truth of the events, and to adapt the words to that truth. But since the events, because of the specificity of their circumstances, when they are narrated effectively stir in the readers different feelings, the fact that in such case the souls are moved by the historian's narrative does not contradict the candor and truthfulness of the historian, since this is an effect of the narrated event, and truth is in no case offended because of this."[104]

What is, then, the principal rhetorical artifice with which the historian can accomplish this task of narrating the past events and impressing them in the readers' mind? This is the *enargeia*, or *evidentia*, which for Mascardi is "the virtue of elocution by which the narrated things are represented so accurately as to be posed, in a way, before the readers' eyes."[105] The reason why vividness in historical narrative is so important is that it allows the historian "to fulfill his duty, and to use his pen so that the truth of the events is recognized in the accuracy of his narrative, and the more accurate and precise the narrative is, the more vividly the readers will perceive it, since readers will, in a sense, see the narrative with their own eyes, portrayed naturally, almost as in a painting, in the writer's writing."[106]

Behind the trite trope of the *ut pictura poesis*, Mascardi's considerations on *enargeia* are here quite interesting. First of all, the effect of reality produced by the *enargeia* is distinct, in Mascardi's work, from the truthfulness of the events narrated, which is based on the authors and documents containing the traces of the past. Indeed, in his epistle to the reader at the beginning of *Dell'arte historica* Mascardi openly declared that his work was longer and less elegant than it could have been because "the number of the authors I use is too dense, and the quotations of their names, reported in the margins, is too ambitious." The reason, however, why he decided to give so many references was not only to give credit to the authority of his predecessors but also to give credibility to his own account, after his credibility had been questioned in the past. In his other works, in particular in his *Discorsi morali*, Mascardi had mentioned "many authors, especially Greek, of whom we do not have the entire works but only some fragments." Since some of his readers had complained that they had not been able to find the works he quoted in any library and bookstore, "they started to believe that in order to suit my subject I was making up names and doctrines of authors at will. . . in order, therefore, to give clarity to the less learned men and to the young, not yet expert in famous authors, I gave in the margin the name and place of publication."[107]

The task of vividness, therefore, is not to persuade the readers of the truthfulness of the account, since this task is fulfilled by the marginal quotations, that is, by the evidence provided by the sources consulted. Rather, vividness enables the historian to narrate true events in a manner that "impresses" the events themselves in the reader's minds. In other words, while the *enargeia* does not provide the evidence needed for a truthful historical account, it truly impresses the "energy"[108] that the historical narrative needs to move beyond the narrative itself and into the territory of the reader, the final recipient history.

The question of vividness thus points directly to the question of the aim of history. It is precisely because the goal of historians is very different from that of orators that historians can use rhetorical techniques without compromising the specificity of their own discipline.[109] Those *ars historiae* theorists who encouraged historians to persuade their readers did so because they believed that the ultimate aim of history was to present examples of good and bad deeds, so that the readers might learn how to imitate the former and avoid the latter. Instilling virtue in the readers was thus the main utility of history, and since this aim was best attained through elegant and catchy prose, the utility of history was conjoined, in different ways and in different degrees, with the readers' pleasure. While Mascardi discussed the question of the aim of history framing it along the same terminological poles of utility and pleasure, nevertheless behind the terminological similarities there was a very different conception of history.

In his discussion of the subject, Mascardi specified that the most obvious result of history is "preserving human events in the memory of posterity." This result, however, might properly be called not the end of history but rather "the means by which history arrives at its real end."[110] As far as this real end is concerned, Mascardi first argued, along traditional lines, that "the utility of the readers is the true aim of history, but this is so strictly conjoined with pleasure, that in a good work one cannot be found separate from the other and each of them is great in its own way."[111] But what exactly is the utility (and pleasure) of history? Here is Mascardi's reply: "I would say that the unparalleled utility of history is that it consigns the deeds of valorous men, indeed of people, to the immortality of glory. Those deeds would otherwise remain buried together with the corpses, imprisoned as they are inside the short span of a very brief life." It is usually the poets who boast that their pens are the only means for men to attain immortality, but for Mascardi poets are not entitled to this honor. Their writings are all the more beautiful, the more they are filled with "noble lies" and "*leggiadria d'invenzione*." History, on the other hand, provides "*verità di fatto*," the truthful account of what did in fact happen, and thus it is the only means to rescue true events from the death of oblivion.[112]

Once again, then, the theme of the past as a sepulchre returns, this time in the context of the aim of history. At the beginning of his treatise, while discussing whether or not history should concern itself with public events only, Mascardi argued that some private stories need to be recorded. As an example, he mentioned Guicciardini, who in the middle of his account of the French defeat in the first phase of the Italian wars (1494–1498) interrupted the thread of his narrative to tell the story of the young son of Gilbert of Montpensier, one of the leaders of the French army, who died in 1496. Gilbert's son had gone to Pozzuoli (near Naples) to visit his father's tomb; while crying over the grave, Guicciardini reported, the young man dropped dead of heartbreak. Mascardi commended Guicciardini because "this exceptional natural piety deserved not to remain buried, even though it was born above a sepulchre."[113] Surely these kinds of examples, Mascardi pointed out, represent examples of noble deeds that posterity could benefit from learning, but this traditional pedagogical function of history should not overshadow the other aim that Mascardi here attributed to the story—that is, the capability to save the past from its sepulchral destiny and to hand it over to the present reader.

In this respect, Guicciardini's report of the story of Gilbert's son becomes almost a synecdoche for the general function of the historical narrative. While a truthful historical narrative ensures the transmission of the past, otherwise dead, to the reader, it is the reader herself who completes and fulfills the purpose of history by acquiring "memory" and "understanding" of the past, thus saving the dead past from its sepulchral destiny. In order for the "magic of history" to happen, then, the reader needs the historian's *giudicio* to understand what happened and the historian's ability to write a vivid account, so that the past events can remain "impressed" in her mind. Because of vividness of the historical narrative, Mascardi continued, the reader is present as King Belus founded the Assyrian monarchy, as Tyre was being put under siege, as Saguntum was being conquered.[114] The fact that in this passage the semimythical figure of Belus coexisted with historical facts such as the sieges of Tyre and Saguntum should not detract from the core of Mascardi's argument—that history is not so much *magistra vitae* as *magistra mortis*, in the sense that through the vivid impression made on a reader's mind by means of a truthful historical account, the dead past can master its own death.

Mascardi's view of the reader who, by being affected by the past by means of the vividness of the narrative, fulfills the fundamental function of acquiring knowledge and memory of the past, has some striking similarities, in terms of theoretical questions, with Ricoeur's notion of the historical representational character as something "analogous to" events as they truly happened, insofar as the historical narrative "stands for" the past. As such, Mascardi's view constitutes a sort of middle way between the notion of the historical narrative as a reenactment of the past in the present, à la Collingwood, and the notion of the historical narrative as an expression of the negative ontology of the past, à la Certeau. In other words, Mascardi's view of historical narrative truly mediates between the present life of the reader and the irrecoverable death of the past events, and as such it maintains an autonomous place between what is alive and present and what is dead and past.[115] In this representational role, historical narrative needs the aid of rhetoric to place before the readers' eyes the events as they happened, which the readers hold as true because of the narrative's truthfulness. Historical narrative, therefore, is characterized by a complex and multifaceted dialectic between absence and presence and between distance and proximity.[116] The fragmentary documentary traces, framed by the historian's *giudicio*, are a testament to the distance between the reader and the lost past. The vividness of the historical narrative creates complicity and makes the readers believe they are actually seeing the siege of a city that truly happened at some point in the past but that is also no longer present. This dialectic, in turn, is not only the essence of history writing as Mascardi conceived it, but it also becomes an expression of the epistemological and existential anxiety of humans insofar as they simultaneously exist in time and are devoured by it.

Mascardi's view of history writing as exemplary of the temporal dimension of the human condition can be considered one of the effects brought about by what I defined, at the end of the previous chapter, as an embryonic early modern doubt concerning the bond between language and reality. Mascardi, as we have seen, did not share the confidence that some of his contemporaries had in the capability of humans to reconstruct the past as it really happened, because he did not share their faith in the nature of documentary traces as a direct entryway into the reality of the past. In this respect, therefore, the representational function of language becomes instrumental in mediating between what is past and what is present, what is dead and what is alive, what is lost in time and what remains through time. Mascardi's view of history writing concerns a particular kind of history: human history. Mascardi's own time, however, was characterized by important developments not only in this kind of historical production but also in the realm of ecclesiastical, or "divine," history. This second kind of history dealt not simply with the reality of past human events but also with the atemporal theological reality of the Church insofar as this was both a divine and a human institution. Did the same embryonic doubt that affected Mascardi have any effect on this other kind of historiography?

3

Writing the Truth: Ecclesiastical History and its Critics

Whoever wants to discuss early modern Catholic ecclesiastical history needs to reckon with Cesare Baronio. This chapter therefore begins with an examination of his historical methodology, which represents one of the clearest and most influential examples of the alliance between documentary criticism and theological certainty. To put it differently, Baronio's confidence in the certainty of the Truth of Catholic theology gave him a distinctive epistemological certainty regarding the possibility of understanding human documents and testimonies as evidence of the history of the Church. The epistemological premises of Baronio's work are fundamental in the development of post-Reformation Catholic ecclesiastical history, indeed in the development of historiography more generally. This does not mean, however, that there were no dissenting voices over Baronio's view of ecclesiastical history. Thus, the second part of this chapter focuses on Paolo Beni, a largely unknown Catholic intellectual who criticized Baronio's view of ecclesiastical history precisely on the basis of a profound epistemological anxiety over the very possibility of overcoming human doubt when writing the history of a divine institution. The sections of this chapter devoted to Beni also show that his view of ecclesiastical history was part of a larger set of reflections on the relationship between the true, the probable, and the verisimilar, which Beni expressed in many works on a variety of topics. Beni, just as Mascardi, is therefore another representative of the shadowy side of the post-Reformation elaborations on truth and language, and as was the case with Mascardi, Beni's works remained marginal with respect to the core of post-Reformation Catholic culture. However, and again as in the case of Mascardi, recentering Beni's intellectual contribution to post-Reformation Catholic culture provides fascinating insights into both the early modern intellectual context and our own way of thinking about history and truth.

The Candles of Jerome: Criticism and Dogma in Cesare Baronio's *Annales*

To Baronio and his contemporaries the first centuries of the Christian Church appeared rather dark, in more than one sense. The so-called edict of Milan allowed Christians to emerge from the catacomb state in which they were forced to practice their religion because of Roman persecution. When this happened, the Christian intellectual leaders were left with the task of articulating the identity of the Christian Church, as opposed to both Judaism and paganism, while at the same time finding a suitable way to shine in the political and cultural context of the late Roman Empire. In this delicate transitional phase, early Christian theologians and apologists carried out the immense labor of defining, enforcing, and defending Christianity on a variety of issues, ranging from theologically controversial doctrines to specific aspects of the Christian liturgical life. Among the latter, one especially contentious issue was the use of candles in Christian rituals, which early modern Catholics believed was a practical necessity in the very first centuries of the Church, when religious services were mostly performed in the dark profundities of the catacombs. According to Vigilantius, the somewhat mysterious Gallic presbyter who lived in the late fourth and early fifth century and who can boast of having made Jerome lose his polemical cool, the fact that Western Christians maintained the custom of using candles in broad daylight as a form of adoration of the relics of the martyrs was an example of idolatry and pagan superstition, which the Christian Church had inexcusably embraced instead of challenging.[1]

Jerome used two partially contradictory arguments to reply to Vigilantius. First, he remarked that lighting candles during daytime rituals was not necessarily a sign of idolatrous superstition; it could rather be seen as a ritual of symbolic and even mystical significance. As an example, Jerome mentioned the liturgical practice of lighting candles during the reading of the Gospel, especially widespread in the Eastern Church: "throughout all the churches in the East candles are lit whenever the Gospel is to be read even when the sun is shining and there are no relics of martyrs. This is done not in order to chase away the darkness, but as a sign of our joy."[2]

The second argument referred more specifically to the Western Church and to the practice of lighting candles in front of the relics of martyrs. First, Jerome remarked, Vigilantius's accusation was a "useless calumny," since "we do not light candles in broad daylight, but only as an aid to alleviate the darkness of the night, so that we might not sleep, as you do, but we can rather watch and be sober."[3] Secondly, Jerome continued, even if "some laymen, out of ignorance or naïveté, or indeed some religious women, of whom we can truly say that they have 'a zeal of God, but not according to knowledge' (Romans 10:2), light candles in honor of martyrs, what harm is it to you?" The Gospel of Matthew (26:7–12) and the Gospel of Mark (14:3–9), Jerome continued, reported the story of the Apostles rebuking a woman who was trying to pour ointment over Christ, since they thought that rather than waste money on a superfluous thing she should have sold the ointment and given the money to the poor. Christ, however, defended the woman, because even though her gesture might have been superfluous and inappropriate, her intention of honoring Jesus was sincere and commendable. Therefore, Jerome concluded, those ignorant men and women who lit candles to honor the martyrs should be granted the same indulgence that Jesus granted that woman in the Gospel. According to Jerome, Western Christianity undoubtedly came from a world of superstition and idolatry: "we are not born Christians, but we become Christians by being born again." Nevertheless, the pagan way of worshipping gods could not be equated to the Christian way of worshipping martyrs: the former was to be condemned because it was a form of veneration directed to false idols; the latter was to be commended because it was a form of veneration directed to the witnesses of the true God.[4]

In the early modern world, this early-fifth-century controversy over candles reemerged from the dark past of the Church and acquired a new, potent, polemical significance. Condemning the Catholic cult of relics of saints and martyrs as superstitious and idolatrous was a relatively common trope in the Protestant anti-Catholic propaganda. As Milton put it, relics, together with "beads, indulgences, dispenses, pardons, bulls," were a common ornament of the Paradise of Fools whom the Catholic Church mercilessly took advantage of (*Paradise Lost*, III, 491–2). The Catholic cult of relics was also attacked on historical grounds: the authors of the Magdeburg Centuries argued in several places that such cult was not consonant with the use of the primitive Church, since it began in the fourth century, when Julian the Apostate ordered the removal of the relics of St. Babyla, and continued to spread after the fifth century.[5] In this polemical context, many Protestant theologians seized the opportunity offered by Jerome's text against Vigilantius in order to further attack the Catholics. For instance, in his 1543 *Traité des reliques* Calvin made an explicit polemical reference to Jerome's argument that the women who lit candles to honor the relics of the martyrs did so out of ignorant zeal. According to Calvin, this kind of justification did not excuse but indeed proved that the Catholic cult was idolatrous.[6]

Cesare Baronio decided to tackle Jerome's opinion on the use of candles in the first volume of his *Annales Ecclesiastici* when describing the first century of the Christian Church. Baronio's *Annales* occupied a special place between past and present, history and theology, textual criticism and dogmatic concerns. Baronio's main aim was to present a comprehensive and critically scrutinized catalogue of documents demonstrating the identity between the *ecclesia primitiva* and the Roman Church of his own time. As Simon Ditchfield put it, *semper eadem,* "always the same," was both Baronio's view of the Catholic Church and the principle that informed the entire argumentative structure of his historical work.[7] In this special place occupied by Baronio's text, historical questions were plotted against theological debates, and the exegesis of a historical document could not be disjointed from the contemporary polemical context. So how did Baronio deal with Jerome's candles in this context?

In his first manuscript version of the *Annales,* Baronio started by summarizing Jerome's arguments. First, Baronio repeated Jerome's suggestion that lighting candles during Christian rituals could be taken as a symbolic manifestation of faith: "usually candles are lit in churches not only to cast away the darkness, but in order to show the solemnity of the sacred ritual, which, as Jerome attests against Vigilantius. . . usually happened in the Eastern Church. . . in a mystic sense."[8] As for the Western Church, Baronio acknowledged that Jerome seemed to have considered the usage of candles in honor of the martyrs as a Christian translation of a pagan and superstitious ritual, due to the ignorant zeal of some men and women. Such ignorant zeal was nevertheless to be excused since it was directed to the honor of the martyrs of the true Church.[9]

After reporting faithfully Jerome's points, Baronio evidently thought that he should have offered some justification for Jerome's second argument, whose weakness Calvin, among others, had already singled out and leveraged polemically. That is why at this point in his manuscript Baronio wrote up a long addition, in the margin of the page. Baronio first admitted that there could be good historical reasons to explain the fact that Jerome mentioned pagan superstition in connection with the lighting of candles: "Without a doubt the pagans used to light candles for that reason [i.e., as a sign of honor]....Indeed even Juvenal in his satire XII writes 'our early-morning lamps join in our thanksgiving.'" In fact, Baronio continued, Tertullian in his *Apologeticus* wrote that unlike the pagan worshippers of the emperors, Christians did not "violate the day with lamps."[10] But since in this, as well as in many other cases, the Jews also had the same custom of celebrating their rituals by means of lighting candles "out of pious religiosity," "why couldn't we say that we borrowed this ritual from the Jews, just as with many other rituals, rather than from the pagans?" In any case, Baronio continued, "it would certainly not be absurd if these rituals had been transferred to the cult of the true God!"[11]

Attributing the lighting of the candles to the pagans rather than to the Jews, however, was not the only error in Jerome's text. Baronio recognized that while on the one hand Jerome justified convincingly the mystical use of candles in the Eastern Church, on the other hand he attributed the same use of candles in the West "to the naïveté of laymen, or to the ignorant zeal of women." Baronio's judgment of this latter part of Jerome's work is trenchant: "that passage is certainly scabrous." Nevertheless, Baronio believed that it was possible to make

sense of that passage without offending Jerome unduly.[12] There were many factors, Baronio continued, which could justify Jerome's mistake: Jerome himself
at the end of his *Contra Vigilantium* admitted to having "composed that piece
of writing in the short space of one night" while his secretary, about to go to
Egypt, was hustling him. Moreover, Jerome explicitly acknowledged that the
Contra Vigilantium, hasty as it was, might not have been sufficient to answer all
of Vigilantius's objections, and this is why in the text Jerome promised "that if
this work had not been enough to restrain that man's [i.e., Vigilantius's] impu-
dence, he would certainly resume all his effort against him."[13] Thus, "given such a
short time (I would say this with the good leave of such a Father of the Church)
it was not easy [for Jerome] to look over and check everything," and given that
Jerome was working from memory, it was natural to find some small mistakes
here and there. For instance, in his *Contra Vigilantium* Jerome had written that
the relics of Andrew, Luke, and Timothy had been moved to Constantinople by
Constantine, while in his earlier work *De viris illustribus* he had written that those
relics were brought to Constantinople by Constantius. The fact that Constantius,
rather than Constantine, was the correct name can be proved not only "from history, but indeed out of Jerome's own testimony": in the appendix of his translation of Eusebius's chronicle Jerome confirmed that those relics had indeed been
transferred to Constantinople by Constantius.[14]

Having thus dismissed Jerome's remarks about the fact that lighting candles
was something done by ignorant men and women, Baronio concluded his discussion by adducing various other testimonies to prove that the mystical use
of candles, "far from being a ceremony of simple-minded men or of those who
have zeal not according to knowledge," was indeed a proper and holy ceremony
recommended by Augustine, celebrated by Paulinus of Nola in his Carmen XIV
dedicated to St. Felix, and widely practiced in the times of Gregory the Great
and Gregory of Tours.[15]

Jerome's passage was indeed difficult to deal with for post-Reformation
Catholic intellectuals. Baronio decided to treat it as a mistake on Jerome's
part: by applying a measure of textual criticism and by collating Jerome's *Contra
Vigilantium* with some of Jerome's other texts, Baronio showed that the former
work was somewhat unreliable, and therefore Jerome's remarks on the pagan
and superstitious flavor of the ceremonial lighting of candles could be easily
dismissed as a minor slip within a text that contained many such slips. Other
equally high-profile Catholic theologians chose different strategies. Bellarmine,
for instance, tackled Jerome's passage in the second book of his *Controversia de
ecclesia triumphante* devoted to defending the cult of saints against Protestant
attacks. In that context, Bellarmine decided not to dismiss Jerome's argument as
a slip but to offer an alternative explanation of its meaning: "Regarding candles,
I affirm that the candles lit in front of the sepulchres of martyrs are not a sign of

adoration, which is due to God: indeed, the candles are not offered as a sacrifice, but they are lit as a sign of joy." Therefore, "when Jerome says that those who light candles in front of relics have a zeal of God, but not according to knowledge, he refers to those who light candles in order to illuminate the martyrs" and not to those who light candles with the right intention; that is, in order to manifest their joy.[16]

Bellarmine was motivated less by the need to find a form of textual coherence and precision within Jerome's opus than by the need to find a harmonious concordance between Jerome's words and the orthodox theology of the Catholic Church. Bellarmine took for granted that Jerome could not have made a mistake, and thus the words of the text were to be taken as correct. However, Bellarmine remarked, those words could not have been taken literally. First of all, both in the *Contra Vigilantium* and in his other works Jerome openly defended the liturgical practices of the Christian Church from the accusation of superstition. In addition, Bellarmine noted that the practice of lighting candles was not limited to ignorant woman, since it was done also "by Bishops and the whole Church, as is clear from Paulinus, Theodoretus, and others." On this score, Bellarmine added that if lighting candles in front of the relics of martyrs was superstitious, lighting candles during the reading of the Gospel would also be superstitious, which was impossible since Jerome himself, together with many other authors, commended the latter practice. Finally, according to Bellarmine, Jerome's ironic criticism of people who thought that dead martyrs actually needed to be illuminated by the light of candles resonated with the sarcastic tone that Vigilantius had used to condemn the practice of lighting candles.[17]

Baronio's and Bellarmine's solutions to the problem presented by Jerome's passage were animated by the same apologetic purpose, since both sought to interpret Jerome's words as a defense of the Catholic cult of relics against the Protestants' attack. The ways in which Baronio and Bellarmine went about defending their similar polemical purpose, however, were very different. In a sense, we can say that for Baronio the question of the *Contra Vigilantium* was a matter of textual criticism; for Bellarmine it was a matter involving more broadly the theo-historical structure of Catholic doctrine. Baronio's solution had the benefit of explaining a number of small mistakes found in the *Contra Vigilantium* in a way that safeguarded the overall integrity of Jerome's opus as well as the theological legitimacy of the candles. The flip side was that Baronio needed to admit openly that Jerome had indeed made mistakes. Bellarmine, by contrast, refused to admit that Jerome might have simply used the wrong words and instead tried to interpret what the text actually said in a way that was consonant with Jerome's own arguments, the practice of the primitive Church, and Catholic theology.

As Baronio was working on the first manuscript version of the first volume of the *Annales*, he must have communicated the difficulties concerning

Jerome's passage to Antonio Talpa. Talpa was one of the founders of the Congregation of the Oratorians in Naples, a personal friend of Baronio's, and one of the people in charge of helping him revise the *Annales*, correct the proofs, and oversee the indexing of the volumes. Talpa had always been supportive of Baronio's enterprise, since he was well aware of its importance for the future of the Catholic Church and of the young Congregation of the Oratorians, but when he heard how Baronio was dealing with that passage from Jerome, he was less than pleased. Talpa must have complained that Baronio's solution had the dangerous drawback of admitting that Jerome had made a mistake, and he must have suggested Bellarmine's *Controversia* as a good model on how to rescue Jerome. In the spring of 1588, only months before the publication of the first volume of the *Annales*, Baronio sent a letter to Talpa in which he tried to defend himself from Talpa's criticism: "As for Jerome's passage, Father Bellarmine dodges the problem of lighting candles during the night and not during the day, and this is precisely my objection. Please look carefully at my writing, and let me know if you think there is indeed a way to excuse Jerome." Baronio admitted that drawing attention to Jerome's mistake was not ideal, but he also seemed convinced that his interpretation was the only correct one: "it pains me to come to similar terms when dealing with the Fathers; and yet I cannot do otherwise, for the sake of the truth of history and of the Catholic doctrines."[18]

Talpa, however, was not the only person who disliked Baronio's decision to blame Jerome for the sake of "the truth of history and of the Catholic doctrines." Other people in the Roman Curia, including the *compagno* of the *Magister Sacri Palatii* (who was responsible for licensing books printed in Rome and who then was the Dominican Tommaso Zobbia), had complained about that part of Baronio's text. Baronio was therefore feeling some pressure to modify his position and to take Bellarmine's elegant way out as a model, which he seemed willing, albeit reluctantly, to consider: "in any case, I will put all my effort into mitigating, or, to tell the truth, into smudging this objection, if at all possible, because it does not sound well to pious ears. I have not refrained from examining, whenever appropriate, the *Controversiae* of the said Father [Bellarmine], which I received as a present from the printer."[19]

And "smudge" Baronio did, for in the printed edition of the first volume of the *Annales* we find a completely different interpretation of Jerome's controversial passage. Gone are the references to Jerome's slips and to the haste with which Jerome composed his *Contra Vigilantium*. Instead, just as Bellarmine had done, Baronio opted to interpret Jerome's passage as an ironic response to Vigilantius's sarcasm. The whole passage, Baronio now argued, needed to be interpreted as a "metaphor." Just as Jerome had joked about the name of Vigilantius, who should rather have been called "Dormitantius," since he was hopelessly sleeping instead of staying awake waiting for the message of Christ, so now Jerome was making a play on the mystical light of the candles as a symbol of the Christians' joy and celebration, which had absolutely nothing to do with illuminating the relics of the martyrs with actual light.[20] Besides, Baronio added, Jerome could not have meant to deny altogether the legitimacy of a practice that he himself had reported as commendable in the Eastern Church and that other early Christian writers attested.[21] Therefore, given that Jerome's principal aim was that of defending the mystical use of candles, when Jerome brought up the ignorant zeal of men and women, "it is as if he said: let me grant you that things stand as you [Vigilantius] say, i.e., let us assume that these simple-minded men and women, as you say, think that the martyrs are actually illuminated by the candles, and let us assume that they have zeal but not according to knowledge, what harm is it to you?"[22] This way of speaking, Baronio explained, is commonly found in Jerome, who "when fighting against the heretics, does not want to concede them even a nail's breadth. Besides, in the same work as well as in his letter to Riparius, he approves openly and clearly the manifestation of such religiosity."[23] Baronio concluded this section by repeating the same words that he used to conclude the corresponding section in the manuscript version. That is, he explained that the practice of lighting candles in front of the relics of martyrs was explicitly recommended by Augustine, Paulinus of Nola, and others. The fact that Baronio revised his initial interpretation in order to satisfy the Master of the Sacred Palace can be gathered from the very end of this new passage. In his conclusion, in fact, Baronio remarked that there was no need to give a long list of people who praised the pious use of candles during religious ceremonies, because the Dominican Vincenzo Bonardo, *collega* of Zobbia and destined to succeed him in the office of *Magister* in 1589, "has written an erudite book on the same argument."[24]

At first sight, from this episode Baronio seems to emerge as a sort of double-headed Janus. On the one hand, there is the philologist, the rigorous critic who, on the basis of an analysis of the evidence internal to the text, seems unafraid to admit that a work written by a Father of the Church contained mistakes. This side of Baronio resonates with his incredible scholarly energy and skills, which can be seen, for instance, in his ability to collect a massive number of documents, in his success in forming a scholarly network of collaborators that cut across confessional and geographical boundaries, and in his acknowledgement of the importance of antiquarian sources for historical research.[25] The other side of Baronio is the apologist, the unrelenting defender of papal authority, the tenacious promoter of the theological and ideological program of the Counter-Reformation papacy, in the name of which he was ultimately willing to sacrifice some of the results that could come from the application of principles derived from textual criticism.[26]

Almost all the historians working on Baronio seem to confirm this somewhat schizophrenic picture of the significance of his work, characterized by ideological commitment and philological criticism as by two forces that pulled Baronio in opposite directions. In Arsenio Frugoni's still influential judgment, for instance, Baronio's ideological commitment completely erases any trace of historical criticism, so much so that Baronio's *Annales*, as Frugoni put it, are not history, but "something else."[27] By contrast, while Stefano Zen grants that Baronio actively participated in the papalist Counter-Reformation project, he nevertheless notes that Baronio manifested, "in the realm of historiography, philological scruples that were not common" in the ideologically charged post-Tridentine Catholic culture. Thus, Zen contends that Baronio's scholarship was characterized by a "heroic use of philology"—heroic, that is to say, because destined to be sacrificed on the altar of the dogmatic culture of the Counter-Reformation.[28]

Even though Zen and Frugoni arrive at almost diametrically opposed judgments regarding the significance of Baronio's historical production, they share the same theoretical presupposition; that is, that ideological commitment and philological criticism are like death and man in Epicurus's philosophy: when one is, the other is no longer. Or to put it differently, the relationship between ideological commitment and philological scruples in a work of history must be a zero-sum game. This theoretical presupposition is the fruit of a specific and thoroughly modern way of thinking about historical research, which implies that a lack of ideological objectivity (or the presence of an ideological bias) is in essence opposite to the historian's primary duty to offer a "true" analysis of her documents.

Contemporary scholarship is discussing, refining, and in certain cases, denying the hermeneutical value of this notion of objectivity in current historical scholarship. Quite aside from the debate involving the current historical practice, however, it seems certain that setting up this notion of objectivity as the benchmark against which premodern works of history should be assessed does not fit Baronio's historiography, and indeed it might not be a good framework for understanding early modern historical scholarship and ecclesiastical history in particular. As Arnaldo Momigliano has argued, the interrelation between dogma and fact in ecclesiastical history is so profound that "any ecclesiastical historian who believes in Christianity is bound also to be a theologian. But if he is challenged on facts, he *must* produce evidence."[29] When we come to early modern ecclesiastical history more specifically, Anthony Grafton has warned us that "heavy documentation did not confer—or imply—strict objectivity."[30] Regarding Cesare Baronio in particular, moreover, it is important to realize that for him sacred history was a distinctive form of history writing that cannot be easily disjoined from liturgy.[31] It is clear, therefore, that the Janus-like portrait of Baronio, based as it is on an anachronistic view of the relationship between documentary criticism and ideological commitment, is not an entirely satisfactory explanation of the significance of his work and that a different explanation is needed.

Fragments, Gems, and Documents: Baronio's View of History and Truth

I would like to argue that if we want to abandon this Janus-like view of Baronio we should start by abandoning the underlying assumption that Baronio's theological views were in tension with his commitment to heavy documentation. Rather, we should start by taking Baronio seriously when he contended that the Truth of the Catholic religion stirred him toward, not away from, the truth of history. As we saw in the case of Jerome's candles, Baronio explicitly wrote that, based on his analysis of the *Contra Vigilantium* and of Jerome's other works, the only option he had was to admit that Jerome made a mistake, "for the sake of the truth of history and of Catholic doctrines." This means that Baronio thought that the truth of history and the Truth of the Catholic doctrines both stirred him in the same direction, that is, away from Bellarmine's solution, which was nevertheless more consonant with the Counter-Reformation apologetic atmosphere. In other words, Baronio's ideological and theological convictions represented not a sort of limitation of but instead the very condition for his textual criticism. It was his firm belief in the Truth of post-Tridentine Catholic theology that gave Baronio a certain documentary and critical freedom that he would not have otherwise been able to exercise.

Scholarship on Baronio is unanimous in asserting that the cardinal did not write much about historical methodology. Two documents are usually cited as Baronio's scant methodological considerations. The first is the preface to the first volume of the *Annales*, in which Baronio strongly defended the originality of his own work with respect to previous pagan and Christian historians. While the latter were full of long digressions and orations "constructed with immense artifice, and fictitious, and composed and arranged according to the author's personal opinion," the *Annales* privileged the evidence provided by the historical documents. Indeed, Baronio decided to write his historical work in the format of annals precisely because such a format allowed him to substitute the rhetorical and narrative (and therefore fictitious) aspects of history with the documents, which Baronio decided to quote in full, "no matter how rough and inelegant they can sometimes appear . . . in order for the truth to shine more and more clearly."[32]

The second document usually cited regarding Baronio's methodology is a letter written at the end of 1589 by Baronio to Talpa in which Baronio wrote: "the profession of the historian is different from the profession of the

defender of dogmas, and therefore in history we need to let the dogma appear
through the traditions and through the truth, not through the historian's own
arguments, so that we may leave it to the reader, be he Catholic or heretic, to
discover the certainty of the truth from the things that are being said, and from
that certainty of the truth the reader might then find arguments to destroy
heresies."[33]

Contemporary scholars have usually taken those two documents as an indication of Baronio's commitment to documentary evidence in the face of the
mounting pressures of the Counter-Reformation Church,[34] which, as I have
already argued, is not a satisfactory explanation of the significance of Baronio's
work. More interestingly, however, Carlo Ginzburg quoted the preface to the
Annales not so much as a testimony to Baronio's own philological scruples than
as a trace of an important development in early modern historiography more
generally.[35] As we already saw, in Carlo Ginzburg's argument early modern historiography progressively moved away from *evidentia* (the narrative vividness)
and embraced *evidence* as the proper way to reconstruct the past. This change
was originated by and in turn helped to articulate a more and more pronounced
"distrust in the possibility of being able, with the help of rhetoric, to evoke the
past as an accomplished fact. Its place was taken by an awareness that our understanding of the past inevitably was uncertain, discontinuous, lacunar, based only
on fragments and ruins."[36] In Ginzburg's view, then, Baronio, who explicitly
rejected the elegant and organic narratives of other historians in exchange for
the "rough and inelegant" fragments of the past as they appear in primary documents, is an example of exactly this process.

There is another document written by Baronio that, I argue, needs to be jux-
taposed to these two if we want to have a complete picture of Baronio's methodology. This is a letter written by Baronio and addressed to Pope Gregory XIII,
which was supposed to become the dedicatory epistle of Baronio's biography
of Gregory of Nazianzus, written when Baronio was young but never published
during his lifetime.[37] In the letter to the pope, Baronio wrote that as a result of
the 1580 relocation of the relics of Gregory of Nazianzus from Santa Maria in
Campo Marzio to St. Peter's Cathedral, "many people, vigorously inflamed by
the desire to venerate Gregory's memory, manifested the desire to know his
acts and life." In order to satisfy such desire, some of Baronio's friends urged
him to write a new biography of the saint. Initially Baronio refused, since there
already existed a biography of Nazianzus, written by the Byzantine writer called
Gregory the Presbyter in the sixth or seventh century. Baronio's friends, however, remarked that the work of Gregory the Presbyter was "not so much a biography as an encomium": there were many omissions and many things "which
are not in accordance with the truth of history." Convinced by this argument,
Baronio decided to write his own biography of Gregory. In order to explain to

the pope the principles informing his work (a work that, in the intention of its author, was supposed to foster people's veneration of Gregory's life and present a biography "in accordance with the truth of history"), Baronio referred to the intarsia of the Cappella Gregoriana, commissioned by the same Gregory XIII and completed in 1583 by Giacomo della Porta. As Baronio put it, just as in the Cappella "the excellent painter represented most beautifully the image of our Gregory together with other Doctors of the Church by collecting and joining together in a mosaic small pieces of stone and marble with magnificent skill, so I collected accurately selected fragments as if they were gems and little stones, chiefly out of Nazianzus's own works, where he, in passing, wrote something about himself. . . then I have put those fragments in their proper place according to chronological order, and I almost glued them together so that out of them, just as out of the most splendid colors, we could have that man's life completely represented, or at least sketched out." Baronio admitted that the draft he was presenting to the pope was not yet perfect, and in fact he was already thinking of polishing his mosaic further by adding more documentary gems: "especially if, as I hope, I could get my hands on some of Gregory's poems and other unpublished works coming from ancient manuscripts."[38]

If we put this letter alongside the other methodological considerations, we will see that the metaphor of the mosaic that Baronio uses here is really the key to understanding his methodology and his view of history. The documentary evidence, those "rough and inelegant" quotations that Baronio thought should be put in place of the elegant and untruthful narratives of other historians, are not simply fragments of the past but rather gems and stones, which the historian needs to collect and glue together in the mosaic of history. In this respect, then, the documentary evidence is significant and indeed can be called historical *evidence* precisely because it does not exist as a random trace and is not randomly assembled. Or in other words, documents do not become *evidence* until they are arranged and composed on the basis of a preordained design or pattern, just as little pieces of stone and marble need to be put in their proper place in order for them to produce a portrait of people and events. The design or pattern of this mosaic is the Truth of theology, in the sense that for Baronio God's Truth has both drawn the contours of history and left some traces along the way; that is, those small pieces of truths that can be found in repositories of written texts such as the Vatican Library but also among the coins and other ancient objects brought to light by antiquarians and "archaeologists." It is only in the pattern designed by God, then, that these various documentary traces find their very nature qua historical evidence.

The fact that Baronio explicitly foregrounded written and antiquarian sources as opposed to both the other historians' rhetorical tirades and the theologians' dogmatic controversies does not mean, of course, that Baronio *was* an "objective"

historian who never made a willing or unwilling mistake in his critical judgment,[39] nor does it mean that Baronio's philology was "honest" and distinctively
original in its critical methodology *despite* his strong ideological and theological commitment.[40] Rather, it means that for Baronio the commitment to the
Truth of theology was *the condition for* his distinctive documentary approach.
In other words, for Baronio ecclesiastical history was not at the service of theology; rather, theology made possible a kind of ecclesiastical history founded
on documentary criticism. Thus, in Baronio's perspective, to ask whether or not
there was a dichotomy between theological Truth and documentary truth was
not simply *une question mal posée* but indeed a nonsensical question.

Understanding Baronio's concept of historical evidence as gems to be added
to the mosaic of history allows us not only to make sense of the epistemological
and methodological basis of his specific mode of connecting history, truth, and
Truth; it also allows us to see how Baronio fits into the larger development of the
genre of ecclesiastical history in premodern Europe. As Arnaldo Momigliano
argued, in order to understand the developments of post-Reformation ecclesiastical historiography we need to go back to Eusebius of Caesarea. Insofar as
Eusebius was "the model of a universal historian of the Church," post-Reformation
ecclesiastical historiography represented, formally and to a certain extent meth-
odologically, a Eusebian revival.[41] The centrality of Eusebius's work, according
to Momigliano, derives from the fact that it was not only the first attempt to
write the history of the Christian Church but it also presented a new methodological approach in the field of historiography with respect to the pagan past.
The main novelty of the Eusebian model, as Momigliano saw it, was precisely
Eusebius's use of primary sources as the main component of his history.[42] As
Anthony Grafton has observed, expanding on Momigliano's argument, Eusebius
chose to privilege primary documents over the polished narrative of his pagan
predecessors because "Church history, as Eusebius framed it, was not a smooth
narrative. . . but a choral work, in which the voices of many witnesses were heard,
along with that of the author."[43] In a sense, then, the trajectory that leads from
Eusebius's chorus to Baronio's mosaic exemplifies some important aspects of the
development of ecclesiastical historiography and illustrates some of the changes
it underwent in order address the ideological and intellectual needs of the fractured world of post-Reformation Christianity.[44]

Seeing Baronio's historiography in this light has several intriguing implications. First of all, if we take seriously Baronio's claim that the contrast between
ideology and documentary scrupulosity is indeed a false dichotomy, then we
can reframe our own historical understanding of post-Reformation ecclesiastical history. More specifically, looking at Baronio from this perspective would stir
us to abandon the traditional view of the *Annales* as the Catholic counterpart to
the Magdeburg Centuries. In fact, both Baronio and his Protestant "enemies"

were on the same side of the question of the relationship between history and theology, since they all had the same passion for documentary evidence and the same unshakable faith in the Truth of their respective churches. The "enemies" of Baronio, instead, would have to be those (Catholic and Protestant) thinkers who, because of their hermeneutical and epistemological and not just theological anxieties, cultivated a sort of embryonic and fundamental doubt about the very possibility of writing a truthful history of the True Church.

This, in turn, would allow us to see that underneath the philological and theological battles between Protestant and Catholic truths, there was another battle over the very possibility of finding the truth in history. Thus, the theological contrasts between Catholics and Protestants were not simply the historical excuse that prodded post-Reformation historians to produce more documentary evidence and to refine their techniques to find, study, date, and interpret primary sources to be used as apologetic tools.[45] Indeed, the theological backbone of much post-Reformation historical production should not be considered a sort of premodern and unhistorical polemical and ideological baggage that coexisted with and was destined to soon be surpassed by the modern view of history as an "objective" science. Rather, theology was the very fiber of the early modern discussion on truth and history.[46]

In this perspective, theology was also the core of a fundamental conflict that, as Arnaldo Momigliano argued, is not only important for understanding the discipline of ecclesiastical history but is also, in a sense, constitutive of modernity. In his already mentioned study of the origins of ecclesiastical historiography, Momigliano claimed that Eusebius needs to be considered the inventor of ecclesiastical history not only because of his innovative methodology but also insofar as he treated the Christian Church as a universal institution. In this respect, post-Reformation ecclesiastical historians, both a Catholic one like Baronio and a Protestant one like Flacius Illyricus, followed the Eusebian model insofar as they thought that their respective church was the Universal Church. For Momigliano, the Eusebian model started to be abandoned only "when the existence of an invisible, Universal Church was no longer taken for granted" and when the history of the Church "began to be studied as the history of a human community instead of a divine institution"—that is to say, in historical terms, sometime between Pietro Giannone's 1742 draft of the history of the papacy of Gregory the Great and Max Weber's works on the sociology of religion.[47]

According to Momigliano, the decreasing popularity, in modern times, of Eusebius-like ecclesiastical historians (of historians, i.e., who believe they are writing history of a divine institution) does not mean that the field of ecclesiastical history is now solidly in the hands of secular historians of the church, or "unbelievers," to use Momigliano's term. Rather, Momigliano sees a profound conflict between the perspective of unbelievers, who face the difficulty, as Momigliano put it, "of describing without the help of a belief what has existed through the help of the belief," and the perspective of believers, who have to deal with the fact that Church history cannot be easily separated from nonreligious factors. This contrast for Momigliano is not a matter of critical prowess or of ideological bias: "love for truth, respect for evidence, and care for details" can certainly "help mutual understanding and tolerance, even collaboration, of believers and unbelievers," but even taking into account any potential collaboration, "no reconciliation is possible between these two ways of seeing the history of the Church."[48] In this respect, we can say that this unsolvable conflict is at the very core of the distinctive nature of ecclesiastical history.

While Momigliano argues that this contrast came to the fore in modern times and, in a sense, this contrast was a fruit of modernity, I want to argue that the seeds of this contrast can be seen already in the early modern world. While Baronio, in fact, was the perfect model of Momigliano's believers, among Baronio's contemporaries there were also some unbelievers. By questioning the very possibility of finding the True Church in history, these early modern unbelievers ended up questioning the very possibility of writing ecclesiastical history. It is now time to turn to these unbelievers, and to examine what exactly made them the enemies of Baronio's believer-like way of writing ecclesiastical history.

Paolo Beni's Early Years

If we want to look for the early modern equivalents of Momigliano's modern unbelievers, we need to scrape the barrel, so to speak, of post-Reformation Catholicism. This is to say that we have to abandon the solid pillars of certainty that surrounded Santa Maria in Vallicella and to plunge instead into the demimonde of post-Reformation Rome, which was populated by the likes of Agostino Mascardi. Indeed, Mascardi himself can serve as a useful starting point for our inquiry on the enemies of Baronio's ecclesiastical history.

Mascardi made only one brief mention of Baronio's *Annales* in the part of his work where he explained the relationship between historical narrative and the order of historical events. Mascardi set up his argument with a brief and not particularly original discussion of the difference between history and annals, in which the latter appeared as a sort of raw and imperfect step toward the former. In that context, Mascardi might have feared that his detractors could argue that downgrading the annalistic genre meant downgrading Baronio's magnum opus. No person hoping to find patrons in Rome could afford to criticize Baronio, and Mascardi was no exception. This is why, after his discussion of the annalistic genre as something that did not quite deserve the name of history, Mascardi added a few words in defense of Baronio. Mascardi wrote that despite the incredible praise that Baronio's work generated in the Catholic world, one man, Paolo Beni, dared to criticize the cardinal's decision to write annals rather than history, since the annalistic format lacked stylistic elegance and encouraged prolixity. Mascardi, by contrast, praised Baronio's choice of writing annals, because the annalistic format had already been used by illustrious authors such as Thucydides and Tacitus and explicitly approved by Augustine. Indeed, Baronio deserved the credit of being the only modern historian able to refashion the annalistic genre, so much so that the *Annales* have no trace of the "antiquated and emaciated style of the ancient annals," which Baronio's own style had completely superseded.[49] The fact that throughout his work Mascardi completely ignored both Baronio's work and the entire subject of ecclesiastical history suggests that Mascardi's defense of Baronio must be interpreted as a sort of tactical move aimed at avoiding dangerous criticism. If it is true, as I argued in the previous chapter, that Mascardi conceptualized historical narrative as a fragile mediator between the lost past and the present time of the reader, then ecclesiastical history, founded as it is on the principle that the past of the Church always shines through time rather than being mercilessly devoured by it, did not have a place in Mascardi's theoretical framework.

But while Mascardi's fundamental doubts about the hermeneutical value of ecclesiastical history can be gathered only from an argument *a silentio*, let us examine the more explicit criticism of Paolo Beni, whose opinion regarding Baronio's stylistic flaws Mascardi used as an excuse to pay his respects to the *Annales*. Paolo Beni was a rather unpleasant figure in the intellectual landscape of early modern Italy. His naive outbursts of juvenile enthusiasm for the life of the mind were overshadowed by his greed and constant preoccupation with money; his scholarly production was as pedantic as it was eclectic, ranging as it did from poetry to language to history to rhetoric; and even though Pierre Bayle praised Beni's work for showing erudition and "même bien du génie," modern scholarship has almost exclusively ignored it, save for some of Beni's reflections in the realm of literary criticism.[50] In the following pages I examine Beni's considerations on ecclesiastical history in the context of the rest of his eclectic production. Beni's work on ecclesiastical history (and on many other topics) has never been considered worthy of much scholarly attention. While it is undeniably true that Beni was not by any means a canonical or strikingly original thinker, he is nevertheless remarkably interesting as a representative of a certain specific intellectual milieu, which I have already identified with Mascardi. Indeed, Beni's reflections are interesting precisely because they do not belong to the intellectual pantheon of post-Reformation Rome; just as Mascardi's, Beni's ideas represent the dark side of post-Reformation Catholic culture, the roads not taken, the potentialities that remained unexpressed.

In order to assess Beni's role in this shadowy aspect of post-Reformation culture, we should start by investigating his biography, which shares some important
features with Mascardi's. In this respect, as I have already said in my discussion
of Mascardi, while I am not arguing that Beni's historiographical position was
a direct consequence of his biography, I do think that grounding Beni's ideas
in the social context in which he lived will give us a better sense of his role and
significance within post-Reformation Catholicism. First of all, as was the case for
Mascardi, Paolo Beni was in a financially precarious condition for most of his life.
Born in the early 1550s to a relatively prominent and wealthy family in Gubbio,
Paolo was destined to follow in his father's and brothers' footsteps and to study
law. He was sent to the Roman College of the Jesuits for his early education, but
during his stay in Rome he tasted for the first time the alluring flavor of rhetoric
and the humanities. In the 1560s Paolo's family decided to remove him from
Rome, fearing that the young man's interest in the humanities might drive him
away from jurisprudence, and placed Paolo first in Bologna and then in Padua,
from where he graduated in 1576. Even in Padua, however, Paolo continued his
humanistic studies, and indeed after graduation Paolo decided to reject the life
of a lawyer and civil servant, which his father had planned for him, and to pursue
his literary interests on his own. In 1576 he returned to Rome, this time as a sort
of freelance writer. He started to work in the entourage of Cardinal Cristoforo
Madruzzo and later as a secretary of Marc-Antoine Muret. In those years Beni
met some of the most important figures in Rome's literary and erudite circles,
including Muret himself and Carlo Sigonio. He also had firsthand experience of
how hard it was to maintain stable employment, since he had to change patrons
several times over the course of the 1570s.

Rome was an expensive city, and Paolo still owed some money to his family. Thus, in the hope, perhaps, of finding a more stable place for himself, in
1581 Paolo decided to enter the novitiate of the Society of Jesus. In 1584, after
completing his novitiate but before professing the fourth vow, Beni became a
humanities tutor in the Roman College and was then transferred to the Venetian
province and later to Milan as a teacher of rhetoric and philosophy. In another
interesting parallel with Mascardi, in 1593 Beni was dismissed from the Society.
Beni's scholarship has usually viewed his expulsion as a mystery,[51] but P. B.
Diffley has now conclusively established that the general's decision to expel Beni,
albeit facilitated by Beni's intellectual ambitions and lack of tact, was motivated
in large part by Beni's greed and continuous involvement in financial affairs. As
a Jesuit, Beni was supposed to embrace and enjoy poverty, and yet he could not
accept being cut off from his family's relatively ample financial means. Thus, he
spent most of his Jesuit years actively engaged in pleading either with his family
for money or with the Jesuit hierarchy for permission to keep whatever money
he obtained.[52] Seen in this context, Beni's expulsion from the Society was the

reaction to a not uncommon, if not exactly frequent, type of early modern pro-spective Jesuit, whom both Beni and Mascardi embodied. Both of them, in fact, sought the Society as a springboard to a more profitable and ambitious career and as a safety net in case their alternative career suffered some setbacks.

One further element of Beni's Jesuit career, however, deserves attention. In the Beni Archive there is a draft of a letter written by Beni to the General Acquaviva, undated, in which Beni seemed to be negotiating with Acquaviva for a "favor" that the general did not seem willing to grant.[53] In this undated draft, then, Beni wrote that given Acquaviva's reluctance to satisfy Beni's request, he wanted to inform the general of another issue, which presumably might have given Acquaviva better reason to grant Beni his wish. This other issue had nothing to do with money or property but rather with theology. Beni in fact told Acquaviva that "the Father Provincial thought that I should teach cases of conscience, and since this is an important subject, I decided to study them thoroughly." In this study, Beni came across the question of ecclesiastical cen-sures, in particular the bull *Ad evitanda*, issued by Martin V at the Council of Constance. This bull prescribed that not all excommunicated persons needed to be cut off from the community, only those who were formally named as per-sons to be shunned. In his lectures on the topic, then, Beni explained two cor-ollaries of Martin's bull as he interpreted it. The first was that members of the Christian community could safely receive sacraments from an excommunicated priest, provided that the said priest was not declared "*vitandus*"; that is, explicitly shunned. The second corollary was that an excommunicated but not shunned priest who was asked by a third party to administer a sacrament did not sin if he complied with the request. Beni's superiors must have taken issue with both points, and in the rest of the letter Beni defended his interpretation, which was based, he declared, on the authorities he studied in the Jesuit College, in particu-lar Soto, Vitoria, and Aquinas. Moreover, Beni stated that while he was a student in the Roman College he heard the very same interpretation from Carlo Reggio, "my master, from whom I learned it and I heard it very well explained," and since "I am not better than my fathers, I have followed their opinions."[54] However, Beni wrote that in addition to following his masters he also followed "other rea-sons, which right now I am not going to use to justify myself, since I have made it my profession to stick to my master. . . obeying the warning I received from the Father Provincial." Beni must have feared that this last remark would remind the general of Beni's past disobedience, which warranted an explicit warning by the provincial, and thus erased this phrase from his draft.[55]

In order to strengthen his case further, Beni remarked that aside from the fact that his opinion was corroborated by many and illustrious authorities, "the truth is that I argued for it with so many limitations that I almost seemed to favor the contrary opinion." In order to prove this point to Acquaviva, Beni wrote that he

enclosed a copy of his lecture notes together with his letter, but he later changed
his mind (perhaps his lecture notes were not so helpful after all) and erased that
part.[56] Evidently frustrated by these multiple attempts at justifying his position
on excommunication, Beni left the draft unfinished, and it is very probable that
he never sent the letter, since I found no trace of a final version of this letter in
either the Beni Archive or the archive of the Society of Jesus.

We can imagine that in Beni's mind this letter was supposed to convince the
general of Beni's theological orthodoxy, which might have further convinced
the general that Beni was worthy of being rewarded the favor he asked. We
can also certainly understand why Acquaviva and the Jesuit hierarchy would
have been irritated by Beni's liberal interpretation of Martin V's bull: leniency
towards excommunicated people was dangerous in the confessionally divided
landscape of sixteenth-century Europe, and indeed the same bull was one of
the documents at the center of the conflict between English Jesuits and other
English clergymen, most notably Thomas Bell, over occasional conformity in
England in the early 1590s.[57] But aside from possibly shedding some light on
the relationship between Beni and the Jesuit hierarchy, this draft is evidence of
another aspect of Beni's thought, more interesting for my purposes: Beni's fas-
cination with the very Jesuit tradition of dealing with cases of conscience by
debating probable opinions rather than by asserting theological certainties. In
this respect, from this draft we learn that Beni saw as a skill his ability to argue
both sides equally, that Beni had formed his own additional reasons to justify
his position on excommunication, and that this personal judgment had already
been censured by his superiors. All these elements illustrate both Beni's personal
engagement with this specific style of theology, which will remain an important
feature of his intellectual profile even after his expulsion from the Society, and
how difficult and dangerous it was for Beni to move in the minefield of theological debates. This very same difficulty will reappear again in Beni's future career,
with dangerous consequences.

After his expulsion from the Society, Beni was, once again, unemployed
and in need of a patron. He found his patron in Pope Clement VIII, who took
Beni under his wing and offered him a teaching post as a professor of philosophy in Rome. During those years Beni wrote a number of works, most of them
dedicated to the pope, including a series of *Orationes*, a commentary on Plato's
Timaeus, and a *Disputatio* on Baronio's *Annales* that was published in 1596 and
to which I will return. Beni wrote also a couple of short pieces on the flood of
the Tiber that devastated Rome in December 1598.[58] Composed with the intention of, once again, impressing Clement VIII with their author's erudition, these
pieces ended up backfiring on Beni. In his verbose discussion of the history and
significance of floods, Beni mentioned that natural disasters are often God's
way of punishing sins, and therefore also the 1598 flood might have been a sign

that God was not pleased with the current administration of the city of Rome. Clement VIII did not take well this implicit criticism of his leadership, and his support for Beni cooled off considerably.[59]

In 1600, however, a post at the University of Padua opened up, and Beni left Rome for what he hoped would be a safe haven for his scholarship. At the beginning things went well for Beni in the academic environment of Padua. He enjoyed the company of illustrious colleagues (e.g., in the early spring of 1600 Beni was admitted to the Accademia dei Ricovrati, which counted Galileo Galilei among its members),[60] and he was busy preparing a number of scholarly works. Possibly strengthened by this initial success, Beni must have thought that the time had come to patch things up with the pope, and confident in his theological training in debating probable opinions, he wrote a short treatise on the controversy *de auxiliis*.

We have Beni's initial draft of his work, in manuscript, entitled *Qua tandem ratione dirimi ac tuto definiri possit controversia quae de efficaci Dei auxilio inter Religiosas Dominicanorum Iesuitarumque familias agitatur.*[61] The draft, composed of sixteen chapters and left incomplete (the printed version of the work has twenty-seven chapters), began with a dedicatory epistle to Clement VIII. There Beni explained that the aim of his treatise was not to side with either part but to foster "concord and peace among all faithful, and especially among those who are the column and foundation of the Church."[62] Beni continued the introduction to the disputation by admitting that even though he knew that the pope did not want to define the controversy in absolute terms, nevertheless the decrees of the Council of Trent on grace and free will seemed to Beni a clear and solid foundation on which to build a definitive solution to the controversy. Finally, Beni invited the pope to take this solution into account whenever he decided that the moment had come to make a final decision.[63] Despite the promises made in the introductory parts of the text, the arguments presented by Beni in the following pages, far from being equally distant from (or equally close to) Jesuits and Dominicans, were instead a very Jesuit defense of the Pelagian-sounding doctrine of Molina, complete with direct quotations from Molina's work[64] and with a pompous rhetorical tirade on how free will was celebrated not only by Christian theologians but also by Plato, Aristotle, and neo-Platonic philosophers such as Plotinus and Ficino.[65]

Beni gave his draft to Cesare Lippi da Mordano, a Franciscan friar and professor in the University of Padua, who anticipated some problems with the content of the text and with the seemingly arrogant stance of its author and therefore suggested some corrections.[66] Beni did try, albeit to a limited extent, to tone down part of his work. For instance, the words "*ac tuto definiri*" were eliminated from the title, as well as the direct reference to the Jesuits and Dominicans as the two sides of the controversy.[67] Beni also eliminated the quotations from Molina and substituted for them relatively less controversial quotations from Bellarmine, Suárez, and Driedo.[68] The bulk of the arguments, however, remained unchanged, and indeed among the new chapters added to the printed version there was a long digression in which Beni criticized Bellarmine's position for not having defended the freedom of the will forcefully and coherently enough.[69]

Needless to say, Beni's book, just as Beni's discussion of the bull *Ad evitanda*, was exceedingly untimely. The controversy *de auxiliis* had been tearing the Church apart since its beginning, in 1588, with the publication of Molina's *Concordia*, and for this reason Clement VIII had imposed silence on the controversy by forbidding further public debate between Jesuits and Dominicans on grace and free will. Thus, the last thing that the pope and the other leaders of the Church wanted in 1603 was the printing and circulation of yet one more text on the controversy, especially considering that the said text did not come from a trusted and famous theologian but a former Jesuit whom the pope himself did not like. Moreover, the philo-Pelagian thrust of Beni's arguments angered the Dominicans without pleasing the Society of Jesus, whose leadership was actively working, not to defend Molina, but to silence the debate. And of course the fact that Beni felt self-confident enough to criticize Bellarmine did not earn Beni any credit with the Jesuits. In May 1604 the Venetian Inquisition sent notice of Beni's book to the Roman Inquisition, which did not waste time in producing a series of very harsh censures for both the content of Beni's philo-Pelagian argument on the relationship between grace and free will and the ill-advised and arrogant attempt, on Beni's part, to define a controversy that he had no business taking up in the first place. Indeed, Girolamo Pallantieri, a Franciscan friar, Bishop of Bitonto, and former professor of theology in Padua, who wrote one of the censures for the Inquisition, commented that "Beni's book should rather be entitled 'on the rationale for making disturbance in' rather than 'on the rationale for solving' the controversy."[70]

The Roman Inquisition went after Beni with its full force: in the summer of 1604 Beni was summoned to Rome, together with Cesare Lippi (Beni's colleague who had read Beni's initial draft) and Girolamo Zacco, archpriest of the Cathedral Church of Padua and colleague of Beni in the faculty of the university, who had approved the book.[71] Interrogated by the inquisitors, Zacco said that he had read only a few passages of Beni's book without paying very much attention, because he was assured by Beni that Lippi had already approved it.[72] Lippi, on his part, said that prior to the publication of Beni's work he had seen only a partial draft "in which I noticed many things that needed to be amended." Beni had promised to make the corrections requested, but when Lippi saw the printed book he noticed that "there are many things which were not in the original."[73] The Inquisition dismissed Zacco at the end of August and Lippi at the end of

September, and as a punishment, among other spiritual penances, both Zacco and Lippi were prohibited from ever revising and approving books in the future.

Beni also was interrogated over the summer, and the folder in the Inquisition archive contains a full transcription of the inquisitors' questions and of Beni's answers. Most of the interrogation centers on the relatively technical theological question of the relationship between Beni's and Molina's understandings of grace and free will (while the inquisitors accused Beni of being just another Molina, Beni denied that his position had anything to do with Molina's *scientia media*). One of the inquisitors' questions, however, touched not on the content of the treatise but on Beni's personal motivations and aims in writing it. Beni's response to this question provides two important insights into his intellectual profile.

The first has to do with the centrality of controversies and disputations in Beni's understanding of theology, which was perhaps the longest-lasting theological legacy from his Jesuit years: "I had decided to write on this matter in 1601, when I read that the pope, asked about this, did not actually prohibit it, but rather declared that the issue needed to be discussed freely among theologians." Many theologians, both Jesuits and Dominicans, had recently published books on the same topic, "and since I saw that their books were printed and accepted in Rome, and reprinted in many different places, I thought I had even less cause to create offense, since I am neutral and I do not depend on either side."[74] Indeed, Beni added that "in the holy Church, whenever there are controversies, it is an ancient tradition for Catholics to present and suggest their opinions."[75] This, Beni explained, had happened several times throughout the history of the Church and in most delicate and controversial debates; why should his book be punished for doing something that Catholic theologians had always done?[76] Beni thought that the essence of theological disputes was precisely the fact that they needed to be discussed and assessed: if nothing is certain yet, why not leave room for disputation? This statement resonates with the draft of the letter Beni prepared for Acquaviva. From both cases we can see that Beni experienced theology as the realm of debates over truths that needed to be proved rather than the realm of assertions of truths already established (in both cases Beni's opinions in matters of theology were censured by his superiors).

The second element emerging from Beni's response to the Inquisition is, once again, the question of patronage: "what really prompted me to publish this work is that, starting from 1594, every year I have dedicated some works to the pope, as it appears from my printed works. And since in October of that year 1602 I told the pope that I could not pay my usual debt because of an illness, His Holiness, seeing me still pale and with the signs of the illness, and learning of my need, gave me a pension. Hence, since I wanted to repay in some form such benignity, in 1603 I began to make the last revisions of this work with all diligence."[77]

Thus, in a sense, the precarious state of Beni's personal and economic condition mirrors the precarious equilibrium he experienced when discussing contentious theological questions, such as the relationship between grace and free will.

Beni's responses during his interrogation failed to convince the inquisitors that the *Qua tandem* was impartial and theologically sound, and Beni's book was condemned. Beni himself, however, was not released, despite having apologized for the book and having reaffirmed his commitment to obey the pope and the Holy Office. At the end of September Beni wrote directly to the pope, asking for mercy and for permission to go back to Padua. The Venetian ambassador in Rome also interceded on behalf of Beni, writing to the pope and to the Holy Office that Beni was penniless in Rome and needed to return to his job at the University of Padua. Finally the Holy Office decided to close the matter and to grant Beni his wish: on September 30 Beni was commanded by the Inquisition to abjure publicly his book, and on October 1 the book was burned. Soon after Beni returned home to Padua.[78] He definitely gave up any dream he might have had to regain favor with the papal court, and for the next two decades he immersed himself in his scholarly work and in the life of the university and of its faculty.[79]

Uncertainty, Probability, and Verisimilitude: The Central Themes of an Eclectic Intellectual

Even though during his last dramatic sojourn in Rome Beni learned that theology was not the place for debating probable and disputed opinions, nevertheless he did not cease to be concerned with the question of the relationship between certainty and uncertainty. After 1603 he did not write any other theological work, but his quasi obsession with the lines of demarcation between certainty and uncertainty, truth and verisimilitude, and reality and representation returns as a constant theme in his literary works, in his Aristotelian commentaries, and of course in his works on history. This quasi obsession, as I call it, can be seen for example in a peculiar and influential book that Beni completed and published in 1612 on the respective merits of Tasso, Homer, and Virgil and on the overall superiority of Tasso to the other poets.[80] Beni dedicated the ninth chapter of this work to a discussion of the difference between epics and history. He started with the locus classicus for this kind of scholarly debates—that is, Aristotle's opinion that the difference between history and epic poetry is not in the form (i.e., prose vs. verse) but in the content; namely, in the fact that history deals with events as they truly happened, while poetry deals with events as they could have happened. Or to put it differently, history deals with the truth, while poetry (in particular epic poetry) deals with the verisimilar.[81] Does this mean, Beni asked, that the difference between poetry and history is that the former is true and the latter is false? Surely, Beni admitted, many ancient authors seem to agree that the poet is in charge of "fabricating fictions," and indeed Aristotle himself clearly attributed to philosophy the task of dealing with universal truths and to history that of dealing with particular truths, so that "the poet, unless he wants to step into the others' territory, is obliged to invent and feign new events, since he must not, like a historian, explain and represent the true events."[82]

This interpretation, however, posed some problems for Beni. For instance, Aristotle seemed to contradict himself, since "while he commands the poet to attend to the verisimilar, he seems not to have any problem in granting that the poet might also sing true things, as long as they resemble the verisimilar." Would that mean that when the poet happens to mention a true event he would become ipso facto indistinguishable from a historian? Indeed, even the historian sometimes "cannot be easily certain and sure about the truth, and he is obliged to write what he or other people think verisimilar. . . . certainty and security in human affairs (especially with respect to motives and reasons and in general with respect to the circumstances of the events) can be obtained with difficulty and very rarely, so much so that even Thucydides and Livy and other historians very frequently report events and other things, which they confess and propose as verisimilar and probable rather than certain."[83] In Beni's opinion, then, Aristotle's distinction between truth and verisimilitude and, consequently, Aristotle's distinction between the content of history and the content of poetry needed to be corrected. Truth and verisimilitude, in fact, are very much conjoined in history and in any other discipline dealing with human affairs, in which absolute certainty is almost never to be found. Thus, Beni proposed a different interpretation of the *Poetics*; namely, that when Aristotle wrote that poetry deals with the verisimilar he did not mean to "command the poet to narrate or sing the verisimilar or necessary, but that he narrate or sing according to the verisimilar and the necessary, which means in imitation of the verisimilar, not the verisimilar itself."[84]

Beni's notion of the difference between the verisimilar itself and the likeness of the verisimilar allows him to reconceptualize the difference between truth and verisimilitude in the relationship between history and poetry: while the historian deals with his own mixture of true and verisimilar as with the truth, the poet can use the same mixture only by "embracing it as credible or verisimilar." This means that the poet creates his fictions in the image of and by imitating the same raw material the historian uses.[85] Beni's own revision to the Aristotelian category of the poetic verisimilar allowed him not only to differentiate history from poetry but also to redefine their respective relationships with oratory, another area of knowledge in which the relations between the true, the false, and the verisimilar are as essential as they are complex. The historian deals with truth first and foremost, even though the truth he seeks is very often impure—that is, mixed with the verisimilar. The orator "narrates, proves, and concludes the verisimilar," but he is not confined to "the boundary of falsehood," since "as he reasons on the basis of probability, his speech is as if balanced in a scale between truth and falsehood." The poet, on his part, "does not narrate the verisimilar itself, which is in the actual things, but rather the image of the verisimilar which is represented in the actual things. . . and this is what imitating means, that is, telling something false which nevertheless has the appearance and likeness of truth, and therefore the poet's falsehood would be between the verisimilar of the orator, and the false of the liar who tells his lies regardless of any verisimilitude."[86]

Beni therefore interpreted the verisimilar as something that mediates between truth and fiction while containing a little of both. He then applied to the discussion on the respective merits of Homer, Virgil, and Tasso his distinctive conceptualization of the poetic verisimilar as something that imitates, or is constructed in the image of, the "real" verisimilar. As a general rule, Beni argued, the best epic poetry balances the verisimilitude (which comes from the plot) and the *maraviglia*, or wonder (which is created by the poet's fictions). Homer's poems were too skewed in favor of fiction, while Virgil's poems, albeit more sober, contained nevertheless many implausible elements (such as, for instance, the anachronistic timing of the encounter between Aeneas and Dido). Thus, Beni concluded, Tasso's work was better than the other two on this account.[87]

Beni's peculiar reinterpretation of Aristotle's category of the verisimilar has caught the attention of all scholars working on Beni; they offer diverging interpretations of the significance of Beni's verisimilar in the context of Beni's role in the very initial phase of the literary *querelle* between ancients and moderns. For instance, according to Bellini and Scarpati (who are among the most recent representatives of a very well established view of Beni as a Baroque or proto-Baroque critic), Beni's "twisting" of Aristotle originated by his being "beset" with the relationship between truth and falsehood. The result of Beni's interpretation of Aristotle was an "objective abuse which illustrates the obsessive return to the same textual passages, and the exegetic urges to deform their meaning, in the turbulence of the switch from Renaissance to Baroque." Or to put it differently, Beni's enlargement of the category of the verisimilar is a prelude to and one of the theoretical presuppositions of the stylistic experimentalism of Baroque.[88] By contrast, while Diffley grants that Beni indeed stretched the Aristotelian category of the verisimilar to the point of making it "a flexible quantity," he contends that Beni did not do this because he was a "Baroque distorter of Aristotle" but because he wanted to "justify the factual accuracy of poetry." This means, according to Diffley, that it is incorrect to see Beni as the thinker who brought down the curtain on Aristotelianism in Padua and who set the stage for Baroque, since Beni's personal preference for factual accuracy over

wonderful stylistic invention is proof that Beni showed "no interest in the orna-
ments and potentially Baroque elements" of Tasso's poetry.[89]

Even though these scholars do not agree over Beni's early Baroque or
post-Humanist Aristotelian literary preferences, they do agree on the fact that
the relationship between the true, the false, and the verisimilar was a core issue
for Beni, who evidently did not feel comfortable separating the category of truth
and the category of verisimilitude as sharply as Aristotle had seemed to do. This,
I argue, does not simply originate from Beni's controversial and convoluted position on Tasso's poetry. Instead, we should see Beni's insistence on the relationship
between truth and verisimilar in connection with his deep anxiety over the limitations that humans have to face whenever they try to attain the certain knowledge of the truth, which Beni experienced in the realm of theology and which he
carried on to other areas of study. This anxiety was not exclusive to Beni's own
literary views but indeed was common to a certain type of post-Reformation
intellectual who, unlike Baronio, experienced post-Reformation culture not as
the triumph of certainty but as the messy theater of human affairs, inevitably
characterized by a mix of certainty and uncertainty, truth and verisimilar, facts
and interpretations.

The same obsession with this issue can be seen, to give another example, in
Beni's reflections on Aristotle's rhetoric. In 1624 and 1625 Beni published two volumes of commentary on the *Rhetoric*. The first volume contained his commentary
proper, while the second contained a series of rhetorical *orationes* that Beni wrote
in order to elaborate on several points that he saw as problematic.[90] Most of the disputations contained in this second volume are in the form of fictitious dialogues,
and almost all of them addressed the question of the relationship between the
probable, the true, and the credible.[91] In the first volume Beni explored at length
the question of Aristotle's enthymeme, which was also the subject of an oration
Beni gave at the University of Padua.[92] In the oration, as well as in the printed
commentary, Beni declared that Aristotle's explanation of the enthymeme and, by
extension, of the role of the orator could open the way for many problems. The
"greatest" problem of all was that Aristotle seemed to imply that the enthymeme
was the orator's tool for discussing contentious issues—issues, that is, whose judgment is not certain. For this reason, according to Aristotle, such issues cannot be
discussed "by necessary reasons, but only by probable ones." How can it be, Beni
wrote, "that the things that need consultation and deliberation and, therefore, usually can go either way cannot be argued and demonstrated by clear and necessary
arguments?"[93] Or in other words, since the Aristotelian enthymeme was supposed
to be used for probable opinions as opposed to certain and necessary things, does
that mean that oratory cannot but deal with uncertain issues? Does that mean that
truth as such is excluded from the realm of oratory? And if an orator cannot persuade people of the truth, what should he persuade people of?[94]

Throughout his commentary on the *Rhetoric*, Beni identified this as a central issue in understanding Aristotle, who according to Beni seemed to distinguish truth on the one side and probability and plausibility on the other; only the latter, not the former, was the proper concern of the orator. Beni specified that in this respect Aristotle was different from Plato, who believed that truth did belong to the realm of oratory, unless one wanted to equate oratory with sophistry. In the first volume of the commentary Beni explained that he wanted to raise this issue "not in order to confute Aristotle, but to signal that the prince of the Academicians taught very different things," since none of the other commentators and scholars of Aristotle, including Cicero, discussed this issue at length. The one exception was Francesco Patrizi, a predecessor of Beni's in Padua and a fellow Aristotelian, who "following in Plato's footsteps, opposed and confuted Aristotle using the Socratic method."[95]

Beni returned to this issue in the second volume. He dedicated entirely to this theme the fourth and fifth disputations, which are a two-part dialogue in which the ghosts of Plato and Aristotle, ushered in by Mercury, debate their respective positions in front of an audience that includes Marc-Antoine Muret and Beni himself.[96] In Beni's fictitious dialogue, then, Aristotle argued that the realm of probability as opposed to truth was the proper area of the orator with respect to other professions, such as those of the historian (who deals with human truth) and the mathematician (who deals with the truth of logic).[97] The fictitious character of Beni, however, did not accept this distinction. On the one hand, Aristotle, according to Beni, was adamant in stating that the orator's job was to persuade his audience with probable arguments rather than with true knowledge. On the other hand, however, Aristotle explained equally forcefully that the natural inclination to search for truth and the natural inclination to search for probable arguments are one and the same: how can the orator be instructed to limit himself to developing the former and not the latter?[98] If the process of arriving at the truth is the same as the process of arriving at the verisimilar, what is then the relationship between πιθανόν (the persuasive) and ἔνδοξον (the probable and reputable)?[99] Would it then be correct to differentiate persuasion from the process of truth finding (and verisimilitude finding)?

A superficial solution to these questions is offered by Plato, who in Beni's dialogue represents the opinion that unless one wants to confuse oratory with sophistry, truth should remain the main concern of the orator.[100] The solution presented by Beni's Plato, however, also poses its problems: if Plato was right, the distinction between philosophy and rhetoric would be moot, since both would be concerned with demonstrating true things. How, then, would rhetoric, reconfigured in this Platonic manner, differ from other disciplines whose main concern is finding truth, such as mathematics and philosophy itself? In general, Beni noted, Plato did not seem to offer a coherent theory of rhetoric as distinguished from other disciplines: sometimes Plato stressed that rhetoric, just as philosophy, must be concerned with the truth, while at other times, following Aristotle, he suggested that rhetoric must deal with the probable.[101] Beni did specify that despite Plato's inconsistencies, the orators of his days, especially the *Christiani oratores* (i.e., the preachers), must follow Plato's insistence on truth.[102] With remarks of this kind, however, Beni simply paid lip service to the religious climate of his own time; in fact, he did not seem to find a satisfactory solution to his own continuous and obsessive concern with the nature of truth, probability, and persuasion and their respective relationship. His dialogues do not end with a clear winner; they have instead a sort of hall-of-mirrors quality in which the fictitious characters return again and again to the same questions, in different language and from different angles, without ever arriving at the end of the discussion.

Beni's Aristotelian commentaries are certainly significant in the context of the development of this genre within the Aristotelian circles of Padua, and they contain many features that are of great importance for the stylistic and philosophical aspects of the reception of Aristotle and Plato in post-Reformation Italian culture.[103] Aside from these elements, however, I am interested here in underscoring Beni's insistence, once again quasi-obsessive, on the relationship of probability, truth, and persuasion. As Diffley argued, this aspect of Beni's work on rhetoric "shows Beni moving from theories of classical rhetoric to moral and theological questions which concern a Christian society in and after the Counter-Reformation."[104] Such "moral and theological questions," however, do not simply concern the role and definition of rhetoric in a post-Reformation Catholic world. Rather, these "moral and theological questions" are at the core of the question of the relationship between certainty and uncertainty that, as I have argued throughout this work, was central not only to Beni's entire scholarly reflection but indeed to the reflection of many intellectuals who, like Beni and Mascardi, started to doubt the very epistemological and hermeneutical foundations of post-Reformation Catholicism. It is in this intellectual context that we need to interpret Beni's almost neurotic elaboration on the relationship between truth, verisimilitude, and representation; while Beni seemed animated by the need to find a clear line that marked where certainty ended and probability began, he found time and again that all the disciplines and topics he examined contained a distinctive mixture of both. Beni experienced such a mixture in the theological debates he personally engaged in, in the Aristotelian category of the poetic verisimilar, and in the realm of rhetoric. How about ecclesiastical history?

Beni against Baronio, or the Impossibility
of Writing Ecclesiastical History

Beni wrote one work devoted entirely to history as a distinctive discipline, an *ars historiae*–type of treatise entitled *De historia libri quatuor* and printed in Venice in 1611.[105] From what Beni wrote in his work on Homer, Virgil, and Tasso, we already know that for him secular history was concerned with events that truly happened in the past. Nevertheless, a degree of the verisimilar needed to be factored in, given the essential uncertainty by which human events are characterized. In fact, in *De historia* Beni elaborated on this question in a manner that reflected both the distinctive mix of narrativism and attention to proofs that Ginzburg has identified in Robortello (a predecessor of Beni in the Aristotelian school of Padua)[106] and the conjectural epistemology of Mascardi.

For instance, Beni began his work with the question of whether history was the *"memoria"* or the *"narratio"* of the *res gestae*, and he sided decidedly with the latter. People who think that history is the remembering of past events, Beni explained, think that antiquarian relics alone can serve as history. These physical remains of the past, however, whether they are pictures or objects, "do not deserve by any means the name of true history, but they are rather an enigma, as I said, or a symbol or some sort of image and shadow of history, especially since deliberations, motives, speeches, and many other things of this sort, which clearly pertain to historical events, can be explained through a narrative, certainly not by a picture."[107] Beni did not mean to discard antiquarian evidence and other sort of "proofs" in the name of rhetorical narrativism, but he wanted to stress that there is an important difference between the *recordatio* (i.e., the remembrance of the past) and the understanding of the past. While the former can be triggered by objects, the latter needs to be attained through narrative. In historical narratives, the testimonies of past events, both written and not written, must be integrated with the historian's conjectures, which can supply an important source of truth whenever documents are missing: "I would not reproach a historian who might draw his own conjectures out of things," provided that he indicate clearly that his sources of information for a specific event come from conjectures rather than other testimonies. Of course it is not ideal to use conjectures, since the historian should rely first and foremost on primary sources (both written and unwritten), but it can be necessary and useful, provided that the conjectures derive from the observation and study of actual remains and testimonies.[108] Once again, as we saw in Mascardi, for Beni harangues and especially indirect discourses can be a viable way to introduce conjectures, but they need to be used sparingly and attentively, in order to convey "verisimilar" information about the past rather than what the historian himself thinks is probable.[109] How does ecclesiastical history factor into this model?

In the part of his work devoted to explaining the different branches of history, Beni explained that "some historians, I do not know why, divide history into four branches: divine, ecclesiastical, natural, and human. It seems to me that they include natural history unadvisedly, and that they separate divine from ecclesiastical history unnecessarily." In fact, Beni continued, if one distinguished ecclesiastical from divine history, then ecclesiastical history would not be different from "human history," and such division would be therefore "unwise and confused."[110] Other scholars avoid the problem of separating ecclesiastical and divine history and simply divide history into divine, human, and natural: "by divine history they understand God and the things that do not die, by natural history they understand, as they say, the natural causes and progressions of animals and plants, and by human history they understand the actions and precepts of men," and sometimes they add a fourth category, the history of scientific disciplines. Such a partition, however, seemed equally problematic to Beni, because to use the very category of "divine history" is, according to Beni, "to confuse history with divine and human philosophy."[111] So which division is the right one? At the end of this passage Beni declared: "in my opinion, it is better and more convenient to say that in history there is not so much a division into branches, but rather a progression in the matters to be treated, so that whoever wants to acquire knowledge of the universal *res gestae* and of true history would acquire it by degrees." Beni suggested three degrees of knowledge to prospective historians. First, historians must study languages, especially Latin; then geography; and lastly chronology.[112]

Thus, from this passage we already see clearly the problem Beni had with the very category of ecclesiastical history and divine history: to assume that ecclesiastical history is separate from divine history means to assume that ecclesiastical history is no different from human history, and as such it too is subject to the same mixture of truth and probability. To assume that ecclesiastical history and divine history are the same thing means to confuse history with "divine philosophy" or, in other words, to confuse history with theology. Is, thus, ecclesiastical history even possible as a branch of history? In the previously quoted methodological paragraph Beni dodged the question by resorting to a set of pedagogical precepts that did not touch on the essence of ecclesiastical history. Soon after, however, he was forced to return to the issue while recommending, among other books of chronology, Eusebius of Caesarea and some of his Christian continuators. At that point Beni specified that Eusebius was one of those who wrote "sacred history, which I call the kind of history that contains both the sacred texts [*sacrae litterae*] and the ecclesiastical records [*monumenta*], such as the succession of Pontiffs, the Councils, the acts of martyrs, the pontifical sentences, the propagation of the faithful people and the divine worship." In addition, ecclesiastical history for Beni should contain an account of all people and events that occurred in the Christian Church (including "heretics" and "schismatics," together with orthodox Catholics), as well as a summary of the structure of the Church. In general, ecclesiastical history should extend from the beginning of the Church until the present times. As to the question of the specificity of ecclesiastical history with respect to human history, Beni added: "And so as to be able to free myself from the difficulties and hurdles in which this question is entangled, as I said at the beginning when I could not find any satisfactory differentiation, here I am not prohibiting historians from including profane people and events that can be useful for understanding sacred and ecclesiastical matters, just as ecclesiastical or sacred people and events can be used for understanding profane history. Otherwise there is no reason to mix sacred and profane, or to apply the profane to the sacred."[113]

We should note that even in this passage Beni did not offer a theoretical solution to the question of the essential difference between ecclesiastical and secular history. According to Beni's own description, ecclesiastical history seemed to be composed in part of biblical philology and in part of human or secular history, and indeed Beni remarked that both ecclesiastical and secular historians can cross over each other's territory whenever they see fit, thus seemingly erasing the specificity of their respective subject matters. Notice also that in Beni's list any reference to doctrine is absent; no discussion is made of the history of the true Church as opposed to the history of false churches. Mixing sacred and profane, from a theological point of view, was not appropriate, but when it came to history, Beni seemed to suggest that there was no way of clearly demarcating when one ended and the other began.

After this paragraph, Beni continued his discussion by offering a brief examination of the existing ecclesiastical historians. Among those who wrote about the period starting from the creation of the world until the advent of Christ, Beni especially recommended Bede, Ado of Vienne, and Zonaras. As for those who covered the history of the Church starting with the birth of Christ, "aside from the sacred books of the New Testament and Eusebius and other ecclesiastical historians," Beni mentioned several other historians "including Cesare Baronio who could have been nearly the greatest one of all, if he had abbreviated his work." Beni continued by saying that since he already treated Baronio's *Annales* in his early *Disputatio*, there was no need to speak much about them, "but I will warn the reader of one thing only: Baronio's *Annales Ecclesiastici* are superior to all the other historians of this kind for their diligence and abundance and they can therefore instruct and educate the reader far and wide, unless he is deterred by their length and prolixity, and unless the numerous digressions delay and distract him with the innumerable variety of things, and unless Baronio's conjectures sometimes appear to the reader as suspicious and slippery."[114]

This is precisely the passage that Mascardi had referenced as a criticism of Baronio and as the starting point for his own, relatively lukewarm, defense of the *Annales*. Mascardi had interpreted Beni's criticism as a stylistic one, and certainly in this passage Beni mentioned explicitly the length and prolixity of the work, as well as the numerous digressions that might distract the reader. However, Beni also mentioned another element, that is, Baronio's "conjectures," which might appear to the reader "suspicious and slippery." We should not read this reference as a criticism of Baronio's documentary honesty and prowess, which Beni had acknowledged in the same passage when praising Baronio's "diligence" in collecting the copious among of material he included in his work. Rather, behind this criticism there is a deeper issue at stake; namely, the fact that, according to Beni, Baronio fell short in the very places of his work where he wanted to be a proper historian—that is, where Baronio used the mix of documents and conjectures that was the most distinctive tool of the historian of human events. This is so because Baronio, according to Beni, was not a historian: he was a theologian. Baronio was not a historian because ecclesiastical *history* as such for Beni did not exist. If one wanted to write the history of the Church, one could either write theology or secular history: Baronio's work, in Beni's judgment, was decidedly the former.

Beni hinted at this later in this work, when, commenting on the utility of history, he wrote that "I would never separate a theologian from a historian.... In fact, I judge that whoever reads and discusses those sacred books should be considered no less a theologian than a historian, and indeed I think that we should not listen to those who, I do not know why, say that the study of history does not pertain to a theologian."[115] But Beni had said exactly the same many years before, in his *Disputatio* on Baronio's *Annales*, the 1596 work I mentioned at the beginning of this section. This was a rhetorical exercise aimed to flatter the pope, and in fact throughout the work Beni uses Baronio's *Annales* as an excuse to praise Clement VIII. Baronio's work, in Beni's judgment, represented an immense contribution to the Catholic fight against the Protestants because it preserved "the gospel of the sacred scriptures pure and untouched" against the false interpretations of the heretics and because it presented to the Catholic people the history of their Church since its inception in chronological order and in "clear style. . . almost as in a public theater."[116] Since the pope patronized Baronio's work, the pope deserved credit for it. Nevertheless, within the relatively uninteresting pages full of rhetorical flattery, Beni's own opinion of Baronio's work comes to the surface.

According to Beni, the best feature of the *Annales* was that they "instruct the Christian theologian by giving him numerous and important aids." Indeed, as Beni explained with a slightly polemical tone, theology was usually taught by means of Scholastic treatises, such as Melchor Cano's *De locis theologicis*. He himself, while studying theology, had read this work but found it not very accessible. Cano required of a theologian many skills that Beni thought almost impossible to acquire: a profound knowledge of both philosophy and Scholastic theology, a certain familiarity with the acts and decrees of the Councils, a more than superficial knowledge of Latin, Greek, and Hebrew. All this seemed to Beni out of the reach of any student of theology, so that "becoming such a great theologian is more a wishful thinking than something which one should hope to attain." Aware of his own shortcomings with respect to Cano's almost unattainable model, Beni felt discouraged and continued his theological studies "not without pain." But "as soon as I started to look Baronio, I easily changed my opinion for a better one, as I hope. In fact, I understood that a theologian, with Baronio's teaching, could cultivate ecclesiastical history wonderfully, and could get a decent, if not full, knowledge of profane history." Baronio's work would also provide knowledge of the acts and decrees of the popes and Councils, and of the apostolic tradition, not to mention the ritual aspects of the Catholic Church and the significance of Sacred Scripture itself. In sum, for Beni any prospective theologian should save the effort and time that he would have to spend on the almost impossible task of mastering all the skills that Cano suggested; a careful study of the *Annales* provided the same amount of knowledge in less time and in a more efficient way. For these reasons, Beni concluded that "Baronio led theology out of difficulties and penury toward great abundance and richness."[117]

This passage is in part the expression of Beni's personal preferences in matters of theology. For Beni, strict Scholastic theology was excessively and unnecessarily systematic and axiomatic in its approach, while as a Jesuit he was trained in a different theological style, which he thought should be more concerned with debating controversies than asserting dogma. In fact, we should remember that Beni wrote this work a few years after his Jesuit experience and shortly before writing his very Jesuit and very ill advised treatise on the controversy *de auxiliis*, which proved just how wrong Beni had been on his opinion regarding the extent to which theological controversies could be freely debated. But this passage also betrays Beni's intuition that Baronio's work was not history proper: Beni praised the *Annales* not so much as the definitive historical account of the development of the Christian Church but as a new, relatively accessible, and thorough theological manual. Indeed, for Beni it was perhaps too thorough, since as he put it, the long digressions on such a variety of subjects "might be vastly superior to my own forces, to speak frankly."[118]

Beni remained firm in his opinion that Baronio's *Annales* should be considered a work of theology rather than a work of history for his entire life, even when, after leaving Rome for the last time in 1603, he abandoned papal politics and Catholic theology and devoted all his energies to the University of Padua, his home institution. Around 1619 Beni wrote up a proposal to reform the university, which remained unpublished.[119] In his proposal Beni touched on a number of issues, ranging from the duration and frequency of the classes to the most appropriate remuneration for the professors, from how to discipline students to how to organize their curriculum.[120] In the section of his proposal devoted to discussing the general humanities curriculum, Beni took a bitter revenge on Scholastic theology. He wrote that Scholasticism was nothing but a system of fixed axioms that students were supposed, not to discuss, but to learn by heart, digest, and regurgitate to their teachers. Not only did this kind of theology, which deals with "abstract and intricate matters, or rather subtleties," provoke many unnecessary conflicts among theologians of different schools, but it was also detrimental to the free use of one's reason. Beni complained that "these metaphysical lectures are taught by professors who *iurant in verba Magistri*, and who do not allow the free use of such metaphysics, without being obliged to follow entirely either Scotus or Aquinas, and yet it would be expedient that whoever spends so much effort and time in metaphysics, at least would be free to use it in theology... and to reserve for himself the free judgment, which in problematic issues is allowed to anybody who has not sworn allegiance to the master. Therefore now metaphysics is like a large smithy where every school, be it Aquinas's or Scotus's or other famous Scholastic doctors', forges its weapons to defend its own teachers."[121] For this reason, for Beni it would have been better to substitute the professors of metaphysics with "two valiant biblical philologists (for this would be the true Metaphysics, or rather the divine philosophy)," who, by giving pupils some notions of Greek and Hebrew, in addition to Latin, could teach not only how to read Scriptures but also how to interpret the Fathers of the Church, which would be useful not only to Scholastic theologians but also to casuists, preachers, and controversialists.[122]

Beni's plan for the reform of the curriculum in Padua had another chapter especially devoted to discussing theology. Beni cut that chapter short, repeating that the choice in Scholastic theology seemed to be between the school of Scotus and the school of Aquinas. He thought that Scotus's theology was too subtle, and therefore "it opens the way for disputes and conflicts" that are exceedingly technical and therefore useless.[123] At the same time, Beni wrote that he did not feel like praising "those who commit themselves so much to Aquinas's opinion that in discussing theology they are happy with Aquinas's sole authority and they completely give up their own sense and judgment. However, I praise those who, after a diligent examination, are ready to embrace Thomas's opinion and doctrine unless they are led to the opposite opinion by a forceful or very probable reason."[124] In any case, Beni thought that not much time should be devoted to this kind of theology at the expense of other subjects, and indeed he did not feel like spending much time on it himself, since "with one of my Latin disputations entitled *De Ecclesiasticis Baronii Cardinalis Annalibus*, I have already shown how to shape a perfect theologian."[125]

In conclusion, then, Beni was remarkably consistent throughout the years in his view of Baronio's *Annales* as a work of theology, not history. This is so because Beni consistently found that in all disciplines involving human affairs it was impossible to find a clear way to demarcate certainty and uncertainty; ecclesiastical history remained for Beni an area from which it was impossible to purge the human component. In this perspective, it was Beni, not Flacius or Casaubon, who was the real anti-Baronio. Baronio and Beni lived parallel lives of a sort in post-Reformation Catholic culture: they were concerned with the same theological as well as historical questions, but they ended up defending opposite opinions. For Baronio, ecclesiastical history was the area in which humans could find absolutely certain knowledge of the Truth, since it was the area in which the Truth of theology emerged from, and at the same time made sense of, the truth of history. For Beni, by contrast, history, just like any other human endeavor, was marred by the indelible stain of uncertainty, which even ecclesiastical history, insofar as it was a human endeavor, was not free from. On this note, let me conclude with one last and very suggestive example of the opposition between Beni and Baronio, this time centered on the different semantic force each gave to the words *ecclesia* and *memoria*.

For Baronio, the relationship between the memory of men and women and the Truth of the Roman Church was based on such a degree of certainty that even the very words *ecclesia* and *memoria* were, in a certain concrete sense, synonyms. In the first volume of the *Annales*, while writing about the several Latin words for Christian churches (i.e., *domus oratoria, basilica,* etc.), Baronio added that Augustine "frequently used" the word *memoria* to indicate a church, especially a church erected in honor of the martyrs. In particular, Baronio quoted Augustine's *De Civitate Dei*, book XXII, chapter 10, in which Augustine wrote that while pagans "built temples to these gods of theirs, and set up altars, and ordained priests, and appointed sacrifices, to our martyrs we build, not temples as if they were gods, but monuments [*memoriae*] as to dead men whose spirits live with God." Baronio's interpretation of Augustine had been challenged by Joannes Rullensis, a theologian at the Sorbonne, who thought that by "*memoria*" Augustine meant "altar" rather than "church." We know of the debate between Rullensis and Baronio from a letter Baronio wrote in response to Rullensis, in which Baronio summarized his adversary's opinion and reaffirmed that "it is necessary that here by *memoriae* we understand the churches of the martyrs, in which altars are built to honor them." Indeed, Baronio continued, a church is rightly called *memoria* "not only in words, but even in deeds," as it can be seen for instance in the case of the church erected in honor of St. Stephen, the first martyr. The church was in Ancona, not because the body of the martyr was in Ancona but because a rock used to stone the saint was brought to that city by a pious sailor, as Augustine attested. Thus the very building of the church stood for the missing relics of the body of the saint (later found), and therefore the physical building of the church was not a symbol only but indeed became the real memory of the martyr.[126]

Beni also linked the words "memory" and "church," but in a way that could not be farther from Baronio's. Beni's reflections on these two words can be found in a short manuscript treatise devoted to the technique of "local memory."[127] Beni's choice of topic is not particularly original, and it needs to be put in the context of the Aristotelian association between places of memory and topical places, which many other early modern commentators on Aristotle were discussing in their treatises on the art of memory.[128] In this vein, then, Beni constructed his entire discussion of the art of memory by explaining that the technique of the local memory was composed of two distinct parts: "the immobile and the mobile. The immobile is the place [*luogo*] where, by means of the intellect or of the imagination, it is possible to locate the figures that represent the concepts [that need to be remembered]. The mobile is the representing figure, because once it fulfills its function of explaining the concept in the present occurrence, it is no longer used, and we can let it slip our mind and sink into oblivion."[129] Beni devoted the rest of his treatise to giving concrete examples of both parts. He started with the "immobile" and suggested that a perfect example thereof was the church of St. Giustina in Padua: "when I entered the church from the left door I used that whole canvas of walls and chapels all around until the right door, and I established it as an immobile place for 173 places or parts of that said immobile place."[130]

When Beni wanted to give an example of the "mobile," that is, of the figures that the church place could hold, he chose to imagine the parts of a possible disputation on Aristotle's *Rhetoric*: "if, for instance, you want to dispute against Aristotle, who defines rhetoric as the faculty which allows to find the probable in any given thing. . . and you want to oppose his definition saying in the first place that the name 'faculty' is ambiguous. . . then in the first place, which will indeed be the first big column of the chapel you will find on the left-hand side, you will put a man dressed as a philosopher with a pallium, who will have many tongues. And you will use this simulacrum, whatever it may look like, as a reminder of the ambiguity and different meanings of the word 'faculty.' "[131] The disputation would continue with the question of whether rhetoric, rather than a faculty, was more properly an *ars* or a *scientia*, which could be constructed by placing in the second *luogo* an image of an artist or scientist. Then it would deal with whether rhetoric was the same as sophistry, which could be remembered by imagining a symbol representing the ambiguous nature of rhetoric, in between virtue and vice, such as a statue of Athena, goddess of both war and wisdom. Afterward, the disputation would address the parts of rhetoric—*inventio, dispositio, elocutio*—which could be represented by the image of Neptune with a trident and so forth, with the various images representing all the various arguments of the disputations being assigned to a *luogo*, that is, to a specific place in the church.[132]

The final part of Beni's imaginary disputation concerned the "greatest labyrinth" of the discussion, as Beni put it, or the fundamental problem that Beni had already identified in his commentary on Aristotle's *Rhetoric*: namely, the relationship between rhetoric and probable arguments. Aristotle seemed to argue that probable rather than certain arguments were the basis of every form of παιδεία (this is the capability, fostered by education, of making a judgment about something in the absence of ἐπιστήμη, i.e., proper and certain knowledge, of it). If this were right, Beni complained, rhetoric could not be easily distinguished from other disciplines. Indeed, probable arguments seemed to be at the core of any form of human pursuit of knowledge, and "an educated man is described [by Aristotle] as somebody who reasons about anything only in a probable manner."[133] But which image should be associated with this fundamental question of the relationship between rhetoric and other forms of παιδεία? Since παιδεία is rendered in Italian by Beni with *pedia*, which resembles the Italian word *piede* (foot), and since occasionally "in order to locate something one can and should use vulgar and laughable things," Beni wrote that for him the best way to remind himself of this topic was to think of a friend of his who had "such a big and monstrous foot that, as a joke, a poem in his honor, entitled Scarpide, was composed" (the title is a play on the Italian word *scarpa*, i.e., shoe). For this reason, Beni said, "I would put in this sixteenth place my said friend extending his monstrous foot, and hence I would remember the *Pedia*, and that part of the disputation."[134]

Reflecting on this last topic leads to the conclusion of this imaginary disputation, which brings Beni back to something he had always been preoccupied with: the fact that Aristotle's definition of rhetoric as the faculty aimed at finding the probable in any thing is fundamentally flawed, "because the truth is so mixed with the verisimilar that very often they are indivisibly joined, which also happens with falsehood and lies when they resemble the truth." Thus, Beni continued, "limiting our investigation to the probable is impossible," and as we are searching for the probable we will always encounter truth or falsehood. In conclusion, "striving to search only for the probable and for that which is apt to give credence is an endless pursuit, which is more of wishful thinking than something one could hope to attain."[135]

The different use made by Baronio and Beni of the couple church/memory is a most suggestive and stimulating representation of Baronio's theological and epistemological commitment to ecclesiastical history and of Beni's opinion of its fundamental impossibility. Beni in fact treated the church of St. Giustina as an ideal place *of* memory, a place, that is, in which to exercise a quintessentially human faculty and adapt it to the mutable conditions of human existence. For

Baronio, by contrast, churches in themselves *were* memories: the physical place built by men to honor a martyr was the same as the act of remembering and at the same time of making present the eternal time of the Church, *semper eadem*. When it came to choosing an example of a trope that could be placed in the church of memory, moreover, Beni chose the theme of rhetoric, indeed the complex mix of true, false, and probable that the Aristotelian definition of rhetoric did not sort out but rather complicated. For Baronio, by contrast, churches were memories of the undisputable Truth of the Church as it emerged unchanged from history.

Baronio and Beni represent the polarized dimensions of the problem of ecclesiastical history in post-Reformation Rome. On the one hand, Baronio and his likes believed that faith in the Truth of theology made sense of the truths of men; therefore ecclesiastical history was the venue in which both Truth and truth emerged triumphantly and harmoniously. On the other hand, people like Beni or Mascardi started to harbor some doubts about the glue that kept together Truth and truth and instead started to see probability and verisimilitude as necessary components of human life and human time, which no theological or epistemological certainty could ever completely eliminate. In this case, then, ecclesiastical history is almost a contradiction in terms, for how can human uncertainty be used to describe a divine certainty? Or how can divine certainty manifest itself in the midst of uncertain and mutable human affairs? Thus, seeing Beni and Baronio as two opposite poles of this debate allows us to view post-Reformation reflections on historiography and ecclesiastical history as a veritable laboratory of modernity. More specifically, their parallel lives are the early modern expression of the modern dialectic already identified by Momigliano between the unbelievers' and the believers' modes of understanding ecclesiastical history, which is in turn at the very core of the raison d'être of ecclesiastical history as a distinctive discipline.[136]

Beni's unbelief, however, was not limited to the extent to which the Truth of theology could be found in history. Rather, Beni's eclectic production as a whole can be considered as an expression of the initial embryonic doubt regarding the correspondence between reality and our representation of it, just as we saw in the case of Mascardi. Such doubt was not only (or not primarily) theological but fundamentally epistemological and hermeneutical, and this is the theme that runs constantly through Beni's eclectic and confused production: how can the things that we write or say, marred as they are by the mutability and uncertainty that characterizes human productions, refer to a stable and certain truth or Truth? Baronio's belief, on its part, was not only theological but also epistemological and hermeneutical: indeed, his faith in the Truth of Catholicism gave him an unshakable faith not simply in the Catholic Church but also in the possibility of recognizing and interpreting the traces of the past as *evidence* of history.

In this perspective, then, Baronio's belief that the transcendent Truth of theology, far from hindering a critical scrutiny of evidence, is instead the very condition for it might resonate more than one could imagine with the very epistemological core of our own current understanding of the historical profession. We can speculate, in fact, that perhaps even we, historians working in the twenty-first century, believe in something that both transcends and is necessary to make sense of our documents. Our current belief is not a theological Truth but faith in the possibility of representing, resurrecting, explaining, or describing the past—perhaps a theological truth of a sort? On the other side, Beni's view of the fundamental impossibility to find the Truth of the Church in the human world of verisimilitude and uncertainty, which stems from the more general tension that Beni identified between reality and its human representation, might make Beni into not simply the forerunner of modern unbelief insofar as ecclesiastical history is concerned but the forerunner of postmodern doubt more generally. In this sense, Beni's intellectual profile might also resonate with current historians, especially those who manifest a heightened awareness of the representational character of historiography and who are grappling with its epistemological implications. Regardless of which position each of us takes toward the epistemological basis of our own discipline, in this chapter I simply wanted to show that by resuscitating Beni and figures like him from historiographical oblivion and by putting them in the context of their time, in this case alongside Baronio, we can recover the early modern seeds of this late modern question. Recovering these seeds, I think, is crucially important for understanding both early modern and late modern culture.

4

Rhetoric, Truth, and the Truth

In the previous chapters I have shown what seemed to me important moments of hermeneutical and epistemological doubt in post-Reformation Catholic culture. The hermeneutical implications of the doctrines of equivocation and mental reservation, Mascardi's view of historical narrative as an effort to counteract the merciless destruction of time, Beni's fundamental doubt regarding the very possibility of ecclesiastical history: all these instances can be considered unique keyholes from which we can take a look at the underbelly of the same post-Reformation Catholicism that produced Bellarmine's *Controversiae* and Baronio's *Annales*. This chapter is devoted to another opening from which we can take a peek at this same shadowy world of post-Reformation doubt: the teaching of rhetoric in the Roman College of the Jesuits. Post-Reformation rhetoric was, in a sense, the breeding ground for many of the concepts that link the various forms of doubt that I examined earlier in this work. The representational function of language, the relationship between truth and verisimilitude, and the tension between probability and certainty were all at the core of the discipline of rhetoric as it was conceived in the early modern period.

Within this general frame, my analysis of rhetoric in the following pages seeks to demonstrate two specific points. First, I want to argue that rhetoric as it was being taught in the Roman College did not simply result in the construction of the *orator Christianus*; that is, the product of the distinctive alliance between post-Reformation sacred concerns and the classical, especially Ciceronian, rhetorical tradition. Rather, the teaching of rhetoric at the Roman College was a veritable laboratory in which Jesuit intellectuals tried to grapple with the epistemological function of rhetoric as a means to attain knowledge in the unstable and uncertain world of men. Thus, Jesuit (and post-Reformation Catholic) rhetoric had a twofold aim: on the one hand, it was an instrument that post-Tridentine Catholicism used in order to communicate, and to stir people toward, the Truth of theology. On the other hand, as I will argue throughout this chapter, it constituted an original and important attempt to conceptualize the "rhetorical" dimension of human life and the relationship between human language and human truth.

The second point I want to make, which is a partial consequence of the first, concerns the multifaceted nature of the Roman College as an institution that produced both the intellectual leaders of post-Reformation Catholicism and intellectuals whose elaboration was characterized less by theological certainty than by the manifold expressions of human uncertainty. The Roman College was able to forge the tools for asserting the Truth, and at the same time it generated the seeds of doubt. It was a venue in which to construct a language that was supposed to conquer the world, and at the same time it was a venue in which language could reflect on itself and on its own capability of knowing the world and of acting in it and on it. Understanding how these different epistemological and linguistic tensions were elaborated in post-Reformation Jesuit rhetoric provides valuable insight into not only the complexity, but also the centrality of post-Reformation Catholic culture for the development of our own current epistemological and linguistic tensions.

Rhetoric at the Roman College

I would like to start my analysis by using as a background the picture—rather, the fresco—that Marc Fumaroli painted of post-Reformation Catholic rhetoric. Fumaroli's work deserves credit for two main reasons. First, Fumaroli's analysis has rescued rhetoric from the oblivion in which the post-Romantic antirhetorical prejudice had confined it. Far from being simply a culturally sterile and intellectually dishonest set of techniques aimed at embellishing one's speech at the expense of the truth, Fumaroli has shown how rhetoric was indeed a fundamental feature of the political, cultural, and religious life of early modern Europe.[1]

Secondly, and within his more general project of recovering the centrality of rhetoric in the early modern culture, Fumaroli highlighted the distinctive role of the "devout Ciceronianism" elaborated especially but not exclusively by the Society of Jesus. This movement evolved during what Fumaroli has termed the "second Renaissance" as the rhetorical backbone of a distinctive and influential pan-European Catholic cultural project. More specifically, summarizing rather roughly Fumaroli's rich argument, by the middle of the sixteenth century some Jesuit and non-Jesuit intellectuals, mostly based either in the Roman College or in the University of Rome (among them Marc-Antoine Muret, Francesco Benci, and Pedro Juan Perpiñán),[2] had taken stock of and fully absorbed both the Erasmian and the Borromean anti-Ciceronianism. Thus, they decided to refashion Ciceronianism and to adapt it to the new post-Reformation circumstances. From a stylistic point of view, this meant that people like Benci, Muret, and Perpiñán maintained that Cicero should indeed be followed as a model of style, but they argued that imitating Cicero did not mean copying Cicero's style slavishly. Instead, it meant taking inspiration from Cicero's insistence that every orator needed to develop his own style within and around a central idea. By the beginning of the seventeenth century, with the publication of Famiano Strada's *Prolusiones academicae* (1617), this newly revised Ciceronianism had been developed in its fullest intellectual and stylistic form.[3]

In the following pages I do not mean to challenge Fumaroli's general interpretation, which remains a convincing and insightful account of the significance and importance of Jesuit rhetoric in the early modern times.[4] Rather, I offer a complementary view to Fumaroli's argument: I argue that not only did the elaborations on rhetoric of these Jesuit intellectuals provide a new stylistic foundation to the intellectual and cultural structures of post-Reformation Catholicism, but they also offered a new and original perspective on the philosophical and epistemological value of rhetoric.

In order to demonstrate this point, this chapter centers on two Jesuit professors of rhetoric: Pedro Juan Perpiñán and Famiano Strada, who represent respectively the initial phase and the fullest development of Fumaroli's second-Renaissance Jesuit Ciceronianism. In my argument, Perpiñán and Strada also represent two different phases of the development of the question of the relationship between rhetoric and truth. By engaging profoundly with the philosophical role that Aristotle assigned to rhetoric and by blending this Aristotelian strand with Cicero's insistence on the epistemological significance of probability, Perpiñán's theory constituted a significant attempt to grant to rhetoric not simply the function of embellishing speech but also an important epistemological and philosophical value. In this respect Perpiñán laid the groundwork for Strada, in whose work rhetoric became the backbone for a fascinating, if still fragmentary, reflection on the power of language to create, not simply communicate, meaning.

Both Perpiñán and Strada synthesized their views on rhetoric in published collections of orations (respectively, the *Orationes duodeviginti*, edited by Muret and published for the first time in Rome in 1587,[5] and the already quoted *Prolusiones academicae* of 1617). Both Perpiñán and Strada had a great impact on the teaching of rhetoric at the Roman College. Perpiñán taught in the Roman College between 1561 and 1565, and in those years he was heavily involved in the discussions on how to structure the curriculum of the Jesuit schools prior to the finalization of the *Ratio studiorum*. He was also in charge of revising Cipriano Soares's *De arte rhetorica*, first published in 1562 and destined to become the official textbook of rhetoric in the Jesuit colleges and thus an international best seller.[6] Strada's official teaching career as a professor at the Roman College began in 1600 and ended in 1614. However, Strada's influence on the entire cultural

world of seventeenth-century Rome is impossible to overestimate: he continued to study and informally "teach" rhetoric for almost fifty years, until 1649
(the year of his death), thus shaping the *Bildung* of many of the students and
scholars of humanities that gravitated toward the Roman College, including, as
we have already seen, Agostino Mascardi. After the publication of the *Prolusiones*
his fame grew exponentially and ensured him the reputation of being the *maître
à penser* of Roman eloquence.[7]

We are fortunate enough to have a considerable amount of manuscript material containing both Perpiñán's and Strada's lecture notes, as well as numerous
fragments of rhetorical works that they both wrote or sketched but never published. Concerning Perpiñán, among his unpublished works the most important
items for my purpose are a few substantial portions of Perpiñán's own treatise
on rhetoric, entitled *De oratore*, which he wrote during his tenure as professor at
the Roman College.[8] As for Famiano Strada, we have several more or less fragmentary works on rhetoric, his lecture notes for a course on Aristotle's *Poetics* he
taught at the Roman College in 1608, and several orations.[9]

An analysis of the manuscript material against the background provided by
the published orations is useful for a number of reasons, and indeed it can offer
quite interesting surprises to the patient reader who is willing to venture among
hundreds of pages recording incomplete, truncated, and constantly revised
thoughts. First, reading the lecture notes taken by students or the personal notes
jotted down by professors gives a sense of what actually happened in the classrooms of rhetoric in the Roman College, thus allowing us to appreciate more
fully the tenor and vivacity of the intellectual debates regarding rhetoric. Thanks
to the work of Lawrence Green, among others, we know that Renaissance students of rhetoric, who generally took Cicero as the main source for rhetorical precepts, were inclined to read Aristotle through or at least to harmonize
Aristotle with Cicero and, to a certain extent, Quintilian.[10] The Jesuits were not
an exception to this general trend: based on the rules for the teachers of rhetoric
of the *Ratio Studiorum*, we know that Cicero was supposed to be the model of
style for the pupils and that in terms of the more theoretical aspects of rhetoric, Cicero's oratorical works needed to be supplemented by Aristotle's *Rhetoric*
and, "if desired, his *Poetics*."[11] Examining the manuscript material coming from
or linked with the courses that Perpiñán and Strada actually taught provides
us a unique opportunity to see how exactly teachers and pupils of the Roman
College integrated Cicero with Aristotle.

Also, perhaps more importantly in the context of the present work, by limiting our inquiry to Perpiñán's or Strada's published orations, we can certainly
appreciate the intellectual and cultural strength of the stylistic synthesis that
Perpiñán initiated and that Strada completed of the classical rhetorical tradition
on the one hand, and the post-Reformation's intellectual, religious, and political

concerns on the other. If, however, we focus on their notes and unpublished fragments, we will have the opportunity to examine the conceptual labor that came before the stylistic synthesis of the orations. Indeed, the unpublished manuscripts present raw reflections on topics that were later polished, modified, or outright discarded, and as such they are the expression of intellectual preoccupations and concerns that in the published material appear only in their final and, in certain cases, sanitized or truncated form.

Pedro Juan Perpiñán: The Probable, the Verisimilar, and the True

In one of his published orations, Perpiñán described the relationship between knowledge and eloquence in classic Ciceronian terms: there are two features, according to Perpiñán, which "*nos homines reddunt*" (make us human): *ratio* and *sermo*. Reason (*ratio*) "investigates what is unknown, understands what is investigated, arranges and composes what is understood, puts together what is dispersed, redistributes what is assembled, remembers the past, understands the present, infers the future, and by connecting the last things with the first things it grasps the course of all things and the succession of events." The capacity of reason to understand the world, to infer and to deduce, to divide and to compose, however, would remain in the dark, "hidden in our mind and soul," were it not for the "*lumen*" of speech (*oratio*), which allows reason to be communicated among men and thus to be brought into a tangible external existence.[12]

After this preamble on the strict relationship between *ratio* and *oratio*, Perpiñán continued by explaining that both reason and speech can make mistakes, and in order to make sure that they function properly humans make use of two different faculties: the first is the "*vis disserendi,* which we call logic," the second is the "*facultas bene dicendi,* which we call eloquence, and which enriches with words and phrases the speech according to what is more apt to persuade."[13] Here, then, Perpiñán seems to have confined rhetoric and eloquence to the realm of *verba*, while logic and reason were in charge of the *res*, as we can see from the fact that Perpiñán used Quintilian's definition of eloquence as the *facultas bene dicendi* that embellishes speech so as to make it more persuasive (rather than the faculty that finds what is more persuasive).[14]

Such a view of rhetoric is confirmed later in the same work when Perpiñán took issue with another of Quintilian's rhetorical precepts; namely, his definition of the orator as *vir bonus*. Precisely because rhetoric does not deal with knowledge but operates, so to speak, on a pre-given content, already elaborated and provided by reason, if correct reason provides a true and pious content, rhetoric will have the task of embellishing the truth and rendering it persuasive. If, by contrast, evil reason provides an evil content, rhetoric will embellish false or heretical opinions, and it will render those persuasive: "eloquence indeed has the prerogative [*vis*] of being able to present opposite opinions on the same issue."[15] There are "*nonnulli nobilissimi Rhetores*," Perpiñán explained, who believed that eloquence could not be found but "*in bono viro*"; while this might have certainly been "desirable," it was nevertheless not true.[16] Eloquence, in fact, could often be found among impious men, and indeed many heretics of Perpiñán's time were effective orators even if they were most certainly not *boni viri*. This is why, Perpiñán concluded, studying rhetoric in his own time was particularly important: "the lovers of truth and religion" needed to "tear away from the impious and deceitful hands" of the heretics the weapons of rhetoric and use them to defend the Truth. Since "the *copia dicendi* is an aid for both sides, just as the heretics use it to oppress the Church, so we can transform it into a means to defend it powerfully."[17]

Perpiñán's statements are a clear expression of the instrumentality, so to speak, of post-Tridentine rhetoric in general and of Fumaroli's devout Ciceronianism in particular. It is only by sharply differentiating between the content of a speech (provided by philosophy or, in this case, by theology) and the form of a speech (polished and rendered more effective by rhetoric) that classical and Ciceronian rhetoric could be restored to a position of privilege in post-Reformation Jesuit education. Thus, endorsing Quintilian's definition of rhetoric as the art of speaking well and opposing Quintilian's definition of the orator as a *vir bonus* are both necessary steps in order to construct the Christian orator as a man able to persuasively present the truth provided by theology. Once the Christian orator qua orator is relieved from the necessity of being *vir bonus* (the Christian orator must of course be a good man qua Christian), and once rhetoric is completely separated from the task of discovering the truth or something similar to the truth and simply endowed with the task of communicating effectively a truth provided by theology, then ancient rhetoric, which used to occupy a central role in the agora or the senate or wherever political and judicial deliberations took place, can, like a phoenix, rise from the ashes of the ancient *respublica* and find a new central role on the pulpits and in the *aulae* of the *respublica Christiana*, where *movere* was progressively becoming more important than *docere*.[18]

So far, one could say, *nihil sub sole novi*, since Perpiñán seems to sketch a profile of the Christian orator and of Christian rhetoric that is very much in line with the general trend of the development of sacred oratory in sixteenth-century Rome.[19] And yet an analysis of Perpiñán's unpublished treatise on rhetoric changes this perspective significantly. In this manuscript work, in fact, Perpiñán consciously abandoned the view of rhetoric as a series of speech techniques *ad usum* of the Christian orator and instead seemed more interested in exploring the epistemological and philosophical value of rhetoric as a form of knowledge.

Let us start from the definition of rhetoric that Perpiñán uses constantly throughout his manuscripts and that is verbatim the one Aristotle used in the *Rhetoric*; that is, "rhetoric is a *vis* or *facultas* to see in any given case what is accommodated to persuasion."[20] Choosing Aristotle's definition over Quintilian's came with a price: Aristotle's definition of rhetoric as the art of finding what is persuasive implies an attempt on Aristotle's part to establish a connection between rhetoric and philosophy by means of which rhetoric could cease to be simply a set of techniques or figures of speech used to manipulate words at the expense of the truth. Indeed, as Paul Ricoeur put it, it is precisely the deep philosophical scrutiny to which Aristotle subjected the concept of πιθανόν ("that which is persuasive") that makes Aristotle's *Rhetoric* "the most brilliant" attempt to "institutionalize rhetoric from the point of view of philosophy."[21] But putting the accent on the philosophical and epistemological aspects of persuasion and, consequently, of rhetoric is a delicate intellectual operation, for it situates rhetoric in a precarious equilibrium between the certain truths of philosophy on the one hand and the dangerous and suspicious power to manipulate words of sophistry on the other hand. Quintilian's definition of rhetoric (especially in its post-Reformation applications), by highlighting rhetoric's function of "speaking well" rather than of "finding what is persuasive," pushed rhetoric more in the direction of techniques and figures of speech and took some of the philosophical pressures off of it. In fact, post-Reformation theorists of sacred eloquence generally highlighted rhetoric's ability to arrange the words in such a way as to stir the audience towards truths whose origin was distinctively not rhetorical.[22]

Thus, Perpiñán's choice of Aristotle over Quintilian in his manuscript works is not a minor or insignificant issue; not only Soares but with him an entire school of rhetoric had implicitly endorsed Quintilian's definition of rhetoric as *ars bene dicendi*, but Perpiñán himself, in his oration, had resorted to the same definition of rhetoric as the art of communicating effectively. Of course Perpiñán was very aware of and indeed personally involved in the need to rescue ancient rhetoric and make it suitable for the distinctive needs of post-Reformation Catholicism. However, just like his friend Marc-Antoine Muret,[23] Perpiñán's deep involvement with Aristotle also made him aware that rhetoric had an important role in Aristotle's entire philosophical project. In a sense, we can say that Perpiñán blended Aristotle and Cicero by connecting the Ciceronian link between wisdom and rhetoric with the Aristotelian link between philosophy and rhetoric. Thus, insofar as the definition of rhetoric was concerned, Perpiñán took care to specify several times in his manuscript that Cicero himself had followed Aristotle's definition and had always insisted against Quintilian that finding the persuasive, rather than simply communicating in a persuasive manner, was the main aim of rhetoric.[24]

Perpiñán's manuscript leaves some traces of what must have been Perpiñán's effort to cope with two different intellectual impulses, one stirring him toward embracing the obvious advantages of Quintilian's definition from the point of view of Christian oratory and the other stirring him toward the more philosophical and epistemological aspects of rhetoric. At the beginning he seemed to have found a compromise: "at some point I thought that while persuading was the end of the orator, the end of rhetoric was speaking well, since it seems that all the precepts of rhetoric are referred to that end, that is, so that we may speak well. If this opinion were true, that controversy that exists between Quintilian on one side, and Aristotle and Cicero on the other, on the end of rhetoric would be easily reconciled." After giving the matter further thought, however, Perpiñán changed his mind, and indeed "now whoever reads diligently the writing of the orators and considers more accurately the nature of rhetoric will think very differently, since even though the precepts of the art refer to speaking well, speaking well in that same art pertains to persuading, thus it cannot be that speaking well is the final end of that art."[25]

Perpiñán's change of heart had important consequences for his reflections on rhetoric: once we assume that rhetoric is the art of finding that which is persuasive, a number of questions arise. What is the nature of persuasion? Does persuasion produce a proper form of knowledge, or can we be persuaded of whatever the orator wants us to believe? Is there a criterion to distinguish "good" persuasion from "bad" persuasion? Or to put it differently, is Plato's thesis regarding the dangers of rhetoric as the art of make-believe justified?

Perpiñán began his discussion of these issues with the usual question of whether rhetoric was an art (in the Aristotelian sense of τέχνη). For him, following Aristotle and Cicero, rhetoric was an art of the "conjectural" kind; that is, the kind that, despite having a certain and well-established method, does not always attain its end. As examples, Perpiñán mentioned the familiar cases of medicine and statecraft. Every doctor or head of state has at his disposal a set of precepts and well-established rules in order to carry out his *officium* (the doctor for instance has a set of medicaments whose effects on the human body he knows, and there are certain rules that the head of state knows he should follow to keep his people peaceful and well organized). Neither the doctor nor the head of state, however, can always be sure to attain his respective *finis*, for sometimes patients of a very good doctor die and states ruled by effective rulers go to ruin. In the same manner, rhetoric provides the orator a set of rules necessary for him to carry out his *officium*, for any well-trained orator should know how to form arguments and how to present them effectively. Even the best orator, however, can sometime fail to persuade the audience, because rhetoric can sometimes fail to find that which is persuasive, thus failing to attain its end.[26]

Rhetoric then, Perpiñán continued, can give precepts on how to present the persuasive, but just as it cannot assure that its practitioners will always succeed in persuading, so it cannot offer any precepts concerning the morality (or lack thereof) of what is it that people should be persuaded of. Perpiñán admitted that the lack of rhetorical precepts regarding the moral value of rhetorical persuasion has troubling consequences: for example, rhetoric by itself does not prohibit the orator from deceiving the audience. Because of this issue, Perpiñán declared, "eloquence has perturbed the minds of many people."[27] Many tried to defend eloquence from this accusation, and Perpiñán started his discussion on this topic by examining Quintilian's solution, which was twofold. First, Quintilian argued that since the orator could only be a *vir bonus*, then one must assume that a *vir bonus* could, sometimes, lie for good reasons. According to Perpiñán, however, this solution had no value. First of all, eloquence had no intrinsic moral requirement and an orator qua orator was not necessarily a good man. Secondly, justifying lying in this manner for Perpiñán was unacceptable for a Christian society: if one started to justify lying in the context of rhetoric, one could just as easily justify it in other contexts. Many pagan authors did in fact justify lying in this manner, but Christians were held to a higher standard. Thus, for Perpiñán it was better, in this matter, to follow the advice that St. Basilius gave to his pupils— namely, to ignore the parts of the pagan books that seemed to condone lying.[28] The second of Quintilian's remarks quoted by Perpiñán was that whenever an orator uses a false argument, his audience is indeed deceived, but the orator himself is not, since he is aware of the falsity of the argument. However, he protested, "I do not approve Quintilian's argument, since even if we say that the orator is not deceived, we still admit that his speech is false."[29]

In order to rescue rhetoric from being naturally associated with fraud and deceit, Perpiñán stated, we need to follow what the "*Aristotelei veteres et Platonici*" say on the content of rhetoric, which is strictly linked to the question of whether or not rhetoric is a *scientia* as well as (or instead of) an *ars*. First, they divide rhetoric in two branches. The first is the rhetoric "unbound and separated from all causes," as when, for example, an orator discusses whether or not being clement is useful for winning over an audience. The second is the one "linked and attached to a certain issue," as when Cicero declared that he wanted to be clement toward Catilina in order to win over the judges during the actual trial against Catilina.[30]

As for the latter kind of rhetoric, Perpiñán wrote that many Greek and Latin scholars, especially Quintilian, thought that it was neither an *ars* nor a *scientia* but rather a "*vis*" or "*facultas*." Quintilian, however, went a step farther than the others in articulating the substantial difference between rhetoric and other forms of knowledge, for he argued that this kind of rhetoric, neither *ars* nor *scientia*, could have no truth-finding value. Since being able to speak pro and contra the very same issue was indeed one of the main abilities of an orator and since the same issue could not be simultaneously true and false, then rhetoric could not but end up telling falsehoods. Precisely because Quintilian could not make rhetoric immune to falsehood, he attempted to justify orators' lies in the ways we have already seen Perpiñán opposed to. For Perpiñán, by contrast, the entire theoretical principle underpinning Quintilian's discussion of lying orators was wrong: it was not necessary to justify rhetors' use of lies because it was simply not true that rhetoric must necessarily use lies. Rhetoric, for Perpiñán, deals not with the things that can be either false or true; it deals with the *probabile*, which is outside the realm of things that are either false or true and which, albeit being different from true knowledge, nevertheless shares something important with it.

Perpiñán stated that Plato and Aristotle were in agreement on the fact that rhetoric, as well as dialectic, does not seek to instill "proper knowledge in the minds of the audience, but what is probable [*probabilia*] and appropriate to be credible. . . from which disputation it is clear that the causes which the orators discuss do not contain knowledge, but opinion, since opinion is a form of credence and therefore it instructs men to give credence, not to understand and comprehend."[31] It is worth noting that Perpiñán attributed to Plato the argument that Gorgias used and that Socrates was to confute later in the *Gorgias*. Perpiñán, however, gave a positive spin on Gorgias's argument and presented it as consonant with Aristotle's. In this manner, he sought to oppose to Quintilian what he saw as a compact Greek tradition that defended the categories of the probable, the credible, and the opinion as something that, while being definitely different from knowledge, nevertheless could not and should not be relegated to the realm of falsehood. Indeed, as a further indication that rhetoric per se had nothing to do with lies and sophistical manipulations, Perpiñán quoted Socrates's remarks in the *Phaedrus* that "whoever wants to speak well about something should have knowledge of that which he speaks about."[32] Socrates's words, however, can be found in the part of the dialogue where Socrates explicitly contrasted rhetoric as the (false and deceiving) art of persuading by means of opinions (δόξα) with the ability to speak the truth and explicitly attacked those sophists who believed that the probable (τὰ εἰκότα) is to be held in greater esteem than the truth (260a ff.). Perpiñán once again interpreted Plato's passage in Aristotelian terms. After quoting Socrates, he concluded: "Add the fact that whoever does not know the truth cannot see in his mind what is similar to the truth, as Socrates himself later confirms. Truly in fact Aristotle wrote in his first book of *Rhetoric* [1.1.11] that only the man who can see the truth can see what is similar to the truth [*verisimile*], and only the man who has the disposition to know the truth has the disposition to properly infer what is probable [*probabile*] in any given case."[33]

Perpiñán's desire to defend the category of the rhetorical *probabile* from any suspicion of falsehood was so strong as to make him think that even his beloved

Cicero made a small mistake when, through the character of Antonius, he argued in his *De oratore* that orators speak of what they do not know because they can argue pro and contra the exact same issue (*De oratore* 2.30). The reason for Cicero's slip, Perpiñán explained, stems from the "ambiguity" of the word *scientia*, which does not refer simply to certain and true knowledge but also to knowledge of things that cannot be different than what they are. Probable things, on the other hand, are precisely those things that are not necessarily one way or the other, which does not mean that they are necessarily either false or true but that insofar as rhetoric deals with them, they can be either way.[34] For this reason, the fact that this kind of rhetoric is not based on and does not produce any form of *scientia* does not mean that it therefore is based on or produces lies.

As for the rhetoric of the other kind—that is, the capability of finding the persuasive that is not tied to a specific controversy—Perpiñán stated that this is most certainly an *ars* in the Aristotelian sense and, as he had already declared, an *ars coniecturalis* more specifically. How about the relationship between this kind of rhetoric and *scientia*? Once again, Aristotle's reflections on the epistemological value of this second kind of rhetoric take central stage in Perpiñán's discussion. Aristotle, Perpiñán wrote, was evidently so convinced of the continuity between truth and the rhetorical *probabile* that several times in his works he used the label of *scientia* to define both dialectic and rhetoric in this general sense. While Perpiñán shared Aristotle's view of the continuity between true knowledge and "rhetorical" knowledge, he nevertheless refrained from giving to rhetoric the name *scientia*. Aristotle and the Peripatetic philosophers, according to Perpiñán, called *scientia* generically "whatever referred to knowledge." Proper *scientia*, however, was only what referred to the "knowledge of truth," while "all the things that are included in the precepts of rhetoric and dialectic do not pertain to the knowledge [of truth], but to its use, as was the opinion of all the old Platonists and Aristotelians." In other words, the point of the proper *scientiae* is for their practitioners to acquire knowledge in the said *scientiae*, while the well-trained orator does not come out of his rhetorical training "knowledgeable in any given subject."[35]

This, however, does not mean for Perpiñán that rhetoric and dialectic have nothing to do with reason and knowledge, and indeed they can be referred to as *scientiae* "in the vulgar sense" of the term.[36] The difference between *scientiae* proper on the one hand and rhetoric and dialectic on the other is that *scientiae* proper are "*scientiae* of things," that is, they are concerned with producing knowledge regarding a specific discipline, while rhetoric and dialectic are "*scientiae* of reasons and arguments," that is, they are concerned with producing a sort of method of reasoning and arguing.[37] For this reason, Perpiñán concluded, rhetoric and dialectic are both "companions and assistants to the other faculties that bring about human reasoning and understanding."[38]

Not everybody agreed that rhetoric shares with dialectic this important function of *comes* and *administra* of reason, and indeed Perpiñán on this point forcefully attacked Talon, Ramus, and their followers: "some recent dialecticians who
fashion themselves masters of speech" have argued that while dialectic has the
function of constructing arguments to be used in disputations, rhetoric must
instead be confined to the function of embellishing speech, so that the only
thing rhetoric would be "companion of" is "the pleasure in speech." Such division of labor between rhetoric and dialectic is so wrong that "to tell the truth,
it seems to be rhetorically, rather than truthfully, constructed," Perpiñán wrote
with a remarkable pun.[39]

Thus, just to recapitulate what we have so far said, in these manuscript pages
Perpiñán argued that rhetoric, especially rhetoric insofar as it is a general theoretical discipline rather than a set of precepts applied to a specific controversy,
is a conjectural *ars*, whose end, not always attained, is persuasion. We also know
that for Perpiñán, while rhetoric is not properly a *scientia*, it is nevertheless not
completely alien from a certain form of knowledge. We also know that this
form of knowledge concerns the *probabile* rather than the certain and necessary
(which is precisely the reason why rhetoric is not properly a *scientia*, since all
scientiae concern certain and necessary knowledge) and that there is a form of
continuity between the rhetorical *probabile* and the true knowledge, since both
are grounded in the same root. Finally, we know that rhetoric shares an important part of dialectic's nature, since both of them are indeed concerned with the
probable and both of them are *comites* and *administrae* of human reason and
understanding.

At this point the reader who has followed Perpiñán's arguments so far would
expect to find a further elaboration on two issues. First, what is the nature of
the rhetorical *probabile*? Or to put it differently, since Perpiñán in the previously
examined passages had mentioned the probable, the credible, and the opinion
as subjects within the purview of rhetoric and as something not completely
opposite to knowledge proper, the reader would expect Perpiñán to reflect on
the nature of those concepts and on their respective relationships. Second, since
Perpiñán mentioned rhetoric and dialectic as both dealing with the *probabile*
and as such sharing the task of being "assistant" to reason and understanding,
the reader would expect Perpiñán to elaborate more on the relationship between
rhetoric and dialectic. Perpiñán's work does not let its reader down: the Jesuit
professor seemed unable to shake off these two issues, for he returned to them
with an almost obsessive insistence time and again in several points of his manuscripts, writing different versions of the same arguments both in the context
of other discussions and as stand-alone sections specifically devoted to the
two themes.[40] Indeed, Perpiñán's insistence on these themes and the fact that
his reflections thereupon are scattered throughout his works at different stages

in his arguments make the task of the interpreter particularly challenging, but they are also highly indicative of how deeply Perpiñán engaged these questions, because it is precisely through these questions that Perpiñán's theory explored the epistemological and philosophical role of rhetoric.

In order to sort out Perpiñán's reflections on the first theme—that is, the nature of the rhetorical *probabile*—I propose to take as starting point his discussion of Plato's opinion on the nature of persuasion: "According to Plato in *Gorgias* there are two kinds of persuasion, one is the διδασκαλική, that is, the one concerning subjects and sciences conferring to the mind of the audience a true and perfect science of that which it persuades of." Mathematicians, for instance, persuade their audience in this first sense when they demonstrate that the sum of two sides of a triangle is greater than the third side. The other is πιστευτική, which is the kind of persuasion concerning credence and opinion. This second kind of persuasion "does not arrive at the perfect knowledge, but it confers to the minds of the auditors justified credence in whatever it persuades of." Both rhetors and dialecticians use this kind of persuasion when they persuade the audience to give credence to arguments discussed "on the basis of probability" [*probabiliter*].[41]

Let us bracket for a moment the question of the difference between rhetoric and dialectic (I return to it later in this section) and focus on the fact that both, according to Perpiñán, deal with disputations argued "on the basis of probability," whose elaboration generates credence and faith. The "probable [*probabile*]," Perpiñán stated, "is defined by Aristotle in the first book, first chapter, of his *Topics* as what is either approved by all people, such as that one must seek the good. . . or by the majority of the people, such as that prudence should be preferred to riches. . . or by the learned, either all of them. . . or the majority of them. . . or by those whose wisdom is esteemed and well-known."[42] There is no qualitative difference, Perpiñán explained, between the *probabile* founded on the opinion of the common people and that founded on the opinion of the learned people. Sometimes, in fact, one needs to discuss subjects that the people know well, and in those cases "the probability of things needs to be considered on the basis of the opinion of the people." When on the other hand the discussion concerns things that people do not know, then the opinion of the learned should be considered the criterion for establishing probability.[43]

Regardless of whether the *probabile* is established by the learned people or by the common people, Perpiñán continued, the very category of the *probabile* has a specific epistemological autonomy: "the probable insofar as it is probable, however, is not necessarily either true or false, but it can be both, and it is not necessary that probable things be either true or false, but they can be partly true and partly false."[44] Some of the things that the common people hold true are actually true, but some are false, and the same can be said for the opinions that the learned people have. Besides, Perpiñán continued, as Alexander of Aphrodisias wrote: "what is *probabile* differs from what is true not because the *probabile* is false but from the manner and method of judging, which Alexander calls ἐπίκρισις. In fact, truth is judged on the basis of the thing itself, so that the truth is when the thing accords with what is said. Probability [*probabilitas*], by contrast, must be judged not on the basis of the thing itself but on the basis of the minds and opinions of the auditors, so that whatever accords with the audience's opinions is *probabile*, even if things are not what the audience believes they are."[45]

In this part, Perpiñán faithfully followed Alexander's commentary on Aristotle's *Topics*, in particular Alexander's commentary on the first chapter, first section, of Aristotle's work, concerning the difference between dialectical syllogisms, based on generally accepted opinions, and sophistical or contentious syllogisms, based on opinions that look as if they are generally accepted but in reality are not.[46] Perpiñán, however, was not much interested in discussing sophistical syllogisms: in his earlier discussion of the nature of rhetoric he had already dismissed the line of argument that linked rhetorical *probabile* with sophistical manipulations and lies, and at this point in his work he was not evidently interested in bring up this topic again.[47] Rather, in this part of his work Perpiñán was interested in establishing a relationship of continuity between the rhetorical and the dialectical *probabile* on the one hand and truth or true knowledge on the other. This is why, after using Alexander's passage to demonstrate that the category of the *probabile* possesses a certain epistemological autonomy with respect to the true/false dichotomy, Perpiñán continued by reflecting on the relationship between the probable, the verisimilar, and the true.

Before getting to Perpiñán's opinion on this topic, we should make a little detour into the terminological intricacies of Aristotle's concepts of the probable, the verisimilar, and the persuasive. First of all, what Perpiñán translated as *probabile* in this whole section is what Alexander of Aphrodisias in his commentary (and Aristotle in the first chapter of the *Topics*) called ἔνδοξα; that is, opinions that are highly reputed or generally accepted or held in high esteem. Aristotle used same word, ἔνδοξα, several times also in his *Rhetoric*, with the same meaning of generally accepted opinions. In the Aristotelian vocabulary we need to register two more words that belong to the same semantic area. The first is εἰκός, which means the probable in the sense of what happens for the most part (τὸ εἰκός ἐστι τὸ ὡς ἐπὶ τὸ πολὺ γινόμενον), which in *Rhetoric* 1.2.14–15 is mentioned as the backbone (together with "signs," *semeia*) of the rhetorical enthymeme. The second is πιθανόν, that which is persuasive, which as we already seen, Aristotle mentioned (among other places) in his discussion on the aim of rhetoric (in 1.2.1).

Rhetoric, in Aristotle's definition, is that which discovers the persuasive, and the persuasive is usually founded on what is commonly accepted and on what happens in most cases. Thus rhetoric, the realm of the probable/approved/persuasive, on one side borders on sophistry, which, as Aristotle argued in the *Topics* and in the *Sophistical Refutations*, is concerned with what appears to be ἔνδοξα (i.e., generally accepted opinions) but is really not. On the other side rhetoric borders on philosophy and the other proper *scientiae*, which are different from rhetoric in that they are founded on and consequently produce true knowledge rather than approved opinions. However, according to Aristotle there is a tight link between philosophy and rhetoric (and dialectic, in this context), since "it belongs to the same capacity both to see the true (ἀληθὲς) and what resembles the true (τὸ ὅμοιον τῷ ἀληθεῖ), and at the same time humans have a natural disposition for the true and to a large extent hit on the truth; thus an ability to aim at commonly held opinions (ἔνδοξα) is a characteristic of one who also has a similar ability in regard to the truth" (1.1.11).[48] In other words, while rhetoric and sophistry differ in that the former deals with truly commonly held opinions and the latter deals with opinions that look as if they were commonly held but in fact are not, rhetoric and philosophy differ in that the former deals with opinions truly commonly accepted and the latter deals with true knowledge. True ἔνδοξα and true knowledge, however, have an important thing in common: they come from the same human ability that investigates both the true and the verisimilar, in the positive sense of something that, while not properly truth, resembles the truth. We should also note that the Aristotelian verisimilar is very different from the Platonic verisimilar, given that by verisimilar Plato meant, in a pejorative sense, something that has the deceptive appearance of truth while having nothing to do with it.

Perpiñán had already quoted, almost verbatim, this passage from Aristotle's *Rhetoric* (1.1.11) on the common root of truth and verisimilitude when, earlier in his work, he reflected on the nature of the relationship between rhetoric and *scientia* in order to argue that rhetorical persuasion did not necessarily imply the manipulation of the audience.[49] Now, in the section of his manuscript concerned with the nature of the rhetorical *probabile*, he returned to examining the nature of the probable, the persuasive, and the verisimilar, and their respective relationship. Even on this occasion he attempted, once again, to highlight the positive epistemological value that Aristotle gave to the kind of imperfect but not necessarily deceitful knowledge one gains from debating probable opinions and to make it consonant with Cicero's understanding of probability as an epistemologically viable middle way between skepticism and dogmatism.

After his quotation from Alexander of Aphrodisias on the fact that the difference between the *probabile* and the true is not that the *probable* is false but that it is attained by a method different from the one used to find true and false things, Perpiñán continued: "as for the verisimilar, Aristotle, almost at the end of his *Prior Analytics* [2.27], defines it as a probable proposition: what for the most part happens thus and thus, or what for the most part is thus and thus.... From which it is clear that in Aristotle's judgment and opinion the verisimilar rests upon the probable, and that the verisimilar is indeed the same as the probable appears even more clearly in the words of Cicero in the first book of *De inventione* [*Probabile autem est id, quod fere solet fieri aut quod in opinione positum est aut quod habet in se ad haec quandam similitudinem, sive id falsum est sive verum*, 1.46]... Thus Cicero calls *verisimile* what Aristotle called εἰκόν, and what Cicero calls *probabile* Aristotle called ἔνδοξον, from which it is clear that those who distinguish probable from verisimilar as if they were completely different, and as if oratory dealt only with the verisimilar, while dialectic dealt with the probable, are gravely mistaken. . . nothing, in fact, can be accommodated to persuasion unless it be probable, and whatever is probable, is apt for persuasion."[50]

It is relatively well known that Cicero's concept of *probabile*, encompassing the probable, the verisimilar, and the persuasive, is one of the central features of Cicero's epistemology of probability, which characterized his Academic skepticism as a middle way between Pyrrhonism and dogmatism. Since it is nearly impossible for humans to attain perfect knowledge, one must give to probability a measure of epistemological and ethical credit: the more "similar" to the truth and the more "probable" an argument is, the more persuasive it becomes. The wise man can, therefore, use probability not only as an acceptable form of knowledge in uncertain situation but also as an acceptable basis for action.[51] Cicero's reevaluation of the epistemological and ethical value of probability resonated with his early modern interpreters, especially with the Jesuits, who embraced and developed Cicero's rhetorical probabilism as an important theoretical reference point for their own probabilistic system of moral theology.[52] Perpiñán also understood the importance of the Ciceronian spin on Aristotle's theory, but his aim was not so much to apply this newly articulated Aristotelian-Ciceronian epistemology of probability to action and to the realm of moral theology, as we can see from the fact that in these sections Perpiñán made no mention of either prudence or wisdom or of any kind of practical concerns. Rather, he used it to prove that insofar as rhetoric is concerned with the persuasive and insofar as the persuasive is concerned with the verisimilar and insofar as the faculty that finds the verisimilar is the same as the faculty that finds the truth, rhetoric has an intimate relationship with the truth and thus a properly philosophical role to play.

Aristotle's insistence on the fact that "rhetorical" knowledge, although founded on opinion and certainly different from philosophy proper, was nevertheless a positive epistemological tool in certain specific conditions, must be put in the specific context of political and intellectual life in ancient Athens. That is, it must be understood in part as a reply to the attacks against rhetoric mounted by Plato, who denied it any philosophical, political, and ethical value. Perpiñán had a different axe to grind: his polemical stance was directed against those who assigned to rhetoric the function of simply embellishing speech while putting dialectic alone in charge of creating, sorting out, and arranging arguments. He attacked this position several times throughout his work, because the question of the relationship between rhetoric and dialectic was crucially important for him, as I have already mentioned. In fact, he dedicated a specific section of his work to illustrate the "*similitudines et dissimilitudines,*" as he put it, between the two.[53] He also devoted a very long part of another chapter to an interesting exegesis of the first line of Aristotle's *Rhetoric*, in which rhetoric is called the ἀντίστροφος of dialectic.[54]

Let us start from this latter section, which indeed touched upon a much discussed and, to a certain extent, still puzzling part of the Aristotelian text.[55] Perpiñán tackled this issue in the chapter of his work devoted to explaining the parts of rhetoric in the Ciceronian tradition; that is, *inventio, elocutio, dispositio, memoria, pronunciatio*. Among these five parts, Perpiñán, in Aristotelian fashion, devoted the majority of this chapter to *inventio* and explained that both rhetoric and dialectic have their own kind of *inventio*, "since Aristotle in the first book of the *Rhetoric* said that rhetoric was something like a simulacrum of dialectic."[56] The word that Perpiñán translated with "simulacrum" is ὁμοίωμα (1.2.7), which means "likeness" or "image," both in the sense of something similar to something else and in the sense of something having the appearance of the real thing without being the real thing. Plato used this word in this latter meaning, for instance, in the part of his *Phaedrus* where Socrates spoke about the difference between true beauty and its likeness (250a–b). Perpiñán used "simulacrum," or likeness, in a positive sense and specified "in fact, when the new rhetors from this same passage [of Aristotle] try to demonstrate their own opinion and argue that rhetoric has the likeness of dialectic because it borrows from it *inventio* and *dispositio*, they make a serious mistake. If there were no *inventio* and no *dispositio* in rhetoric, and if dialectic only were composed of those two parts, as they think, rhetoric would have nothing similar to dialectic; by contrast, I think Aristotle thought they were similar because just as dialectic has its own *inventio* and its own *dispositio*, so does rhetoric."[57]

After this introduction, Perpiñán attacked the most exegetically contentious first line of Aristotle's *Rhetoric*, starting with a discussion of the semantic problems concerning the word "ἀντίστροφος." Perpiñán was familiar with the tradition of commentaries, both ancient and contemporary, dealing with the contested meaning of the word, and he was especially concerned with the commentary on the *Topics* by Alexander of Aphrodisias, whose explanation of this word was an important reference throughout the Renaissance.[58] Alexander had argued that ἀντίστροφος meant the same as ἰσόστροφος; that is, it implied a sort of similitude between rhetoric and dialectic since, according to Alexander, both rhetoric and dialectic deal with the same things, albeit with a different method. For Perpiñán, while Alexander's solution had the merit of highlighting the similarities of rhetoric and dialectic, it was nevertheless mistaken. Using (without mentioning the source) Guillaume Budé's definition of ἀντίστροφος as a synonym of ἀνάλογος, Perpiñán stated, "I therefore think that ἀντίστροφος is not the same as ἰσόστροφος and thus does not declare the kind of similitude that they [i.e., Alexander and his followers] imply, but that similitude must be taken in a different sense. . . in comparisons, in fact, we call the analogy of proportion what relates proportionally to something else, such as when we say that there is the same proportion between twelve and eight as there is between six and four, so that twelve is the analogue of six, and eight of four."[59] As an example of ἀντίστροφος/ἀνάλογος Perpiñán mentioned a part of Plato's *Gorgias* (465b–e), in which Plato wrote that gymnastics is in the body the analogue of the legislative part of the mind and that medicine is in the body the analogue of justice in the mind. Plato afterward continued by adding four further activities fostered by flattery (self-adornment, sophistry, cookery, and rhetoric) and argued that as self-adornment is to gymnastics, so is sophistry to legislation; and as cookery is to medicine, so is rhetoric to justice. Having set up this set of proportions, Plato drew his definition of rhetoric as ἀντίστροφος of cookery. Thus, according to Perpiñán, since "we call ἀντίστροφος what corresponds to something else proportionally, and since in every proportional comparison there is a similitude in those things which are compared, if rhetoric has the same proportion to justice that cookery has to medicine, necessarily rhetoric has some similarity with cookery and justice with medicine."[60]

A few years after Perpiñán allegedly wrote this manuscript, Marc-Antoine Muret would also stress the parallel use of ἀντίστροφος in Plato and Aristotle. Muret argued that Aristotle used the same word as Plato in an explicit effort to highlight the connection between rhetoric and philosophy against Plato's denigration of rhetoric as cookery.[61] Perpiñán, however, did not pick up on the potential polemic between Aristotle and Plato but rather used the parallelism to argue, against Alexander of Aphrodisias, that the kind of similitude implied by ἀντίστροφος "does not refer to what deals with the same things but rather to what deals with different sorts of things in a similar and indeed almost the same manner."[62]

Once Perpiñán was satisfied with having explained that the word indicated a specific kind of similitude, different from the kind of similitude that Alexander had identified, he moved on to explain the meaning of Aristotle's sentence. First, however, he dealt with the problem posed by Cicero's "translation" of Aristotle's line in *Orator* (32.114), according to which rhetoric "*quasi ex altera parte respondere dialecticae."* Many early modern commentators, including Pietro Vettori and Carlo Sigonio, had interpreted Cicero's phrase to mean that rhetoric was contrary to, or the opposite of, dialectic.[63] Perpiñán was aware that many scholars in his own time interpreted Cicero in opposition to Aristotle, but he was confident he could resolve the issue: "certainly these words were indeed written by Cicero, and they greatly trouble the minds of many learned people. Nevertheless, if we analyze diligently Cicero's whole position, we will find that Cicero thought otherwise [than the opposite of Aristotle]."[64] Since one of the main points of that part of the *Orator* was to argue that orators needed to be familiar with the precepts not only of rhetoric but also of dialectic, it would make no sense for Cicero to stress the dissimilarities between the two functions, while it would be much more to the point to stress their respective similarities. Besides, in *De finibus* (2.17) Cicero mentioned Aristotle explicitly, together with Zeno, as arguing for a certain similarity between rhetoric and dialectic. Indeed, Cicero also reported that Zeno and the Stoics compared rhetoric and dialectic, respectively, to the palm of the hand and the closed fist. Therefore, Perpiñán concluded that not only was it clear that Cicero thought there were some similarities between the two but that by analyzing Cicero's position we could indeed interpret better Aristotle's meaning.[65]

Having thus dispensed with the Ciceronian problem and consequently having demonstrated that there was no doubt that ἀντίστροφος implied a similitude rather than an opposition of rhetoric and dialectic, Perpiñán continued by elaborating on the nature of the similitude in question. He started by mentioning once again—and once again quickly dismissing—those who believed that the similitude rested in the fact that rhetoric needed to borrow its *inventio* from dialectic.[66] Other interpreters argued that the similarity of the two was due to the fact that neither has a specific subject, in the sense that that both deal with all possible subjects. This explanation, Perpiñán glossed, albeit better than the previous one, is nevertheless wrong. Aristotle never said that those two faculties are similar in that they deal with all kinds of subjects but that they come from the same root; that is, the impulse of finding what is "suitable for persuasion" in any given case.[67] Finally, Perpiñán arrived at what he thought was the interpretation closest to the truth: that Alexander of Aphrodisias's already quoted opinion that the similarity of rhetoric and dialectic rests in the fact that both deal with the same kind of probable issues. Based on his previous semantic analysis of the word ἀντίστροφος, however, he proposed a small modification to Alexander's explanation: "in fact, it seems to me that the good interpreter [i.e., Alexander] has not explained fully the force of the Greek word, since ἀντίστροφον is not what deals with the same issues, but what deals in the same way, proportionally, with different issues, which is also called ἀνάλογον by the Greeks."[68]

In other words, while Alexander's opinion implied that rhetoric and dialectic both dealt with probable issues and that the difference between them was in the manner in which they dealt with them (i.e., rhetoric in the context of civil affairs and in a question-and-answer format, dialectic in the context of any discussion and not necessarily tied up in the format of question and answer), Perpiñán argued that they dealt with different issues in the same manner. That same manner, or method, can be defined according to Perpiñán by the Greek word διάλεξις; that is, the process of discussing an argument—that is, something whose knowledge is not certain—with the aim of finding and communicating what is persuasive/probable/verisimilar. Some neo-Platonic philosophers (in particular Perpiñán mentioned Marsilio Ficino in his Platonic commentaries) made the grave mistake of attributing διάλεξις only to reason, whereas for Perpiñán it comprises both reason and speech, as can be seen "from the beautiful Latin translation [of the Greek word as *disserere*], which is to spread and almost to disseminate the speech." The amphibious nature of "discussing," at once a thought process and a speech act, is lost, Perpiñán declared, on the "*novi rhetores atque dialectici*" such as Ramus and Talon, who believed that dialectic did the reasoning while rhetoric did the speaking. Instead, "both these faculties, that is dialectic and rhetoric, are occupied in the method of discussing (that is, of making use of speech)."[69]

Thus, while rhetoric and dialectic use the same method of "arguing" and "discussing," or to put it differently, of finding the persuasive/verisimilar/probable in uncertain things, they apply this method to different areas. As Perpiñán put it, "the dialectician inquires what is more probable in the thing itself, whether this be credible or incredible to humans. He does not care to persuade humans of what he proves, and neither does he accommodate the discussion to the mind of humans but only to the nature of the thing, so that even though he cannot arrive at the perfect knowledge, at least he arrives at something close to it. The orator, on the other hand, does not inquire into what is in the nature of the things but rather into what is apt for the minds of the auditors, in which we have said he is occupied. Therefore there are two different kinds of persuasion generating opinions only: the first is accommodated to the nature of things, which deals with disputations regarding the highest arts; the other is popular and is accommodated to the minds of the people rather than to the nature of things. The former is proper of dialectic, the latter of rhetoric."[70]

This basic difference between rhetoric and dialectic generates a number of other morphological distinctions, so to speak, which Perpiñán explored in the already mentioned part of his work entitled "Similitudines et dissimilitudines logicae atque rhetoricae." For instance—and following here a well-established line of Aristotelian commentators starting once again with Alexander of Aphrodisias—Perpiñán stated that while dialectic deals with arguments concerning any discipline in a general and unstructured way, rhetoric deals with forensic or civic arguments. Moreover, dialectic is mostly used in philosophical disputations, while rhetoric in popular orations; dialectic uses a more stringent and sophisticated logical argumentation, while rhetoric's argumentation is popular and simpler; dialectic uses a more elaborated, more copious, and richer style, while rhetoric's style is more compressed and mostly composed of brief question-and-answer sections.[71]

In addition to these differences, Perpiñán added that rhetoric and dialectic appeal to different anthropological elements. His discussion on this topic started with the fourth book of Plato's *Republic*, in which Plato argued that there are two components in human souls, a rational one that is proper to humans alone and a nonrational or appetitive one, "wild, savage, and uncultivated," which we share with the animals and which contains "the senses and all the movements [*motus*] of the soul." The former "is entirely governed by reason and deliberation," while the latter is ruled by *impetus*.[72] Then Perpiñán switched gear and moved to Aristotle and to his Scholastic commentators: he stated that the sensory part of the human soul is divided into two further branches, the concupiscible and the irascible, and that each of these parts hosts different emotions and therefore produces different emotional responses.[73] Thus, while dialectic deals only with reason, rhetoric deals with both reason and the passions: "[rhetoric uses] arguments and all that is necessary to teach in order to move reason, while it uses the passions in order to move the uncultivated and wild part of the soul."[74]

A medieval Scholastic tradition of commentators of Aristotle's *Rhetoric*, exemplified by Giles of Rome, had used this distinction between rhetoric and dialectic in order to establish a clear hierarchy between the two. Since dialectic appeals to reason alone and rhetoric to both reason and emotions, dialectic is the tool that rational people employ to lead the audience to form a rational opinion about universals, while rhetoric, on the other hand, is the tool that orators use to lead the audience to being persuaded, on the basis of both rational arguments and emotional responses, about a particular issue. Therefore, the kind of opinion produced by rhetoric is inferior to that produced by dialectic, just as in the soul the sensitive part is inferior to the rational one.[75]

Perpiñán, however, at this point parted company with the medieval Scholastic commentators of Aristotle and concluded this section by highlighting the positive contributions of rhetoric in the realm of human understanding. First, Perpiñán sharply attacked the Stoics' opinion that all the passions of the souls are corrupt, which many "*gravissimi authores*," including Augustine, also opposed.[76] Secondly, he appealed to the Aristotelian and Ciceronian notion of "equity" in order to argue that passions were not the enemy of good judgment. When Aristotle, Perpiñán wrote, in the first book of the *Rhetoric* attacked those who tried to persuade the jury by appealing to their emotions rather than by

offering arguments, he simply meant to condemn the abuse of an otherwise positive practice. Indeed, stirring the passions properly might contribute to a better
judgment, more suitable to the actual circumstances of the case: "to those who
claim that strong passions move the minds of the audience away from the truth
we can answer that even though it is pernicious to distract the mind of the judge
from his office by passion, I do not see why it cannot be useful if judges were
bent, so to speak, of their own accord, and, when they are strangers to equity, [I
do not see] why they cannot be brought to a measure of equity."[77]

Thus, from Perpiñán's elaborations on the rhetorical *probabile* and on the
relationship between rhetoric and dialectic, many interesting elements emerge.
First, for Perpiñán there was a strict relationship of that which is persuasive,
that which is probable, and that which is similar to the truth: indeed he treated
the three terms almost as synonyms. Also, according to Perpiñán, the *probabile*
(which for him, as we have seen, was a concept encompassing the persuasive,
the probable, and the verisimilar) fell short of generating true knowledge, and
yet it provided something "similar to" knowledge, or a kind of knowledge necessary for discussing things that are neither necessary nor certain. Moreover, in
opposition to what Alexander of Aphrodisias stated, for Perpiñán the *probabile*
was less a feature characterizing the *issues* targeted by rhetoric and dialectic than
a peculiar characteristic of the *method* of discussing those uncertain issues. Such
issues, moreover, can concern either the nature of things (whenever this nature
is not certain and cannot be discerned by means of proper *scientia*) or people's
opinions, feelings, states of mind. While the former kind of issue belongs to dialectic, the latter belongs to rhetoric. Or to put it differently, dialectic uses a specific method of discussing, on the basis of probability rather than certainty, with
the aim of attaining knowledge of specific things. Rhetoric uses the same specific
method of discussing, on the basis of probability rather than certainty, with the
aim of adapting a specific kind of knowledge to specific kinds of people. Thus,
to persuade, which is the aim of rhetoric, means to adapt things to the mind as
well as to the feelings of the audience. In this respect rhetoric should not be considered a tool whose main aim was to cloud the judgment or to manipulate the
audience: rather, by appealing to both reasons and passions rhetoric contributed
to a better, more "equitable," judgment.

At the end of his own survey of the different positions that Renaissance commentators took on the contentious and mysterious exegesis of the first line of
Aristotle's *Rhetoric*, Lawrence Green asked rhetorically: "Are these all distinctions without a difference?"[78] His reply was that those distinctions are indeed fundamental indicators of how significant the problem of the relationship between
rhetoric and dialectic was for Renaissance scholars. This, in turn, can help us to
understand both the complexity of Aristotle's text and the distinctive intellectual
preoccupations that animated its Renaissance students. I argue that Perpiñán's

variation with respect to Alexander's definition of the relationship between rhetoric and dialectic is also a highly significant distinction, for it helped Perpiñán to articulate a distinctive role to assign to rhetoric. For Perpiñán, rhetoric occupied a special and specific place between reason and speech, between knowledge of things and knowledge of people, between the reasonable and the appetitive soul. In other words, Perpiñán restored rhetoric to the precarious but central position in which Aristotle sought to put it, equally distant from the luminous certainty of philosophy and the shadowy power of language.

When dealing with Perpiñán's work (and in general with works of this kind) we cannot certainly speak about "originality" in the strict sense of the word. Not only are many of Perpiñán's arguments a form of reelaboration on a well-established tradition of Aristotelian commentaries, but many of the themes in which Perpiñán framed his reflections are also part of a much older tradition. Indeed, just to present one example, reflecting on the nature of rhetoric by means of reflecting on its relationship with dialectic was standard fare in the Humanists' thinking about rhetoric.[79] Nevertheless, Perpiñán's effort to think through the philosophical edge of the Aristotelian rhetorical theory is worthy of consideration for at least two reasons. First, we should remember that the lengthy passages I have analyzed all come from a work that Perpiñán entitled *De oratore* and that was inspired by and certainly conceived in part as a commentary to Cicero. In this respect, then, we can see that Perpiñán integrated Aristotle with a specific subset of Cicero's reflections on rhetoric—those concerning the more properly epistemological rather than practical functions of probability. Most of Perpiñán's work, in fact, engaged the question of probability and verisimilitude in a framework that resonates more with the Aristotelian epistemological view of rhetoric than with the Ciceronian emphasis on probability as a proper guide for action.[80] Indeed, while the latter was usually developed by Jesuit theologians mostly in the realm of moral theology, in Perpiñán's work there is little trace of those kinds of practical concerns. In this respect, then, Perpiñán's deep engagement with Aristotle is not a function of the possible applications of rhetoric and of rhetorical concepts to the realm of casuistry or moral probabilism but the expression of his effort to think through the philosophical value of rhetoric as the discipline that connects thought and speech, abstract reasoning and concrete situations, things and people. This of course does not mean that Perpiñán was more Aristotelian than Ciceronian[81] or that the ethical aspect of Ciceronian probabilism had no consequence for the teaching of rhetoric in the Roman College. Rather, this means that Perpiñán chose a specific line of Ciceronianism that resonated with and indeed contributed to highlight a specific line of Aristotelianism. It is useful to keep in mind that while it is true that the Jesuits followed Cicero, it is also true that there were many different ways in which specific Jesuit thinkers decided to go about it.

Secondly, if we put Perpiñán's work next to Soares's textbook (which Perpiñán helped to revise for its second edition), as well as next to Perpiñán's published orations, we will get a sense of the complexity of the functions that Jesuit rhetoric played in the middle of the sixteenth century. In Soares's manual we find no trace of any of the topics that, as we have seen, feature prominently in Perpiñán's manuscript treatise. Soares did not deal with the relationship between rhetoric and dialectic, nor did he deal with the nature of rhetorical persuasion (indeed, Soares defined rhetoric as "*ars vel doctrina dicendi*," and even though he mentioned that its end was persuasion, he ignored altogether the epistemological role of persuasion). In general, Soares's manual did not aim at providing a philosophically rigorous discussion of the rhetorical process of finding arguments but rather at offering a "pleasant, easy, and brief" compendium of what the ancient authorities (especially Aristotle, Cicero, and Quintilian) wrote about rhetoric.[82] Enabling students to get a grasp of the main rhetorical precepts was all the more important because those students needed to quickly and effectively apply what they learned to the needs of post-Reformation Catholicism. As Soares wrote, once the students had mastered the techniques of rhetoric, they needed to "purge" it with religion: just as a good farmer knows how to prune and cut an overgrown vine so as to make it more fruitful and better looking, so students needed to "amputate" eloquence from its classical mistakes by means of Christian principles.[83]

Thus, Soares's manual was truly a militant handbook for a militant Christian rhetoric, the same kind of rhetoric that Perpiñán praised in the published orations I quoted at the beginning of this section. Perpiñán's manuscript work, by contrast, was less suitable for the militant needs of post-Reformation rhetoric, given its insistence on the more philosophical and epistemological value of rhetoric as a truth-finding tool. In fact, Perpiñán was quite aware of the fact that his elaborations did not really provide the advice and precepts that the *orator Christianus* needed in order to carry out his duty. In a part of his manuscript dealing with the definition of rhetoric as the art of persuasion, he anticipated with a curt remark a possible objection from readers who might not find in his work the kinds of considerations on Christian rhetoric that they thought they would: "I am not going to say anything about Christian orators, whom we call preachers. Indeed, their *ratio* is different [from the ancient orators], for while the Christian orators are *magistri vitae*, the ancient orators avoided even the slightest appearance of being such. It is necessary for a *magister* [*vitae*] not to sin in what he preaches, and to say just a few things, since the aim of Christian orators is to incite people to live well, which was not the aim of ancient orators, it is necessary for the Christian ones to live in a most virtuous manner, since men are incited to a virtuous life more by examples than words."[84]

In this perspective, then, it is not surprising that Perpiñán never published his book, while Soares's manual went on to become an incredibly influential text. Nevertheless, these two aspects of Jesuit rhetoric should be seen not as opposite but rather as complementary. This is evident from the fact that when Perpiñán revised Soares's manual he limited his observation to minimal and mostly typographical corrections. Indeed, these two aspects of Jesuit rhetoric, taken together, exemplify most clearly just how rich, complex, and significant rhetoric was for shaping not just Jesuit but indeed modern culture.

Famiano Strada: The rule of the Metaphor and the Sovereignty of the Word

Perpiñán's manuscript work, as we have seen, introduces an interesting and (if one were to judge the core concerns of Jesuit rhetoric in these years only on Soares's manual and on Perpiñán's published text) rather surprising aspect of Jesuit reflections on rhetoric. Perpiñán in fact addressed rhetoric in its epistemological function, as a method of reasoning that provides a specific kind of knowledge, halfway between the stable and certain nature of things and the mutable and changeable nature of people, halfway between reason and emotions, halfway between the linguistic world and the real world. Famiano Strada would develop Perpiñán's view to its full potential, to the point of making rhetoric the linchpin of a complex intellectual structure whose anchor was language understood as a "medium." When I speak of language as a medium, I refer to the particular significance given to this expression by Hans-Georg Gadamer, according to whom language is a medium insofar as it makes possible the mediation between the finitude of the human mind and the infinity of the divine. For Gadamer, as is well known and as I already indicated at the beginning of this book, the concept of Christian incarnation modified substantially the Greek concept of *Logos*: just as Christ's incarnation made it possible to establish a dialectical relationship between the unity of the divine Word and the multiplicity of human words, so thinking of language as a medium makes it possible to establish a dialectical relationship between abstract concepts and the multiplicity and peculiarity of speech. Because of its mediating function, then, language becomes an event in which concepts quite literally come to life and in which the hermeneutic experience, as Gadamer put it, "finds its own, special ground."[85]

I want to argue that Famiano Strada's work is one of the most striking examples of precisely this process of constructing language as the medium of hermeneutic experience, or in other words of constructing language as the only possible mediator between fixed and certain abstract knowledge and the concrete and mutable world of men. Thus, in Strada's elaboration language is not simply a way to articulate thoughts but the event in which thoughts can be formed. Rhetoric, consequently, is not simply a specific discipline in charge of persuading or of teaching how to speak well; it is the discipline in which language is explored in all its hermeneutic potential.

Marc Fumaroli has already identified this capacity to mediate between the unity of the divine Word and the multiplicity of the human words as a fundamental feature of Strada's Ciceronian style. Because of this feature, Strada's version of Ciceronianism, in Fumaroli's reading, became the organizing principle of a comprehensive cultural project, perfectly suited to articulate and make sense of the tension between the multiplicity and complexity of the challenges faced by the post-Reformation Catholic Church and the fundamental wholeness and unicity of the Catholic *Logos*.[86] The Reformation had shaken the Catholic world profoundly because it brought into play what Fumaroli called "the centrifugal forces of individualism, nationalism, and heresy." Catholic intellectual leaders understood that a strict imitation of Cicero's style as prescribed by the first-Renaissance Ciceronians was not suited to this complex and fractured post-Reformation world. By contrast, Strada's second-Renaissance devout Ciceronianism, which far from annulling individual styles, did in fact embrace such diversity by anchoring it to a unique and stable stylistic principle, perfectly responded to the needs of post-Reformation Catholicism.[87]

As Christian Mouchel has shown, in his *Prolusiones academicae* as well as in his unpublished treatise *De contexenda oratione*,[88] Strada applied his general theory of style to the traditional three areas of eloquence: history, poetry, and oratory. Strada demonstrated how each of them had an autonomous and distinctive role with respect to one another, and thus to each of them he applied a particular style. In each case, in particular in the case of history (which is the one Mouchel especially focused on), Strada's stylistic considerations aimed to rescue the power of language from the sophistical exaggerations of the Asianists on the one hand and from the dryness of the Atticists on the other. Strada's Ciceronianism, characterized by a distinctive balance between precision and strength in making arguments and power and inspiration in stirring the passions, became therefore the perfect language for not only the historian and the poet but also the *Christianus orator*, who needed a rhetorical style suitable for communicating effectively the divine Word.[89] Strada could then be rightly considered the pinnacle of that kind of militant rhetoric that post-Reformation Catholicism needed. This militant rhetoric began to be articulated in texts like Soares's *De arte rhetorica* and Perpiñán's published orations in the sixteenth century and reached its full potential in works such as Strada's *Prolusiones academicae* and Carlo Reggio's *Orator Christianus*, probably the most influential seventeenth-century handbook for Catholic preachers. In this perspective, Fumaroli and Mouchel are absolutely right in saying that Carlo Reggio's *Orator Christianus* and Strada's *Prolusiones academicae* are "les deux volets du même tableau,"[90] and mutatis mutandis, we can say that Strada's orations are to Reggio's book what Perpiñán's orations were to Soares's manual.

Nevertheless, just as Perpiñán's manuscript work points toward an engagement with the philosophical and epistemological and not simply stylistic function of rhetoric, so also in Strada's unpublished production can we discern a more philosophical kind of intellectual concern alongside the stylistic considerations examined by Fumaroli and Mouchel. Both Fumaroli and Mouchel base their analysis on the *Prolusiones academicae* and on *De contexenda oratione*, which albeit a manuscript work, was nevertheless very similar in content, if not in structure, to the *Prolusiones*. Also, from the point of view of form, the manuscript is a complete treatise.[91] By contrast, there are other fragmentary, unfinished, or in certain cases barely sketched manuscript works by Strada in which we see that he was preoccupied less with matters of style than with exploring the philosophical potentiality of language.

The first thing to notice as we approach our analysis of Strada's reflections on language is that, in a sense, Strada picked up where Perpiñán left off. A good part of Perpiñán's elaboration was devoted to demonstrating the specific and special place of rhetoric between reason and speech and between the certain and necessary knowledge provided by *scientia* and the mutable and inconsistent realm of human opinions. Perpiñán arrived at this conclusion by means of a profound engagement with the question of the relationship of rhetoric and dialectic. In his discussion on this issue, Perpiñán sought to deny a sharp division of labor between the two (with rhetoric dealing only with embellishing speech and dialectic dealing only with reasonable arguments), and instead he argued that rhetoric shared with dialectic a specific truth-finding aim. For Strada, who lived and worked half a century later than Perpiñán, the fact that rhetoric was not simply a series of speech techniques was not in doubt: in his first *Prolusio* he had clearly stated that "those who relegate the orator only to the realm of speaking elegantly and ornately are mistaken," for the orator has the task of "discovering what he might elegantly say," as Aristotle's *Rhetoric* taught.[92] Indeed, Strada's reflection of the orator's *iudicium* (one of the most central aspects of his rhetorical theory) was centered precisely on the notion that rhetoric's main function was to mediate between the atemporal and stable truths of philosophy and the fickle, varied, and mutable world of humans.[93]

Also, while Perpiñán dedicated a good part of his work to demonstrating that rhetorical persuasion was not a means to manipulate the audience based on falsehood but was rather founded on the probable, which in turn rested upon what was similar to the truth, for Strada the relationship connecting rhetorical persuasion, probability, and verisimilitude was a given. In fact, at the beginning of his *De contexenda oratione*, when Strada was about to explain how to construct the *narratio*, he proposed a revision to the Ciceronian order of the characteristics necessary to form *narratio*. In the *Partitiones oratoriae* 9.31, Cicero stated that a good *narratio* was supposed to be first *dilucida*, then *probabilis*, and lastly *suavis*. According to Strada, by contrast: "while probability [*probabilitas*], or verisimilitude, is the second condition for a *narratio*, it is clearly the most important one, since in fact the *narratio* is done so as to generate credence, just as the *peroratio* is done to stir the passions, it is clear that we must narrate with as much *probabilitas* as possible, and this is why at the beginning we said that the *narratio* is the basis for generating credence, which without truth, or without what is similar to the truth, cannot happen."[94] In this passage, then, Strada solidly links *probabilitas* with what is similar to truth and with truth itself, which is the basis for generating credence. In *De Inventione* (1.29) Cicero had explained briefly that *probabilitas* has something to do with the truth when he wrote that a *narratio* was *probabilis* "if in it we see the elements that usually appear in truth" [*si in ea videbuntur inesse ea quae solent apparere in veritate*]. Strada's variation on this theme has the benefit of making explicit the tight link connecting truth, verisimilitude, and probability and to explicitly set up this bundle of the probable and the verisimilar, indeed the true, as the basis for generating credence, which is the kind of knowledge that rhetoric is uniquely able to foster. In this manner, therefore, Strada fleshed out, as it were, the positive epistemological role that Cicero assigned to probability and persuasion. After reading Perpiñán's manuscript work, we can clearly see that Strada's passage here contains in essence what Perpiñán spent many pages articulating.

Strada, then, used Perpiñán's reflections as a springboard that allowed him to articulate more fully the philosophical role of rhetoric and, more generally, of language. If we want to see this part of Strada's work, we need to turn to the other manuscript works, starting with a treatise entitled *De elocutione*.[95] This text appears as a sort of dry run for Strada's *De contexenda oratione*: approximately the last two thirds of *De elocutione* are remarkably similar in content with respect to *De contexenda oratione* (they are in fact devoted to explaining the different characteristics of *narratio* that an orator needs to master; that is, "*ut clara sit, brevis, probabilis, illustris, suavis*").[96] There are important differences in these two works, however. First, in *De elocutione* Strada's attempt to integrate Cicero with Aristotle is more apparent, while *De contexenda oratione* is more distinctively Ciceronian. In fact, just before beginning the part of *De elocutione* concerned with the various kinds of speech, Strada warns his readers that "we will deal with those virtues [of speech] articulated by Cicero in our own usual way; that is, by inserting what is appropriate out of Aristotle and Demetrius."[97] The Aristotelian edge of this work is apparent in its structure: while *De contexenda* was built around Cicero's precepts on how to construct a speech, *De elocutione* was built as a sort of commentary on book 3 of Aristotle's *Rhetoric*. As such, *De elocutione* began with a discussion of Aristotle's opinion that style was a part of rhetoric and that the style of orators presented certain characteristics that distinguished it from poetic style.[98] Thus, since the specificity of the rhetorical style depended on the manner in which words were put together, Strada began his work by talking about words, which can be divided (as Cicero did in *Partitiones oratoriae* 5.17) into "*propria, addita, nova, antiqua, modificata.*"[99] Strada spent one short chapter elucidating the nature of those words. When it came to discussing the words "*inflexa*" and "*modificata,*" Strada stated that those words concern the tropes and figures of speech and that unlike some authors, especially Quintilian, he did not think it appropriate to discuss every single figure of speech. Rather, Strada thought that all those figures could be subsumed under the overarching Aristotelian category of metaphor, to which Strada devoted the following twelve chapters—that is, the rest of the entire section on words.[100]

But why was metaphor so important for Strada? At the beginning of his discussion of metaphors in general, Strada mentioned two reasons for the usefulness of metaphors, which he took, respectively, out of Cicero and Aristotle. The first, Ciceronian, reason concerned the fact that metaphors (of course if aptly used) embellished speech and in so doing they generated *voluptas*, pleasure, in the audience, who, captivated by admiration for the skills of the orator, would then be more willing to believe his arguments.[101] The other reason, which can be found in chapter 10 of the third book of Aristotle's *Rhetoric*, concerned the fact that the pleasure brought about by metaphors did not simply grant more credit to the orator but indeed facilitated knowledge: "when we learn something by metaphors, we learn more easily and more quickly, but also more effectively." Metaphors allow an orator to condense in one sentence a variety of meanings, and therefore they allow the audience to quickly grasp more concepts at once. Moreover, metaphors are usually the concrete expression of abstract concepts, and learning through examples is easier than learning through abstract reasoning and enthymemes, as Aristotle argued in *Problemata* 18.3. Thus, metaphors put the audience in the best possible position to grasp fully, quickly, and pleasantly the "*causa rei*"; that is, the core reason of any given argument. Since, as Aristotle argued, thinking through an issue by examining its core reason is most appropriate to human nature, then learning things by metaphor means learning things "perfectly."[102]

Even though Strada endorsed fully Aristotle's opinion that metaphors not only embellish our speech but in fact aid our understanding, he did not find in Aristotle a satisfactory explanation of why this was the case. Thus, he supplied his own reason why learning through metaphors "is most consonant with human nature": the "*modus,*" or the method, of constructing metaphors was for Strada the quintessential form of "*ratiocinatio,*" or reasoning, which in turn distinguishes humans from other creatures.[103] But where did this equivalence between reasoning and "metaphorizing" come from? Strada must have been puzzled by this question, and initially in his manuscript he explained this link as such: "this operation of reasoning appears chiefly in metaphors when we perceive a similitude and connection of two things. . . thus we compare one thing with another and we perceive what is similar in both."[104] Strada must have thought that this rationale was a good description of the mechanism by which we learn things through metaphors, not a good explanation of why it happened. This is why he added in the margins of the manuscript: "This act of reasoning is then exercised when from one thing the intellect deduces another, and thus the thing which was previously known becomes a step toward the next thing, so that the mind, while it is investigating something, finally ties all together in a sort of shrewd link by putting together many things at once."[105] For Strada, therefore, metaphors are not simply passive vehicles for words that signify things we already know; rather, they produce new knowledge: in this respect, they are a form of reasoning because they allow the intellect to move from the knowledge we already have toward the knowledge of something new.

Strada returned to this question later in his treatise, when discussing the well-known Aristotelian critique of farfetched and obscure metaphors in the third book of the *Rhetoric*, chapter 3. Strada was familiar with many of the existing commentaries on this passage, and all of them seemed to interpret the Aristotelian precept as an indication that metaphors should involve things of the same genus (Marcantonio Maioragio) or things that are generally related to one another (Carlo Sigonio) or things that have a common origin (Ermolao Barbaro) or, finally, things that are not only of the same genus but also of the same species (Victorinus).[106] For Strada, by contrast, the precept of Aristotle should not be understood as a sort of strict limitation of the kind of things that one might compare in a metaphor but rather as an indication of how metaphors work in producing knowledge. Thus, Strada argued that when Aristotle cautioned against the use of certain metaphors, he meant to discourage metaphors dealing with "those arguments that are obvious (and by obvious we mean the things that nobody ignores and for whose understanding there is no need of any discussion)" and to discourage also metaphors that "are impossible to understand." Instead, Aristotle wanted to commend those metaphors that "either as soon as they are uttered bring us to a knowledge that we before did not have, or those that our intellect needs a short interval of time to comprehend." If, Strada continued, the things expressed in a metaphor are too obscure, then we learn nothing at all; if, by contrast, they are too obvious, then we learn nothing new. For this reason, Strada concluded, in that passage of his *Rhetoric* Aristotle did not mean to condemn *tout court* the use of similitude and comparisons between things of different genus and species, since indeed in the same book 3, chapter 11, of the *Rhetoric* he argued that in philosophy it was the prerogative of an acute mind to perceive resemblance in dissimilar things, which is why Aristotle praised Archytas's metaphor assimilating an arbitrator to an altar, given that both are the refuge of the wronged. Rather, Aristotle wanted to discourage farfetched and obvious metaphors that failed to bring new knowledge.[107]

There are several things in these passages that deserve attention. First, Strada refused to consider metaphors simply an embellishment of speech but instead treated them as peculiar features of language that have a strong relationship to knowledge. Since for Strada, in a sense, to produce metaphors was the same as to reason, metaphors belong not only to rhetoric or poetics but also to philosophy. In this respect, Strada restored metaphors to the position of philosophical privilege they had in Aristotle against a Roman tradition that, especially with Quintilian, had restricted metaphors to a subcategory of the simile among the figures of speech. Also noteworthy here is that for Strada metaphors do not only convey meaning but also assist in producing it: the process set in motion by metaphors, as Strada described it, is not a process by which the metaphorical meaning is simply added to or substituted for the literal meaning but rather a process of acquiring new knowledge through the metaphor. On this score, it is also important to notice that Strada did not frame his discussion on metaphors in terms of opposition between literal and metaphorical language (in fact in Strada's work there is no engagement with such opposition). Rather, he described the process of producing metaphors as a cognitive and heuristic activity, indeed as the human cognitive and heuristic activity par excellence.

At this point the reader will start to see some similarities between Strada's take on metaphors and Paul Ricoeur's theory of metaphor as "the rhetorical process by which discourse unleashes the power that certain fictions have to redescribe reality."[108] Such similarities are firmly rooted in both Strada's and Ricoeur's respective engagements with Aristotle. As Ricoeur has argued, in fact, his own attempt to consider metaphors heuristic tools that language has at its disposal in order to produce meaning is a development of Aristotle's intuition that metaphors do not simply belong to the realm of poetics but also to the realm of ontology.[109] Seen in this perspective, then, Strada's sustained attempt to recover the Aristotelian view on metaphor against Quintilian and a specific Roman rhetorical tradition explains why Strada deserves a place in the intellectual tradition that saw metaphor as the key to understanding the heuristic power of language.

Moreover, Strada's reflections on metaphors (just as, mutatis mutandis, Ricoeur's) stem from a more general attitude toward language: language, for Strada, possessed a "fundamental metaphorical nature," in Gadamer's sense.[110] The metaphorical nature of language, in Gadamer's thought, is not opposed to a "real" or "literal" meaning of language, and as such stressing the metaphorical does not mean discarding the logical. Rather, the metaphorical in this case refers to the capability of language to act as a medium between reality and thought.

Gadamer's concept of language as a medium, then, does not imply that the world is simply an object of language, nor does it imply that language *is* the world to the point of denying the existence of an extralinguistic reality. Rather, language's metaphorical nature is a manifestation of the quintessentially amphibious aspect of language, at once referential and creative. In this view, then, language becomes an "event" insofar as it expresses the dialectic relationship between reality and thought and between objectivity and subjectivity.[111]

Strada, I argue, was very much aware of this peculiar eventlike aspect of language. We have seen this already when Strada discussed history writing, in which the *narratio rerum gestarum* (the historical narrative) acted as a medium between the *res gestae* (the historical events) and the present time of the audience.[112] We have seen this same feature in Strada's discussion of rhetoric, in which the orator's *iudicium* ensured that rhetoric functioned as a medium between the immutable truths of philosophy and the mutable world of human affairs.[113] Strada elaborated on this same issue in another of his unpublished works, a treatise devoted to explaining Aristotle's *Poetics*, to which we now should turn. Strada's treatise was supposed to be composed of five books. The first was devoted to explaining poetics in general, and the following four books were devoted to the specific kinds of poetry; namely, epic, tragic, comic, and lyric. In 1608 Strada gave a course on the topic of the first book.[114] We have a draft of Strada's lecture notes in the course, and a draft (somewhat modified) of this first book can be found in another autograph manuscript by Strada, which also contains a draft of the second book, on epic.[115] Evidently Strada lost interest in the work, which he neither completed nor published.

The first book of this treatise starts with a seemingly unoriginal explanation of the specificity of poetry with respect to other literary forms. Theologians, philosophers, historians, orators, Strada claimed, "bring to light nothing new, but rather they receive a preexisting subject." While they can certainly reelaborate and change their subject and in some sense they can "add something new," nevertheless "they do not produce new things, but rather rearrange old things, and therefore we must say that they change and modify, rather than create, facts." Poets, by contrast, are the only ones that "produce out of their own wit something that before did not exist and that will exist in the future."[116]

After this introduction of the creative power of poets, who, "emulating God, create new kinds of things ex nihilo,"[117] Strada tackled the question of imitation, which both Plato and Aristotle put at the core of poetry. How can the poet both create reality ex nihilo and at the same time imitate reality? Strada chose to begin his discussion on poetic imitation from the *Sophist*, the dialogue in which Plato explored the link between poetry and sophistry as imitative arts to be opposed to philosophy.[118] Strada started by quoting Plato's passage in which the Eleatic visitor distinguishes two kinds of imitation or two species of image making (235d–236c): "the first is the art of likeness making (*ars assimulandi*), whose task is to fabricate an imitation by following the proportions of the original in length, breadth, depth, and appropriate colors."[119] The second one is not so much a process of "imitating" the original as a process of creating appearances (*fantasma*). For instance, this second kind of image making can make something appear a beautiful thing that in reality is not beautiful.[120]

After making this distinction between types of imitation, which Strada reported faithfully enough, Plato continued by introducing the core argument of the dialogue: the difference between a sophist and a philosopher. The sophist, like the poet in the *Republic*, is like an appearance maker who distorts proportions and creates something that has the appearance of beauty but that, in reality, is not beautiful. The philosopher, by contrast, makes true images, and by means of this kind of likeness he can investigate the truth. Strada was not willing to follow Plato in his sharp division between the likeness-making task of the philosophers and the appearance-making task of poets and sophists. Strada's own view of language as a medium between thought and reality, as we have seen, excluded the possibility of relegating rhetoric to the art of creating *fantasma* made of words, as opposed to philosophy, which uses words to get to the truth. Likewise, Strada could not support Plato's assimilation of poetry to sophistry. This is why Strada, after quoting Plato's distinction, continued by claiming that if we really want to understand what kind of imitation characterizes poetry, we have to discard such a rigid division. Poetry cannot "imitate" in the first sense of likeness making, since this kind of imitation "is more appropriate to the historian, who narrates faithfully events as they happened" and not as they ought to have happened, which is Aristotle's definition of poetry. Poetic imitation, however, cannot be considered the art of appearance making either, "since this second kind is not a form of imitation: if to imitate means to conform one's work to an original, how can the poet be said to imitate, since he has nothing similar to the original but rather departs so far from the original?"[121] The solution, according to Strada, is that poetic imitation is something between likeness making and appearance making: "the poet has an exemplar to which he partly conforms and from which he partly departs." For this reason, the "fantastic imitation" proper to poets is not, as Plato would have it, an art of making appearances that have nothing to do with truth but rather an art of creating something that is both like the original and distant from it.[122]

This is, in other words, Strada's opinion of the specific poetic verisimilar, halfway between reality and creation. The solid Aristotelian anchor of Strada's theory of poetry indicates that Strada was not interested in constructing poetic language as simply the creator of an "alternative" reality that has no ties to the extralinguistic reality. In this respect, then, poetic language is similar to the language of history and to the language of rhetoric, insofar as it too mediates between what exists in the world and what is created in the mind of the writer or the speaker. At the same time, however, the link with reality that poetic language maintains is different from the link with reality expressed by the language of historical narratives. The historical narrative, in fact, is a creative product of the historian, whose scope is restricted by the reality of the past, since it is a faithful narrative constructed by the historian of events that truly happened in the past. The very nature of the historical narrative implies the aim of reconstructing the reality of the past, and in this respect the occasional falsehoods that can be found in historical narratives are to be considered limited flaws that do not distort or invalidate the core of history writing.[123] Poetry, by contrast, is a creative activity whose aim is to represent, not the reality of events as they happened, but the reality of events as they could happen. This is what, according to Strada, Aristotle meant when he insisted that poets must create "according to the verisimilar and to the necessary": "he [Aristotle] did not mean that the subject of poetry is verisimilar and necessary in the same way as the matter of history, whose subject is necessary insofar as the truth is necessary." Rather, Aristotle meant to say that poets "must express actions. . . constructed so that one necessarily follows the other", just as Achilles's rage and revenge against the Greeks necessarily followed Agamemnon's offense. Thus, Strada concluded, the "necessity" Aristotle mentioned "must be referred not to actual things (*res naturales*) but to the nexus among actual things."[124] In other words, for Strada poetic imitation is neither the production of a copy of reality nor the creation of *fantasma* that have nothing to do with reality. Rather, poetry is a creative form that refers and, to an extent, is submitted to reality without being bound by it, or as Ricoeur put it, for poetry (unlike for history) "reality remains a reference, without ever becoming a restriction."[125]

In conclusion, then, this peculiar aspect of language, which is both anchored to the extralinguistic reality and able to create meaning, is a central characteristic of Strada's reflections on rhetoric, poetry, and history, insofar as language for Strada truly mediates the uncertain and mutable world of men and the creative power of the divine. As Strada put it in his work on poetry, the category of the poetic verisimilar allows the poet to remain anchored to the human reality while sharing some of the creative power of the divine insofar as he, "emulating God," creates new things ex nihilo. At the end of another unpublished work in which he described the different emotions and how orators could stir them in the audience, Strada commented that according to Aristotle the capability of moving men's passion was the main task of the orator because it allowed him to "descend into other men's souls and move them at will, which is the power [*imperium*] of God alone."[126] In other words, for Strada language has a divine component insofar as it allows humans to create, re-create, or generate events and emotions. In parallel, however, language for Strada is a quintessentially human activity insofar as it cannot be disjointed from human reality. Thus, through language humans can partake of the divine while remaining solidly grounded in their own world. The fact that language is not a simple mirror of reality does not mean, however, that language folds over itself and creates a "linguistic" world alternative to the real one. It means that the world of humans for Strada truly comes to life as a linguistic event: as Gadamer put it, "whoever has language 'has' the world"; that is, whoever can master language can achieve the delicate balance between reality and thought that is the unique marker of the human condition insofar as humans are both creatures living in and creators of the world.[127]

Once we abandon the historiographical prejudice according to which Strada's work was simply an early expression of Baroque conceptism at the service of the theological and ideological program of the Counter-Reformation[128] and once we recognize the centrality and importance of Strada's intuition that language was a mediator between reality and thought, we will be able to see that one of the great achievements of Jesuit rhetoric was precisely this process of constructing the world as a linguistic event. Jesuit rhetoric undeniably constructed the language of the *orator Christianus* as a weapon at the service of post-Tridentine theology, but it also articulated a vision according to which language and reality are not like subject and object. Rather, they are intertwined and linked in a delicate and complex dialectical relationship with one another. This complex relationship between words and reality, in turn, originated the need to renegotiate the epistemological relationship between certainty and uncertainty, knowledge and opinion, truth and verisimilitude. In a sense, both Beni and Mascardi represent some of the possible outcomes of this process. They were both alumni of the Roman College, and as such they absorbed and were engaged in the kind of questions discussed in the classrooms of rhetoric—indeed, Beni took a course with Carlo Reggio and Mascardi's years as a student at the College overlapped with Strada's years as a professor there. Both Beni and Mascardi were fascinated and indeed obsessed with the concept of verisimilitude and with its relationship to truth and to falsehood, and they were both fully aware of the marvelous and sinister power of language to represent—that is, make present—reality.

Perpiñán's and Strada's works on rhetoric manifest both the militant aspect of the language that post-Tridentine Catholicism wanted to be at the service of the divine Truth and the more shadowy aspect of language insofar as language reflects on its own ability to know, create, shape, and represent human truths. While in the first case neither Perpiñán nor Strada had any doubt about where truth ended and falsehood began, in the second case the relationship between truth and falsehood was less clear, because the relationship between reality and language was not a simple case of the latter mirroring the former. The fact that we are able to find so many shades of gray in post-Tridentine Catholic culture and indeed in an institution such as the Roman College, which generally instructed people to see the world in black and white, is one of the most interesting testimonies to the centrality of early modern Catholic rhetoric and culture in the history of Western thought.

The Sacrament of Language and the Curse of Speech

I began this book with a reflection on what I thought were the radical hermeneutical and epistemological implications of the doctrines of equivocation
and mental reservation. I argued that by thinking through these doctrines
post-Reformation Catholic intellectuals and theologians explored not only the
ethical tension between conflicting moral imperatives but also the ambiguities
and potentialities of language and its unstable relationship with thought on
the one hand and with reality on the other. I then took a number of detours
into intellectual debates and cultural phenomena that seemed to express various manifestations of the same hermeneutical and epistemological instability
that I saw creeping into post-Reformation Catholic culture. It is now time, in
this final chapter, to come back home, as it were. Thus, in the conclusion of this
study I want to come back to the question of language as it was theorized by
post-Reformation Catholic intellectuals. I want to do this by examining a specific linguistic event that, in ways that will soon be apparent, can be considered
the synecdoche of the entire human experience of language: the oath.

The oath is a special and powerful kind of performative speech act in which,
generally speaking, humans invoke or call as witness the divinity, in order to
attest either the truth of an assertion or the sincerity of a promise. Canonists and
theologians, starting from around the thirteenth century, systematically defined
the oath that accompanied an assertion as *iuramentum assertorium* and the oath
that accompanied a promise as *iuramentum promissorium*. The origins of the oath
are still somewhat mysterious: while many of the juridical and religious aspects
of the oath were fully discussed in ancient Greece and ancient Rome, some
anthropologists and linguists at the end of the nineteenth and the beginning of
the twentieth century sought to find the origins of the oath in the dark past of the
Indo-European people, on "the fringe of ultra-history," as Dumézil famously put
it.[1] The question of the anthropological significance of the oath, tightly linked
with the question of its origin, is still an open one, one that I do not wish to

address here. Suffice it to say that in the Western tradition the oath has been generally understood as both a powerful way to connect humans with the divinity (in this respect oaths are intrinsically linked to the sphere of the sacred) and an equally powerful way to connect humans with one another (in this respect oaths are intrinsically linked to the sphere of law). The ways in which the oath connects the sphere of the sacred and that of the law, however, are still very much in dispute among scholars from a variety of disciplines, from anthropologists to philosophers to historians to jurists.[2]

From a more specifically historical perspective, in 1992 Paolo Prodi published what is still the most influential account of the evolution of the oath in late medieval and early modern Europe. Rather than addressing what he defined as the "a-historical and immobile nucleus of the oath-event," Prodi focused on the historical evolution of oaths as "sacraments of power."[3] In other words, Prodi claimed that the institution, theory, and practice of oaths as they evolved over time are important lenses through which we can understand the development of the concepts of power and authority in late medieval and early modern Europe. Within this general project, Prodi's study especially highlighted the late sixteenth and early seventeenth centuries: in that period, Prodi argued, the theological and political understanding of the oath as the sacrament of power changed dramatically with respect to the medieval past and, in a sense, planted the seeds of political and religious modernity. As a result of the pressure exercised on the *corpus mysticum* of the Church by the Reformation and because of the parallel pressure exercised on the *corpus politicum* of the Christian commonwealth by the growing strength of early modern states, oaths in early modern Europe were no longer used as an expression of a diverse set of bonds within a society in which political and religious authorities were not yet fully differentiated theoretically and juridically, as happened in the Middle Ages. Instead, oaths started to express the modern duality between the sphere of public authority and the sphere of private conscience.

In this general trajectory, Prodi in particular singled out three Catholic theologians who expressed most clearly the main milestones of the evolution of the oath in the sixteenth and seventeenth centuries: Domingo de Soto, Francisco Suárez, and Leonardus Lessius. Soto was the first Catholic theologian to identify and discuss systematically the dual function of the oath. In his view, insofar as the oath was a form of internal correspondence between the speaker, who intended to assert or promise the truth, and God, who stood as a silent witness of the sincerity of the speaker's intention, the oath involved the internal forum of the conscience and as such it was under the regulative power of religion. Insofar as the oath was publicly uttered and thus served as a kind of sacred seal of the speaker's true intention for the sake of the hearers, however, the oath involved the external forum that was regulated by the political authority, in charge of making sure that promises solemnly made were in fact respected.[4]

From the end of the sixteenth through the beginning of the seventeenth century, however, states and churches were still fighting about jurisdiction over both the consciences and the bodies of European men and women. In this context, the debate over the English Oath of Allegiance represents a crucial moment of tension for the institution of the oath in Western society. James's act was an attempt on the part of the political authority to use the oath as a bond between the sovereign and the consciences, and not just the bodies, of the subjects.[5] Insofar as James's oath effectively attempted to make the community of the subjects of the English king into the community of the faithful to the English sovereign power, it proposed a novel and potentially crucial tool for sacralizing political power and thus to unify what Soto had initially distinguished; that is, the internal forum of the conscience and the external forum of public authority. In this respect, then, the English oath threatened the Catholic dualistic understanding of the oath and stirred the Catholic reaction, which in Prodi's argument was expressed by the other two theologians, Francisco Suárez and Leonardus Lessius. It is with them, Prodi contends, that the dual nature of the oath was fully articulated: on the one hand, the oath as an act of conscience became strictly confined to the realm of theology and as such regulated by the Church. On the other hand, the oath as a juridical act progressively assumed the nature of pact or contract among individuals and as such was strictly regulated by the political authority.[6]

Giorgio Agamben took up Prodi's argument in an important and stimulating essay on the nature and significance of the oath. While Agamben did not question Prodi's historical interpretation of the oath as the sacrament of power, he contended that simply focusing on the historical developments of the oath does not help us understand "what is at stake" in the oath or "what is it in its structure and its history that has made it possible for it to be invested" with the function of sacrament of power.[7] By opposing a "philosophical archaeology" of the oath as a language event to Prodi's "history" of the oath as a religio-political tool, Agamben argued that the oath needs to be considered primarily as an expression of the human experience of language. In this respect, rather than the sacrament of power, the oath is more properly the sacrament of language. In other words, aside from and before tying men to either God or to each other, for Agamben the oath ties men to their words. Thus the oath represents the "verification of words in facts"; that is, the "precise correspondence between words and reality."[8] Because the words of God, insofar as they always correspond perfectly with reality (indeed they become reality), are always properly speaking "oaths," whenever men perform this specific and special speech act, they imitate their Creator by committing themselves to their own language and to its truthfulness. Thus, when one swears by God, she does not properly call Him as a witness; rather, she invokes Him as the original "oath-taker in the language of which man is only the speaker."[9] As a result, in human oaths God's testimony is nothing but "the very signifying force of language."[10] Because oaths are the quintessential expression of the bond connecting humans, language, and reality, they cannot be said to be a product of either law or religion. Indeed, according to Agamben it is the oath that does in fact predate and even, to a certain extent, create law and religion.

In this chapter I take seriously Agamben's interpretation of the oath as first and foremost a linguistic phenomenon, since I think that Agamben is correct in arguing that oaths tell us something important about the ways in which humans conceptualize the relationship between language, thought, and reality. However, my argument is that in order to understand fully the significance of this aspect of oaths, we need to examine its historical, not simply philosophical, manifestations. In other words, I want to plot Agamben's perspective on Prodi's historical trajectory: I argue that by focusing on the early modern elaborations on the oath as the sacrament of language, we can get a historically and philosophically significant sense of an important evolution in the ways in which Western civilization articulated the links connecting language, thought, and reality. In order to do this, I examine the same three Catholic theologians (Soto, Suárez, and Lessius) that Prodi singled out as emblematic of the evolution of the oath as the sacrament of power, and I show how they also demonstrate a fundamental evolution of the oath as the sacrament of language.

There are two main issues at stake in my argument. First, I think that by analyzing how Soto, Suárez, and Lessius, respectively, conceptualized the oath as sacrament of language, we can appreciate an aspect of early modern theological and intellectual debates that has been mainly neglected so far and that I have been seeking to recover throughout this book. While it is undeniable that the oath had an important role to play in the processes of confessionalization and sacralization of power, we should remember that the oath was also invested with important hermeneutical functions. Post-Reformation Catholic culture, as I have been arguing throughout my work, was a fundamental moment in the political and religious history of Western civilization precisely because it planted the seeds of epistemological and hermeneutical doubt that still preoccupy us today and because it forged many of the tools we still use to understand the relationship between language and reality.

The second issue at stake in my argument concerns the relationship between philosophy and history. More specifically, I think that Agamben's philosophical archaeology of the oath needs to be thickened, so to speak, with a specific historical analysis. Agamben explicitly contends that swearing—that is, taking the oath as the sacrament of language—is a constitutive characteristic of humans as speaking beings. For this reason, he argues, the philosophical investigation of the linguistic sacrality of oaths "is always under way, because *Homo sapiens* never stops becoming man, has perhaps not yet finished entering language and swearing to his nature as a speaking being."[11] Nevertheless, I think that if we pay more attention to certain specific historical junctures within the ever-lasting development of men as speaking beings, we will be able to understand how over the course of time this feature of human language and human nature was suited to engage distinctive historical, not just philosophical or anthropological, challenges.

Domingo the Soto: Identifying the Cracks

By the middle of the sixteenth century, when Soto published most of his works, Catholic theologians who wrote on the oath needed to address two main concerns. The first one originated from the proliferation of oaths created by the "sworn society" of the Middle Ages.[12] In their effort to make the oath into an instrument by which the Church could firm up the believers' faith and allegiance (in a move parallel to the states, which sought to use the oath as an instrument to firm up the subjects' faith and allegiance), early modern Catholic theologians needed to curb the tendency of overswearing in order to institutionalize and regulate the oath more firmly as a sacrament of power. The second concern, to an extent the opposite of the first, came from the hostility toward the oath as an unnecessary act that directly contravened Christ's precept, "Swear not at all. . . . But let your communication be, Yea, yea; Nay, nay: for whatsoever is more then these cometh of evil" (Matthew 5:34–37). Christian humanists had already started to attack the oath rather vigorously on this basis. For instance, Lorenzo Valla, in *De professione religiosorum*, had argued that oaths and vows not only added nothing to the obligations that a Christian had in her conscience but also cheapened the value of any act done or promised in honor of God. Swearing or vowing to commit a good deed, in fact, introduced an element of the fear of punishment and thus limited the freedom with which any Christian should choose to perform good deeds. It was indeed paradoxical, Valla glossed, that men continued to offer God oaths that God himself had forbidden.[13] Besides, according to Valla, even the value of oaths for the consolidation of political life needed to be reconsidered. People were required to respect oaths because they were supposed to fear God's punishment in case they failed to uphold their oath, but what happened "if the gods did not get angry" after all? Since the fear of the gods was the main reason for the binding force of the oath, if the fear disappeared, the force of the oath would disappear also.[14]

Thus, faced with this double jeopardy, Soto (and post-Reformation Catholic theologians in general) needed not only to reassert the religious and theological legitimacy of oaths but also to grant oaths a special place, attentively circumscribed to a series of specific occasions and instances. Soto entered this discussion with a short treatise, published in 1551 in Latin and Spanish, entitled *De cómo se ha da evitar el abuso de los juramentos.*[15] The work was dedicated to prince Philip (future king Philip II): since, as Soto wrote in the dedicatory epistle, abusing oaths was a way to disrespect not only the *"Divina majestad"* but also the *"humana majestad,"* the task of eradicating such a practice was entrusted to both theologians and political leaders. Soto divided his treatise into three parts. The first concerned the nature of the oath, which for Soto (who in this case closely followed Aquinas) was not only pious and licit but indeed in certain cases necessary. When discussing the origin of the oath, Soto began by relating Aristotle's precept that man is by nature a social animal, which means that men need to live in society. Original sin, however, had deprived human words from the "authority" to firm up pacts amongst men, which they had in the state of innocence. Therefore, God's providence made possible "that with the strength of the oath in His name we can strengthen our authority, which because of sin was weak and ill."[16] This is how, Soto claimed, we should interpret Christ's command against swearing in the Gospel: the oath is born out of sin as out of a disease, but the oath itself is not sinful, just as the medicine one takes to cure the disease is not evil. The fact that the oath did not contravene any religious precept, according to Soto, could also be gathered from the fact that God himself swore (e.g., to Abraham in Genesis 22:16–17), and that St. Paul not only swore but explicitly commended the oath as "an end of all strife" (Hebrews 6:16). Indeed, God gave to men "permission to swear because of His great love and care toward us. . . so as to free us from strife and so that we might be able to pacify our controversies and live in peace and tranquility."[17]

However, just as to swear legitimately means to honor God as "the supreme principle and source of truth,"[18] by contrast to swear improperly means to contravene the second precept of the Decalogue; that is, to utter God's name in vain. Thus, the second part of Soto's treatise is devoted to explaining just how dangerous it is to use the oath improperly, since the oath could change from a medicine into a poison.[19] When one does not swear legitimately, Soto explained, one commits the sin of blasphemy, which in the case of a sworn assertion is linked to the sin of perjury and is always a mortal sin. Even in the case of a sworn promise, swearing improperly or unnecessarily is always a sin (whether it was a mortal or a venial one depended on the nature of the promise and on a set of possibly mitigating circumstances).

Because of the gravity of the sin of using oaths improperly, Soto devoted a third section to explaining the manifold ways in which one could be guilty of blasphemy and to give a few suggestions on how to avoid it. For instance, Soto declared that blasphemy starts in the family, and thus the husband should check on the wife and the parents on the children, so as to make sure that they do not abuse the practice of swearing and that they are suitably punished when they do. Moreover, priests and preachers should do their best to instill in their parishioners just how dangerous it is to sin against the second commandment, and so on.[20]

In a nutshell, then, Soto's treatise seems to present all the elements that Paolo Prodi has identified as constitutive of the oath as the sacrament of power. Soto asserted vigorously the religio-political legitimacy of the oath as a providential tool to bond sinful humans into a civil society. Soto also started to circumscribe the oath within certain limits in order to curb the proliferation of oaths—a necessary step in order to legitimize the use of the oath as a profession of (political and religious) faith. Soto, however, must not have been entirely satisfied with his treatment of oaths in this work, for he decided to come back to the issue in a more systematic fashion. In fact, he wrote an entire book devoted to oaths that he added to the second edition of *De iustitia et iure*, published in 1556 (the first edition, published in 1553, did not discuss the oath).

As we saw in the first chapter of this book when I examined the doctrines of equivocation and mental reservation, Soto was very much interested in exploring the potentialities and limitations of human language as both an internal bond between the speaker's words and the speaker's tongue and as an external link between speakers and hearers. Thus, by analyzing Soto's revised treatment of the oath in *De iustitia et iure*, we can really appreciate how he blended his reflections on the political and theological significance of the oath with its hermeneutical and linguistic aspects. Indeed, in the process of strengthening the oath as the sacrament of power, Soto started to perceive both the power of the oath as the sacrament of language and the fragility of the bond that linked men to their words.

Let me start my analysis of Soto's intuition regarding the significance of the oath as the sacrament of language with his discussion of the oath's definition: "the oath is a statement confirmed by divine testimony."[21] In order to understand the significance of Soto's definition, we need to go back to Aquinas, Soto's main interlocutor throughout the treatise. In the *quaestio* 89 of the *IIa IIae*, Aquinas started his own reflections by proposing the following definition as a basis for discussion: "to swear is to call God as a witness." Aquinas, however, realized that the status of God in the oath was somewhat problematic: in what sense should God perform His duties as witness? Should He be called in order to attest to the truthfulness of a human affirmation or promise, or should He be called in order to judge the truthfulness of human affirmations and promises? Should humans expect God to give some external signs of the truthfulness of their oath or lack thereof and to visibly punish the transgressors? Aquinas solved the problem by saying that there are actually two kinds of oath: the first is the proper oath, when men call God as a witness; the second is a sort of curse or imprecation, when men bind themselves to God's punishment in case of perjury.

In Soto's discussion of Aquinas's definition of oath, we can immediately see that Soto felt somewhat uneasy with Aquinas's distinction between God as a witness and God as a judge, especially with the issue of God as a judge. Lorenzo Valla, as we have seen, had already asked what would happen to the strength of the oath in case the gods did not decide to get angry, and we should note that Valla's question has implications in two main areas. The first, which is what Valla had in mind in the previously quoted passage, had to do with the oath as a sacrament of power; namely, with the question of what kind of authority can actually oversee and regulate the oath. This question was not too problematic for Soto, who suggested that the political or religious authority on earth might step in for God, so to speak, and fill the role of the judge of oaths. In fact, as a response to the question of whether or not oaths were necessary, Soto declared that the main proof of their necessity was that "any public authority, whether civil or spiritual, has the right by law and by custom to demand from a citizen or any subject an oath in order to disclose and restrain the evil that can arise either to the detriment of the commonwealth or of other men." Whoever abuses the oath requested by the public authority, Soto continued, sinned against both king and God, and thus both the political and the religious authority had the right and the duty to impose certain penalties on those who committed perjury.[22]

However, Valla's point is also relevant for another question, concerning not the oath as the sacrament of power but the oath as the sacrament of language. In a nutshell, what is the role of God in the oath if we consider the oath as a peculiar kind of speech act? Is God supposed to judge from the outside, as it were, whether or not men's language corresponds to men's thought and to reality? Or is God supposed to represent a sort of ideal model of truthfulness? To put it differently, when men swear, do they put their language in the hands of God, as if asking Him to judge whether or not they swore the truth, or do they imitate God as the original oath taker, as Agamben put it? When Soto considered the oath as the sacrament of language, he forcefully rejected the possibility that God might be acting as a judge. In fact, qualifying Aquinas's statements on this matter, Soto declared that the distinction between God as a witness and God as a judge was only an apparent distinction: in reality, God was never supposed to be a judge but always a witness. The difference, brought up by Aquinas, between oaths and imprecations was for Soto like the difference between a black-skinned animal and a white-skinned animal of the same species: different colors but same kind.[23] And what was God supposed to "witness" exactly? For Soto, when one swears by God one invites God to witness the "manifestation of truth." Original sin made language unstable and thus created the *"vulnus,"* the wound, of "incredulity." Because God was mindful of the necessity of being able to trust one another in order to live in society, He gave the gift of the oath to men. Thus the God of Truth gave men an instrument for expressing human truth, and every time men swear—that is, whenever they express the truth—they show their honor, gratitude, and veneration for the Truth.[24]

Soto was very strong in asserting that the core significance of the oath was that it linked human language and divine Truth rather than (or before) linking men to one another. On this point he aggressively attacked Cajetan, who had remarked that one could not say that the end of the oath is the manifestation of human truth. Cajetan thought that in order for the oath to be considered a pious and religious act, it needed to have the honor of God as its end. Thus, since the manifestation of human truth was of an inferior order with respect to the honor due to God, one could not say that the proper end of the oath was the manifestation of human truth but rather that such manifestation was simply a product of the oath. To this argument Soto remarked: "Cajetan complicates the matter by means of a certain kind of metaphysical distinction, which is possibly unnecessary, on the question of whether the manifestation of truth is the effect or the end of the oath." Cajetan's scruples, according to Soto, made no sense: first of all, the necessity of manifesting the truth through the oath was a product of sin, which corrupted human nature and human language; thus the very act of swearing—that is, of manifesting the truth—is not simply a side effect of the oath but its very core and raison d'être. It is precisely insofar as the oath is the manifestation of truth that it can be said to be a form of veneration for the God of Truth. Besides, Soto continued, there is nothing absurd in thinking that the God of Truth can be venerated through the manifestation of the human truth: after all, God died for our salvation, and in this respect we can say that the glory of God (an end of the highest order) is achieved through human salvation, which was definitely of an inferior order.[25] At stake here was the very core of the oath as the sacrament of language: for Soto, God does not function as a judge of human language in the oath but rather as a model of truthful language par excellence. Human language used to be similar to this model in the state of innocence but lost its "authority" with original sin. Swearing, thus, was a gift of God given to men in order to recover their lost confidence in human words.

Just as humans can get closer to God by means of the gift of the oath, so in a sense for Soto, oaths make God closer to humans. Recall that in his early short treatise Soto had mentioned God's oath to Abraham in Genesis 22 as a proof that oaths were not evil. In *De iustitia et iure* Soto returned to the question of God's oaths, but this time he did not limit himself to mentioning the episode as evidence of the religiously acceptable nature of oath. If oaths are the gift of God by which human language can recover its authority, why does God swear, since His words never endured the loss that original sin inflicted on men's words? To this question, Soto first specified that "God does not swear for the same reason as men; that is, because He needs to confirm His truth by means of the oath. Indeed God's simple assertion is as solid [*firma*] as an oath: He swears by Himself."[26] If the assertions of God are oaths, why does God need to swear then? Soto responded by referring to one of the canons of the eighth council of Toledo (celebrated in 653), which then became one of the canons of the second part of Gratian's *Decretum*.[27] Using the example of God's oaths as evidence of the sacrality of oaths in general, the canon explained that God's oath signified that whatever He promised to do was "*immutabilis*"; that is, not subject to change. Sometimes, in fact, God changed His mind, and as an example the canon referred to Jeremiah 18:7–8, where God threatened "to pluck up, and to pull down, and to destroy" the people of Israel but soon after added that "if that nation, against whom I have pronounced, turn from their evil, I will repent of the evil that I thought to do unto them." Thus, Soto explained, "whenever God asserts something without an oath, sometimes He changes it because He declares it as a threat; whenever, by contrast, He asserts something by oath, He confirms it as immutable." Even Paul, in his epistle to the Hebrews, explained that by swearing God expressed the "immutability of his counsel" so that "by two immutable things, in which it was impossible for God to lie, we might have a strong consolation" [Hebrews 6:17–18].[28]

As Grotius would notice a few decades later, to explain God's oaths in such terms meant "to attribute to Him human passions, rather in conformity to our finite capacities than to His infinite nature." According to Grotius, in fact, God never changes His mind and never repents; what may change is the "occasion" in which He utters his assertions.[29] The interesting aspect of this passage, however, is that Soto not only attributed to God the very human characteristic of changing His mind—which after all was part of the relationship between God's *potestas ordinata* and God's *potestas absoluta*, which in turn was part of Soto's Scholastic understanding of the nature of God and His relationship with His creatures.[30] Rather, we should notice that Soto put God, by extension the oath, at the center of a conversation—or a dialogue in Gadamer's sense. All of Soto's Biblical quotations (Genesis, Jeremiah, and Paul's epistle to the Hebrews), in fact, imply that God swore to make His intention of changing or of not changing His mind manifest to the hearers. In this context, then, the oath of men and the oath of God have an important characteristic in common: they are significant insofar as they are speech acts that imply the presence of a speaker and the presence of a hearer. Thus, oaths are supposed to guarantee the firmness and the "*immutabilitas*" of both men's and God's intentions for the sake of the audience.

The fact that the oath is at the center of the hermeneutical experience of language conceived as a dialogue has several intriguing implications. First of all, the very existence of the oath implies that language is an unstable means of communication between a speaker and a hearer, and oaths are needed precisely insofar as they can stabilize what is by its very nature unstable. In the case of God's language, the "instability" that God's oaths are supposed to eliminate has its origin in God's self-imposed *immutabilitas* or lack thereof. Thus, it is God Himself who can decide to bind Himself by His own words and who then signals His intention to men by swearing. In the case of human language, however, the instability is a fruit of original sin, and as such it involves the very nature of the language of humans after the Fall. In this respect, then, human oaths are the means by which men can bind themselves to their own words by imitating the God of Truth. But since human language is flawed, can oaths ever completely eliminate any possible doubt about the correspondence between intention and reality? This is where the hermeneutical aspect of the oath gets more complex, and this is also where Soto's reflections become quite interesting, for they begin to expose possible moments of fracture involving men's thought, men's words, and men's world.

Since the primary function of the oath, as Soto discussed it in *De iustitia et iure,* is to ensure the "manifestation of truth," the oath should serve as a seal of the truthfulness of the language spoken. Thus, the truth of one's assertion or of one's promise is, as Soto declared, the first and foremost reason for the binding force of the oath. Aquinas had argued that the assertory oath cannot be binding insofar as truthfulness is concerned, since one is always bound to do something in the future and since the assertory oath simply attests to the truth of a past or present assertion. Against this position, Soto declared that even though in an assertory oath "nobody swears to make his assertion true, nevertheless one swears what is absolutely true." For this reason, according to Soto, we should interpret Aquinas as if he meant to say that both the promissory oath and the assertory oath bind the speaker to the truth and that "the difference is that in the assertory oath the obligation [to truth] is not born out of the oath but precedes it, since everybody is bound to swear the truth. In the promissory oath, however, the obligation [to truth] is an effect of the oath: the obligation to fulfill the promise arises from the fact that one swears."[31]

Once Soto firmed up the obligation to truth as the binding force of both kinds of oaths, he set out to describe in details how such obligation to truth might work in the oath. Since the oath is an act of human will, in order for this special kind of speech act to be practiced, the oath taker must intend to actually perform this speech act. Thus, the speaker's intention to swear is a necessary condition for the oath to happen as a language event. On the other side of the oath, as it were, we have the hearer, for the sake of whom the speech act of swearing is practiced. Thus, the ideal case is when a speaker has the intention of committing to the truth of her assertion or promise, then seals such intention with an oath that, insofar as it is a speech act performed externally, serves as a certain and stable sign of the truthfulness of the speaker's utterance for the sake of the hearer. However, what happens when the bond between the speaker's intention and the speaker's performance of the speech act of the oath is broken?

Soto could clearly see how the complexity of the world in which he lived would prompt a speaker to utter an oath that she did not mean to utter; for instance, a man could be forced to swear to give money that he had no intention to give to a robber who threatened him, or a man could swear to marry a woman he had no intention to marry. In both cases, there is a fracture between the speaker's intention and the speaker's speech act, and in both cases the hearer, prompted by the seal of the oath, is bound to believe the speaker's speech and therefore would be deceived as to the speaker's intention. How then could one preserve, Soto asked, the sacrament of language in those cases?[32]

Soto and the Catholic theologians who thought about this issue had at their disposal two partially contradictory authorities, both of them sanctioned by canon law. The first was Gregory the Great's statement in his commentary on the Book of Job, which became canon 11, question V, *causa* XXII, of the second part of Gratian's *Decretum*. We already encountered this text in the first chapter, since it was the canon Navarrus commented on in his treatise on equivocation and mental reservation: "The ears of men judge our words as they sound outside. The ears of God, however, judge our words as they are uttered from the inside. Among men the heart is judged by the words, but for God the words are judged by the heart."[33] Following Gregory's authority, since an oath is such only when the speaker has the intention to swear—that is, to commit herself to the truthfulnes of her assertion by invoking God as the model of Truth—whenever a speaker performs the speech act of swearing without intending to do so the oath is not valid. The speaker is thus released in conscience from the obligation to tell the truth or to make good on the promise that would have arisen from a valid oath.

The second authority was Isidore of Seville, who in the second book of his *Sententiae* had declared: "Notwithstanding any verbal trick a person might use when swearing, God, who sees the conscience [*qui conscientiae testis est*], considers the oath in the sense in which the person receiving the oath understands it." This also became part of canon law, as canon 9 of the same question and *causa* of Gregory's words.[34] Following Isidore's words, then, since the validity of an oath, in God's judgment, depends not on the intention of the speaker but rather on the speech act actually performed, it follows that the binding force of the oath does not depend on the speaker's intention or lack thereof; God is not on the side of the speaker, so to speak, but on the side of the receiver of the meaning of the speech act of swearing.

Soto did not find either of those solutions especially satisfactory. To follow Gregory meant to deny the very origin of the oath, which is to restore the "authority" that human language lost with original sin: if the words pronounced in an oath did not have to correspond to the real intention of the speaker, how can men trust each other's words? To follow Isidore, by contrast, meant to deny free will and agency of the speaker in the performance of the speech act of swearing, which had troubling consequences, both morally and hermeneutically. The solution for Soto was to combine Isidore and Gregory by distinguishing between internal and external forum. Thus, when a speaker pronounces an oath without the intention of swearing, he is not bound to the truth of his assertion "by the force of the oath, since in that case there wouldn't be an oath and if he contravenes his utterance he would not be committing the sin of perjury. However, he can be bound by other laws. For instance, if a man promised a girl to marry her only in order to take advantage of her. . . if he pronounces the words of the oath, he is bound to make good on the promise by the law of justice. The same would happen in any other contract whenever there is a pact involved. Also, one would be bound to make good on the promise in order to avoid scandal: if a man swears solemnly, albeit fictitiously, in something important, unless he can convince people clearly that he did not truly swear, without a doubt he has to be bound to his words under pain of mortal sin, so as not to give scandal and not to be perceived as a perjurer in other people's opinion."[35]

Distinguishing between internal and external forum in the way Soto did was the only way to ensure both the binding force and the main end of the speech act of swearing: "the intention of swearing is always included in the external words of the oath, provided that this is done by purpose and that whoever swears does not exclude in his mind such intention specifically and directly. Thus whoever does not have an intention to bind himself to his oath lies regarding the substance of the oath, which is the promise, but he does not lie insofar as the actual swearing is concerned, therefore he truly swears."[36] Swearing the truth by oath, Soto continued, is different from just telling the truth: "when one says 'I swear' this is not simply an assertion in words [*in actu signato*], as the logicians say; that is, one does not simply assert to be swearing. . . but it is an oath in deed [*in actu exercito*]. Indeed when you say 'I speak' you are not only signifying that you speak but you are indeed truly speaking."[37]

The special force of the speech act of swearing is such that whenever an oath is invoked, an obligation to truth arises, and while the speaker's lack of intention eliminates this obligation in the internal forum of the conscience, the obligation remains in the external forum. Or to put it differently, for Soto swearing without intention does not make the sworn promise or the sworn assertion "*void*, though it is given *in bad faith*." It makes it "unhappy," or "infelicitous"[38] : the effects of such infelicity should be evaluated by the external public authority insofar as the oath binds the speaker and the hearer, and by the Church insofar as the oath binds the speaker's conscience to her own words through God.

Soto's attempt to define the double nature of the oath as both an internal and an external act, as Prodi argued, articulated and indeed consolidated the dualism between the Church and the state as the respective authorities in charge of

enforcing the oath's obligations in the internal and external forum.[39] However—
and this is my main point in this section—the duality identified by Soto in the
oath also originated a potentially upsetting instability in language itself. As Soto
had argued, the oath was given to men precisely as an antidote to this instability, but distinguishing between the words inside and the words outside reintroduced this instability to the point that it now could upset not only human
language but the very core of the oath itself. In other words, to integrate Austin
with Wittgenstein, if I pronounce an oath without intention, I am generating a
series of multiple language games. I am playing one language game with God,
which takes place in the forum of the conscience. This game can be regulated
only by the Church, which can impose its penalties for my sin of swearing an
oath outwardly without an inward intention, even though no obligation to truth
arises in my conscience. In parallel, I am playing a different language game with
my hearers, who will take my external words as a (misguided) indication of my
intention. The hearers' interpretation can be protected by the political authority,
which in cases of contracts or pacts can make me stand by my words by the law
of justice or for reasons of scandal, even though I am not bound by my words
in the internal forum. Thus, while Soto's solution had the benefit of assigning,
respectively, to the Church and to the state the prerogative of punishing any
instance in which my intention does not correspond to my words, neither the
religious nor the political authority can restore to language the function of stable
bond connecting thought, tongue, and reality that the oath was supposed to
give. In a sense, then, Soto's dualistic understanding of the oath has a powerful
and troubling effect on the oath as a sacrament of language: in Soto's elaboration
the oath ceases to "manifest the truth" and becomes rather a manifestation of
the complex and fractured relationship of one's intentions, one's words, and the
world outside.

Soto showed a certain awareness of this potentially troubling consequence
when he addressed a specific case of problematic oaths; that is, oaths sworn in
ambiguous terms. Soto knew that the entire theological discussion regarding fictitious, invalid, and false oaths was a dangerous territory, and he remarked that
previous theologians had usually solved the issue by invoking either Gregory or
Isidore (two solutions that, as we saw, he did not entirely approve). Thus he proposed to address the issue by making two preliminary distinctions. The first concerned the very words used in the oath, which could be either false or equivocal;
that is, "in one sense true, and in another false." The second concerned the person
to whom the oath is sworn, who could either have a legitimate reason to ask for an
oath or request an oath unlawfully and by violence.[40] Soto then continued: "once
we assume this distinction, then we first establish a general rule: if the words pronounced outwardly are false with respect to the intention of the speaker, that is,
they do not accord with his mind, swearing in such case would be absolutely and

without any exception a mortal sin," regardless of whether the oath was asked lawfully or unlawfully and regardless of whether the speaker mentally posed some conditions restricting her words, since the words pronounced do not allow for an interpretation that takes mental restrictions into account.[41] The political authority, in certain cases, could still hold the speaker to the fulfillment of her promise in the external forum, as we have seen.

But what happens when "there is a simulation in the words, which are pronounced in an equivocal manner or in such a way as they could accommodate the meaning of the speaker even though the hearer might not be able to understand it"? How can the oath function as a sacrament of language when the oath itself is pronounced in such an ambiguous and instable manner? Soto had already argued that pronouncing the words of an oath means to actually and truly swear. Thus, when one uses ambigous words to swear one also transforms the oath into an ambiguous speech act: in that case, the oath as sacrament of language would cease to represent the bond connecting words, thought, and reality, because it would be marred by the same instability of human language that it was supposed to counteract in the first place. Thus, how can we save the oath as the sacrament of language? Soto seemed to admit that there was no easy way to save the oath as sacrament of language from the stain of instability, or to put it differently, to save human language from itself. He saw only two possible remedies. The first was, once again, the external public authority; the second was constituted by the semantic limitations intrinsic to language itself. As Soto explained, if one swears in ambiguous terms in front of a legitimate authority, the oath must be taken in the sense in which the words are taken by the hearer, "because of the wrong that would happen to the person who has the right to demand the oath." If, by contrast, the person asking the oath did so unlawfully or by violence, then "it is licit to deceive the person with this fraud." For instance, if a robber asked me for money, I could licitly swear that I would "count," *numerare*, the money, without either committing perjury or incurring any obligation to make my promise true, since the verb *numerare* means both "to count" as in "I will count my money whenever I can do so on my own," and "to count" as in "I will count out for you as I pay you the money." Because of the fact that the verb actually means what the speaker intends, the speaker does not commit perjury. The unlawful status of the person requesting the oath will free the speaker from the sin she would incur with the fraud, thus releasing her from the obligation to make good on a promise that she did not swear to make even though she actually did.[42]

Notice that the semantic argument is virtually the same that Soto had used in a different part on his treatise; namely, in the book devoted to the rights and duties of a defendant. There Soto used it in order to justify the use of amphibology and equivocation whenever one needed to conceal a secret but could not avoid lying.[43] The fact that Soto used precisely the same semantic argument when he needed to protect the oath from the instability of language is indicative of the fact that in Soto's elaboration the oath had started to lose its sacred power to bind men's minds, men's tongues, and the world outside. Indeed, the oath had become as unstable as language itself: the semantic rules of language provide a crutch to the oath, which, however, had been given to men by God precisely in support of language. Thus, even though for Soto the oath was supposed to bind men to their words in the likeness and honor of the God of Truth, in his work we start to see a scenario in which the words men intend to utter, the words they actually utter, and the ways in which words are perceived by the hearers do not match. The force of the oath as the sacrament of language is not enough to save this bond anymore; the only things saving humans from a world of incommunicability are the semantic idiosyncrasies of spoken language and external authority, which acts as the police of men's words and which can bind men to their words for extralinguistic reasons. Soto's remedies, then, do not manage to close the wound completely. The external authority can certainly protect the interest of the hearer, and as such it can correct, to a certain extent, the infelicitous outcome of a "broken" oath, but it cannot restore the bond that a broken oath originates. The semantic rules of spoken language, on their part, make the oath subject to the same instability that language itself is subject to; this instability erases the specific force of the oath as the sacrament of language. Thus, behind these thin bandages there is an open and deep fracture. Soto caught a glimpse of it; it was up to Suárez to fully expose it.

Francisco Suárez: Exposing the Fracture

Everybody knows that Suárez was one of the great theologians of the Society of Jesus, and as such many of his philosophical and theological propositions became the backbone of early modern Jesuit theology and moral philosophy. Yet the significance of Suárez's theological and philosophical views is more complex than that. Some of Suárez's early modern detractors, undoubtedly with a hint of malevolence but with much insight, had already noted that Suárez's thought departed in many and important ways not only from that of Aquinas (a common accusation against Jesuit theologians) but also from that of his fellow Jesuits. Indeed, Suárez was so different from anybody else that his enemies accused him of founding his own, entirely new, school of theology.[44] Even the strongest supporters of Suárez's doctrines realized that some of them could be potentially divisive for the Catholic camp, and time and again they had to defend him from the attacks coming from the intellectual and institutional leadership of his own religious order.[45] I do not intend here to examine in detail just how radical and, to a certain extent, upsetting some of Suárez's theories were in the context of Suárez's own theological tradition.[46] I would like, however, to cite only one, remarkably interesting and very little known, example of Suárez's intellectual freedom, which should serve as a way to frame the specific considerations I am going to make regarding his positions on oaths.

Suárez was born in Granada in 1548. After completing his studies in Salamanca, Suárez remained in Castile for the first half of his life, teaching in prestigious institutions such as Ávila and Valladolid. During that time Suárez acquired a great reputation for his precocious intelligence, as well as a growing number of detractors. In 1580, as Suárez's academic stardom was rising in parallel with the anger of his intellectual and personal enemies, Acquaviva (then Provincial of Rome) called Suárez to the Roman College as a professor of theology. During his five-year sojourn in Rome Suárez enjoyed some professional success (Pope Gregory XIII had heard so much about Suárez that he supposedly went to the college to listen to his inaugural lecture)[47] while rubbing shoulders with some of the most important Catholic intellectuals of the time (among Suárez's colleagues in the faculty of the college in those years were Robert Bellarmine and Christopher Clavius). Eventually Suárez's health, which had always been frail, started to suffer from the Roman climate, and Suárez's ego started to suffer from the competitive scene of the Roman College.[48] Thus in 1585 Suárez was sent back first to Spain and then to Portugal, more specifically to the University of Coimbra, where he lived and taught for twenty years, until he died in 1617. The episode I am about to relate refers to Suárez's years in Rome, during which he had the opportunity of working with some of the brightest young minds. One of them was Leonardus Lessius, whom Suárez influenced a great deal and in a controversial way.

We know about this controversial influence from the somewhat troubled publishing history of a biography of Lessius, which eventually appeared in 1640. The editor of the biography, Thomas Courtois, explained in the dedicatory epistle to the Belgian fathers of the Society of Jesus that he had received the manuscript biography from a nephew of Lessius, a regular clergyman by the name of Leonard Schoofs. After sitting on it for some time, Courtois realized that 1640 was the jubilee year for the Society of Jesus in Belgium, and thus the time had come to publish the manuscript, which could have served as an appropriate contribution to the celebration.[49] What Courtois, understandably, did not say, is that in those years the Jesuits were busy not only celebrating their jubilee but also fending off the attacks by the Jansenists, who of course in Belgium were especially strong. This is why the publication of Lessius's biography was closely watched in Rome: the Congregation of the Index of Prohibited Books had the manuscript read and censured by several different theologians, and in addition to the censors appointed by the Congregation other important personalities in the Roman Curia were involved in the discussion of this book.[50]

In general, the censors took issue with the more "Jesuitical" aspects of Lessius's biography; they suggested toning down the harsh words the biographer used against Lessius's detractors and cutting out the parts where the biographer praised Lessius's teaching on grace and free will, whose radical anti-Baianist flavor had worried even Robert Bellarmine.[51] The censors devoted a great deal of attention also to the chapter about Lessius's studies at the Roman College. This chapter narrated that at the beginning of his studies, Lessius was plagued by "hesitation" and "scruples" concerning the fact that "it looked like one had to swear by the words of the old doctors, and that it was not allowed to disagree with the opinion of the majority of the doctors or of the greatest ones." In sum, Lessius was deeply upset because he started to realize that in matters of theology "authority" seemed to count more than "reason."[52] Francisco Suárez, Lessius's teacher, saved the student from his scruples: "Suárez prudently responded that it was not a sacrilege to diverge from the opinion of learned doctors in issues that do not pertain to either faith or morality. Indeed, (as Horace said) sometimes even the great Homer nods, and it is easy to forgive when somnolence creeps into a long work. Nobody can be so insightful as to be able to investigate everything carefully enough, and the truth is not so easy to discern, therefore even the most intelligent authors might miss or overlook the truth in many things. Thus, just as many eyes see more than two, so many minds see more than one."[53] The world, Suárez continued, was full of hidden treasures: there were veins of gold and silver hidden in the depth of the earth, pearls hidden in their shells, precious stones hidden inside rocks. Just because nobody had found them yet did not mean that one person at some point might not find them by searching more thoroughly in places where nobody had ever searched before. The same was true when it came to knowledge.[54] Suárez concluded by saying that there were plenty of people who refused to investigate the truth and preferred to follow others' opinion, as a sheep follows another sheep. Lessius, however, should not feel restricted by any intellectual "*vincula*" coming from authority, but he should be free to explore the truth with the guidance of his own reason. Truly liberated from his scruples by this speech, Lessius, the biographer concluded, reimmersed himself with newly found enthusiasm in his theological and philosophical studies.[55]

Evidently the Roman censors thought that this passage was not good either for Lessius or for Suárez, which is why they proposed to eliminate this entire episode.[56] The printed version of this chapter, in fact, is much shorter and sanitized: the biographer mentioned Lessius's scruples and Suárez's fatherly intervention but eliminated completely the references to Homer's nods, the hidden treasures waiting to be discovered, the need to avoid behaving like a sheep, and the invitation to free one's judgment from the constraints of authority in order to follow one's reason as the only guide in matters of knowledge. Suárez's pep talk was now limited to the following sentence: "it is not a sacrilege to disagree with the opinion of some great scholars in certain issues that do not concern either faith or morality."[57]

I have resurrected this expunged chapter from scholarly oblivion because I think that it offers a vivid snapshot of Suárez's approach to the relationship between reason and authority in discussing matters of theology and moral philosophy; as we will see in the following pages, his reflections on the oath were informed by the same lack of reverential fear toward well-established intellectual traditions and by the same inquisitive attitude. Suárez's elaborations regarding the oath as a sacrament of language were novel and profound, which is why we are still grappling with its philosophical and historical implications.

Suárez devoted to the oath a treatise included in the second volume of his *De religione*, first published in Coimbra in 1609.[58] As we can see from the very beginning of his discussion, Suárez was especially interested in the relationship of oaths, truth, and language. He proposed to define the oath as "an enunciation in which we take God as a witness," whose main end is the "confirmation of truth."[59] Indeed, recalling the polemic between Soto and Cajetan about whether confirming the truth was the end or simply the effect of the oath, Suárez decidedly sided with Soto and even added: "to explain this better, I think that the oath should be first examined insofar as it is an action apt to confirm the truth, without taking into consideration its repercussions on the honor of Him Who is invoked as a witness, but examining only the utility and effect of that action for the sake of the confirmation of truth." Only after we examine the oath's effect in verifying language, Suárez argued, can we see how such verification of language achieved through the oath contributes to the honor of God.[60]

After establishing the tight link between swearing and confirming the truth, however, Suárez added that insofar as the oath is an act of conscience, such an enunciation, made in order to confirm the truth, does not have to be a verbal proposition but can be expressed through other nonverbal signs, even not expressed at all. It is only insofar as the oath is a sacrament of power—that is, insofar as the oath is an act that confirms human pacts or agreement—that words are necessary: "thus words are required by human law only, so that the oath might give credence, or induce obligation, where the human law has established this specific form of swearing in order to achieve a specific effect."[61] By contrast, the speaker's intention to swear, not the speaker's verbal expression of her intention to swear, is the necessary condition for the existence of oaths: "in fact, the oath properly signifies a human action, and nobody could say that a man swears while asleep, even though he uttered a verbal oath, and the same could be said in the case of a crazy man and other similar cases."[62]

Up until now, it seems that Suárez simply assigned the speaker's intention to swear and the speaker's verbal utterance to the two fora identified by Prodi: the intention to swear is a necessary condition for the performance of the oath in the internal forum of the conscience, while the verbal expression of the oath is necessary for the performance of the oath in the external forum. However, Suárez's reflection on oaths cannot be reduced to an expression of Prodi's dualism. Suárez went beyond this and indeed used the tension between intention and expression as the springboard for an interesting hermeneutical reflection on the power of words.

The verbal expression of the oath, according to Suárez, is distinctively useful as a means for binding human societies because it has the effect of convincing the hearer about the speaker's intention to commit herself to her words, so that whenever an oath is pronounced, "the hearers are moved to believe that what the speaker says is true." Even though the oath becomes valid only if the intention of the speaker is present, the effect produced by the oath's words on the hearers "is equally achieved whether or not the speaker uttering such words has the intention to swear." It is not true, Suárez glossed, that the force of the oath rests on the fear that God might punish the transgressors, since God is never invoked so that He might show some tangible signs of the truthfulness of the oath pronounced by men. Indeed, we can say that the oath is forceful regardless of whether it is actually a real oath: it is only because of the verbal expression of the oath that men believe each other, and there is nothing in the verbal expression of the oath that can prevent men from being mistaken in their belief in case the speaker lacks the intention to swear.[63]

In this passage, then, Suárez introduced a fundamental hermeneutical imbalance between the perspective of the speaker as the producer of meaning and the perspective of the hearer as the receiver of meaning. The speaker's intention is the only measure by which we can distinguish a real oath from a fake one, and as such it is the only thing that creates a real oath, regardless of how the hearers perceive it. The hearers' interpretation, however, is the only source of the oath's binding force, and as such it is the only thing that makes humans believe in one another, regardless of how the speaker intended her words. This imbalance, in turn, results in a fundamental fracture between what the speaker thinks and what the speaker says: the oath, far from being able to fix this imbalance, is indeed one of its clearest manifestations.

Soto had already treated the question of what happens whenever one swears an oath she does not mean to make, but Soto had treated this question as an exception to the general rule that oaths are supposed to seal the true intention of the speaker and thus to confirm the true meaning for the sake of the hearer. Indeed, Soto introduced his discussion on false, fictive, and ambiguous oaths by talking about the motives that a person might have for rendering the speech act of the oath infelicitous (a man, for instance, could be pressured to swear by a robber or by his desire to have sex with a girl he did not want to marry). For Suárez, by contrast, oaths always imply the possibility of a fracture between thought and language, because this fracture is inscribed in the very nature of the oath.

Suárez was fully aware that his position had the effect of exposing such a fracture in a rather dramatic manner. He explicitly argued that those people who might object to his view should realize that "the certainty that results from the oath is not of such kind and of such strength as to be protected from the deceits and frauds of men. Thus a man can lie even if he swears, and likewise he can swear deceitfully and fictitiously even if he speaks otherwise outwardly." The fact that the oath cannot mend the broken link between thought and reality, however, does not make the oath useless. Its utility, for Suárez, is that of offering a sort of reminder of the need for men to commit to their words, and in this respect the oath is an incentive to, rather than a sure sign of, truth: "it is enough that men are bound to the particular obligation to tell the truth whenever they adduce God as a witness."[64]

Suárez thus saw clearly and exposed lucidly the fracture separating human thought, human language, and human reality. He also forcefully argued that the oath could not function effectively as a means for restoring the lost bond because the oath as a linguistic event does not have the strength to repair this fracture. This consideration led Suárez to rethink the origin of the oath, which for Soto, as we remember, had to be traced back to original sin. Because of original sin, Soto thought, human words had lost their "authority," which was partially restored by God's benevolence through the gift of the oath. For Suárez, by contrast, "the oath is not one of those things that necessarily presuppose sin or its effect on human nature." In fact, according to Suárez, "even if human nature were intact and innocent, it still would ignore many things, and especially the contingent, the past, and the future." Humans, even in the state of innocence, would also be ignorant of the present: in a discussion concerning an event they could ignore the time, or in a discussion concerning the place they could ignore the distance, or in a discussion concerning "internal acts" they could ignore the "hidden" motives and intentions. Thus, Suárez continued, "even in that state [of innocence] a man could speak with another man about things the speaker knows and the hearer does not, and the hearer could believe the speaker on the speaker's own testimony. Such testimony would not be infallible even in the state of innocence, since the speaker would not be exempt from sin even in the state of innocence: he could lie if, say, he was not as well versed in the topic of conversation as he was in other things." Given all this, Suárez argued that the need to swear comes from the "*moralis necessitas,*" "moral necessity," that humans have to believe each other's words and from the "*fallibilitas*" of human language; that is, the fact that human words cannot be always and necessarily true. Human beings' capability of failing each other when speaking and their necessity to believe one another "do not refer to the effects of the original sin, but are per se conjoined to the human condition." For this reason, the oath is not a medicine for the illness of original sin but the act that represents an intrinsic characteristic of humans, torn between the need to believe and the impossibility of grounding such belief in infallible truth.[65] Even God, Suárez glossed, realized that such tension between the "*fallibilitas*" of language and the "*necessitas*" to believe was part of human nature, and indeed this is the reason why He swore: He used the oath "as an external aid," "in order to comfort men in their faith or in order to make them believe." Adam, for his part, could have used God's reassurance both before and after original sin.[66]

Once again, the question of how to save humans from a world of incommunicability returns, in Suárez much more strongly than in Soto. Recall that Soto, in addition to stressing the external pressure of the public authority that could make humans stand by their word, also pointed to the semantic idiosyncrasies of language itself as a very tenuous link between intention and words. While Suárez agreed and, indeed, went even further than Soto in establishing the right and the duty of the public authority to enforce oaths, he denied that language could provide any remedy for its own fallibility. Language by itself "has no binding force unless because of men's consent, as happens in the case of marriage and all contracts, as well as religious professions and vows. The reason is that the interior will is almost the soul of words, and words have no strength unless insofar as they are signs of the mind. This has to be interpreted as concerning the obligation per se, and on the basis of the strength of the oath: in fact obligation can arise out of external oaths because of extrinsic reasons, even though the intention is not present."[67]

Soto's last resort—that is, Soto's desperate attempt to bind together the intention of the speaker and the words she utters by using the semantic argument—for Suárez made no sense. Soto and his followers, Suárez declared, were disturbed by the fact that if there were no linguistic means to bind the speaker's thought and the speaker's words, then "the whole benefit and end of the oath would be enervated: the end of the oath is to confirm the truth and to firm up pacts amongst men, but when men cannot understand each other's minds, given that the oath would depend entirely on the speaker's intention rather than on the meaning of the words, then oaths would be useless since the obligation would be so uncertain and obscure that it would be almost as if it never existed."[68] Because of this, Soto and his followers tried to "put some limitation" on the freedom a speaker has to think something and say something else: splitting intention and verbal expression was licit, according to Soto, only "when the deceitful intention of the speaker can easily be adapted to the words according to their own proper meaning, or whenever one could understand the speaker's intention out of other circumstances or conjectures or proofs." According to Suárez, however, such a limitation had no bearing on the forum of the conscience, since regardless of whether the speaker used ambiguous, false, or plain words, the oath was valid only if the intention was present.[69] It is too bad, Suárez seemed to say, that the oath cannot ensure the correspondence between words, intentions, and reality, but this is part and parcel of the very nature of the oath, which is part and parcel of the human condition: when we swear we do not expect God to validate our words, but we commit ourselves to our words. Whenever we do not intend to commit ourselves, there is no force in the words that can make us do what we do not intend to do. The only force is, once again, the external public authority that can correct the external effect of the broken oath.[70]

Suárez came back, with even more polemical force, to the same topic of the impossibility of limiting the freedom men have to commit or not to commit to their words in his specific discussion of ambiguous oaths. In that context, he first reported Soto's and Navarrus's positions on whether or not one was allowed to use only equivocation as opposed to equivocation and mental reservation.[71] He recognized that accepting Navarrus—that is, allowing mental reservation—had potentially upsetting consequences, and he understood where Soto and like-minded theologians were coming from when they denied mental reservation: if one allowed mental reservation "there would be no certain speech among men, but anybody could say and write whatever he wanted, reserving in his mind the meaning that the words according to their sense do not have, which is against human fidelity and is no less obnoxious to human society than open lies."[72] Nevertheless, Suárez thought that Navarrus's solution was the correct one. He also, to an extent, supported Navarrus's justification for mental reservation as *"probabilis"* (as we recall, Navarrus's justification was based on the argument that mixed propositions exist as an intrinsic feature of language, which anybody can take advantage of, regardless of motive). Suárez, however, understood that to accept Navarrus's reasoning meant to allow the possibility of mixing and matching heterogeneous signs, which was not entirely uncontroversial. Thus, Suárez offered what he thought was a better justification for mental reservation: "because men are free to express or not to express their intention, therefore they are free to begin a phrase and not to finish it. Thus when I conceive in my mind the whole phrase: 'I did not do something today,' I can begin to express this concept without actually finishing it, thus even if I said 'I did not do something' and stopped there, without finishing my mental proposition, effectively I am not lying."[73]

Once again, then, Suárez returned to the argument that the freedom of the conscience cannot be limited by language, since it is this freedom that indeed gives language its "soul." The oath as a speech act finds its raison d'être neither in God's power to verify men's words nor in language's own power to link intentions and reality. Rather, the oath is the verbal expression of the free decision of men to commit themselves to their own words. Thus, without men's will to commit, their words remain "soulless," idle signs of the broken bond between words and thoughts. To put it differently, the price we pay for the freedom to commit to our language is a world of hidden intentions and of soulless speech. For Suárez, then, every oath contains both a blessing and a curse. As Agamben put it, language is a blessing if "there is a correspondence between the signifier and the signified, between words and things; a curse if the word is empty, if there remains, between the semiotic and the semantic, a void and a gap."[74] For Suárez, oaths are the blessing of speech whenever they signal the correspondence between intention and words; that is, whenever they attest to the speaker's free and voluntary choice to commit to her language. Oaths embody also the curse of speech, whenever they signal a broken bond between intention and words.

In Suárez's extraordinarily lucid understanding of the double-sided nature of the oath, we can hear an echo of the problem identified by Austin for all performative speech acts of the same kind as the oath; namely, that one cannot judge them simply on the truth or falsehood of the verbal assertion or on the ethically correct or ethically reproachable character of the moral intention. As Austin put it, whoever claims that the external words of an oath must correspond to an internal act "appears as a solid moralist" and yet provides "the bigamist with an excuse for his 'I do' and the welsher with a defence for his 'I bet.' Accuracy and morality alike are on the side of the plain saying that *our word is our bond*."[75] Suárez refrained from using either accuracy or morality as a rigid criterion to conceptualize the oath, because rather than attempting to erase the complexity of oaths, Suárez embraced the oath's capability to be both a blessing and a curse as a fundamental feature of the human condition, in which the broken link between words and things is the price one must pay for the freedom to commit oneself to one's words.

The oath was not the only occasion for Suárez to reflect on the broken link between words and things; rather, his profoundly modern (in a sense we could say postmodern) understanding of the human condition as one in which thought, speech, and reality do not perfectly correspond to one another is also visible in another aspect of Suárez's doctrine, which potentially could have cost him his career. This aspect concerns the sacrament of confession, which is another case, much like that of the oath, where words acquire a sort of surplus of value. In order for the sacrament of confession to take place, in fact, the words uttered by the penitent in front of the confessor must correspond to the penitent's sincere repentance and the words of absolution uttered by the confessor act as a sort of performative in that they have the effect of actually absolving the penitent.

The sacrament of confession, specifically in its verbal aspect, was at the center of a profound controversy between two competing models in post-Reformation Catholicism, eventually destined to merge in some measure. The first, especially favored by the Roman Inquisition, sought to transform the confessor into a judge of the conscience and the confession into a trial. Thus, in the confession-trial the words of absolution pronounced by the confessor were neither a form of pastoral ministry such as preaching, nor a simple declaration of forgiveness, but rather a proper sentence pronounced by the confessor on behalf of God. The second model, especially favored by the Society of Jesus, saw the confessor as a doctor rather than as a judge of the conscience: in this model a confessor would be required not to sentence the penitent for her sins but to understand the penitent's sins as symptoms of a spiritual disease, to offer a diagnosis of the disease, and eventually to provide a cure.[76]

There are many instances in which the contrast between those two models manifested itself, and a particularly interesting one concerns the modes in which the actual words of both the penitent and the confessor are expressed. In the confessor-judge model, in fact, both the confession of and the absolution from sins need to be expressed orally in a specific setting, just as in order for a case to be discussed in the juridical forum, one needs a proper tribunal, with properly appointed judges, in a properly appointed time. The confessor-doctor model, by contrast, is centered on the penitent's duty to examine his conscience thoroughly and on the confessor's duty to examine the penitent's symptoms of spiritual disease equally thoroughly; in this case, then, a written report on one's sins could have been more useful than a hasty and possibly incomplete verbal account.[77]

It is well known that Ignatius Loyola was personally and acutely aware of how lacerating examining one's conscience could be and of how important it was to do it carefully in order to save one's soul. He was also fond of the practice of writing down rather than just recounting one's experiences: the very format of the *Spiritual Exercises* encouraged an accurate examination of conscience on the part of the penitent and implied that writing was best suited for such practice. The Jesuits were also aware that writing could sometimes help confessors do their job better. In 1595 Rutilio Benzoni, bishop of Recanati and alumnus of the German College, wrote a treatise on the duties of people in government, prompted by the plague that had hit northern and central Italy in the 1590s and that had caused many secular and clerical officials to leave their post in order to avoid contagion. Benzoni wrote that clergymen, in charge of ministering to their flock, could not flee, but at the same time they should try to protect themselves as much as possible. One of the most difficult cases was that of confession: it was true that a sick and possibly dying penitent could not be left without the comfort of confession, but it was also true that a verbal confession exposed the priest to a high risk of contagion, so why couldn't the penitent write his confession and send it to the priest, who could then read it at a safe distance from the sick penitent? After all, the confession was valid regardless of whether it was expressed orally or in writing.[78]

Another case in which a nonverbal confession or even a confession orally expressed by a third party could come in handy was that of a penitent who, in her last hours, could not speak anymore. This specific case had a place in canon law and a long history: as Pope Leo the Great had already noted in the fifth century, confession was very important and should never be denied, especially when somebody was close to death. Indeed, it could happen that right before dying penitents could not have enough strength to speak and thus to confess their sins verbally, but because confession at that point was as necessary as ever, the confessor should not deny the sacrament to the penitents "if they demand it with the indication of full understanding even when they have lost the use of their voice" or even if there were witnesses willing to attest to the penitents' desire to confess.[79]

Since, as I said, the Roman Inquisition was especially invested in transforming the sacrament of confession into a proper juridical act involving an initial investigation and a conclusive trial and sentence, it needed to curb the tendency of allowing a written confession instead of a verbal one. In fact, on 20 June 1602 the Holy Office issued a decree by which Pope Clement VIII prohibited the confessor "from confessing sacramentally and from absolving" a penitent who had communicated his confession not orally but "through letter or through an intermediary."[80] Just as this decree was being published, Suárez had sent to press a treatise entitled De poenitentia, which was part of his commentary on the third part of Aquinas's Summa. In it Suárez argued that since a verbal confession was not absolutely necessary for the sacrament of confession to be valid, in same cases of extreme necessity, such as Leo's case concerning penitents in their final hours, an exception should be made, and a nonverbal confession, or a confession by a third party, should be considered valid. When, however, Suárez learned about the 1602 decree he quickly decided to change what he initially wrote on verbal and nonverbal confession so as to make clear that he was aware of and, of course, upheld the papal decree, and devoted a specific section (the fourth section of the Disputatio XXI) to discussing why his opinion did not contradict it.[81] In order to accommodate both Clement's intransigence and Leo's mercy, Suárez argued that the canon taken from Leo's letter allowed, only in case of extreme necessity, a nonverbal confession but not a nonverbal absolution. Clement's decree, on its part, also forbade nonverbal absolution while allowing nonverbal confession, since the particle "and" in the text of the decree, "from confessing sacramentally and from absolving," needed to be interpreted not as if the decree prohibited both the confession and the absolution but as if the decree prohibited the two actions together—that is, the confession followed by absolution—while allowing the confession if in fact it was not followed by the absolution.[82]

Suárez's attempt to reinterpret Clement's decree in such a way as to allow some room for discretion within the general rule regarding oral confession did not go unnoticed. At the beginning of summer 1603 the Inquisition began to examine Suárez's *De poenitentia* in order to establish whether or not Suárez's interpretation was to be allowed.[83] On 31 July 1603 the Inquisition completed its deliberation. It declared that Suárez's interpretation, especially as it was articulated in the fourth section of *Disputatio XXI*, did in fact contradict Clement's intention, and thus Suárez's book "should be suspended *donec emendetur ac corrigatur*," and Suárez should be ordered to send to the Roman Inquisition the corrections he would make and to wait for the inquisitors' approval before printing other editions of the work. The copies of *De poenitentia* that were already published were to be collected and dealt with in "the usual manner" in which the Inquisition dealt with such books; that is, the condemned passages were to be erased. In the meantime, Suárez "cannot write or publish any book dealing with sacred theology unless he sends the books he wants to publish to Rome and to the Sacred Congregation of the Inquisition prior to publication and unless those books are formally approved." The inquisitors must have decided to really make clear to Suárez just how dangerous it was for him to meddle in such affairs: Suárez, they stated, should be reminded that the decree of Clement VIII imposed the punishment of excommunication for those who violated it and thus "Suárez should be advised to take care of his conscience."[84]

This was a slap in the face for Suárez—and in effect for the entire Jesuit order and for the friends and supporters of the Spanish branch of the Society, including the Spanish crown, with which Suárez had always had a tight relationship. Philip II, in fact, had personally sought and forcefully recruited Suárez as the star professor of the University of Coimbra, which Philip had decided would become the leading academic institution in Portugal, the most recent addition to his kingdom. Philip III, on his part, showed the same respect toward Suárez that his father had shown and successfully retained Suárez in Coimbra at the beginning of the seventeenth century, when Suárez had expressed his intention to resign from his chair of *Prima*.[85] As for Suárez's position on nonverbal confession and on confession by third party, the issue that most worried both Acquaviva and Philip III was the inquisitors' order to remove the condemned section from the copies of *De poenitentia* that were already printed. This visible and permanent correction to the book, in fact, would stand as a public reminder of the fact that Suárez had received a condemnation by the Inquisition. As Acquaviva wrote to the pope and the inquisitors, he was more than willing to see to it that Suárez's interpretation of Clement's decree be removed or revised in the following editions of Suárez's work, but he asked permission to leave the current editions untouched, in order to save "the reputation of this doctor which is among the greatest and most exemplary and better respected" members of the Society of Jesus. The book, Acquaviva continued, had been approved by the king's advisers, and all the "learned and conscientious people" knew how much the king appreciated Suárez's "sincerity" and "lack of malice."[86]

The general's plea did not change the pope's and the inquisitors' minds regarding the need to expunge the condemned sections from Suárez's work.[87] Suárez, however, was not ready to concede, and in the months following the censure he composed a long and articulate defense of his doctrine.[88] All through 1604 the Congregation of the Inquisition discussed this defense, together with various additional documents presented in Suárez's support by the hierarchy of the Society of Jesus and even by the Spanish ambassador.[89] Finally, at the end of 1604, Clement VIII decided to reconvene a meeting with the same theologians who censored Suárez's doctrine in the first place, so as to evaluate whether or not Suárez's defense had any ground. Before the pope could see the result of the evaluation, he died at the beginning of March 1605. After Paul V ascended to the papacy, he resumed the discussion, which ended in the summer of 1605 with a final declaration of the Inquisition confirming the previous condemnation of Suárez's book.[90]

Now, what is interesting about this episode for my purpose is the document Suárez wrote and presented to the Inquisition in defense of his position, from which we can glimpse the same hermeneutical fracture we saw in Suárez's elaboration on the oath. Suárez mainly defended his interpretation of Clement's decree as the only possible solution in order to avoid admitting a contradiction between the decree and Leo's epistle, which was part of canon law. If we grant that Clement really intended to abolish both nonverbal confession and nonverbal absolution, Suárez argued, we would have to admit that either the canon was wrong or that it contradicted the new papal decree. Another option, no less problematic than the former two, would be to argue that Leo's words really referred to nonsacramental confession, which would contradict the canons issued on the sacrament of penitence at several general councils, including the Council of Trent, and which would present a number of theologically difficult and potentially thorny questions concerning the role of the priest in absolving a sinner. In addition to defending his opinion as the only means to accommodate both Leo's and Clement's decrees, however, Suárez decided to make an argument concerning the significance and role of language in the sacrament of confession. On this note, Suárez wrote that nonverbal confession should be considered legitimate "because it is certain that even though the form of this sacrament is essentially defined by the specific words expressed by human voice, which by their very nature postulate the presence of the speaker, nevertheless the substance of the sacrament, which is the confession of sins, is not essentially defined by the specific words, indeed by any word at all, since it can be expressed by any physical sign and in any way possible; that is, even by means of an interpreter or a witness if it cannot happen in any other way."[91]

This difference between the form and the substance of the sacrament of confession, Suárez continued, was recognized also in other contexts. For instance, while ideally a penitent should offer an *integra confessio*—that is, a complete confession of her sins—in order to receive absolution, there were cases where it was impossible for this to happen because the confessor did not have enough time to hear a full confession. In those cases it was allowed for the penitent to shorten her confession and for the confessor to provide absolution.[92] Couldn't the same argument be used regarding confessions expressed nonverbally or by a third party? Given that the substance of the sacrament prescribes that the confessor absolve the penitent in person after learning of her sins and her intention of repentance, absolution in absentia would contravene the substance of the sacrament, but a nonverbal confession or a confession by a third party would not. In fact, since the point of the confession is to make the confessor aware of the penitent's sins, if the penitent has no other means of communicating the sins but nonverbally or by a third party, the confessor should still be able to use this knowledge to perform the sacrament and absolve the penitent, just as a confessor who had no other means of learning the sins but in haste and in an incomplete manner could still perform the sacrament and absolve the penitent.[93]

In other words, just as the validity of the oath depends on the speaker's intention, regardless of the verbal expression, so the sacrament of confession depends on the confessor's absolution in the presence of the penitent, which in turn depends on the confessor's awareness of the penitent's intention to repent of her sins, regardless of whether such intention is expressed in words or by a third party or by a letter or by a physical gesture. The flip side of this argument regarding the oath was that since the oath as a speech act could not guarantee the correspondence between intention and words, there was nothing in the nature of the oath as a sacrament of language that prevented the possibility of swearing without intention. As for confession, assuming that the external expression of one's intention of repenting is not substantially relevant for the validity of the sacrament can plant a seed of uncertainty in the communication between confessor and penitent. Certainly, even if one insisted that confessions should only be oral, there would still be the question of how to make sure that a penitent truly and sincerely confessed. Indeed, much of the reason why by the end of the seventeenth century even the more aggressive defenders of the confessor-doctor model ended up accepting the Inquisition's juridical model was precisely because the latter could offer a set of investigative tools that could aid the former in deciphering and exposing secret intentions, or in "opening a window into the heart."[94] Nevertheless, once we sever the link between the intention to repent and the oral expression of repentance, we open the proverbial Pandora's box: the same incommunicability we saw creeping into human language could creep also into the confessional. The confessional, however, was a special place devoted to laying one's soul open, and thus it could not become the setting for empty words and hidden intentions.

Suárez must have realized that defending his position by differentiating between inward intention and outside words was dangerous territory, this is why after the passages I just quoted he quickly added that regardless of his argument concerning the relationship between intentions and language, his general theory never supported absolution in absentia; it simply defended the legitimacy of the confession done nonverbally or by a third party only in extreme and exceptional situations. Because his position had so many limitations and thus could not be invoked save in a very limited number of cases, Suárez did not think that he deserved such a harsh punishment.[95] After this brief parenthesis, Suárez went back to more solid grounds; that is, the presumed contradiction between Clement and Leo that his position would have avoided.

To conclude, then, I argue that Suárez's reflections on the relationship between words and intentions in the sacrament of confession resonate with his more general view of the human condition, which for Suárez was characterized by a radical fracture separating words, things, and thoughts. He articulated this view fully in his elaboration on the oath, which for Suárez, far from being a tool that men have for restoring the broken link between language, thought, and reality, became instead an expression of the radical inability of language to act as a bond. Because the oath simultaneously manifests the blessing and the curse of language—that is, because the oath as sacrament of language cannot restore the broken bond connecting language, thought, and reality—the oath must become sacrament of power in order to keep these amphibious and upsetting features in check. As Agamben argued, once the oath is no longer able to guarantee that men commit to their words by its own force as sacrament of language, then the political and religious authorities need to police speech by regulating the "anthropogenic experience of the word in the oath and the curse as historical institutions, separating and opposing point by point truth and lie, true name and false name, efficacious formula and incorrect formula."[96] Suárez realized this, which is why, as he exposed the dark side of the oath as a sacrament of language, he firmed up and strengthened the authority of both Church and state to regulate oaths and to punish perjuries. As Prodi already noted, on the one hand Suárez devoted lengthy sections of his work to explaining the different sins associated with an oath performed illegitimately and the different kinds of punishment that the Church could impose for perjury in the internal forum of the conscience.[97] On the other hand, Suárez wrote equally lengthy sections in order to explain, define, and establish the power of the public authority to enforce or to dissolve oaths in the external forum. Both questions received but a cursory treatment in Soto's and other Catholic theologians' works prior to Suárez.[98] Indeed, Suárez's main polemical position against

James's Oath of Allegiance stemmed precisely from the fact that the oath of the king of England, according to Suárez, failed to respect the dual jurisdiction of the religious and the political authority in matters of oaths and instead merged the forum of the conscience and the external forum under the sole authority of the temporal sovereign.[99] Suárez's effort to police language by strengthening the authority of Church and state over the oath, I insist, originated within the irreparable fracture between men and their words that Suárez lucidly and dramatically exposed. Suárez's attempt to put this kind of band-aid over a wound that could never permanently heal, however, was just the beginning: Leonardus Lessius, Suárez's former student, completed the job.

Leonardus Lessius: Putting on the Band-aid

We have already met Leonardus Lessius through his 1640 biography, in which he appeared as a precocious student, although somewhat troubled by the fact that his teachers and fellow students of theology seemed to place too much emphasis on authority at the expense of reason. Francisco Suárez, as we remember, liberated young Lessius from his scruples. Indeed, if we were to judge from the development of Lessius's intellectual trajectory, we would have to conclude that Suárez's pep talk must have been very effective, given that Lessius, after completing his studies, would go on to become one of the enfants terribles of early modern Jesuit thought. Lessius spent most of his adult life in Louvain, a Catholic island in the middle of a complex confessional geography: most of his theological production mirrored, resonated with, and indeed was intended for the specific theological and cultural needs of the Catholic Low Countries, which often did not coincide with the needs of the Catholic hierarchy in Rome. This conflictual aspect of Lessius's theology is evident in what is probably the best-known and the most thoroughly studied among his views; that is, Lessius's position on grace and free will. Lessius's philo-Pelagianism, in fact, was radical enough to disturb the Roman leaders of the Society of Jesus, because they saw clearly the negative repercussions that Lessius's position could have on the controversy *de auxiliis*. By contrast, the Jesuit leaders in Louvain defended Lessius's strong anti-Baianism because they saw how useful it could be in the Catholic fight against the Calvinists; in Louvain the echo of the controversy *de auxiliis* was distant and feeble, while the fight against the heretics was a much more pressing and urgent matter.[100]

Grace and free will, however, were not the only doctrines in which Lessius manifested a sort of bold irreverence. Lessius systematized most of his theological views, including his view on the oath, in a treatise entitled *De iustitia et iure*, first published in Louvain in 1605 and then revised often throughout the first

half of the seventeenth century, both during Lessius's time and even after his
death (the entire section 42 of the second book of this work is devoted to the
topic of oaths). Thus, in order to get a sense of the larger theological and intellectual context in which Lessius embedded his reflections on the oath and in order
to appreciate some of the most controversial features of Lessius's production,
I think it would be worth considering briefly the reception that Lessius's treatise
enjoyed in the Catholic world by examining some of the censures written by the
intellectual leaders of the Society of Jesus, both in and outside Rome, before the
publication of the first edition.[101]

The first element we should note is that Lessius's work was judged very differently in Rome and in Lessius's own province. Virtually all the censures coming from Louvain and Antwerp praised Lessius's work for the "solid doctrine,"
the "clarity, brevity, and method," and the accuracy with which Lessius always
supported his arguments by quoting "the most learned doctors."[102] The Jesuit
father and natural philosopher François d'Aguilon, who in the early 1600s was
counselor to the rector of the Jesuit college at Antwerp (he became rector of that
college a few years later, in 1614), was assigned specifically the parts of Lessius's
work dealing with "contracts and judgments," among which Lessius's chapters
on the oath were included. His evaluation chimed with that of his Flemish colleagues: "I liked immensely the entire treatment."[103]

If we read the censures written by Jesuits based in Rome, however, we will
immediately see that the tone is very different. Because of the fact that Lessius's
treatise *De iustitia et iure* was relatively long and complex, the general of the
Society assigned its examination to a group of theologians, who were supposed
to read the treatise in batches. As was common practice with collective evalu-
ations of this kind, the group would produce a common censure. If, however,
there were discrepancies among the members of the group or if one of the members felt strongly about something that the other members did not think was
a problem, each member of the group had the opportunity to write a personal
additional censure, addressed directly to the general of the Society. This is what
happened in the case of Lessius.

The group assigned to Lessius's treatise was composed of Juan de Salas, Jean
Lorin, Cristovão Gil, and Antonio Maria Menù, and it deliberated on the book
in 1603 and 1604. In their collective judgment, the censors seemed to understand Lessius's aim of writing a treatise on moral theology that was simultaneously "eloquent, brief, and clear," but they noted that "sometimes, because of
the need to be brief especially in difficult matters, he [Lessius] does not offer a
detailed enough explanation." This was especially troublesome because "often he
follows the more liberal opinions, and moreover he frequently says that the opinions he does not follow are nevertheless probable, and yet their use in practice
should not be encouraged." Moreover, the censors added that "often he neglects

to quote supporting authors even when he asserts the most difficult opinions, those that leave the reader doubtful."[104]

To this general judgment the censors added a long list of propositions that exemplified the main problems with Lessius's work and that spanned the entire text. A couple of propositions in particular concerned the section on oaths. The first was Lessius's statement that whoever was obliged to swear by violence and therefore used equivocation or mental reservation committed neither perjury nor any other sin originating from the fraud. As we have seen, Suárez had already taken this position, not wholly uncontroversial in the Catholic world. The censors did not openly attack the content of Lessius's opinion but were disturbed by the fact that Lessius had taken such a controversial position for granted: "it is not expedient to say this [i.e., that whoever uses mental reservation commits no sin], at least without quoting supporting authors."[105] The second observation concerned the chapter in which Lessius had defended most forcefully the right and duty of political authorities to manage oaths. At the beginning of that section Lessius had argued that political authorities could by law both establish oaths and render oaths void, and as an example he mentioned a case quoted by Luis de Molina regarding the kingdom of Portugal (and, with certain limitations, also the kingdom of Castile), where "all contracts, obligations, agreements, promises, remissions, and dissolutions of contracts confirmed by oath are void, if their cognizance pertained to the secular forum, unless the oath had been sanctioned with royal privilege."[106] It is not difficult to see that the Jesuit censors must have thought that Lessius granted too much authority to the temporal sovereigns in matters of oaths. Given the intrinsically religious nature of the act of swearing, Lessius's position could have been problematic, and this is why the censors suggested that "the author [Lessius] consider how exactly Molina's quotation must be interpreted, and what contracts he [Molina] is actually talking about," since Lessius's interpretation "is not universally true."[107]

While the four Jesuit censors were unanimous in noting that Lessius often took some liberty with opinions and authors, which he used in order to support somewhat liberal and controversial positions, they disagreed about whether or not the book should be approved for publication. Menù and Salas thought that despite these problems the book should be approved; Gil "agreed with them, although with some hesitation"; Lorin refused to approve the book for publication and requested to see a corrected version before pronouncing a definitive judgment.[108]

Lorin, the most critical of the four, sent a personal letter to the general of the Society in which he wrote what he really thought about the book. Lorin knew that Lessius's fame was growing in Louvain, and thus many people were anxiously waiting for the magnum opus of such a respected author. Even though Lorin understood Lessius's impulse to publish a relatively brief work quickly in

order to capitalize on such expectations, he also knew that the more brief a treatise is, the more readable it will be, and thus he expected Lessius's work to be
a great success. All the more reason why Lessius's work should be thoroughly
checked to avoid mistakes due to haste. The chief mistake, as Lorin saw it, concerned Lessius's liberal opinions: "the common censure does not say just how
broad, in my judgment, the doctrine he seems to be supporting is. I understand,
from what I have been told, that the praise Lessius receives from merchants and
traders comes precisely from this reason, which nevertheless will grow bigger
and bigger, to the detriment of the author himself and of the Society of Jesus."[109]
Lorin knew that Lessius's fan club included not only merchants and traders but
also the Jesuits living in Louvain and Antwerp ("from Flanders we have received
no censures, only encomia," he wrote to the general), but he was also aware that
curbing Lessius's theological exuberance was better "for the sake of the common
good of the Church, of the Society and of the author himself." Lorin was French,
and thus he understood better than most the needs of the *"tramontani"*—that is,
of those living across the Alps—and yet he firmly believed that giving Lessius a
free pass was not useful for the transalpine Catholics while being detrimental for
those on the near side of the Alps.[110]

     Evidently the leadership of the Society of Jesus did not take Lorin's preoccu-
pations seriously enough, for in Lessius's printed treatise all the propositions that
the censors had explicitly suggested should be modified were left untouched.
Lorin's opinion, however, really put the finger on the main problems with
Lessius's work but also on its main contributions. Lessius's approach to moral
theology resonated with the general approach taken by all moral theologians of
the Society of Jesus, who were distinctively aware of the need to adapt moral
principles to the specific political, religious, and cultural needs of the world in
which they lived.[111] Lessius's doctrine, however, was peculiarly "liberal" and
"broad" even by Jesuit standards, as we have seen, because it was suited to a society of merchants and traders and missionaries and intellectuals who lived at the
frontiers of the Catholic world and who, while defending their own confessional
identity, could not refrain from interacting with their Protestant neighbors and
from seeking the protection of the political authority.

     How did the general elasticity I identified in Lessius's theology manifest itself
in the question of oaths? In other words, what kinds of oaths did those Flemish
merchants, traders, and Jesuits need? What kinds of oaths were needed in a society in which the links between territorial Churches and early modern states was
growing stronger and stronger under the pressures of the confessional battle and
in which, in parallel, both states and churches were strengthening their means to
control people's bodies and souls? In a nutshell, we can say that Lessius believed
that his own people needed fewer sacraments of language and more sacraments
of power, and Lessius happily obliged. To put it differently, Lessius's reflections

on the oath demonstrate that Lessius took for granted what Suárez had spent many agonizing pages discussing; that is, that there was a fracture separating language, thought, and things, which the oath as sacrament of language could not heal. Instead of beating the dead horse, so to speak, of the oath as sacrament of language, Lessius decided to articulate, strengthen, and defend the oath as sacrament of power.

We can begin to appreciate the radical character of Lessius's position just by examining the definition of the oath that Lessius used throughout his treatise. Recall that for both Soto and Suárez the oath's main end was the confirmation of truth; for Lessius "the oath is nothing other than invoking or calling the divinity as a witness in order to generate trust or to firm up pacts."[112] Thus, for Lessius the core of the oath did not reside in the truthfulness of human language, and thus the main aim of oaths was not to bind the speaker to her words; rather, the end of oaths, indeed their very raison d'être, was to be found in the effects they had insofar as they could strengthen the bond among men.

The fact that Lessius was not interested in exploring the hermeneutical aspects of the oath appears clearly throughout his text. Lessius, in fact, reasserted without much discussion the importance of the speaker's intention in originating a valid oath. He also insisted, again without much discussion, on the fact that regardless of the validity of the oath in one's conscience, even an oath pronounced without intention needed to be carried out in the external forum both in order to avoid an obvious damage to the person who received the oath and in order to avoid scandal.[113] Lessius also devoted a short section of his work to ambiguous oaths; he briefly reasserted the validity of using mental reservation and equivocation, citing Navarrus "*et alii multi*" and spending no time discussing the implications of the fracture of thought and speech that mental reservation manifested and that Suárez had already explored. Moreover, as Lorin and his colleagues had already noted in 1603/4, Lessius did not even mention any of the controversies around this position. Instead, Lessius asserted that whoever was afraid of allowing mental reservation should rest assured that regardless of what the speaker meant in the forum of the conscience, in the external forum the oath was to be taken as the hearers took it, "so as not to give cause for damage or scandal." Indeed, Lessius even enlarged the conditions under which a speaker could use mental reservation without perjury: he in fact included *utilitas* alongside *necessitas* as criteria for discerning when it is permissible to think one thing and say another thing.[114]

Thus, for Lessius the oath ceased to be the sacrament of language, and as such its function had nothing to do with ensuring the correspondence of language, thought, and reality, since such correspondence could not be ensured by any linguistic means, so to speak, and indeed anybody could take advantage of this fracture whenever it appeared "useful" and not just "necessary." In parallel, indeed precisely because the oath ceased to be the sacrament of language, Lessius saw that the oath could and should become first and foremost the sacrament of power, by which pacts and contracts are regulated by the public authority. This is why Lessius was less interested in exploring the hermeneutical consequences of the weakness of the oath as sacrament of language, which by contrast Soto and especially Suárez explored at length and at times in dramatic terms, than in exploring the mechanisms by which the oath as sacrament of power could be strengthened, implemented, and regulated. Or to put it differently, once Suárez exposed the fracture between speech and thought and once he asserted the oath's fundamental incapability of mending it, Lessius, far from attempting to find a cure, focused instead on applying some band-aids, so that the oath could become a fully functional sacrament of power.

We can see clearly just how much attention Lessius paid to the function of the oath as the sacrament of power from the long chapter he devoted to the authority in charge of invalidating oaths, which is the *Dubitatio XII*. This section is not only the most ample and original treatment of this question in post-Reformation Catholic theology,[115] but it is also the one chapter Lessius revised the most in the following editions of his work. In order to appreciate the substance and significance of Lessius's revisions, let us briefly compare the text of the *Dubitatio XII* as it appeared in the first edition of *De iustitia et iure* (Louvain 1605) and the same text as it appeared in the Lyon 1622 edition, which was the last one to be printed in Lessius's lifetime (Lessius died in 1623). This *Dubitatio* started with the passage that the Roman censors had already noted in 1603/4, in which Lessius stated that the political authority had full authority to void oaths, as happened in Portugal and Castile. Lessius then continued: "but there is a difficulty here, namely how can a human authority void the oath, given that the obligation arises from the oath naturally and necessarily, since by the law of nature we must avoid making God witness of a falsehood?"[116]

In the 1605 version of this chapter, Lessius replied that there were two ways of voiding an oath: the first was to render the person to whom the oath was sworn "unable to accept it," and the second was to remove the obligation arising from the oath. As to the first, Lessius remarked that it since it was possible for the *lex civilis* to declare that a person was unfit to occupy public offices or to buy and sell goods, by the same token it should also be possible for the civil law to declare a person unable to accept an oath.[117] As Lessius revised this section, he thought that framing the question of the authority to render oaths void in this way was not strong enough. In fact, in the Lyon 1622 edition he specified that "this method of voiding oaths is not sufficient," because there could have been many gray areas and exceptions. As an example, Lessius mentioned the case of a minor who swore to alienate property that he could not legitimately dispose of without a judge's permission. Even though civil law would make the minor's act invalid, nevertheless the minor's oath might be considered valid and legally binding, which could also happen when the minor was approaching the age of puberty.[118]

Definitely more solid was the second ground for voiding an oath; that is, when the obligation arising from the oath was condoned, remitted, or annulled. In the Louvain 1605 edition Lessius wrote that there were five ways in which the obligation could be removed. The first concerned the "changing of the matter" of the oath; that is, "when the thing that has been sworn becomes impossible for the speaker to perform, or illicit, whenever a superior authority prevents it." In the Lyon 1622 edition Lessius added the following phrase after this one: "and this is the manner which the secular authority can use."[119] The second method is by "condonation"; that is, whenever the receiver of the oath gives up her right to obtain whatever was promised. In the Louvain 1605 edition Lessius justified this method in the following way: "whoever makes a vow or an oath does not mean to commit himself except with the tacit condition 'if the person for the sake of whom I am doing this is willing to accept it.'" In the Lyon 1622 edition, after explaining his justification, he added: "and the civil authority can use this same method, if there is a just cause."[120] Thirdly, an oath can be rendered invalid by "commutation"; that is, whenever the receiver of the oath accepts receipt of something different from what the speaker originally swore. Since the oath is a promise sworn to men and confirmed by God, men can always release the promise in the external forum, but only the ecclesiastical authority can settle things with God in the forum of the conscience, because only the ecclesiastical authority can, on behalf of God, consider the commutation valid.[121] Fourthly, an oath can be considered invalid because of *irritatio*; that is, whenever the matter of the oath falls under the jurisdiction of a superior authority. Since the superior authority has the final word on whatever the matter of the oath is, it follows that the same superior authority, whether lay or ecclesiastical and whether public or private, has also the authority to annul the oath.[122]

In general, then, Lessius seemed less interested in discussing the origin and nature of oaths than in exploring the authority that ecclesiastical and political leaders have to regulate them. Moreover, as we can see from the changes Lessius made between the 1605 and the 1622 editions, he consistently sought to reinforce the capability of the political authority, not just of the religious authority, to void oaths; as Lessius specified several times in the Lyon 1622 edition, both political and ecclesiastical authority could void oaths in different ways, and the difference between those two authorities was the forum in which each authority was competent (the ecclesiastical was in charge of the forum of conscience, and the political was in charge of the external forum). It is easy to see how these developments might indeed please merchants and traders, who could count on a firm authority in charge of managing the external effects of oaths and as such able to regulate and protect the validity of pacts and contracts firmed up by oaths. It is also easy to see how some of these developments, generally speaking, might please the Roman Curia, since they contributed to strengthening the supreme authority of the pope and the Church for regulating and protecting the validity of the oaths in the forum of the conscience.

Lessius was aware of the importance of enclosing the oath as the sacrament of power between the political authority working outside the conscience and the religious authority working inside the conscience. In fact, he clarified this point in a more articulated manner in his discussion on the fifth method of voiding an oath; that is, by dispensation or absolution. In the Louvain 1605 edition Lessius explained that such a method of voiding oaths "happens by authority of the superior" (Lessius strengthened his point in the Lyon 1622 edition, where he wrote that such method "happens by authority of the superior *only*").[123] But— this is really the core issue—by what authority can the superior dispese from the obligation, since the obligation of the oath is also to God?

In the Louvain 1605 edition Lessius wrote that in certain cases an inferior can perform some functions on behalf of the superior, and thus since the pope and, in certain cases, even the bishops can perform functions on behalf of God, then the Pope and the bishops can dispense from oaths in the forum of the con-science.[124] In other cases, Lessius continued, the obligation arising from oaths can be erased as a form of punishment, such as the cases of oaths "by which subjects are bound to their prince or to another superior," which can be elimi-nated "whenever the prince is deprived of his authority or office by the supreme Pontiff or by some other superior."[125] Finally, the obligation of the oath can be nullified "by reason of the common good," whenever a speaker swears to do or say something that, for the sake of the common good, should not be done or said. The pope can make use of this method "and even the secular prince, since the ground of his office requires the capability of removing obligations that might hinder good government."[126] In conclusion, Lessius wrote, the absolution concerning the obligations arising from the oath in conscience "concerns only the ecclesiastical forum," whereas "whenever the question clearly concerns the unlawful or unjust status of the person who receives the oath or whenever an oath is clearly detrimental to the public good, the secular prince and sometimes even an inferior judge can not only oblige the receiver of the oath to condone the promise, but he can also remit and annul it by his own authority, which by itself is not spiritual, but is generally founded on the power to govern. Without such power, civil government would be imperfect and lame and unable to avoid many troublesome occurrences."[127]

As Lessius revised this section, he must have found that his approach might open up a few problems. As we have seen, in his 1605 discussion Lessius argued that secular princes had the power to invalidate oaths in certain cases and for certain reasons, while the pope and the bishops had the power to invalidate oaths in other cases and for other reasons. Both the prince's and the pope's authorities, however, came from the same root—that is, they were both supreme rulers of a government—and in order to rule their respective governments they needed to exercise, among other faculties, that of being able to absolve their subjects and the faithful from the obligations arising from oaths. Now, if Lessius wanted to firmly attach the power of regulating oaths to the secular and religious authorities in their respective and distinctive fora, he needed to address more clearly the question of the origin and specificity of their respective authorities insofar as oaths were concerned. This is why in the 1622 edition Lessius decided to explain the question of absolution in a different manner: instead of the 1605 discussion of the different cases in which either the secular or the religious authority could and should invalidate an oath, in the 1622 edition we find a more detailed analysis of the kind of authority required to invalidate oaths.

Lessius started this new version by asserting that the kind of authority that secular princes enjoyed was qualitatively different from the kind of authority that the pope and, in some cases, bishops enjoyed: "the obligation of the oath can be removed in two ways, namely indirectly and directly. It is removed indirectly whenever the promise or its execution is condoned, and in that case as a consequence the obligation of the oath disappears [as soon as the promise and execution are condoned]. It is removed directly when the very obligation arising from the oath to execute a promise is condoned."[128] In other words, a superior authority can void either the actual obligation originated by the oath or the execution of the promise that is a consequence of the actual obligation. The end result is similar in both cases—the person who swore to do something would not be bound to do it—but the grounds for absolving and, consequently, the kind of authority required in order to absolve is different in the two cases. Thus, Lessius continued, since Christ as the supreme Lord of all can absolve directly anybody from any oath, then "the supreme Pontiff, as Christ's Vicar and superior of all Christians, can immediately remove and condone all obligations originated by a promissory oath toward anybody, whenever there is a just reason."[129] The political authority, Lessius continued, could still absolve someone from the obligations arising from an oath for the sake of the common good, which was the same argument he used in the 1605 edition. This time, however, Lessius decided to add a specification: those cases are not properly dispensations from the oath but rather dispensations from the obligation to fulfill the sworn promise. For instance, a man to whom a promise was sworn could condone the man who swore and absolve him from the duty of fulfilling his promise, "but this is not a dispensation, and it is not a spiritual act, but a simple [*nuda*] condonation." The same happened in the case of a moneylender who lent money "without permission from the prince" and who had been promised the money back with an oath. If a judge, wanting to punish the moneylender for conducting his business unlawfully, declared the oath void, he would not properly dispense from the oath but simply condone the debt and thus the promise. Therefore, while the political authority can void oaths by a form of indirect dispensation or "simple condonation," a direct dispensation only occurs "whenever the ecclesiastical leader or another clergyman who received authority from him condones the obligation and dissolves the bond originated by the oath in his capacity of vicar of God and on behalf of God. Hence it is clear that only the ecclesiastical authority can properly dispense from oaths."[130]

With these modifications, which are consistent with many other additional modifications that Lessius made and that I have no time to examine in detail now, Lessius assigned more and more firmly the jurisdiction over the oath as an act of conscience to the Church: insofar as the oath as an act of conscience was properly annulled only if the obligation, not simply the promise, was condoned, only the ecclesiastical authority could properly dispense from oaths. In parallel, however, Lessius also assigned more and more firmly the jurisdiction over the oath as a means to firm up pacts to the secular authority: insofar as the oath confirmed a promise and thus was invoked precisely *ad fidem faciendam vel promissionem firmandam*, the public authority in charge of fostering trust and confirming promises could regulate, oversee, annul, or enforce the external effects of the oath. In sum, we can say that Lessius really buried the oath as the sacrament of language, which had died from the fracture that Suárez opened up among thoughts, words, and things. Lessius also christened the oath as the sacrament of power, which he fortified by giving it the double crutch of Church and state.

While everybody in the Roman Curia was pleased with Lessius's attempt to reinforce the Church as the ultimate authority in charge of oaths in the forum of the conscience, somebody must have felt uneasy with Lessius's attempt to strengthen, in parallel, the authority of the secular authority to oversee oaths in the external forum. We have evidence of this in the comments the censors made in 1603/4, but this was not the only instance in which this issue was brought up in Rome. In 1624 the Congregation of the Index met to examine Lessius's 1622 Lyon edition, prompted by the attacks against Lessius's opinion on equivocation and mental reservation launched by the English Benedictine John Barnes. At that meeting, the Congregation once again noted the problem: the censors, together with suggesting the removal of the world *utilitas* on the question of equivocation and mental reservation, ordered Lessius "to remove from his work the parts where he argued that temporal princes can absolve [their subjects] from oaths," which were the parts that, as we saw, Lessius had added to the 1605 edition precisely in order to strengthen the authority of the temporal sovereigns.[131]

The demise of the oath as sacrament of language, however, was now definitive, because the fracture separating words, things, and thoughts could not be mended. In parallel, the process of firming up the oath as sacrament of power could not be stopped, because the growth of the hegemonic power of the centralized states could not be resisted. Thus, just as in the case of *utilitas*, even in the case of the princes' power to absolve subjects from oaths the requests of the censors fell on deaf ears. In 1626 a reprint, virtually identical, of the 1622 Lyon edition was made in Antwerp. Lessius's *De iustitia et iure* was also reprinted in Lyon in 1653 (this was the edition with Raynaud's *Splendor veritatis* as an appendix), and even in that last edition the *Dubitatio XII* is identical to the 1622 version.[132]

At the beginning of his book Paolo Prodi stated that he was prompted to study the history of oaths because he realized that "today we not only face a crisis involving the institutional and constitutional mechanism of politics. . . but also a crisis involving the very being of man as political animal, a crisis that puts in jeopardy not only the rule of law and liberal democracy, but also the entire development of the Western political system." Our generation, Prodi continued, is the first to "live its collective life without the oath as a solemn, absolute, and sacred bond sanctioning our being part of a political body." The disappearance of the sacred bond of the oath linking men to their political body, according to Prodi, has led to new forms of political organizations, whose contours and mechanisms are still unfolding and, to an extent, difficult to define.[133] To these considerations Agamben replied that we are indeed experiencing a modification in the significance and value of oaths but that the risk inherent in this development is not simply and not primarily of a political nature but indeed of a linguistic, hermeneutical, and epistemological one. As Agamben put it, "humanity finds itself today before a disjunction or, at least, a loosening of the bond that, by means of the oath, united the living being to its language." This fracture, according to Agamben, has crucial ethical and existential implications: "when the ethical—and not simply cognitive—connection that unites words, things, and human action is broken, this in fact promotes a spectacular and unprecedented proliferation of vain words on the one hand and, on the other, of legislative apparatuses that seek obstinately to legislate on every aspect of that life on which they seem no longer to have any hold."[134]

I am writing this chapter as I prepare to take an oath myself, the oath of allegiance to the United States of America, which is one of the requirements the American government imposes on all who want to become American citizens and which I must swear to take "freely without any mental reservation." While in this instance the government of the United States still holds on to the oath as to a form of quasi-sacred political bond, there are other contexts in which that very same government seems to embody the vanity of oaths in contemporary society. As an example, one need only recall the political debates concerning the impeachment of former president Clinton, which are a clear evidence of the loss of the sacrality of perjury. Thus I am peculiarly aware of and preoccupied with both developments identified by Prodi and Agamben because I am choosing to subject myself to a legislative apparatus that regulates the words and, consequently, the life of its citizens insofar as they are part of a political system but that does not and cannot entirely protect them from the proliferation of vain words. Or to put it differently, I am experiencing directly both the blessing of language, that is, the extraordinary power that words assume when they mean something, and the curse of speech, that is, the extraordinary danger that humans incur when they are disconnected from their words.

As I hope I have shown in this chapter, both the erosion of the oath as the sacrament of language and the development of the oath as the sacrament of power started in the early modern world. Indeed, as I hope I have shown throughout this entire book, the fragility of the relationship between truth and language that characterizes our current intellectual and cultural horizon originated in the early modern world. All the case studies I examined in this book are evidence of the embryonic cracks that started to appear in the system linking language, truth, and Truth. The thinkers I analyzed began to perceive these cracks and reflected on their significance and implications in their respective intellectual, cultural, and social contexts. I find their arguments incredibly interesting precisely because they open a window into an aspect of post-Reformation Catholic culture that we are not accustomed to take into account, which is why I decided to write about them. But what I find especially noteworthy and, indeed, personally moving is that despite the difference in social and cultural milieu, none of the thinkers I analyzed, from Mascardi to Beni to Navarrus to Suárez, tried to obliterate the shadows of doubt they perceived by resorting to either a form of extreme hermeneutical and theological dogmatism or a form of skepticism. Rather, they all tried to grapple with, rather than erase, the tension between the fallibility of language and the necessity to believe, as Suárez put it. We live in a world full of words, which can simultaneously mirror, describe, express, and create reality and which can be simultaneously devoid of meaning and charged with a surplus of meaning. As we also try to grapple with the dangers, limitations, and potentialities of our current world, dominated as it is by language in its various incarnations, I believe we can find much insight if we turn our attention to the early modern world: to look back to early modernity, in this respect, means to look back to the future.

NOTES

Introduction

1. The papers presented at that conference were later published in Saul Friedlander, ed., *Probing the limits of representation. Nazism and the "Final Solution,"* Cambridge, MA: Harvard University Press, 1992.

2. See Michel de Certeau, "The Black Sun of Language: Foucault," English trans. in *Heterologies: Discourse on the Other*, Minneapolis: University of Minnesota Press, 1986, pp. 171–184, at 183, and id., "Micro-techniques and Panoptic discourse: a Quid pro Quo," English transl. in ibid., pp. 185–192, at 189. On the significance of this image in the context of the relationship between narrative and reality in historiography, see also Roger Chartier, *On the Edge of the Cliff*, English trans., Baltimore: Johns Hopkins University Press, 1997.

3. Elizabeth A. Clark, *History, Theory, Text: Historians and the Linguistic Turn*, Cambridge, MA: Harvard University Press, 2004; Constantin Fasolt, *The Limits of History*, Chicago: University of Chicago Press, 2003; Gabrielle M. Spiegel, *Romancing the Past: The Rise of Vernacular Prose Historiography in Thirteenth-Century France*, Berkeley: University of California Press, 1995, and *The Past as Text: The Theory and Practice of Medieval Historiography*, Baltimore: Johns Hopkins University Press, 1999; Susan E. Schreiner, *Are you Alone Wise? The Search for Certainty in the Early modern Era*, Oxford: Oxford University Press, 2011.

4. John Lewis Gaddis, *The Landscape of History. How historians map the past*, Oxford: Oxford University Press, 2002, quot. at 139, but see his entire ch. 8. On the historical development of the conceptualization of the past, see also Reinhart Koselleck, *Futures Past: On the Semantics of Historical Time*, English trans., Cambridge, MA: MIT Press, 1985; Donald J. Wilcox, *The Measure of Times Past. Pre-Newtonian Chronologies and the Rhetoric of Time*, Chicago: University of Chicago Press, 1987; and Zachary Sayre Schiffman, *The Birth of the Past*, Baltimore: Johns Hopkins University Press, 2011.

5. For a thought-provoking reflection on the category of distance in historical thought see Mark Salber Phillips, *On Historical Distance*, New Haven, CT: Yale University Press 2013.

6. Jean-François Lyotard, *The Postmodern Condition: A Report on Knowledge*, English trans., Minneapolis: University of Minnesota Press, 1974, p. 79.

7. *The Historian's Craft*, English trans., Manchester: Manchester University Press, 1992, p. 53.

8. Sigonio's quotation comes from a letter written by Sigonio to his fellow historian Onofrio Panvinio, November 26, 1558, in Sigonio's *Opera omnia*, Milan, 1732–1737, vol. 6, cols. 1001–1002 at 1002.

9. Caroline Bynum, "Why all the fuss about the body? A medievalist's perspective," in Victoria E. Bonnell and Lynn Hunt, eds., *Beyond the cultural turn*, Berkeley: University of California Press, 1999, pp. 241–280, at 265.

10. *Judgments on History and Historians*, English trans. by Harry Zohn, Indianapolis: Liberty Fund 1999, p. 168.

11. I have explored some of those tensions in *Empire of Souls. Bellarmine and the Christian commonwealth*, Oxford: Oxford University Press, 2010.
12. On this point see, e.g., Carlo Ginzburg, "Alien Voices: the Dialogic Element in Early Modern Jesuit Historiography," in id., *History, Rhetoric, and Proof*, Hanover NH: University Press of New England, 1999, pp. 71–91; id., "The European Discover (or Rediscover) the Shamans," in *Threads and Traces. True, False, Fictive*, trans. by Anne C. Tedeschi and John Tedeschi, Berkeley: University of California Press, 2011, pp. 83–95; Peter Burke, "The Jesuits and the art of translation in early modern Europe," in John W. O'Malley, ed., *The Jesuits: cultures, sciences, and the arts, 1540–1773*, vol. II, Toronto: University of Toronto Press, 2006, pp. 24–32; Ronnie Po-chia Hsia, "The Catholic mission and translations in China, 1583–1700," in Peter Burke and Ronnie Po-chia Hsia, eds., *Cultural Translation in early modern Europe*, Cambridge: Cambridge University Press, 2007, pp. 39–51. On the cultural significance of translations in general, together with the above-mentioned collection of essays, see also Peter Burke, *Languages and Communities in early modern Europe*, Cambridge: Cambridge University Press, 2004.
13. F. Fernández-Armesto, *Truth: A History and a Guide for the Perplexed*, New York: St Martin's Press, 2001, pp. 163–164.
14. Important exceptions to this traditional view are Anthony Grafton, *What was History? The Art of History in Early Modern Europe*, Cambridge: Cambridge University Press, 2007; and Carlo Ginzburg, "Description and citation," in *Threads and Traces*, pp. 7–24.
15. *The Sacrament of Language: An Archaeology of the Oath*, English trans. by Adam Kotsko, Stanford, CA: Stanford University Press, 2011.
16. *Il Sacramento del Potere: Il Giuramento Politico nella Storia Costituzionale dell'Occidente*, Bologna: Il Mulino, 1992.

Chapter 1

1. For insightful and accurate accounts of the role of the Jesuits in the development of the doctrine of equivocation, see Perez Zagorin, *Ways of Lying. Dissimulation, Persecution and Conformity in Early Modern Europe*, Cambridge, MA: Harvard University Press, 1990, pp. 153–185; Johann P. Sommerville, "The 'new art of lying': Equivocation, mental reservation, and casuistry," in *Conscience and Casuistry in Early Modern Europe*, ed. Edmund Leites, Cambridge: Cambridge University Press, 2002, pp. 159–184; Harro Höpfl, *Jesuit political thought. The Society of Jesus and the State, c.1540–1630*, Cambridge: Cambridge University Press, 2004, pp. 142–145.
2. See, e.g., Pascal's ninth provincial letter, in which Pascal's criticism of equivocation is embedded into a larger criticism of probabilism and casuistry (*Lettres écrites à un provincial*, Lettre IX, July 3, 1656, and *Litterae Provinciales*, Cologne, 1658, pp. 202–216).
3. Both Zagorin and Sommerville understand equivocation and mental reservation as parts of moral theology and a spin-off, so to speak, of the early modern development of casuistry. Even more explicitly "moral" is the reading of equivocation offered by Albert R. Jonsen and Stephen Toulmin, *The abuse of casuistry. A history of moral reasoning*. Berkeley: University of California Press, 1988, esp. pp. 195–215.
4. The literature on Augustine's views regarding lying is quite extensive. I found particularly useful Paul J. Griffiths, *Lying. An Augustinian theology of duplicity*, Grand Rapids, MI: Brazos Press, 2004, pp. 25–39; Thomas D. Feehan, "Augustine on lying and deception," *Augustinian Studies* 19 (1988), pp. 131–139; Alan Brinton, "St. Augustine and the problem of deception in religious persuasion," *Religious Studies* 19 (1983), pp. 437–450.
5. On the distinction between truth and truthfulness in this context, see esp. Sissela Bok, *Lying. Moral choice in public and private life*, New York: Vintage, 1978, esp. pp. 5–31.
6. Griffiths, *Lying*, pp. 73–100 (quot. at 89).
7. Ibid., p. 85.
8. See Hans-Georg Gadamer, *Truth and Method*, London: Continuum, 2006, pp. 418–426.
9. On language as coming to an understanding, see ibid., pp. 442–452.
10. See, in particular, *IIa IIae, quaestio* 110.
11. See ibid., *quaestio* 33, articles 7 and 8.

12. On the juridical and theological importance of the question of the *correctio fraterna* in mid-sixteenth century Spain, see Stefania Pastore, "A proposito di *Matteo 18,15*. *Correctio fraterna* e Inquisitione nella Spagna del Cinquecento," *Rivista Storica Italiana*, 113 (2001), pp. 323–368, esp. 332–341 on Carranza. On Carranza's trial, see also José Ignacio Tellechea Idígoras, *El Arzobispo Carranza y su tiempo*, 2 vols., Madrid: Ediciones Guadarrama, 1968, and, more recently, id., *El Arzobispo Carranza: "Tiempos Recios,"* 4 vols., Salamanca: Universidad Pontificia de Salamanca, 2003-2007. On the exegesis of the evangelical precept expressed in Matthew 18:15, see also Piero Bellini, *"Denunciatio evangelica" e "Denunciatio iudicialis." Un capitolo di storia disciplinare della Chiesa*, Milan: Giuffrè, 1986.

13. For an overview of the treatment of the question of equivocation in the procedures of the medieval Inquisition, see Jean-Pierre Cavaillé, "L'art des équivoques: hérésie, inquisition et casuistique. Questions sur la transmission d'une doctrine médiévale à l'époque moderne," *Médiévales* 43 (2002), pp. 119–146.

14. On the tension between "correction" and "infamy" in the theological and juridical debate in sixteenth-century Catholicism, see Vincenzo Lavenia, *L'infamia e il perdono. Tributi, pene e confessione nella teologia morale della prima età moderna*, Bologna: Il Mulino, 2004.

15. For an overview of the Spanish theological debate over the *correctio fraterna*, see Stefania Pastore, *Il Vangelo e la Spada. L'inquisizione di Castiglia e i suoi critici*, Rome: Edizioni di Storia e Letteratura, 2003, esp. pp. 213–253 (222–224 on Soto). On the significance of Soto's treatise for the definition of inquisitorial proceeding, see also Jean-Pierre Dedieu, *L'administration de la foi. L'Inquisition en Tolède XVIe–XVIIIe siècle*, Madrid: Casa de Velázquez, 1989, pp. 111ff.

16. Domingo de Soto, *De ratione tegendi et detegendi secretum*, Salamanca, 1541, esp. pp. LXXVIr–LXXXVr.

17. Ad tegendum secretum confessionis licitum est ubique sacerdoti, dum ea interrogatur quae in confessione novit, respondere se nescire, nec alia opus habet verborum arte: quia id potest in tali casu citra mendacium respondere. Ibid., p. LXXVIIv.

18. Nam sacerdos ea quae audivit in sacramento, quanquam noverit ut particularis persona, novit tamen ea in foro & iudicio Dei: quod quidem Deus voluit esse adeo occultum, ut peccata illic confessa habeantur omnino pro oblitis: acsi non fuissent. . . Quare sacerdos, quemadmodum Deus, dicens 'Ego te absolvo,' promittit habere peccata acsi nunquam audivisset: atque adeo in foro exteriori citra mendacium potest dicere se illa nescire. Et hic est sensus illorum verborum: 'sacerdos scit ut Deus,' idest scit tanquam minister Dei & ad modum eius. Ibid, pp. LXXVIIIv-LXXIXr.

19. Scire, quamvis vulgari sermone dicatur etiam illud quod idoneis testibus credimus, tamen proprie id solum sciri dicimus, quod mentis firma ratione comprehendimus (verba sunt Augustini 1 Retrac., cap.14 [3]) & tamen quod aliorum relatione novimus, profecto non certo cognoscimus: quia, cum sit omnis homo mendax, potuit qui retulit mentiri, quare proprie non dicimur illud scire, sicut loquitur Aristoteles de scientia 1 Post. [see Aristotle's *Posterior Analytics,* 1.1-2, and Aquinas's commentary on it, especially lecture 4]. Nam scientia est certa & evidens cognitio veritatis. Ibid, p. LXXIXr.

20. Si qui interrogatur solum id noverit ex aliorum relatione, ambigi non potest quin possit simpliciter respondere se nescire.... Immo non solum si iniuste, sed dum iure & ratione interrogatur, nullam iniuriam facit qui respondet se nescire quod aliorum relatu novit. Ibid., p. LXXXr.

21. Nam citra necessitatem non licet uti huiusmodi amphibologiis: non quod essent mendacia, sed quod hominum convictus & societas id exposcat, ut homines usitatioribus atque perspicacioribus verbis in seriis utantur: ne se fallant. Ibid., p. LXXXVr.

22. Quid si improbissimus homo interrogaret testem: 'dic mihi quicquid scis de hac re, quantumcunque secretum sit, nec possit iure revelari'? Videtur enim tunc responderi non posse: 'nescio' . . . Re vera orte tunc responsio illa, 'nescio,' non careret mendacio. Ibid., pp. LXXXIv–LXXXIIr.

23. Reo, cum iniuste interrogatur de proprio, sed secreto, crimine, nec prodest respondere se nescire, nec licet negare verum crimen, dicendo: 'non feci'. . . . nam ridicula esset responsio, si homo diceret se nescire, dum interrogatur de proprio opere. Ibid., p. LXXXIIIr.

24. Sed instas adhuc pressius, quid faciet miser homo qui mortem comminante tyranno nisi verum fateatur, non habet qua se amphibologia protegat? Aut adultera: quam maritus nudo

gladio petit fateri adulterium, ut iuret an adulterium fecerit? Respondetur quod plures sunt homines, nequitiae, & violentiae, quam ut possit omnibus obviam iri. Ob idque in tali casu mori opus est: quemadmodum si tyrannus mihi comminaretur mortem nisi peierarem aut levissime mentirer, mortem prius deberem oppetere, quam mentiri. Ibid., p. LXXXIVv.

25. Gadamer, *Truth and method*, pp. 359–363, quot. at 361.

26. The first edition of *De iustitia et iure* was published in Salamanca in 1553. Soto enlarged and modified the text in a second edition, which appeared in Salamanca in 1556 and was reprinted several times in the course of the sixteenth century. I am quoting from the reprint of the second edition which was published in Lyon in 1569.

27. Soto, *De iustitia et iure*, p. 163v.

28. Enimvero cum voces sint conceptuum signa, oratio illa 'nescio' recipere hunc sensum citra mendacium potest: 'Nescio ut tibi modo dicam.' Quare non adversatur alteri veritati, scio simpliciter: etiam si propriis oculis id de quo interrogatur vidisset. Nam si tantum auditu illud teneret, dubium non est, quin posset respondere se nescire. Quandoquidem quod credimus, non proprie scimus. Ibid.

29. Facere enim non habet eandem connexionem cum eo quod est, ut dicam, quam habet scire. Ibid.

30. Quare nec adulterae a marito nudo gladio interrogatae, an amicum admiserit, dicere fas est non admisisse si id modum factum est. Neque posset a mendacio excusari si cum eum admisisset... absolute respondisset non admisisse, intelligens heri: nam illa negatio universalis est. Quid ergo remedii est? profecto nullum... sed miseris necesse est mortem, veluti martyres perpeti, antequam ius naturale & divinum mentiendo transgrediantur. Quod enim remedium excogitare potest misera puella, cum mortem tyrannus ei minatur, nisi secum turpiter consentiat? profecto nullum: sed gladio potius succumbendi illi est. Ibid.

31. Cf. Navarrus, *Commentarius in cap. Humanae Aures*. In *Commentaria*, 3 vols., vol. I, Venice 1588, pp. 218v–224r, at 220r.

32. See P. Zagorin, *Ways of Lying*, pp. 165–166, and esp. Lavenia, *L'infamia e il perdono*, pp. 219–264.

33. On this episode, see S. Pastore, "A proposito di *Matteo*," pp. 352–363; and Antonio Astrain, *Historia de la Compañia de Jesús en la asistencia de España*, 7 vols., Madrid: Razón y Fe, 1912–1925, vol. III, pp. 368–410. On the legal, religious, and cultural implications of the crime of *sollicitatio ad turpia* in early modern Spanish Catholicism, see Stephen Haliczer, *Sexuality in the Confessional. A Sacrament Profaned*, Oxford: Oxford University Press, 1999.

34. On the relationship between inquisitors and confessors in post-Tridentine Catholicism, see Adriano Prosperi, *Tribunali della coscienza*, Turin: Einaudi, 1996, pp. 226–289 passim.

35. On the circumstances of composition of Navarrus's commentary on the canon *Humanae Aures*, see Eloy Tejero, "El Doctor Navarro en la historia de la doctrina canónica y moral," in *Estudios sobre el Doctor Navarro en el IV centenario de la muerte de Martín de Azpilcueta*, Pamplona: EUNSA, 1988, pp. 125–180, esp. 153–154.

36. An excellent summary of the entire commentary can be found in Zagorin, *Ways of Lying*, pp. 168–175.

37. Una & eadem ratio potest componi ex diversis partibus, quarum aliae sint expresse vocales vel scriptae, & aliae tacitae & mentales: & quod ipsa tota sit vera, & partes eius separatae sint falsae & haereticae. Navarrus, *Humanae Aures*, p. 219r.

38. See Ludwig Wittgenstein, *Philosophical Investigations*, trans. G. E. M. Anscombe. Upper Saddle River, NJ: Prentice Hall, 1958, I 249, II xi.

39. Quod autem iudex male faceret, si intenderet, ut N. simpliciter responderet, probatur eo quod intendebat munire & parare viam ad ferendam sententiam iniustam, videlicet quod erat matrimonium inter illos contractum, quod erat falsum: quoniam confitenti ei se illa verba dixisse creditum fuisset: non autem si addidisset animum contrahendi sibi defuisse: quoniam confitenti se aliquid fecisse ad sui defensionem creditur quidem ei fecisse illud; sed non creditur quod fecisset ad defensionem...& ideo non tenebatur ei respondere ita, ut volebat, sed ut velle debebat, & huic rectae voluntati satisfacit respondendo se illa non dixisse, subintelligendo animo contrahendi matrimonium: & ita non peieravit. Navarrus, *Humanae Aures*, p. 221r.

40. Secundum remedium est. . . credere ipsi iuranti, si videtur verisimile viris sapientibus, prudentibus, & moribus egregie probatis, quod iuste credi possit ex circumstantiis personarum, temporum, & locorum, puta quia statim post illa verba prolata, vel paulo postea contraxit cum alia palam & publice, vel quod tanto intervallo esset nobilior, potentior, vel ditior ipsa, quod eis videtur verisimile eum verbis fictis contraxisse. Ibid., p. 223r.
41. See Wittgenstein, *Philosophical Investigations*, II xi.
42. For Gadamer's notion of play within his theory of interpretation, see *Truth and Method*, pp. 102–130.
43. In stressing the multiplicity and complexity of language-games, I am following Jean-François Lyotard's interpretation of Wittgenstein: see, e.g., Jean-François Lyotard, "Wittgenstein 'After,'" in *Political writings*, trans. Bill Readings and Kevin P. Geiman, Minneapolis: University of Minnesota Press, 1993, pp. 19–22, and id., *The Postmodern Condition*, pp. 9–11, 40–41.
44. On the question of motive in Wittgenstein's interpretation of lying, see Dale Jacquette, "Wittgenstein on lying as a language-game," in Danièle Moyal-Sharrock, ed., *The Third Wittgenstein. The post-"Investigations" works*, Farnham: Ashgate, 2004, pp. 159–176.
45. Navarrus, *Humanae Aures*, pp. 223v–224r; and Zagorin, *Ways of Lying*, pp. 173–175.
46. Zagorin, *Ways of Lying*, p. 175.
47. On the multiform uses and cultural significances of dissimulation in early modern Europe, see, in addition to the already quoted works by Zagorin and Sommerville, Carlo Ginzburg, *Il Nicodemismo: simulazione e dissimulazione religiosa nell'Europa del '500*, Turin: Einaudi, 1970; Jean-Pierre Cavaillé, *Dis/simulations. Jules-César Vanini, François La Mothe Le Vayer, Gabriel Naudé, Louis Machon et Torquato Accetto. Religion, morale et politique au XVIIe siècle*, Paris: Champion, 2002; Jon R. Snyder, *Dissimulation and the Culture of Secrecy in early modern Europe*, Berkeley: University of California Press, 2009.
48. On these authors and on some more early modern Catholic theologians who rejected Navarrus's theory, see Sommerville, "The 'new art of lying,'" pp. 170–173.
49. Gregory of Valencia, *Commentariorum Theologicorum*, 4 vols, Ingolstadt, 1591–7, vol. III (Ingolstadt, 1595), Disputatio V, Quaest. XIII de Reo, Punctum II, cols. 1397–1404.
50. In tali casu cum quis scilicet *inique* interrogatur, non minus licet alicui usurpare verba ad significandum sensum, quem vult, quam si a nullo prorsus de aliqua re determinata interrogaretur. . . Unde. . . nego id esse mendacium, sed solum est, *non dicere* unam determinatam veritatem, sed aliam disparatam, cum ad dicendam certam illam & determinatam, quam alius perperam interrogat quis non tenetur. Ibid., col. 1403. Emphasis in the original.
51. Nego sequi inde ulla incommoda in conversatione communi. Nam quamvis verba usurpare ad aliquem sensum alienum significandum in conversatione communi, non esse mendacium proprie contra *negativum* praeceptum; esset tamen peccatum *omissionis* contra praeceptum *affirmativum* illius virtutis, *Veritatis*. Ibid., col. 1404. Emphasis in the original.
52. In aliqua propositione possunt intelligi & suppleri aliquae particulae ex circunstantia loci & temporis & personarum. . . in casu posito omnes illae particulae intelliguntur ex circunstantia personarum, ergo vera est illa propositio, ergo non feci. Domingo Bañez, *Decisiones de iure & iustitia*, Venice, 1595, Quaestio LXIX, de rei accusati iniustitia, pp. 284–292 (quot. at 290–291).
53. In Austin's terms, one could say that these theologians treated the utterance of the man under interrogation as an expositional performative, in which the happiness of the performative (i.e., the truth of the utterance) depended on the absence of infelicities that would otherwise make the utterance void, rather than on the sincerity or insincerity of the speaker's thoughts and feelings: see John L. Austin, *How to do things with words*, Cambridge, MA: Harvard University Press, 1975, esp. pp. 1–11, 83–93. In Searle's terms, one could say that for Valencia and Bañez the utterance of the man under interrogation needed to be analyzed as an indirect speech act, and thus the communication of meaning depends on the background information shared by the hearer and the speaker, together with the capacity of the hearer to make inferences: see John R. Searle, *Speech Acts. An essay in the philosophy of language*, Cambridge: Cambridge University Press, 1969, pp. 54–71, and esp. id., *Expression and Meaning: Studies in the theory of speech acts*, Cambridge: Cambridge University Press, 1979, pp. 30–57. I am aware of significant differences between Searle's and Austin's speech act theories; here, however, I would like to simply emphasize the distance between them and

Wittgenstein with respect to the relationship between context and meaning, which I think mirrors well the distance between Navarrus and these later theologians.

54. For an overview of the controversy over mental reservation in England, see Zagorin, *Ways of Lying*, pp. 186–220.

55. On this part of Southwell's trial, see Christopher Devlin, *The life of Robert Southwell, Poet and Martyr*, London: Longmans, Green, 1956, pp. 311–314; and A. E. Malloch, "Father Henry Garnet's *Treatise of equivocation*," *Recusant History*, 15 (1981), pp. 387–395 (esp. 387).

56. fraudes, imposturas, dolos. . . quippe qua non modo mendacio, sed et periurio porta aperitur. George Abbot, *Quaestiones sex*, Oxford, 1598, "Praefatio ad lectorem," pp. 4–5.

57. Thomas Morton, *A full satisfaction concerning a double Romish iniquitie*, London, 1606, pp. 47–103 (quot. at 47).

58. On the Protestant propaganda against equivocation, see J. P. Sommerville, "The 'new art of lying,'" pp. 179–182. The fact that the early modern English Protestant establishment seemed compact in condemning equivocation does not mean that the doctrine and practice of equivocation was not defended by English Protestants as well, esp. when, during the reign of Mary, the roles in the confessional game of cat-and-mouse switched: on this topic, see Susan Wabuda, "Equivocation and recantation during the English Reformation: the 'subtle shadow' of Dr. Edward Crome," *Journal of Ecclesiastical History* 44 (1993), pp. 224–242, and Andrew Pettegree, "Nicodemism and the English Reformation," in id. *Marian Protestantism: Six Studies*, Farnham: Ashgate, 1996.

59. On this, see S. Tutino, "Between Nicodemism and 'Honest' Dissimulation: The Society of Jesus in England," *Historical Research*, vol. 79, no. 206 (2006), pp. 534–553, at pp. 545 and 552–553.

60. On this topic, see Alexandra Walsham, "'Yielding to the Extremity of the Time': Conformity, Orthodoxy and the post-Reformation Catholic Community," in *Conformity and Orthodoxy in the English Church, c. 1560–1660*, eds. Peter Lake and Michael C. Questier, Woodbridge: Boydell Press, 2000, pp. 211–236, and id., "Ordeals of Conscience: Casuistry, Conformity and Confessional Identity in Post-Reformation England," in *Contexts of Conscience in Early Modern Europe*, eds. Harald E. Braun and Edward Vallance, Basingstoke: Palgrave Macmillan, 2004, pp. 32–48. The definition of nicodemism and dissimulation as "behavioral equivalents" of verbal equivocation is Lowell Gallagher's, in *Medusa's Gaze: Casuistry and Conscience in Early Modern Europe*, Stanford, CA: Stanford University Press, 1991, p. 89.

61. On this and many other dilemmas faced by the Catholic laity in Elizabethan and Jacobean England, see Peter Holmes, ed., *Elizabethan Casuistry*, Catholic Record Society, vol. 67, 1981, and Elliot Rose, *Cases of Conscience. Alternatives open to Recusants and Puritans under Elizabeth I and James I*, Cambridge: Cambridge University Press, 1975, pp. 11–113.

62. On the phenomenon of the "recusant wives," see Alexandra Walsham, *Church Papists: Catholicism, Conformity and Confessional Polemic in Early Modern England*, Woodbridge: Boydell Press, 1993, pp. 77–81.

63. On Thomas Bell, see P. Holmes, *Resistance and Compromise: the Political Thought of the Elizabethan Catholics*, Cambridge: Cambridge University Press, 1982, pp. 95–98; A. Walsham, "'Yielding to the Extremity of the Time;'" Michael C. Questier, *Conversion, Politics and Religion in England, 1580–1625*, Cambridge: Cambridge University Press, 1996, pp. 45–48.

64. Henry Garnet, *A treatise of equivocation*, ed. David Jardine, London: Longmans, 1851, pp. 12–13.

65. Ibid., p. 15.

66. Ibid.

67. Ibid., p. 17.

68. Ibid., p. 53, my italics.

69. Robert Persons, *A treatise tending to mitigation*. [Saint Omer], 1607, pp. 273ff.

70. On the polemical context of Persons's text, see S. Tutino, "Between Nicodemism and 'Honest' Dissimulation."

71. R. Persons, *A treatise*, p. 279.

72. Ibid., p. 419. Italics in the original.

73. Ibid.

74. Ibid., pp. 420–425.
75. For a biography of Lessius, see Charles van Sull, *Leonard Lessius, 1554–1623*, Louvain: Museum Lessianum, 1930. On Lessius's moral theology, see J. P. Sommerville, "The 'new art of lying,'" pp. 167–177, and H. Höpfl, *Jesuit political thought*, pp. 142–145 and passim. For an overview of the tense theological debates that took place in Louvain during Lessius's time, see Edmond J. M. Van Eijl, "La controverse louvaniste autour de la grâce et du libre arbitre à la fin du XVIe siècle," in *L'Augustinisme à l'ancienne faculté de théologie de Louvain*, eds. Mathijs Lamberigts and Leo Kenis, Louvain: Leuven University Press, 1994, pp. 208–282
76. This is the *Dubitatio IX* of chapter 42, book II, of *De iustitia et iure*, Louvain, 1605, pp. 556–558.
77. See, e.g., Lessius's statement, in the same section of his work: "Whenever somebody is unjustly obliged to swear, or has an otherwise just reason to conceal his mind through an ambiguous speech or through a silent [mental] restriction, he does not sin even though he swears in another sense [with respect to the sense intended by the interlocutor]. *Note that this is valid if necessity or utility requires the oath*." Ibid., p. 557, my italics. Even the Congregation of the Index singled out this very statement as problematic because of the reference to utility: see infra, note no. 86.
78. The documentary evidence concerning the censures of these books can be found in ACDF, Index, Protocolli KK, passim. These censures have to be put in the context of the shifting attitude of the Congregation of the Index, which starting in the 1640s assumed a more pronounced anti-Jesuit and antiprobabilistic character: on this, see Pietro Stella, *Il Giansenismo in Italia*, 3 vols., Rome: Edizioni di Storia e Letteratura, 2006, vol. I, pp. 82–86.
79. The first edition of the *Splendor veritatis* was published in Lyon in 1627. The text was reprinted as an appendix of the 1653 Lyon edition of Lessius's *De iustitia et iure*, pp. 667–790. I will be quoting from this latter edition. There are some differences between the first and the second editions (in general, the second edition is a much enlarged version of the first), but the passages I discuss below are virtually identical in both.
80. Ita ille ex mendacio non mendacium, ex periurio non periurium. . . & mirabili metamorphosi nigrum in album, tenebras in lucem, falsitatem in veritatem transformat. John Barnes, *Dissertatio contra aequivocatores*, Paris, 1625, pp. 15–16. For a summary of Barnes's arguments, see Zagorin, *Ways of Lying*, pp. 213–215.
81. [Navarrus's *ratio*] fere enim gratis assumit, dari absque culpa posse orationem mixtam ex terminis vocalibus & mentalibus: cum tamen hoc sit ipsum de quo controvertitur. Raynaud, *Splendor veritatis*, p. 752.
82. Probandum igitur ac declarandum fuerat, illam compositionem orationis ex parte una vocali aliaque mentali, sive ex signo & non signo, apte cohaerere. Ibid.
83. Sic igitur argumentor. Dimidiata illa conceptus expressio, *suppetente iusta eius causa, & urgentiore lege quam veracitatis*. . . nullo igitur modo est illicita. Ibid., my italics.
84. Et quia. . . quaecumque verba. . . ambigua sunt & pluribus gravida sensibus, incredibilis anxietas oboriretur, quoties proferenda essent verba, nitendumque foret, ut nutibus aliisque signis tolleretur verborum ambiguitas. Cui scrupulositati occurritur, rejecta universaliter improbatione vocum ambiguarum, & concesso ex causa iusta earum usu. Ibid., pp. 709–710.
85. Imo contra fraudes, dolos, mendacia, & periuria quae miseris hisce temporibus sub aequivocationum specie orbem Christianum inundarunt, apprime utilem & salutarem censemus. J. Barnes, *Dissertatio*, "Approbatio Doctorum in sacra Theologiae facultate Parisiensi," unfol.
86. Ill. DD. mandarunt librum prohiberi, sed moneri suaviter R.mum Patrem Generalem Jesuitarum ut moneat d. Lessium ad amovendum a suo opere de iustitia et iure verbum illum utilitas. . . c.42 disputatione 9a. ACDF, Index, Diarii III, "Congregatio habita 17 Julii 1624," fos. 125r–v.
87. Cf., e.g., Lessius's *De iustitia et iure* ed. 1605, pp. 556–558; and Lessius's *De iustitia et iure* ed. 1653, pp. 515–516.
88. The decree of this condemnation can be found in ACDF, SO Decreta 1679, f. 46r. The text of the propositions condemned can be found in Heinrich Denzinger et alii, eds., *Enchiridion Symbolorum*, Freiburg, 2001, nn. 1176–1178. The discussion held by the members of the Congregation of the Inquisition over the condemned propositions can be found in ACDF, St. St. UV 45.

89. The first censure, anonymous, can be found in ACDF, Index, Protocolli RR, fos. 226r–229r. The second censure, done by Laurentius Bulbulius, can be found in ibid., fos. 231r–234r.

90. For a biography of Tomasi, an important protagonist of the erudite culture of his time, see Francesco Andreu, *Pellegrino alle sorgenti. San Giuseppe Maria Tomasi*, Rome: Curia Generalizia dei Chierici Regolari, 1987. Domenico Stefano Bernini, son and biographer of Gian Lorenzo, wrote a biography of Tomasi, *Ragguaglio della vita del venerabile D. Giuseppe Maria Tomasi* (1st ed., Rome, 1714), at the request of Pope Clement XI, who in 1713, immediately after Tomasi's death, initiated Tomasi's beatification process.

91. ACDF, Index, Protocolli RR, fos. 235r–236r, at f. 236r.

92. *Verum quum. . . iste quinquaginta plus annis scripserit ante huiusmodi proscriptionem, excusandus hinc ipse. . . Quumque ipse solus non fuerit in hac sententia, vel in ea non ignobiles scriptores sit secutus, non video cur huius tantummodo scriptoris liber sit prohibendus, et non item et coeterorum.* Ibid., fos. 235r–v.

93. The memo can be found in ARSI, Instit. 186e, fos. 43r–44r.

94. *Aliquando licere, imo et necessariam esse restrictionem, quam vocant realem. . . quo pacto munus ipsum confessarii est res quaedam et circumstantia, unde illa responsio, nihil scio de tali crimine, verum et legitimum sensum habeat, etiam si illud ex confessione noverit.* Ibid., fos. 43v–44r. Emphasis in the original ms.

95. On the debates over probabilism in Society of Jesus in the years of the leadership of Tirso González, see Jean-Pascal Gay, *Jesuit Civil Wars. Theology, Politics and Government under Tirso González (1687–1705)*, Farnham: Ashgate, 2012. I thank Dr. Gay for the stimulating conversations he and I had on this topic.

96. The complete title of Alfaro's treatise is *Observationes in librum cui titulus: Controversia Theologica Tripartita Academicae Disputationi subiecta de recto usu opinionum probabilium: Authore Patre Christophoro Rassler*, and it remained in manuscript form (a copy of it, in Alfaro's own handwriting, can be found in APUG, Fondo Curia—hereafter FC—2056E). Alfaro finished writing it on August 18, 1695, as it is written in the manuscript itself (f. 62)

97. On the complex editorial vicissitudes of Rassler's treatise, see C. Sommervogel, *Bibliothèque de la Compagnie de Jésus*. Bruxelles: Schepens; Paris: Pichard, 1890–1912, vol VI, col. 1462. As far as I know, only one copy of Rassler's *Controversia Theologica* survived the Jesuits' purge, and it can be found in the Biblioteca Casanatense in Rome.

98. J. Alfaro, *Observationes*, fos. 17–22.

99. *Licet maior propositio praedicti sillogismi sit vera: at minor est saepe falsa, et in ea potest aliquis culpabiliter decipi, existimando se omnibus rite ac sine passione perpensis iudicare prudenter aliquid esse licitum et honestum, cum tamen non rite, ac recte, sed temere et imprudenter et passione aliqua deceptus ita iudicet, sicuti de facto decipiuntur illi omnes, qui conscientiam erroneam vincibilem sibi formant existimantes se rectam conscientiam habere, et recte ac prudenter agere, ut in conscientia Iudaeorum et Haereticorum omnium et seductorum conspicitur.* Ibid., f. 18. Emphasis in the original ms.

100. *Deinde etiam tunc, cum ille sillogismus non fallit, sed ambae ipsius praemissae sunt verae, nihilominus certitudinem et evidentiam plerumque non habet, sed solam probabilitatem, quia regulariter nemo potest esse omnino certus quod adhibuerit omnem debitam diligentiam ad inquirendam veritatem, sed metuere potest ac debet, ne in studio virtutis ac veritatis defecerat, ne a proprio commodo aut privato affectu aut animi perturbatione obscuritas aliqua in mentem irrepserit, et error, qui forte latet, poena sit negligentiae ad Deum pie et perseveranter recurrendi, rem attente considerandi, consilium capiendi, quo casu conscientia errantem non excusat. Haec enim erat perpetua solicitudo et anxietas sanctorum omnium.* Ibid., fos. 19–20.

101. *Vana igitur est phantastica et perniciosa evidentia illa et securitas, qua regulariter omnes etiam communis vitae homines possint esse certi, se non ex passione vel negligentia in inquirenda veritate, sed omnibus rite perpensis prudenter iudicare rem esse licitam, praesertim in rebus de quibus est controversia, an licere necne.* Ibid., f. 21.

102. See Ibid., fos. 22–23.

Chapter 2

1. An investigation into the genre of the *ars historiae* should start with these collections: Johann Wolf, ed., *Artis historicae penus*, 2 vols., Basel 1579, and Eckhard Kessler, ed., *Theoretiker humanistischer Geschichtsschreibung*, Munich: Fink 1971. As examples of traditional scholarship on post-Reformation historiography and esp. on the *ars historiae* genre, I will mention only Giorgio Spini, "I trattatisti dell'arte storica della Controriforma Italiana," *Quaderni di Belfagor* 1 (1948), pp. 109–136 (translated into English by Eric Cochrane as "Historiography: The art of history in the Italian Counter Reformation," in *The Late Italian Renaissance, 1525–1630*, London: Macmillan, 1970, pp. 91–133); Girolamo Cotroneo, *I Trattatisti dell'ars historica*, Naples: Giannini, 1971; Sergio Bertelli, *Ribelli, Libertini e Ortodossi nella storiografia barocca*, Florence: La Nuova Italia, 1973; Eric Cochrane, *Historians and Historiography in the Italian Renaissance*, Chicago: University of Chicago Press 1981, esp. pp. 479ff. For recent attempts to revise this traditional assessment, see Anthony Grafton, *What was History?* and Carlo Ginzburg, "Description and citation." On the French school of historical jurisprudence, see at least Julian H. Franklin, *Jean Bodin and the sixteenth-century Revolution in the Methodology of Law and History*, New York: Columbia University Press, 1963; George Huppert, *The Idea of Perfect History: Historical Erudition and Historical Philosophy in Renaissance France*, Urbana: University of Illinois Press, 1970; Donald R. Kelley, *Foundations of Modern Historical Scholarship: Language, Law, and History in the French Renaissance*, New York: Columbia University Press, 1970, and, more recently, "Between history and system," in Gianna Pomata and Nancy Siraisi (eds.), *Historia: Empiricism and Erudition in early modern Europe*, Cambridge, MA: Harvard University Press, 2005, pp. 211–237. For a different perspective, cf. Zachary Sayre Schiffman, *On the Threshold of Modernity: Relativism in the French Renaissance*, Baltimore: Johns Hopkins University Press, 1991. On Humanist and early Renaissance historiography, see also Joseph Levine, *Humanism and History: Origins of modern English historiography*, Ithaca: Cornell University Press, 1987; Robert Black, "The new laws of history," in *Renaissance Studies* 1 (1987), pp. 126–156; Gary Ianziti, *Humanistic Historiography under the Sforzas: Politics and Propaganda in Fifteenth-Century Milan*, Oxford: Oxford University Press, 1988, and id., *Writing History in Renaissance Italy: Leonardo Bruni and the Uses of the Past*, Cambridge, MA: Harvard University Press 2012. For the contribution of the antiquarians' methodology to the development of modern historiography, see the seminal work of Arnaldo Momigliano, "Ancient history and the antiquarian," *Journal of the Warburg and Courtauld Institutes* 13 (1950), pp. 282–315, now in *Studies in Historiography*, London: Weidenfeld and Nicolson, 1966, pp. 1–39. Finally, an important study to situate post-Reformation historical scholarship within the larger intellectual context of post-Reformation Catholicism is William McCuaig, *Carlo Sigonio. The changing world of the late Renaissance*, Princeton, NJ: Princeton University Press, 1989.

2. Sergio Bertelli expressed a relatively widespread opinion when he remarked that Mascardi's work "certainly did not have the gift of originality" (*Ribelli, Libertini e Ortodossi*, p. 176), and Eric Cochrane gives a clear sense of the place that traditional scholarship has assigned to Mascardi and to "Baroque" historiography in "The Transition from Renaissance to Baroque: The Case of Italian Historiography," *History and Theory* 19, no. 1 (1980), pp. 21–38.

3. On this point, see Irena Dorota Backus, *Historical Method and Confessional Identity in the Era of the Reformation (1378–1615)*, Leiden: Brill, 2003. Backus's work is, in part, a response to the classic thesis of Pontien Polman, who in *L'élément historique dans la controverse religieuse du XVIe siècle*, Gembloux: Duclot, 1932, argued that post-Reformation historical research was a function of and subordinated to the confessional conflict between Protestants and Catholics.

4. Mascardi's most exhaustive biography is Francesco Luigi Mannucci's *La vita e le opere di Agostino Mascardi*, Atti della Società Ligure di Storia Patria, vol. XLII, Genoa, 1908, which, although very much dated, contains a useful appendix of primary sources. Recent reconsiderations of the importance of Agostino Mascardi in the context of the literary culture of his time are Manuela Doni Garfagnini, " 'Dell'arte historica' di Agostino Mascardi. Saggio teorico di storiografia del primo Seicento," in id., *Il teatro della storia fra rappresentazione e realtà*, Rome: Edizioni di Storia e Letteratura, 2002, pp. 325–370, and Eraldo Bellini, *Agostino Mascardi tra "ars poetica" e "ars historica,"* Milan: Vita e Pensiero, 2002.

5. Mascardi disliked Galluzzi since his time as a student in the Roman College, and the conflict between the two continued and intensified over time. At the end of the 1620s Galluzzi was one of the most vocal detractors of Mascardi's *Congiura del conte Gio. Luigi de' Fieschi*, and Mascardi responded by circulating a pamphlet, written under the pseudonym of "Nardini" and entitled "Storia della rivoluzione del Seminario Romano avvenuta il 5 Gennaio 1631." This work narrated a rebellion of some of the students of the Roman College, of which Galluzzi was rector, that exploded in January 1631. The reason for the students' insubordination, according to the text, was the faulty leadership of Galluzzi, who because of his evil character and ignoble birth was not well suited to govern "the most virtuous and noble" students in Italy. The text of the manuscript has been published by Mannucci, *La vita e le opere*, pp. 541–562 (quot. at 544–545). For the context of this manuscript, see ibid., pp. 164–166.

6. L'ostinazione della fortuna m'ha costretto a deporre quell'abito che per undici anni ho portato con tanto mio gusto, ed in ciò non trovo motivo che mi consoli, fuor che d'averlo onoratamente deposto, come onoratamente il portava. La più principale cagione di tanta calamità è stata la servitù con la Serenissima Casa d'Este; così sentono i periti di queste parti. Mascardi to Molza, Rome, November 2, 1617, Mannucci, *La vita e le opere*, doc. 37.

7. The catalog of the *"Dismissi"* from the Society of Jesus simply states that Mascardi was expelled "iustis de causis" on November 1, 1617 (see ARSI, Hist. Soc. 54, f. 26r).

8. The *Silvarum libri IV* were published in Antwerp in 1622. The Jesuit father Gualfreducci was secretary of the general and author of several Latin poems of religious content and of some theatrical pieces that were performed at the Roman College.

9. Iuvenilia P. Augustini Mascardi non videntur seorsim imprimenda, sed cum accesserint plura vel pia vel moralia magis, cuiusmodi expectantur a persona religiosa, poterint edi ut pars aliqua iusti voluminis. Interim auctor ex intervallo recognita sine dubio etiam haec ipsa faciet meliora. ARSI, Fondo Gesuitico 662, Censurae Librorum, f. 219r. The document is undated, but it is included in a folder containing censures from the 1610s and 1620s. Also, because the *Censurae Librorum* were internal censures done by Jesuits on the work of their confreres, this censure should be dated before 1617, the year of Mascardi's expulsion from the Society.

10. On the Accademia dei Desiosi there is a short entry in Michele Maylender, *Storia delle Accademie d'Italia*, 5 vols., Bologna: Cappelli, 1926–30, vol. II, pp. 173–174. The most recent and exhaustive contribution on the Accademia dei Desiosi is Riccardo Merolla, "L'Accademia dei Desiosi," in id. (ed.), *L'Accademia dei Desiosi. Storia e Testo*, Rome: Carocci, 2008, pp. 5–43. On Mascardi's role in the Accademia, see esp. pp. 30–33. The manuscript *Diario* of the Accademia has been edited and published by Merolla in ibid., pp. 50–112. On the larger implications of the cultural project of Maurizio di Savoia, see Laura Alemanno, "La politica culturale di Maurizio di Savoia," in Merolla, ed., *L'Accademia dei Desiosi*, pp. 123–129.

11. Fabrici's oration can be found in the collection *Saggi accademici*, edited by Mascardi and published in Venice in 1630. For the date of the oration, see a letter by Mario Guiducci to Galileo Galilei, February 8, 1625, in which Guiducci informed Galileo that "last Thursday, in the accademia which meets every week at the palace of Card. Savoia, Giuliano Fabrici. . . gave a very good lecture and struck at all the Aristotelians, especially the most authoritative ones" (*Le Opere. Edizione Nazionale*, 20 vols., Florence: Barbera, 1929–39, vol. XIII, pp. 253–254). On the date of this event in the context of the formative years of the Accademia dei Desiosi, see Merolla "L'Accademia," pp. 27–28. On the importance of the oration in the context of the philo-Galilean position of the Accademia, see ibid., pp. 34–37.

12. Mario Biagioli, *Galileo courtier. The practice of science in the culture of absolutism*, Chicago: University of Chicago Press, 1993, quot. at 261, but see the entire chapter, pp. 245–265.

13. una delle più necessarie qualità dell'huomo di Corte è la flessibilità nell'accommodarsi alle altrui nature. The inaugural oration for the Accademia dei Desiosi, entitled "Che gli essercitii di lettere sono in Corte non pur dicevoli, ma necessarii" ("That the practice of letters at court is not only appropriate, but necessary"), can be found at pp. 1–35 of the *Prose vulgari*, Venice, 1626 (I, ed. 1625), quot. at 11.

14. On the several ups and downs of Mascardi's career, see Mannucci, *La vita e le opere*, pp. 67ff., and for a more synthetic summary, see Doni Garfagnini, " 'Dell'arte historica'," pp. 353–360, and Bellini, *Agostino Mascardi*, pp. 1–15.

15. Mascardi, *Discorsi morali su la Tavola di Cebete Tebano*, Venice, 1627. On the importance of this work for the early seventeenth-century literary debates, see Bellini, *Agostino Mascardi*, pp. 68–99.
16. Mannucci, *La vita e le opere*, docs. 128, 129 and 130, letters dated respectively January 12, February 7, and February 26, 1626. The salami finally reached Mascardi in the spring of that year (see Mannucci, *La vita e le opere*, doc. 131).
17. Gli studi ch'ho per le mani non lasciano che ne possa far senza, onde ho voluto supplicar V.S.Ill.ma che, nel farsi di nuovo conceder la facoltà, secondo che pur sarà a lei necessario, per molti libri ch'ella ha, si compiaccia di chiederla con la solita riserva di porterla partecipare ad un suo servitore, perché in tal maniera V.S.Ill.ma verrà a promuover gli studi miei senza sua spesa. Mascardi to Cardinal d'Este, Genoa, February 2, 1623, Mannucci, *La vita e le opere*, doc. 113.
18. Tutino, *Empire of Souls*, ch. 2.
19. E, perché nel giro d'un secolo intiero avrò occasione di parlar frequentemente di cotesta eccelsa Repubblica e degli accidenti occorsi tanto nelle riforme del Governo quanto nello stabilimento della libertà, supplico umilmente le SS. VV. Ser.me ad accennarmi il loro senso ed a somministrarmi le notizie opportune; con la sicurezza d'esser da me servite con la fede ed affetto ch'io debbo loro per ogni titolo, salva la verità prescrittami dalla coscienza, dalla riputazione e dal fine che debbo avere del publico beneficio. Mascardi to the Senate of the Republic of Genoa, Rome, November 12, 1627, Mannucci, *La vita e le opere*, doc. 135.
20. Assicuro V.A. che dopo quello che per riputazione e coscienza si dee alla verità, io non avrò oggetto più proporzionato alla mia vera divozione che la gloria de' Principi Estensi: onde la supplico riverentemente a somministrarmi quelle notizie che possono meglio abilitarmi al conseguimento di questo fine; e perché dai fatti d'Alfonso primo e del Cardinale Ippolito nella guerra di Siena sono state scritte cose diverse, desidero d'intendere se posso in tutto riferimi alla vita dell'uno, a quello che dell'altro vien notato dagli scrittori fiorentini, o se V.S. può dagli archivi farmi saper di vantaggio; e, con ricordarle la mia umilissima servitù, le bacio con ogni riverenza le mani. Mascardi to the Duke of Modena, Rome, December 8, 1627, Mannucci, *La vita e le opere*, doc. 137.
21. L'oggetto della mia penna è la verità: la quale havrà ne' miei fogli luogo incontaminato, senza esser violata dalle passioni mal regolate. Agostino Mascardi, *La Congiura del Conte Gio: Luigi de' Fieschi*, Venice, 1629, epistle to the reader, unfol.
22. Quelle poche debolezze mie già publicate nacquero a caso; frettolosamente, per servire all'occasione, senza fine di stamparle, come che pur sieno uscite alla luce. In quelle il non riuscir a proposito poco montava alla somma de' miei pensieri, che le presero per trastullo. Ma l'impresa ch'io tento è indirizzata al ben publico; porta seco la necessità d'ammaestrare i Lettori; conserva le memorie degli homini valorosi; ed è una autentica testimonianza delle cose passate. Ibid.
23. Parrà forse ad alcuno ch'io non dovessi publicare una parte sì picciola d'un intero volume. Rispondo che la congiura del Fieschi scritta nel modo che qui si legge non è parte d'un tutto, ma sta da sé; e nel corpo dell'historia si vede sotto altra forma; non dovendo io nel racconto universale sminuzzar tanto ogni particolare accidente. L'intention mia è di scrivere una compita attione con le sue parti, per haver occasione di tentar in essa tutti quei luoghi, che in una lunga historia possono appresentarsi. Né ciò da me si fa senza esempio tralascio gli antichi, e specialmente quel di Salustio. Ibid.
24. On Mascardi's Sallustian harangues, see Ginzburg, "Alien Voices," at p. 75. On Sallust's role in early modern political thought, see Patricia J. Osmond, "*Princeps Historiae Romanae*: Sallust in Renaissance Political Thought," *Memoirs of the American Academy in Rome* XL (1995), pp. 101–143, esp. 127–129, on the moralizing and stylistic (as opposed to the political) use of Sallust on the part of Mascardi and other historians and theorists of history.
25. Francesco Patrizi had already noted that historical narrative needed to be arranged according to the "attione" of the story rather than simply according to the chronological order of the events, see Patrizi, *Della Historia diece dialoghi*, Venice, 1560, pp. 62–63. On this aspect of Patrizi's work see Cotroneo, *I Trattatisti*, pp. 266–267. On the fact that occasionally historians need to neglect the chronological order of historical events in order to preserve the

"fabric" of the text of the narrative see also Giovanni Antonio Viperano, *De scribenda historia liber*, Antwerp 1569, p. 35.

26. Le concioni saranno per ventura stimate lunghe e frequenti. Io havrei molto che dire in discolpa, ma basti solo accennarti, ch'io medesimo ho considerati i difetti, e che non voglio far la difesa prima d'udir le accuse. Mascardi, *Congiura*, epistle to the reader, unfol.

27. Volendo dare un saggio di tutto quello che può cadere in historia, faceva di mestiere incontrar anche le occasioni, che per altro si potevano lasciar correre; e nella deliberatione d'un negotio gravissimo, dove sono contrarie le opinioni, non è così agevole l'uscir di briga con sei parole, se si hanno a pesar le ragioni. Ibid.

28. On the harangues as hermeneutical and heuristic tools, see Grafton, *What was History?* pp. 34–49.

29. Non per tanto mi rapporto alla sentenza, che tu ne darai; la quale aspettando avidamente, & a fine di riceverne giovamento, ti prego a somministrarmi insieme quelle notitie, che possono agevolarmi il camino. Mascardi, *Congiura*, epistle to the reader.

30. Trattano di questa materia il Foglietta, il Sigonio, il Campanacci, il Bonfandio, il Tuano, e molte scritture private. Mascardi, *Congiura*, p. 1.

31. [Fieschi era] un giovane di grand'animo, e di pensieri turbulenti. Mascardi, *Congiura*, p. 16. Sallust's description of Catilina can be found in *Catilinae Coniuratio*, 5.1.

32. Si diede Gio: Luigi per consiglio de suoi amici, a leggere diligentemente la vita di Nerone, la congiura di Catilina, e l'operetta del Principe di Nicolò Machiavello. Da questi libri sentì pian piano instillarsi nell'animo la crudeltà, la perfidia, e l'amore del privato interesse sopra ogni ragione humana e divina. Mascardi, *Congiura*, p. 18. When Cardinal de Retz translated or, better, adapted Mascardi's *Congiura* into French, he completely changed Mascardi's interpretation and portrayed Fieschi as the hero rather than as the villain of the story; see Derek A. Watts, *Cardinal de Retz: The ambiguities of a seventeenth-century mind*, Oxford: Oxford University Press, 1980, pp. 134–135. For a discussion of this episode in the context of early modern translation theory, see P. Burke, "Cultures of translation in early modern Europe," in *Cultural Translation in early modern Europe*, pp. 32–34.

33. Trivulzio's harangue can be found in Mascardi, *Congiura*, pp. 21–26.

34. A pamphlet containing a letter to Mascardi from Bruno Taverna (a courtier in the service of Cardinal Teodoro Trivulzio, who had accused Mascardi of having misread and mistreated Agostino Trivulzio) and Mascardi's reply to Taverna was published in Venice in 1630, with the title *Oppositioni e difesa alla "Congiura del conte Gio. Luigi de' Fieschi" descritta da Agostino Mascardi*.

35. Che se doppo la pubblicatione della *Congiura del Fieschi* è rimasto nell'animo di V.S. illustrissima qualche vestigio d'amaritudine (come mi presuppongono alcuni amici), non mi dorrò mai a bastanza della mia sorte che mi fa parer mancante al mio debito, dove io mi studiai di soprabondare in termini di riverenza e di cautela. A V.S. illustrissima prima d'ogni altro fu presentata quella scrittura, a' cenni suoi dalle mia carte ciò che non le piaceva si cancellò, per suo comandamento stette sepolta l'opera per molti mesi, né senza il suo consentimento fu publicata. Mascardi to Barberini, ed in *Dell'arte historica* (Florence, 1859), pp. ix–xv, quot. at xi. The letter is undated, but it was written in the years 1629–30; see Bellini, *Agostino Mascardi*, p. 106.

36. Nel rimanente resti persuasa che i Principi interessati nella Congiura da me descritta hanno cortesemente abbracciato non meno la veracità dell'historia, che la candidezza dell'historico, et in testimonio di voluntà ben inclinata all'impresa c'ho per le mani, alcuno m'ha favorito di notitie opportune, altri me l'ha benignamente promesse. Mascardi to Barberini, p. xii.

37. Bellini, *Agostino Mascardi*, pp. 110–111.

38. [Mascardi] nel fiorir dell'età sua dichiarossi publicamente di voler seguitare la sostanziosissima *Storia* del Giucciardino e ne fe' trascorrere le notizie a molte corti europee; anzi de chiederne a' principi scaltramente le memorie come materiali dell'ideata sua frabbrica. . . quasi ogni grande, con le memorie, felli trasmettere un edonativo che fu un soccorso per ingagiar quell'autore a ricambiarlo con la gratitudine. . . accumulò questi nel giro di pochi mesi una somma di scudi assai rilevante, ma non curandosi più d'intraprender con quel fervor che promesso avea la storica tessitura, richiesto del perché da un suo intimo confidente, li rispose che avea conseguito il suo fine, poiché, trovandosi egli mal assistito da casa sua, con

quel mezo termine si trovava la sua necessità rimediata. Frugoni, *De' ritratti critici abbozzati e contornati da Francesco Fulvio Frugoni. Ripartimento primo*, Venice, 1669, pp. 422–423. Sergio Bertelli, among other modern scholars, seem to share Frugoni's opinion that Mascardi's historiographical enterprise was motivated mostly by greed (see *Ribelli, Libertini e Ortodossi*, pp. 175–176).

39. The first edition of this work was published in Rome. A modern edition containing some primary sources (Florence, 1859) was edited by Adolfo Bartoli. All my quotations from this work, unless otherwise noted, come from this latter edition.

40. On this last phase of Mascardi's career, see Mannucci, *La vita e le opere*, 175–223.

41. See Ginzburg, "Aristotle and History, Once More," in id., *History, Rhetoric, and Proof*, pp. 38–53, and id., "Lorenzo Valla on the 'Donation of Constantine'," in ibid., pp. 54–70. On this topic, see also Momigliano, "Ancient history and the antiquarian" and "The Herodotean and the Thucydidean Tradition," in *The Classical Foundations of Modern Historiography*, Berkeley: University of California Press, 1990, pp. 29–53, and "The rise of antiquarian research," in ibid., pp. 54–79, to which Ginzburg responds.

42. The seminal work to understand seventeenth-century Jesuit rhetoric remains Marc Fumaroli, *L'Âge de l'éloquence: Rhétorique et res literaria de la Renaissance au seuil de l'époque classique*. Paris: Champion, 1994. On this topic, see also Fumaroli, "The Fertility and Shortcomings of Renaissance Rhetoric: The Jesuit Case," in John W. O'Malley, ed., *The Jesuits: Cultures, sciences, and the arts, 1540–1773*, Toronto: University of Toronto Press, 1999, vol. I, pp. 90–106; Frederick J. McGinness, *Right Thinking and Sacred Oratory in Counter-Reformation Rome*, Princeton, NJ: Princeton University Press, 1995; and John O'Malley, *Praise and Blame in Renaissance Rome: Rhetoric, Doctrine, and Reform in the Sacred Orators of the Papal Court, c. 1450–1521*, Durham, NC: Duke University Press, 1979. On Strada in particular, see Fumaroli, *L'Âge*, pp. 190–202 and passim, and id., "Cicero Pontifex Romanus. La tradition rhétorique du Collège romain et les principes inspirateurs du mécénat de Barberini," *Mélanges de l'École Française de Rome, Moyen-Age, Temps modernes* 90, no. 2 (1978), pp. 797–835; and infra, ch. 4. For a useful overview of Renaissance rhetoric in general, see Peter Mack, *A History of Renaissance Rhetoric 1380–1620*, Oxford: Oxford University Press, 2011.

43. For a more thorough discussion of the Jesuits' Ciceronianism, see infra, ch. 4.

44. Paul Ricoeur, *Time and Narrative*, English trans., Chicago: University of Chicago Press, 1984–5, 3 vols., vol. I, p. 162.

45. Strada's *De bello Belgico*, in two volumes, was published several times in the course of the seventeenth century. The first edition of the first volume was published in Rome in 1632, and the first edition of the second volume appeared in Rome in 1647. The first volume was reprinted in Bologna in 1646 and then again in Rome in 1653. The second volume was published again in Rome in 1658. The work received rave reviews even before publication from the hierarchy of the Society of Jesus. Antoine Jordin, one of the Jesuit fathers in charge of writing the censure for Strada's work, approved it enthusiastically: "cum omnia in eo non solum. . . orthodoxa doctrina, bonisque moribus omnino consentiunt, sed sint etiam scripta ea fide, quae in historia requiritur, eaque doctrina ac facundia, quae futura est et auctori suo, societatique gloriosa et lectoribus utilissima et iucundissima." Jordin's censure, dated August 6, 1632, can be found in ARSI, Fondo Gesuitico 664, Censurae Librorum, fos. 44r–v (quot. at 44r). Another censure, equally enthusiastic, was written by Girolamo Petrucci (in ibid., fos. 43r–v). Cardinal Mazarin was also very enthusiastic because of the favorable portrait that Strada had painted of the French monarchy, and in fact he personally wrote to Strada on a number of occasions to compliment him on his work and to ask for his scholarly opinion (see ARSI, Rom. 132, I, fos. 194r–v). Strada's *De bello Belgico* became an international best seller: in 1646 the first volume was translated into Dutch; in 1650 the entire work was translated into English and was widely discussed by Clarendon and others in the context of the debate over Tacitist history (on this topic, see Paul Seaward, "Clarendon, Tacitism, and the Civil Wars of Europe," *Huntington Library Quarterly* 68 (2005), pp. 289–311). The following year a French translation appeared also.

46. Strada, *Prolusiones academicae*, Rome 1617, "Muretus," pp. 141–142. On this dialogue in particular and on its significance in the context of Strada's stylistic views, see Christian

Mouchel, *Cicéron et Sénèque dans la rhétorique de la Renaissance*, Marburg: Hitzeroth, 1990, pp. 271–296.

47. Strada, "Muretus," pp. 149–151. After a few back-and-forths between Benci, Muret, and Antoniano, this part of the text ended by endorsing the position defended by Muret, who limited the historian's freedom in revealing other people's secrets and argued that revealing secrets was possible only if there was a just reason to do it and if the secret in question was corroborated by several sources.

48. For more details on Strada's notion of poetic imitation, see infra, ch. 4, pp. 144–146.

49. Nec alium Annibalem historicus habet, cum quo verum Annibalem comparare possit, non enim veri Annibalis conformare similacrum studet historicus, in quo similitudo cernatur, sed studet lectorem a se historiaque sua avocare, ac declinare ad res ipsas, quas lector inspectet, iisque intersit potius, quam absens legat. APUG, Fondo APUG (hereafter APUG) 1188, fos.27r–v.

50. Atque haec causa est, cur author Herennianus historiam lib. primo difiniens dixerit Historia est res gesta ab aetatis nostrae memoria remota; quis autem non videt nisi ad hoc alludatur historiam non esse rem ipsam sed narrationem rei. APUG 1163, f.18r (cf. APUG 1188, f.27v)

51. On Strada's concept of *Mythistoriae* and on his example of the story of King Arthur, see "Muretus," pp. 152–154.

52. Bertelli, *Ribelli, Libertini e Ortodossi*, p. 24.

53. il Castelvetro confonde col suo soggetto l'istoria, che non è piccolo errore; perché non è l'istoria, com'egli crede, cosa rappresentata, ma rappresentante; essendo *narrazione secondo la verità di azioni umane memorevoli avvenute*; che questa è la diffinizione da lui medesimo portata; sicché la cosa rappresentata saranno le azioni umane, la rappresentante sarà l'istoria che le racconta; tanto che l'istoria, né paragonata con la poesia, né in riguardo a se stessa ed al suo soggetto, potrà dirsi cosa rappresentata. Mascardi, *Dell'arte historica*, p. 348 (emphasis in the original).

54. un'esatta notizia del tempo in cui le cose ristrette dentro al giro che si propone accadettero. Mascardi, *Dell'arte*, pp. 66–68 at 67. On Scaliger and his work on chronology, see Anthony Grafton, "Joseph Scaliger and Historical Chronology: The Rise and Fall of a Discipline," *History and Theory* 14 (1975), pp. 156–185, and *Joseph Scaliger. A study in the history of classical scholarship*, vol. II, "Historical Chronology," Oxford: Oxford University Press, 1994.

55. Segue dunque l'istoria, per quanto può, l'ordine somministrato dal tempo, e di ciò manifestissima è la ragione: perché, se propria impresa dell'istorico esser crediamo il rappresentar tanto vivamente gli avvenimenti passati al leggente, che di veder gli argomenti, certo è che, si come una cosa dopo l'altra accadette, così una dopo l'altra narrar si dee. Mascardi, *Dell'arte*, p. 368.

56. Né mi si dica in contrario, che quando si riguardasse all'ordine di natura (cominciando per cagion d'esempio dall'autor della impresa, poscia narrando i motivi che l'indussero ad affrontarla, indi l'occasione, e poi gli strumenti ed i mezzi, e finalmente il successo), l'istoria sarebbe giustamente ordinata, senza aver mira al tempo; perché nell'argomento si nasconde un equivoco grande; conciossiacosaché cotal ordine di natura, è inseparabile dall'ordine del tempo, il quale, come trascendentale, svaga e per i motivi e per l'occasione e per l'uso degli strumenti. Ibid.

57. L'istoria può talora, anzi dee, tralasciato il rigor di quell'ordine, ch'accompagna la successione del tempo, anticipare e posporre nel suo racconti gli avvenimenti, secondo che, per agevolar a' leggenti l'intelligenza e la memoria delle cose avvenute, riuscirà più profittevole e piano. Ibid., p. 371.

58. Notice that in this passage Mascardi does not mention the question of the precepts of wisdom that history was supposed to bring, and as such he does not reduce the function of the reader to that of a passive recipient of moral lessons. Rather, he imagines the present time of the reader as the temporal point in which the past events, mediated through the historical narrative, are re-presented—that is, made present, recovered. For a discussion of the exact nature of the representational character of historical narrative from the point of view of the reader, see below.

59. On the question of emplotment in historical narratives, see at least Hayden White, *Metahistory: The Historical Imagination in Nineteenth-Century Europe*, Baltimore: Johns

Hopkins University Press, 1973, but esp. his most recent works, such as *Figural Realism: Studies in the mimesis effect*, Baltimore: Johns Hopkins University Press, 1999. The trajectory and evolution of White's thought on this issue can be traced through the essays written by White and collected by Robert Doran, *The Fiction of Narrative: Essays on History, Literature and Theory, 1957–2007*, Baltimore: Johns Hopkins University Press, 2010. On emplotment and historical narrative, see also Ricoeur, *Time and narrative*, vol. I, ch. 2.

60. Ricoeur, *Time and Narrative*, vol. I, esp. ch. 3.

61. Ricoeur, *Time and Narrative*, vol. III, chs. 1–4, but see also Koselleck, *Futures Past*, pp. 255–275.

62. Le pitture, le sculture, le iscrizioni, gli archi, le colonne, e somiglianti memorie pubbliche, erano un mutolo raconto d'imprese nobili e grandi, dalle quali senza rivolger libri, altri apprendeva ed apprende i fatti degli uomini valorosi. Mascardi, *Dell'arte*, 9–10.

63. Ma ne anche cotal sorte di memorie mi son proposto per oggetto dell'arte historica che compongo. Quando dunque nomino in questi fogli l'istoria, intendo, popolarmente e senza metafisica, quel racconto che far si suole degli accidenti che occorrono, e si conserva ne' libri. Mascardi, *Dell'arte*, p. 11

64. See Ginzburg, "Description and citation," pp. 22ff. According to Ginzburg, in this passage Mascardi alluded to the *Museo Cartaceo* of Cassiano dal Pozzo, who incidentally attended the same Accademie as Mascardi; see ibid., p. 22. This passage was also noted by Francis Haskell in *History and its Images. Art and the Interpretation of the Past*, New Haven, CT: Yale University Press, 1993, pp. 93–94.

65. Che non può ad onta del tempo divorator de' marmi e de' bronzi la magia dell'istoria? Mascardi, *Dell'arte*, p. 77

66. non avendo chi dovrà scrivere capitale più certo per arricchire di sodi ammaestramenti la posterità, che la sicurezza delle notizie, le quali come in sacrario dovrebbono negli archivi delle repubbliche e dei principati serbarsi. Ibid., p. 36. Interestingly enough, Mascardi quoted "Vopiscus," one of the fake authors of the *Historiae augustae*, as a supporting authority on the need to keep accurate, complete, and truthful documentary accounts of events ("E l'istesso Vopisco, rendendo conto della sua diligenza in compor le Vite de' Cesari, accenna i fonti da' quali aveva le notizie ritratte: *usus autem sum, praecipue libris ex bibliotheca Ulpia, aetate mea Thermis Diocletianis, item ex domo Tiberiana*," p. 36; emphasis in the original). In taking a fake author as an authority on original sources Mascardi was in good company: even François Baudouin, in fact, quoted Vopiscus as an authority on the question of original documents as the proper sources of history (see Grafton, "Traditions of Invention and Inventions of Tradition in Renaissance Italy: Annius of Viterbo," now in *Defenders of the Text. The Traditions of Scholarship in an Age of Science, 1450–1800*, Cambridge, MA: Harvard University Press, 1991, pp. 76–103, esp. 95–96).

67. Mascardi, *Dell'arte*, pp. 92–93.

68. Fra le merci che di luogo in luogo, e di tempo in tempo si tramandano, niuna più agevolmente della verità si corrompe: e Saturno, cioè il tempo, si dice esser padre della verità, perché quella insieme con gli altri figliuoli si divora e consuma; non è da maravigliarsi, se con la lunghezza degli anni corra quel medesimo risico la verità, a che veggiamo soggetti gli stessi marmi nelle fabbriche sontuose; poiché talora alle statue mancano gli occhi, un braccio, una gamba, il capo, che sono stati rosi dal tempo, ed in modo cancellano la prima conoscenza, che quei tronchi rimangono senza nome. Ibid., p. 91.

69. On the trope of *veritas filia temporis*, the following are still useful: Erwin Panofsky, "Father Time," in id., *Studies in Iconology. Humanistic Themes in the art of the Renaissance*, Oxford: Oxford University Press, 1939, pp. 69–94; Fritz Saxl, "Veritas filia temporis," in Raymond Klibansky and H. J. Paton (eds.), *Philosophy and History. Essays presented to Ernst Cassirer*, Oxford: Clarendon Press, 1936, pp. 197–222; and Ginzburg, "Contributo ad un dizionario storico. In margine al motto 'veritas filia temporis,'" *Rivista Storica Italiana* 78 (1966), pp. 969–973. On Mascardi's use of this trope in his other works, see Bellini, *Agostino Mascardi*, pp. 115–116.

70. Potrà dunque, anzi dovrà il savio scrittor d'istorie, dalle parti fra loro nemiche ritrar tutto quel lume, che gli sarà conceduto; e con la bilancia d'un pesato giudicio librar esattamente i motivi dell'una e dell'altra, adattandogli con gran riguardo alle circostanze, che accompagnarono

quel negozio; e poi come giudice ben informato in contraddittorio, pronunzierà francamente la sua sentenza. Mascardi, *Dell'arte*, pp. 94–95.

71. La verità è di sua natura sfuggevole e lubrica. Ibid., p. 95.
72. See Michel de Certeau, *The writing of history*, English trans., New York: Columbia University Press, 1988, pp. 99–102, and *L'absent de l'histoire*, Paris: Mame, 1973, pp. 7–11 and 156–159. On this aspect of Certeau's work, see also Paul Ricoeur, *Memory, History, Forgetting*, English trans., Chicago: University of Chicago Press, 2004, pp. 361–369.
73. Ricoeur, *Memory, History, Forgetting*, p. 141; also, Jacques Derrida, "Plato's Pharmacy," now in *Dissemination*, trans. by Barbara Johnson, Chicago: University of Chicago Press, 1981, pp. 61–171.
74. Derrida, "Plato's Pharmacy," pp. 95–117.
75. For a different opinion, cf. Brendan Dooley, who considers Mascardi a skeptic who "pick[ed] up where Patrizi left off"; see his "*Veritas filia temporis*: Experience and Belief in early modern culture," *Journal of the History of Ideas* 6 no. 3 (1999), pp. 487–504 (quot. at 494), and *Social history of skepticism. Experience and doubt in early modern culture*, Baltimore: Johns Hopkins University Press, 1999, pp. 114ff.
76. Non si lasci il discreto lettore portare a quelle estreme risoluzioni di Lodovico Vives e di Giovan Francesco Pico, che negano agli storici ogni credenza, e sappia porre la dovuta differenza fra l'errore e l'inganno. Mascardi, *Dell'arte*, p. 97. On Vives's skepticism, see J. A. Fernández Santamaría, *Juan Luis Vives. Escepticismo y prudencia en el Renacimiento*, Salamanca: Ediciones Universidad de Salamanca, 1990, and more recently, *Theater of Man: J. L. Vives on Society*, Philadelphia: Transactions of the American Philosophical Society, 1998. On Pico's skepticism, see Charles B. Schmitt, *Gianfrancesco Pico della Mirandola (1469–1533) and his critique of Aristotle*, The Hague: Martinus Nijhoff, 1967, and Gian Mario Cao, *Scepticism and Orthodoxy: Gianfrancesco Pico as a reader of Sextus Empiricus*, Pisa: Fabrizio Serra Editore, 2007. As a background to the history of early modern skepticism, still most useful is Richard H. Popkin, *The history of scepticism from Savonarola to Bayle*. Oxford: Oxford University Press, 2003.
77. La fede che si presta all'istorie è fede umana, cioè a dire sempre congiunta col dubbio; poiché nell'essenza non s'allontana dall'opinione. È dunque ingiurioso il lettore, se chiede all'istorico la certezza infallibile, appoggiata all'autorità che non riceva contrasto. Si lasci alla fede divina la verità tanto indubitata, quanto si dee alla divinità che la rivela. Mascardi, *Dell'arte*, p. 96
78. Ibid., p. 95.
79. On the theme of the historian as a judge of her documents, see Ginzburg, *The Judge and the Historian*, New York: Verso, 1999, and also "Clues: Roots on an evidential paradigm," in *Clues, Myths, and the Historical Method*, Baltimore: Johns Hopkins University Press, 1989, pp. 96–125.
80. Qui accedit ad Historicum, ad cognoscendam antiquitatem accedit, est enim ille testis antiquitatis: male igitur occupat judicis partes is, a quo testimonium quaeritur, non judicium. Strada, "Muretus," p. 158.
81. Mascardi, *Dell'arte*, p. 227.
82. Pericoloso non tutto ciò è 'l mestiere che giudicando intraprende; e sì come egli si vale della libertà concedutagli in dar sentenza dell'operazioni altrui, così corre gran risico d'esser giudicato dagli altri; onde sarebbe necessario ch'andasse con l'occhio risvegliato ed aperto, né fosse facile a pronunziare, come coloro che a poche cose rimirano. Perché, dipendendo la verità del giudicio dall'esatta notizia delle circostanze ch'accompagnano il fatto, una di loro per disavventura o non si risappia o non si consideri, può render fallacissima la sentenza dello scrittore. Né riputerei se non molto utile quella cautela, di portar il suo giudicio con termini, che lo propongano, ma non l'affermino; quando però non sia nella materia di maniera sicuro, che non gli cada nell'animo il dubitarne. Ibid., pp. 228–229.
83. See Ricoeur, *Memory, History, Forgetting*, pp. 314–333, on the problems of the historian-as-a-judge trope. In this context I also found useful Collingwood's considerations on the difference between analyzing historical sources as "testimony" and as "evidence" (*The Idea of History*, pp. 252ff., passim) and Koselleck's reflections on the historical development of historiographical "perspective" (*Futures Past*, pp. 128–151).

84. Strada, "Prolusio I," pp. 14–19 (quot. at 16), and Fumaroli, *L'Âge*, pp. 193–196.
85. Certeau, *The writing of history*, p. 93.
86. Ibid., pp. 86–102, and Chartier, "Michel de Certeau: History, or Knowledge of the Other," in *On the edge of the cliff*, 39–74. On this point, see also Koselleck's discussion of the significance of description and narration in historical representation (*Futures Past*, pp. 105–114 and 205–221) and White's notion of "middle voice" as expressed, e.g., in "Historical emplotment and the problem of truth in historical representation," now in *Figural Realism*, pp. 27–42, and "Writing in the middle voice," now in *The Fiction of Narrative*, pp. 255–262. Cf. also Martin Jay's criticism of White's notion in "Of Plots, Witnesses, and Judgments," in Saul Friedlander (ed.), *Probing the limits of representation*, pp. 97–107, esp. 100–101.
87. Il buon giudicio. . . è bastevole, a far accorto l'istorico, quanto sia necessario il vedere, ciò che ridire, ciò che tralasciare nella narrazione si debbia; quali cose in passando toccar si vogliono, quali diligentemente spiegare. Mascardi, *Dell'arte*, 57.
88. Tutti i negozi umani, la cui manifesta notizia sotto la conoscenza de' sentimenti non cade, han di mestiere che la loro occulta verità con studiosa esamina si rinvenga. Strumenti di ciò molto efficaci sono le congetture; le quali se giudiciosamente alle circostanze del negozio s'adattano, o di rado o non mai ingannano chi discorre; anzi fermando prima un verisimile universale, con la scorta di lui a ritrovar il vero particolare infallibilmente conducono. Ibid., p. 114. On fact that harangues and conjectures are necessary tools for historians to investigate obscure truths see also the interesting considerations in Viperano, *De scribenda historia*, p. 28 and pp. 41-42. In Viperano's reflections, however, we do not find the same attention to the temporal dimension of historiography that we find in Mascardi. Viperano, in fact, attributed the obscurity of historical truths simply to the complexities and difficulties inherent in the task of representing human events by means of human language, without taking into account the peculiar loss time inflicts on historical records and historical events. On Viperano's understanding of conjectures and harangues as hermeneutical tools also Grafton, *What was History?*, pp. 40-42. In order to appreciate the importance of Mascardi's reflections on the historian's judgment and conjectures, cf. also the much more limited role assigned by Vossius to the same tools (Nicholas Wickenden, *G. J. Vossius and the Humanist Concept of History*, Assen, Netherlands: Van Gorcum, 1993, pp. 120–123).
89. Chiunque per tanto valendosi delle congetture ben applicate alle circostanze del negozio che si maneggia forma senza fallacia di discorso le conchiusioni, non può dirsi rinvenir solo il verisimile, ma il vero, che nelle cose umane, sottoposte alla varietà di mille accidenti, si può trovare. Mascardi, *Dell'arte*, pp. 114–115.
90. In this sense, Mascardi's view of the historian's *giudicio* crosses over in an interesting way the subjective/objective dichotomy of the historian's craft without conflating the two; see Ricoeur, *Memory, History, Forgetting*, pp. 333–342.
91. L'ufficio dell'istorico, dicono gli avversari, è di raccontare schiettamente la verità, facendo che le cose accadute si ravvisino per l'appunto nelle memorie, senza ch'in esse si scorga divario; ma le concioni introdotte dagli scrittori non sono altro, che un parto del loro ingegno, per ostentazion di facondia, né si confanno con le cose accadute; dunque non debbono dal buon istorico, in adempimento dell'ufficio suo, essere adoprate già mai. Mascardi, *Dell'arte*, pp. 107–108.
92. Perché non nasce bene spesso dalla varietà delle parole con cui si narra, la varietà degli accidenti narrati; potendosi gli avvenimenti medesimi raccontare con maggiore o con minore eleganza; con maniere più ristrette, o più ampie; con l'ornamento di figure, o con la schiettezza del parlar naturale, senza mutazione alcuna che tocchi ed alteri la sostanza del vero. Ibid., p. 110.
93. Ibid., pp. 112–113.
94. L'istorico all'incontro il verisimile falso aborrisce, né già mai gli dà luogo nelle sue carte; perché ha per oggetto la verità, di cui la falsa somiglianza è nemica; adopra talora il verisimil vero, ma come strumento da rinvenire la verità. Ibid., p. 113. On the question of the poetic verisimilar as it was discussed among intellectuals in Mascardi's time, I found esp. useful Claudio Scarpati and Eraldo Bellini, *Il vero e il falso dei poeti. Tasso Tesauro Pallavicino Muratori*, Milan: Vita e Pensiero, 1990.

95. che il verisimile vero, nel modo che dall'istorico si pone in uso, equivocamente verisimile s'addimanda; poiché non esce fuori da quei termini della verità, che nelle cose civili l'umana diligenza prescrive; onde vero semplicemente può dirsi. Mascardi, *Dell'arte*, p. 114.

96. Ricoeur, *Memory History Forgetting*, pp. 274–280, quot. at 280. See also Ricoeur, *Time and Narrative*, vol. III, ch. 6.

97. Ginzburg, "Description and citation," p. 12; Ginzburg's italics.

98. Ibid.

99. Momigliano, "Ancient history and the antiquarian" and "The rise of antiquarian research."

100. Ginzburg, "Description and citation," pp. 22–23.

101. Strada, "Muretus," pp. 170–171. The first oration of the second book of the *Prolusiones academicae*, entitled "De stylo Oratorio: & an acumina dictorum vellicantesque sententiae Oratoribus usurpanda sint" (pp. 121–139), started with the discussion of the different styles that oratory, poetry, and history, respectively, needed to follow. In this initial section Strada complained because "quoties Historiam lego poetice nimis ac tragica lamentatione dolentem, aut exaggerato Oratorum more magnificeque narrantem, in permovendis animis, argumentorumque telis intorquendis insistentem, ubique certa per intervalla numerorum, percussionumque modos, verba modulantem" (p. 122).

102. Atque ut in marginatis librorum paginis appositus identidem manus index legentem monet, ut illud animo non indiligente, omissove praetereat: sic adjectae historicorum interpreta- tiones, iudicia sunt ac nota; quae vel oscitantes, aut sopitos exsuscitent, eisque documenti aliquid ultro ingerant. Strada, "Muretus," p. 155.

103. Strada, "Muretus," pp. 158–159.

104. All'incontro l'istorico studiandosi, secondo la sua obbligazione, di rappresentar per l'appunto, ma vivamente le materie che narra, procura che nell'animo de' leggenti s'imprimano quali sono: onde il suo primo fine è d'esprimer la verità degli accidenti, e d'adeguargli con le parole; i quali, perché secondo la diversità delle lor circostanze, quando efficacemente si narrino, destano in chi legge diversi affetti, non ripugna al candore e alla veracità dell'istorico, che in caso tale sieno commossi gli animi da' suoi racconti, perché ciò viene ad essere effetto della materia narrata; né per sua colpa rimane in parte alcuna offesa la verità. Mascardi, *Dell'arte*, pp. 295–296.

105. L'energia dunque, o vogliam dir l'evidenza, è una virtù dell'elocuzione, rappresentante tanto per minuto le cose narrate, che sotto a gli occhi de' leggenti in un certo modo le pone. Ibid., pp. 297–298. On the way in which early modern historians spoke of *enargeia*, a rhetorical tool discussed in Aristotle's *Rhetoric* and much debated in the context of ancient oratory, see Ginzburg, "Description and citation," pp. 8–12.

106. Che sia virtù all'istorico necessaria è manifesto; perché dovendo egli in adempimento delle sue parti adoperar con la penna, che la verità de' fatti nella sincerità delle sue narrazioni per l'appunto si riconosca, con quanto maggior accuratezza e puntualità l'anderà descrivendo, tanto più vivamente potrà ella ravvisarsi da' leggitori, perché la vederanno ad un certo modo con gl'occhi ritratta al naturale, quasi in pittura, nelle carte dello scrittore. Mascardi, *Dell'arte*, p. 298.

107. Alcuni acerbamente mordono l'opera mia, perché troppo denso stimano il numero degli autori de' quali mi vaglio, e troppo ambizioso il racconto de' nomi loro, che nel margine si rapportano. . . ne' miei discorsi morali su la Tavola di Cebete io nomino di molti antichi autori, specialmente greci, de' quali non abbiamo l'opere intere ma qualche frammento.... Alcuni uomini tondi sono iti per le botteghe de' librari limosinando l'opere di coloro, e ne portavano una breve nota de' nomi; e perché non solo non trovarono i libri, ma videro non esser di loro presso il libraro notizia alcuna, si diero a credere ch'io, per servire alla materia mi fabricassi e le dottrine ed i nomi degli scrittori a capriccio.... Per disinganno dunque degli uomini più naturali, e de' giovani non ancor introdotti negli scrittori famosi, io porto il nome di ciascuno nel margine del mio libro, insieme col luogo. Ibid., epistle to the reader, pp. 3–4.

108. Scaliger failed to distinguish between *enargeia* and *energeia* and thus translated the former as the latter (see his *Poetices libri septem*, Geneva, 1561, pp. 116ff.). Mascardi knew of this error, but he remarked that perhaps it was not simply due to a mistake "nell'interpretazione grammaticale." Rather, for Mascardi "vide lo Scaligero la necessaria corrispondenza dell'una con l'altra, in virtù di cui l'energia nasce in gran parte dall'enargia. Perché la favella che nel

racconto più generale, e senza il caldo dell'evidenza, riman languida e fredda, illustrata da questa virtù, ch'innanzi agli occhi rappresenta gli oggetti, tutta s'invigorisce ed infiamma. . . onde può ben talora intervenire che l'energia, o vogliam dir l'efficacia, sia disaccompagnata dell'enargia, cioè dell'evidenza; e nasca d'altronde, come vuole Aristotele; ma non è per trovarsi mai enargia senza energia" (*Dell'arte*, pp. 301–302).

109. Conchiudasi dunque non esser vero ciò che per indubitato ci prescrivevano que' valent'uomini, che dall'istoria tanto l'amplificazione quanto il commovimento degli animi debbono esser tenuti lontani; perché dell'una e dell'altro ella è senza dubbio capace, tuttoché con maniera differente ed a fine molto diverso da quello degli oratori l'adopri, quando dentro a' suoi propri termini si contiene. Mascardi, *Dell'arte*, p. 307.

110. Onde s'alcuno rispondesse al quisito con dire, il fine dell'istoria esser la conservazione degli avvenimenti umani nella memoria de' posteri, direbbero vero in suo senso, perché questo è il fine primo, ma non primario, che vien proposto all'istoria; ma io all'incontro direi, che il conservar nella memoria degli uomini gli avvenimenti memorevoli è un mezzo, per cui l'istoria arriva al suo vero fine. Ibid., p. 74.

111. L'utile dunque de' leggenti è il vero fine che si propone l'istoria, ma tanto strettamente col diletto congiunto, che l'uno, per lo più, non può in componimento di buona mano separatamente trovarsi; e ciascun di loro nel proprio genere è grande. Ibid. Here Mascardi quotes Dionysius of Halicarnassus and Lucian as representatives of the side of *voluptas* and of the side of *utilitas*, respectively.

112. Potrei dire essere utilità impareggiabile dell'istoria ch'ella riserba all'immortalità della gloria le prodezze degli uomini, anzi de' popoli valorosi; le quali per altro, dentro all'angusto giro d'una brevissima vita imprigionate, rimaner dovevano co' cadaveri seppellite. . . In somma o sieno Greci, o sien Latini gli autori di poesie, tutti unitamente questo vanto si danno, che per lor cagione vive presso de' posteri il nome degli uomini più singolari; i quali abbandonati dall'aiuto delle penne poetiche, non potevano con la fama oltrepassare i termini della vita. Ma sia con vostra pace, o anime pellegrine, questa è lode dovuta all'istoria, perché se belle e prezione le vostre scritture non sono, quando con nobili menzogne non arricchiscono la materia; quanto meglio adempirete le vostre parti fingendo, tanto minor credenza è da prestarvi il leggente; sicuro allora di non trovar verità di fatto, dove s'incontra leggiadria d'invenzione. Mascardi, *Dell'arte*, pp. 75–76.

113. perché meritava questo eccesso di pietà naturale di non rimaner seppellito, benché fosse nato sopra un sepolcro. Ibid., p. 64. (Presumably, then, and following the hint of John Lewis Gaddis, since Guicciardini liberated Gilbert's son from oblivion, the young man has now become one of the grateful dead; see *The Landscape of History*, p. 139 and n. 13).

114. Non veggiamo ancor oggi, dopo secoli innumerabili, Belo fabricator di Babilonia fondar la monarchia sopra gli Assiri?. . . Non siamo, in virtù dell'istoria, presenti all'assedio di Tiro. . . alla presura di Sagunto?. . . ma che vad'io inutilmente aggirandomi per lodi improprie all'istoria, e poco profittevoli a chi legge, mentre la sola curiosità con legger cibo nodriscono, non alimentan l'animo con la sostanza delle virtù? Mascardi, *Dell'arte*, p. 77.

115. See Ricoeur, *Time and Narrative*, vol. III, ch. 6.

116. On the dialectic between distance and proximity in historical thought, see also Mark Salber Phillips, "Distance and Historical Representation," *History Workshop Journal*, no. 57 (2004), pp. 123–141 and id., *On Historical Distance*.

Chapter 3

1. Most of what we know of Vigilantius comes from Jerome himself in his *Contra Vigilantium*. Among the recent attempts to place Vigilantius in his own theological and historical context, I found useful David G. Hunter, "Vigilantius of Calagurris and Victricius of Rouen: Ascetics, Relics, and Clerics in Late Roman Gaul," *Journal of Early Christian Studies* 7, no. 3 (1999), pp. 401–430.

2. The text of Jerome's *Contra Vigilantium* can be found in PL, vol. XXIII, cols. 337–352. The quote comes from §7, col. 346. An accessible English translation of this work can be found in *A Select Library of Nicene and Post-Nicene Fathers*, vol. VI (New York, 1893), pp. 417–23 (the passage quoted is on p. 420). The translation used here is my own.

3. Ibid., col. 345. In this passage Jerome refers to 1 Thessalonians 5:6 and to a sarcastic joke on Vigilantius's name made at the beginning of the text: for Jerome, Vigilantius should rather be named "Dormitantius," given his opposition to the liturgical practice of the *"vigilia"* (cf. PL, vol. XXIII, cols. 339–340).

4. Ibid., cols. 345–346.

5. See Flacius Illyricus et al., eds., *Ecclesiastica Historia*, 7 vols., Basel 1561–74, *Centuria* IV (esp. ch. XIII), and *Centuria* V (esp. ch. VI).

6. Si l'idolâtrie n'est sinon transférer l'honneur de Dieu ailleurs, nierons-nous que cela ne soit idolâtrie? Et ne faut excuser que ce a été un zèle désordonné de quelques rudes et idiots ou de simple femmes. Car ce a été un désordre général, approuvé de ceux qui avaient le gouvernement et conduit de l'Église. Calvin, *Traité des reliques*, pp. 20–21, ed. Irena Backus, Geneva, 2000.

7. Simon Ditchfield, *Liturgy, Sanctity, and History in Tridentine Italy. Pietro Maria Campi and the Preservation of the Particular*, Cambridge: Cambridge University Press, 1995, esp. pp. 273–285.

8. exploratum habetur adhiberi solita in ecclesia luminaria non ad tenebras tantum propellendas, sed sacri cultus celebritatem illustrandam. Id quidem in Orientis ecclesiis fieri solitum, Hieronymus agens contra Vigilantium fidei desertorem isthaec in catholicos exprobrantem plane testatur his verbis: absque martyrum reliquiis per totas Orientis ecclesias, quando legendum est Evangelium, acccenduntur luminaria iam sole rutilante, non idque ad fugandas tenebras, sed ad signum laetitiae demonstrandum etc. agere pergit de luminum mystico sensu. Manoscritti Vaticani Latini (henceforth Vat. Lat.) 5684, f. 335.

9. Quodvero de aliis locis quod ad diuturnum spectat lumen, sic dicit: cereos autem non clara luce accendimus, sicut frustra calumniaris, sed ut noctis tenebras hoc solatio temperemus et vigilemus ad lumen, nec caeci tecum dormiamus in tenebris. Quod si aliqui propter imperitiam et simplicitatem secularium hominum, vel certe religiosarum feminarum, de quibus vere possumus dicere: confiteor zelum Dei habent, sed non secundum scientiam, hoc pro honore martyrum faciunt. Quid inde perdis? Causantur quondam et Apostoli, quod periret unguentum, sed Domini voce correpti sunt; neque enim Christus indigebat unguento, nec martyres lumine cereorum; et tamen illa mulier in honore Christi hoc facit, devotioque mentis eius recipitur: et quicumque accendunt cereos, secundum fidem suam habent mercedem dicente Apostolo: unusquisque in suo sensu abundet [Romans 14:5]. Idolatras appellas huiusmodi homines! Non diffiteor, omnes nos qui in Christo credimus de errore Idolatriae venisse; non enim nascimur, sed renascimur Christiani. Et quia quondam celebramus idola, num colere Deum non debemus, ne simili eum videamur cum idolis honore venerari! Illud fiebat idolis, et idcirco detestandum est: hoc fit martyribus, et idcirco recipiendum est. Haec Hieronymus. Ibid.

10. Haud dubium Gentiles etiam (quod et Iudaei pia religione agebant), incendere consuevisse eadem ex causa lucernas. Unde et Iuvenalis satyr.12 [v.92] et matutinis operantur festa lucernis. Docet hoc ipsum Tertullianus saepius, ut in Apologetico c.35 Nec lucernis, inquit, diem infringimus. Ibid.

11. Sed cum haec ipsa (ut vidimus) aeque Iudaei factitarent atque Gentiles, cur non potius a Iudaeis ea sicut et pleraque alia, quam a Gentilibus ecclesiam mutuatam esse dixerimus. Et si velimus accepta ab his esse: quid absurdum si eadem in veri Dei cultum conversa fuerint! Ibid.

12. Quod vero dicat cereos non incendi solitos die, nisi in ecclesiis Orientis, quod in sup. addat de cereis honore martyrum incendi solitis, idque totum tribuat secularium hominum simplicitati, vel feminarum zelo non secundum scientiam: scabrosus plane locus est; quem non nisi levi offensa Hieronymi, quis inoffenso pede valeat penitus superare. Ibid.

13. Certe quidem perspicitur quod in fine eiusdem scriptionis habet, se tabellario properante scriptionem illam unius noctis brevi lucubratiunculam dictasse, pollicitus nimirum si ea ad compescendum hominis procaciam non sufficissent, rursus in eundem omne studium impensurum. Ibid. See also Jerome's text in PL, vol. XXIII, col. 352.

14. Quamobrem sicut properantis hominis non est omnia facile pervidere vel omnium reminisci: brevi illo temporis spatio (pace tanti patris id dixerim) illum multa praeterivisse oportuit. Sit in exemplum, quod in eodem libro dixit reliquias Andreae, Lucae, et Timothei

translatas esse a Constantino Costantinopolim, immemor se in libro quem antea scripserat de autoribus ecclesiasticis, id factum anno vigesimo Constantii tradidisset. Constantii enim ut habet verior lectio et non Constantini legenda est: nam non tantum spectum habetur, ex rei gestae historia, sed eiusdem Hieronymi testimonio, qui in appendice sui chronici ad Eusebium id factum sub Constantio manifeste testatur. Vat. Lat. 5684, f. 335.

15. Ibid., fos. 335–336.

16. Ad illud de cereis, dico cereos accensos coram tumulis Martyrum non esse signum adorationis, Deo debitae; nam non offeruntur cerei Martyribus tamquam sacrificia, sed accenduntur in signum laetitiae. . . ad Hieronymum dico, eum, cum ait de iis qui accendunt cereos coram reliquiis "Confiteor, zelum Dei habent, sed non secundum scientiam" loqui de iis, qui cereos accendunt, existimantes inde Martyres illustrari. R. Bellarmine, *Opera Omnia*, ed. Justin Fèvre, Paris: L. Vivès, 1870–1876, 12 vols., vol. III, p. 211.

17. Ibid.

18. In quanto al loco di S. Hieronimo, il P. Bellarmino lassa di toccare quella difficultà dell'accendere i lumi di notte, & non di giorno, nel che verte la mia obiettione: come prego vediate attentamente & me ne rescriviate, se vi è risposta da poter scusar S. Hieronimo. Et in quanto al P. Bellarmino, lui lo scusa nell'altro capo: *Quoniam zelum habet*, & c. Mi pesa quando bisogna venir a simil termini di toccare gli Padri; pur per la verità del'istoria, & dogmi Cattolici non si può far di mando. Baronio to Talpa, Rome March 4, 1588, in Raymundus Albericius, ed., *Venerabilis Caesaris Baronii. . . Epistolae et Opuscula*, 3 vols., Rome 1759–1770, vol. III, Epistola VIII. Italics in the original.

19. Tutte simili obiettioni sono state fatte al R.P. Bernardo Compagno del Mastro Sacri Palatii, a tal fine è rimasto capace della ragione; pur mi affatigarò, se si potesse detta objettione in qualche modo mitigare, overo per dir il vero, impiastrare. Che in vero non fa bon sono alle orecchie pie. Io non ho mancato di vedere secondo le occorrentie le Controversie del detto Padre, quali dal Stampatore mi forno mandate a donare. Ibid. "Bernardo" might here be a mispelled version of "Bonardo," who was then Zobbia's *collega* and whom Baronio mentioned in the printed version of the *Annales* (see infra, note no. 24).

20. Certe quidem testimonio etiam Vigilantii, moles, ut ait, cereorum Sole fulgente, accendi solere in ecclesiis, satis liquet: licet ipse pium cultum derideat; perinde ac si id fideles facerent ad martyres illuminandos. In quem haec iure Hieronymus: Cereos non clara luce accendimus (sicut frustra calumniaris) nimirum ut hoc pietatis officio putemus martyres e tenebris vindicari, quorum lucerna est Agnus. Sed mysterium docet, scilicet sic facere, ut (quod sequitur) noctis tenebras hoc solatio temperemus: nempe (quod ait Apostolus) Nox praecessit, dies autem appropinquavit, abiiciamus ergo opera tenebrarum, & induamur arma lucis [Romans 13:12]. Ac proinde (quod subdit) vigilemus ad lumen, ne caeci tantum dormiamus in tenebris. Perstat enim in metaphora, qua superius iam quarto eundem non Vigilantium, sed Dorminantium nominaverat; & paulo superius dixerat: Tu vigilans dormis, & dormiens scribis. Vel adhuc etiam dicere possumus, quod ait: Cereos non clara luce accendimus non ipsum diem per lucem claram intellexisse, sed lumen ipsum, quo cerei accenduntur, ut sit sensus: non fulgenti lumine accendimus cereos, ut tu dicis, ad illustrandos martyres; sicque nihil de die esse locutum. *Annales Ecclesiastici*, vol. I, Rome, 1588, anno Christi 58, Petri 14, Imperatori 2, p. 519.

21. Nam quonam pacto negasse potuit, interdiu a fidelibus accendi lumina, qui paulo post de toto Oriente, ubi ipse agebat, haec ait: per totas Orientis ecclesias quando legendum est Evangelium, accenduntur luminaria, iam sole rutilante, non idque ad fugandas tenebras, sed ad signum laetitiae demonstrandum. Immo & id ipsum factitari solitum in ecclesia Hierosolymitana, sub qua vivebat ipse Hieronymus, Epiphanius scribens ad Ioannem tunc temporis eius sedis Episcopum, demonstrat. . . . Ac nec rursum potuit eum dixisse de ecclesia Occidentali, in qua pariter accendi solita lumina interdiu, S. Paolinus illi aequalis docet. Ibid., p. 519.

22. Sic pariter quod idem subdit Hieronymus: Quod si aliqui, propter imperitiam & simplicitatem saecularium hominum, vel certe religiosarum feminarum, de quibus possumus dicere: Confiteor Dei zelum habent, sed non secundum scientiam: hoc pro honore martyris faciunt, quid inde perdis? Idem est ac si diceret; esto quod tu dicis, id eo modo, quod asseris, faciant simpliciores, ut putent cereis martyres illustrandos, sicque habeant zelum non secundum scientiam: quid tamen inde perdis? Ibid., p. 519.

23. Usitatus est disserendi modus Hieronymi, ut adversus haereticos pugnans, nec latum unguem eisdem loco cedat. Caeterum eiusmodi pietatis cultum a se probari, in eodem commentario paulo inferius & supra eodem argumento ad Riparium scribens, aperte aeque ac libere profitetur. Ibid., p. 519.

24. Sed in his non immoramur, quod sciamus R.P. Vincentium Bonardum, Magistri Sacri Palatii collegam, novarum ex officio scriptionum cognitionem, eiusdem argumenti eruditum scripsisse libellum. Ibid., p. 520. The title of Bonardo's book was *Discorso intorno all'origine, antichità et virtù degli Agnus Dei di cera benedetti*, published for the first time in Rome in 1586. The book, which aimed at regulating the semisuperstitious use of the wax *Agnus Dei* according to the post-Tridentine principle of disciplining and controlling phenomena of popular religion, became an editorial success, and it was reprinted again in 1591, 1621, 1624, and several other times during the seventeenth and eighteenth centuries. On the developments and significance of the rituals linked to the wax *Agnus Dei*, see Agostino Paravicini-Bagliani, *The Pope's Body*, Chicago: University of Chicago Press, 2000, pp. 75–81, and Sergio Bertelli, *The King's Body: Sacred rituals of power in medieval and early modern Europe*, University Park, PA: Pennsylvania State University Press, 2001, pp. 128–138.

25. On Baronio's research method and skills, see, among others, Stefano Zen, *Baronio storico. Controriforma e crisi del metodo umanistico*, Naples: Vivarium, 1994, and Giuseppe Antonio Guazzelli, "La documentazione numismatica negli *Annali ecclesiastici* di Cesare Baronio," in Luigi Gulia, ed., *Baronio e le sue fonti*, Sora: Centro di Studi Sorani "Vincenzo Patriarca," 2009, pp. 489–548. On the role of Baronio's Congregation in fostering research in ecclesiastical history, see Ditchfield, *Liturgy, Sanctity, and History*, pp. 273ff. As a testament to the reputation that Baronio's immense erudition enjoyed even among his Protestant contemporaries, I would cite briefly the example of Degory Wheare, the first Camden Professor of ancient history at Oxford and the author of a very popular *ars historiae*–type of treatise, one of the last of its kind. The first edition of this work, entitled *De ratione et methodo* and published in 1623, contained nothing on ecclesiastical history. The second edition, published two years later, although much enlarged, still remained silent on the question of ecclesiastical history. In 1637 Wheare decided to revise substantially his work, and the new version, entitled *Relectiones hyemales de ratione et methodo*, did include a long section devoted to discussing ecclesiastical history. In this part of his work Wheare explicitly referred to Casaubon as the main authority on the history of Judaism and on Hebrew sources and to Baronio as the main authority on the history of Christianity. Wheare wrote that while the Magdeburg Centuries were a "very useful work" even though they contained "not a few things that leave much to be desired," Baronio's *Annales* was "a work simply stupendous (by the admission of the most learned men, including Casaubon himself)." Baronio, according to Wheare, deserved the credit of having "collected all the things that pertained to the Church in a continuous series of years," so that Baronio's annals of the Church looked "almost like the annals of one city." Wheare admitted that Baronio's work had an ideological agenda that his Protestant students could not afford to ignore: "it is fair to say that Casaubon spoke without temerity when he said that the great merits of that Cardinal were partly stained by his zeal. For this reason any student of ecclesiastical history should know that Baronio's *Annales* cannot be read without caution, and indeed how much caution one should use is indicated very well by the most learned Casaubon in his prolegomena to the *Exercitationes*." Nevertheless, Wheare's admiration for Baronio's erudition and scholarly energy is palpable in this text: "[Baronio] is the only one who first brought to light so many things, out of I don't know what obscure place, which before were completely unknown" (D. Wheare, *Relectiones*, Oxford, 1637, pp. 211–216). Indeed, well before writing this text Wheare seemed to have considered Baronio, perhaps with a slight touch of irony, as the erudite par excellence. In 1601, while Wheare was in Oxford as tutor of John Pym, he wrote a playful note to his friend Charles Fitzgeffry, a fellow Cornishman and Oxford student who was part of the same Broadgates Hall circle in which Wheare was active, to describe a trip that Wheare had planned and that the unfavorable weather had obliged him to postpone. The destination of the trip was supposed to be a little town in Somerset, a place so obscure, Wheare joked, that only Baronio could shed some light on it: "Hodie mane fascinulas collegerem ipsius iussu, et libellos omnes in arculam commodum composueram, Stoam hinc (non platonicam illam sed sommersetensem nescio quam)

opidulum satis obscurum nisi quod Baronius huius nomen aliquid ei luminis addiderit disce-dendi certus, stabant prae foribus clitellarii sarcinae ferendae parati: ecce autem de subito mutata est ei sententia mihi iter dilatum, placet divitius hic immorari," Wheare to Fitzgeffry, October 23, 1601, BOD, MS. Seld. Supra 81, Ep. 77).

26. On this, see esp. Arsenio Frugoni, "La 'Storia' del Baronio," in id., *Incontri nel Rinascimento*, Brescia: La Scuola, 1954, pp. 191–208.

27. Ibid., quot. at p. 192.

28. Stefano Zen, *Baronio storico*, quot. at pp. 229-230, but see the entire ch. 5. For an insightful criticism of Zen's argument and for an attempt to rebalance Baronio's contribution more on the side of theology and less on the side of historical criticism and philology, see Riccardo Fubini, "Baronio e la tradizione umanistica. Note su un libro recente," in id., *Storiografia dell'Umanesimo in Italia da Leonardo Bruni ad Annio da Viterbo*, Rome: Edizioni di Storia e Letteratura, 2003, pp. 360–371; and Simon Ditchfield, "Baronio storico nel suo tempo," forthcoming, in G. A. Guazzelli, R. Michetti, and F. Scorza Barcellona, eds., *Cesare Baronio fra santità e scrittura storica* (I thank Dr. Ditchfield for sending me a copy of this essay in advance of its publication).

29. Arnaldo Momigliano, "The Origins of Ecclesiastical Historiography," in id., *The classical foundations*, pp. 132–152, quot. at 137. Momigliano's emphasis.

30. Anthony Grafton, *The footnote. A curious history*, Cambridge, MA: Harvard University Press, 1997, p. 166, but see his entire ch. 6. See also Anthony Grafton and Joanna Weinberg, *"I have always loved the holy tongue": Isaac Casaubon, the Jews, and a forgotten chapter in Renaissance scholarship*, Cambridge, MA: Harvard University Press, 2011, pp. 164–230.

31. On the nature, uses, and aims of Baronio's historical work and of post-Reformation Catholic sacred history more generally, see the work of Simon Ditchfield, esp. *Liturgy, Sanctity and History*; " 'Historia magistra sanctitatis'? The relationship between historiography and hagiography in Italy after the Council of Trent (1564–1743 ca.)," in Massimo Firpo, ed., *Nunc alia tempora, alii mores. Storici e storia in età postridentina*, Florence: Olschki, 2005, pp. 3–23; "Baronio storico nel suo tempo" and "What was sacred history? (Mostly Roman) Catholic uses of the Christian past after Trent," in Katherine Van Liere, Simon Ditchfield, and Howard Louthan, eds., *Sacred History. Uses of the Christian Past in the Renaissance World*, Oxford: Oxford University Press, 2012, pp. 72–97. On the link between liturgy and history in Baronio's *Martyrologium*, see Guazzelli, "Cesare Baronio e il *Martyrologium Romanum*: problemi interpretativi e linee evolutive di un rapporto diacronico," in *Nunc alia tempora*, pp. 47–89.

32. Nos autem, quoniam non tantum res antiquas, sed Ecclesiasticas potissimum pertractamus, in quibus non solum, ut in caeteris historiis, ipsa veritas primum sibi vendicare locum debet; sed vel latum unguem ab ea recessisse, religio est: hanc ob causam ne proditae veritatis, vel levi saltem suspicione pulsemur; Christianis legibus obsequentes praecipientibus: sit sermo vester: est est, non non; quod autem his abundantius est, a malo est [Matthew 5:37]: relinquemus historicis Ethnicis locutiones illas, per longiorem ambitum periphrastice circunductas, orationesque summa arte concinnatas, & fictas, ex sententia cuiusque compositas, ad libitumque dispositas, & Annales potius, quam historiam scribemus, & quod Ecclesiasticam maiestatem ac gravitatem maxime decet, dicendi genus sectantes: quae dicenda sunt sancte, pure, sincereque absque ullo prorsus fuco, vel figmento, prout gesta sunt, per annos singulos digesta enarrabimus.... Quamobrem res ipas ecclesiasticas ad suum principium reducentes, sic res gestas recensebimus, ut ecclesiastica ecclesiastice pertractemus; cumque in ommibus testimonio nitamur antiquorum, veritatique consultum velimus, illorum potius verba singula reddere, quamvis horridula, & incomposita aliquando videri possint, quam nostra apponere, ac describere, a nobis est constitutum. Atque ut magis magisque eadem veritas elucescat, indiscussum nihil, quod ambiguum, vel veritati contrarium esse senserimus, uspiam relinquemus. *Annales*, vol. I (1588), pp. 1–6, quot. at 3–4.

33. Et perché altra è la professione del historico da quella del defensore de' dogmi, in tal maniera bisogna nel'historia mostrare per le traditioni, & verità li dogmi, che non para haver voluto far quello istesso, ma lassar al lettore, o catholico o heretico che sia, dalle cose dette & ben fondate cavarne la certezza della verità, & da quella formarne argumenti in destruttione delle heresie. Baronio to Talpa, Rome, 9 December 1589, in Albericius, *Epistolae et Opuscula*, vol. III, Epistola XXXVIII.

34. See Zen, *Baronio storico*, ch. 2.
35. See Ginzburg, "Description and citation," esp. pp. 20ff.
36. Ibid., p. 24. On the question of the relationship between evidence and *evidentia* see also supra, ch. 2, pp. 67ff.
37. Baronio's biography was composed in the early 1580s, but it remained in manuscript for about a century. It was edited and published for the first time in 1680 in the Bollandists' *Acta Sanctorum*. The work was also reprinted in Albericius, *Epistolae et Opuscula*, vol. II, pp. 241ff. On this work, see Generoso Calenzio, *La vita e gli scritti del cardinale Cesare Baronio*, Rome: Tipografia Vaticana, 1907, pp. 216–217.
38. Ex ea tam ingenti Reliquiarum translatione, & collocatione factum est, Pater Beatissime, ut multi ad Sancti huius memoriam colendam vehementius inflammati, eius & res gestas, vitamque cognoscere percuperent; e quorum numero nonnulli amici, saepius ea de re mecum egerunt, rogaveruntque impensius, ut onus hoc susciperem: quibus cum responderem, non esse hoc imbecillitatis meae, tum extare Orationem Gregorii Presbyteri de laudibus Nazianzeni, non accipiebant excusationem meam. Gregorium vero Presbyterum, ajebant, non tam vitam, quam laudationem conscripsisse, multa itidem ab eo omissa, brevius, quam par erat, nonnulla alieno loco narrata, quaedam etiam parum cum historiae veritate consentanea: quid multa? pervicerunt, & perpulerunt. Itaque non tam volens, quam obediens, opus magnum aggressus, Vitam Gregorii Nazianzeni scribere institui. Conatus sum autem, etsi rudis plane artifex, egregias illas Gregoriani Sacelli picturas aliquo modo imitari. Ut enim ibi pictor eximius ex tesserulis, & lapillis miro artificio musivo opere compositis, & coagmentatis, cum aliorum quorumdam Ecclesiae Doctorum, tum Gregorii nostri effigiem venustissime expressit; ita ego ex ipsius Nazianzeni potissimum scriptis, quae ille de se ipso variis in locis alio currens, aliud agens, obiter scripsit, aut etiam data opera commemorat, selecta fragmenta, tanquam gemmas & lapillos, accurate collegi; quos, servato temporum ordine, suis locis collocavi, & quasi inter se conglutinavi, ut ex iis, velut ex splendisissimis coloribus, vitam viri omnino expressam, saltem adumbratam haberemus. Neque enim diffiteor, multa adhuc desiderari posse: & nos fortasse aliquando opus diligentius perpoliemus, praesertim si quamplurima Gregorii carmina, & alia quaedam ex vetustis codicibus nondum edita, ad manus nostras, ut speramus, pervenerint. Baronio to Gregory XIII, undated, in Albericius, *Epistolae et Opuscula*, vol. I, epistola II.
39. As Glen W. Bowersock has argued, Baronio misrepresented the archaeological evidence found in the apse of the old St. Peter's Basilica in order to present what he thought was proof of the fact that the church was founded by Constantine as a token of his reverence toward St. Peter and his successors; see "Peter and Constantine," in William Tronzo, ed., *St. Peter's in the Vatican*, Cambridge: Cambridge University Press, 2005, pp. 5–15, at 11–12.
40. Cf. Zen, *Baronio storico*, pp. 80–92.
41. Momigliano, "The Origins," quot. at p. 150.
42. Momigliano, "Pagan and Christian historiography in the fourth century A.D.," in id., *Terzo contributo alla storia degli studi classici e del mondo antico*, Rome: Edizioni di Storia e Letteratura, 1966, vol. I, pp. 87–109 (orig. pub. as "The conflict between Paganism and Christianity in the fourth century," Oxford: Clarendon Press, 1963, pp. 79–99).
43. Grafton, "Church History in Early Modern Europe: Tradition and Innovation," in Katherine Van Liere, Simon Ditchfield, and Howard Louthan, eds., *Sacred History*, pp. 3–26 (quot. at 18).
44. For a more detailed analysis of Baronio's neo-Eusebian historical methodology in the context of post-Reformation ecclesiastical history see Tutino, "'For the sake of the truth of history and of the Catholic doctrines': History, documents, and dogma in Cesare Baronio's *Annales Ecclesiastici*," *Journal of Early Modern History*, no. 17 (2013), pp. 125–159.
45. Polman, *L'élément historique*.
46. On the importance of the post-Reformation confessional battles for the development of ecclesiastical history, see Backus, *Historical method*; Grafton, "Where was Salomon's House? Ecclesiastical history and the intellectual origins of Bacon's *New Atlantis*," in id., *Worlds made by Words. Scholarship and Community in the Modern West*, Cambridge, MA: Harvard University Press, 2009, pp. 98–113; Ditchfield, *Liturgy, Sanctity, and History*.
47. Momigliano, "The Origins," p. 151.

48. Ibid., p. 152.

49. Con l'esempio e con l'autorità di questi grandi, il cardinal Baronio, di gloriosa ed immortal ricordanza, nell'opera utilissima degli *Annali Ecclesiastici*, calpesta il medesimo sentiero; e tutto inteso alla distinzione e all'ordine de' tempi, conduce per dodici secoli felicemente la sua dottissima impresa. E nondimeno s'è trovato qualche scrittor moderno, che l'ha di ciò molto agramente ripreso; e perché s'avvedeva non dover esser dagli uomini scienziati approvata la sua censura, come all'uso de' grandi ed alla ragione ripugnante, riduce, per sua discolpa, la testura degli Annali a quell'antica seccaggine ricordata da Tullio; quando da' sacerdoti, o vogliam dir da' pontefici, nudamente gli avvenimenti si descrivevano, e venivano esposti al popolo per ammaestramento comune; perciò conchiude, che il cardinal Baronio elegger doveva materia proporzionata agli Annali, o diversamente ordinar la testura di quel che ha scritto. Ma quel dottissimo cardinale non aveva bisogno dell'insegnamento del Beni, a cui esser poteva in ogni materia, senza paragone, maestro; perché avendo ben esaminata la disposizione a' suoi racconti dicevole, con l'osservazione degli scrittori più celebri, a bello studio elesse il modo tenuto negli Annali da Tacito, e da Tucidide nell'Istoria, a lui consigliata dall'autorità di Sant'Agostino, come nella prefazione del primo tomo ci lasciò scritto. Perché quella vieta e smunta narrazione degli antichissimi Annali è ita in dimenticanza; né v'ha scrittore d'intendimento gentile, che di rinnovarne in questo secolo le sembianze, impresa vile e perduta non riputasse. Mascardi, *Dell'arte historica*, p. 367. The reference to Augustine is from *De doctrina Christiana*, (book II chap.28, text in PL vol.XXXIV) which Baronio quoted as a testament to the importance and usefulness of annals for historical knowledge (Baronio's quote can be found on p. 4 of the preface to the 1588 edition of the *Annales*). Soon after this quotation, on p. 6, Baronio returned to Augustine and referred to his epistle 101 to Memorius (section 2, text in PL vol.XXXIII) on the importance of truth and truthfulness for historians.

50. *Dictionnaire historique et critique*, Rotterdam 1697, 2 vols.: the article on Beni is in vol. I, pp. 541-542, quot. at 541. The scholarship on Beni is very scant and usually limited to a cursory mention of Paolo Beni as an early Baroque interpreter of Aristotle's *Poetics* and as one of the most representative defenders of the moderns in the early stage of the *querelle des anciens et des modernes*. More recently, however, Beni has been the subject of an accurate reconsideration by P. B. Diffley, who, on the basis of his research in the Beni Archive (contained in the ASV), has done much to clarify certain key features of Beni's biography and intellectual production (*Paolo Beni. A Biographical and Critical Study*, Oxford: Clarendon Press, 1988). On the Beni Archive within the ASV, see also Pier Paolo Piergentili, *L'Archivio dei Conti Beni di Gubbio (note storiche e inventario)*, Vatican City: Archivio Segreto Vaticano, 2003.

51. The "mysterious" nature of Beni's expulsion is heightened by the fact that in the archive of the Society of Jesus we have a note saying that Beni was dismissed "iustas ob causas," and in that same document a few lines containing a longer explanation for Beni's expulsion were scratched out (see ARSI, Hist. Soc. 54, f. 13r).

52. See Diffley, *Paolo Beni*, pp. 31-39, on Beni's experience as a Jesuit, but see Diffley's entire biographical section, pp. 9-117. For a different explanation for Beni's expulsion, see Maurizio Sangalli, "Paolo Beni: Da gesuita a Ricovrato," in Ezio Riondato, ed., *Dall'Accademia dei Ricovrati all'Accademia Galileiana*, Padua: Accademia Galileiana di Scienze, Lettere ed Arti, 2001, pp. 491-503, in which Sangalli argued that Beni's not entirely orthodox Platonism was the reason for his dismissal. Bayle too suggested that the expulsion of Beni had something to do with Plato: according to Bayle, Beni wanted to publish a commentary on Plato's *Symposium*, but because of the "obscenity of the subject" the Society of Jesus refused Beni permission to publish the work and expelled him (see *Dictionnaire*, vol. I, p. 541).

53. Già che V.R. ha giudicato che di presente non si possa prender risoluzione sopra la gratia ch'io le dimandava, son forzato a scoprir quello che per non annoiarla tacqui nell'altra mia. E mi perdoni se per avventura le paressi alquanto lungo, che il travaglio nel qual mi trovo me ne sforza. ASV, Beni II 137, fos. 247r–248v at 247r. I propose to date this draft to 1592 or early 1593, when Beni, who was assigned to the faculty of the Jesuit College in Milan, wanted to leave his post and either move back to Rome or go back to Gubbio so as to be able to deal with some financial issues involving his family. According to Diffley, Acquaviva refused to let Beni go, and Beni went to Gubbio without permission before being definitely dismissed by the Society in 1593 (see *Paolo Beni*, pp. 37–38).

54. la quale opinione è di Soto in 4 d.22 q.c. a.4 di Victoria Tract. de exc.ar. 13 in f.e Medina de confes. q.22. . . et altri antichi i quali se bene non trattano ciò ex professo, mostrano d'haver presa l'estravagante in questo senso. . . del P. Carlo Reggio mio M.ro dal quale io l'appresi e sentii dechiarar molto bene. Anzi è in tutto conforme a S. Tom. . . Talché io il quale non sum melior patribus meis ho sequitato la loro opinione. ASV Beni II 137, fos. 247r–248r. In the draft Beni erased the words "dal quale io l'appresi e sentii dechiarar molto bene," possibly trying to avoid pitting too openly Acquaviva against Reggio. The notes from Carlo Reggio's lecture on excommunication during his time as professor at the Roman College can be found in APUG, FC 899, fos. 206r–224v.

55. [erased: "altre ragioni, che perora non voglio che mi vagliano punto, havendo fatto professione d'attenermi al mio M.ro. . . conforme all'avvertimento ch'io haveva havuto dal P.N. Provinciale"] ASV Beni II 137, f. 248r.

56. Vero è ch'io l'ho letta con tante limitationi che quasi quasi mi sono accordato con la parte contraria si come V.R. intenderà [erased: "per un capo descritto nell'inchiuso foglio dalle mie lettioni ad verbum"]. Ibid.

57. See Questier, *Conversion, Politics and Religion in England*; Walsham, "'Yielding to the Extremity of the Time'"; also supra, ch. 1.

58. These pieces were published together in a work entitled *Discorsi sopra l'inondation del Tevere*, Rome, 1599.

59. On this, see Diffley, *Paolo Beni*, pp. 55–57.

60. On Beni's role in the Accademia, see Maurizio Sangalli, "Paolo Beni: Da gesuita a Ricovrato."

61. The manuscript draft of this work can be found in ASV, Beni II 117, folder 2. Folder 1 in the same document contains some preparatory notes for the draft.

62. Quae tibi Pater Beatissime pro communi Ecclesiae bono ac tranquillitate offero, si (quod maxime opto) e re Christiana erunt, Deo accepta referantur qui unus dat velle et perficere. Ego certe illud affirmare possum, me nulli aut mancipatum aut infensum scripsisse; sed eo inprimis studio incensum, ut concordia et pax cum inter fideles omnes, tum inter eos maxime, qui columnae sunt Ecclesiae ac firmamentum, diutissime floreat. ASV Beni II 117, folder 2, f. 2r.

63. Ita me Deus amet, tanta in Tridentinis Decretis illis suboriri, seque obiicere lux visa est unde propositae controversiae tenebrae dissipentur, ut mihi quidem nihil clarius, nihil explicatius expeti posse videatur. Sive enim cupias difficilia loca omnia commode atque perspicue enodari, quae in divinis literis modo divinam gratiam modo liberum arbitrium extollunt; sive quaestiones universas explanari quae divinae gratiae ac liberi arbitrii occasione a patribus, praesertim scholasticis, excitantur (haec enim omnia cum proposita controversia arctissime iuncta sunt) sive denique controversiam ipsam per se dilucidari ac dirimi, hoc est qua plane divinum auxilium, qua liberum arbitrium ad supernaturales hominis actus concurrat, doceri atque perspicue doceri, Tridentina doctrina occurrit, quae (si eius vis et efficacitas undequaque recolatur, ac debita attentione aestimetur) nobis cumulatissime satisfaciat. Ut propterea si tu forte Beatissime Pater istiusmodi litem ac dubitationem in praesens omnino tollendam, ac definiendam iudicaveris, Tridentinam rationem ac viam, hoc est, gravem nobilem atque perspicuam; habeas quod ineas, et amplectaris. Quam rem totam a me (quod non te fugit, Pater Sanctissime) superiore anno inchoatam, nunc vero omni ex parte (quantum tamen ingenii mei tenuitas petitur) absolutam atque perfectam. Tu pro tua sapientia et auctoritate iudicato. Ibid., fos. 5v–6r.

64. Ibid., f. 7v and folder 1, f. 6vr.

65. Ibid. folder 2, fos. 109r–122v.

66. See ACDF, Stanza Storica (hereafter St. St.) O 1-n, folder no. 2, unfol.

67. *Qua tandem ratione dirimi possit Controversia quae inpresens de efficaci Dei auxilio & libero arbitrio inter nonnullos Catholicos agitatur*, Padua, 1603.

68. Cf. pp. 9–10 of the printed edition with f. 7v of the manuscript draft in ASV Beni II 117, folder 2.

69. See pp. 440–449 of the printed *Qua tandem*.

70. Ex his paucis, B.me Pater, facile constare potest, quod libellus Bennii satius inscriberetur de ratione interturbandi, quam de ratione dirimendi. Pallantieri's censure is also included in the folder of the Beni trial (ACDF, St. St. O 1-n, folder no. 2, unfol).

71. Zacco's and Lippi's approbations were printed at the beginning of Beni's book, unfol. The various steps of the inquisitorial procedure against Beni can be followed in ACDF, SO Decreta 1604–1605, fos. 88r–179v passim.

72. Sacerdos Hieronymus Bartholomaeus Zacchi Archipresbiter Ecclesiae Cathedralis Paduae deposuit, se per saltum solum legisse praefatum librum sibi delatum a Paulo Benio... et eum a preafato Benio dictum fuisset approbatum esse a P. Mordano Theologo primario Studii Patavii, dedit suam approbationem in scriptis. ACDF, St. St. O 1-n, folder no. 2, unfol.

73. P. Caesar de Lippis de Mordano Ordinis Minor. Conventual. Lector primarius Universitatis Patavinae deposuit se... legisse medietatem solum libri manuscripti sibi delati, in quem animadvertit plura emendanda, ea per scriptis in folio exhibito Auctori, qui rediens significavit eum emendasse juxta ejus correctionem... librum impressum continere plura, quae non erant in originali. Ibid.

74. ch'io l'anno 1601 mi posi a scrivere sopra tal materia per haver letto che N.S. consultus sopra ciò, non solamente non habbia ciò proibito, ma habbia risposto che rem totam liberae Theologorum disputationi committit... Soarez et di poi il Vaschez, che sono Gesuiti, con venir i lor libri publicati, et accettati in Roma et ristampati in più luoghi, molto meno havrei pensato di far alcuna offesa io che son neutrale, et non dipendente da alcuna parte. Ibid.

75. Oltre che nella S.ta Chiesa in occasione di controversie ab antiquo è stato costume, che i Cattolici rappresentino, et suggeriscano quello, che gl'occorresse. Ibid.

76. si come per lasciar gl'esempi troppo antichi... Così Caterino, Vega, et altri presentarono in stampa lunghi trattati al sacro Conc.o di Trento in diverse materie et il Conc.o veduto il tutto risolse quello che giudicò in Domino: Così alquanto avanti Caietano presentò a Sisto Quarto un opuscolo persuadendo che non si deffinisse cosa alcuna intorno alla concettione della B.V. Anzi Gregorio XIII di S.ta Mem.a nell'voler mutare il Calendario non solamente udì volentieri qualunque diede consiglio alcuno etiamdio opponendosi, ma ancora con un breve sollecitò tutti i Principi Cattolici a far scrivere sopra ciò, come fu fatto, risolvendo poi quello, che giudicò più espediente, si che stimando io che qui appunto mirasse la risposta di N.S.re sperai che il mio libro non dovessi esser discaro: massime essendo io (come ho detto) neutrale, et independente, et rimettendo sempre il tutto al giuditio, et arbitrio di S.S.tà. Si aggionge 2.o che l'anno 1601 fu predicata in Roma questa materia... con molta acrimonia, et dottrina, et in particolare dal Padre Bernardo Olgiano Giesuita, il quale più volte disse, et replicò la sua opinione esser fede catholica: l'istesso si è fatto in altri luoghi senza che mai ne sia nata prohibitione. Anzi l'anno 1602 in Roma il Padre Benedetto Giustiniani publicamente alla presenza di molte nationi disputò et dettò il suo parare sopra questa materia istessa più d'un mese senza che li fusse interdetto cosa alcuna. Si com'anco in Roma hanno fatto i Padri Domenicani anch'essi nelle loro scuole et l'istesso hanno fatto altri, et ne' pulpiti, et nelle Catedre tanto in Roma, quanto in molti altri luoghi. Ibid.

77. Finalmente quello che mi ha indotto a dar fuori quest'opra è stato che dal '94 indietro io ogn'anno sono stato solito a dedicare qualche opera a S.S.tà sicome è noto per le opere stampate. Et per questo l'anno 1602 del mese di 8bre esponendoli io di non potere per l'infirmità che mi era sopra giunta pagar per quell'anno il mio solito tributo S.S.tà, vedutomi ancor pallido, et fresco del male, et saputo il mio bisogno, per sua benignità mi fece dare una pensione. Ond'io desideroso di corrispondere in qualche parte a tanta benignità dal 1603 attesi a dar l'utima mano a quest'opera con ogni mia diligenza. Ibid.

78. Ibid.

79. Just to give a sense of Beni's substantial scholarly output in his years in Padua, I mention only that in 1612 Beni published his controversial and relatively famous *Anticrusca*, in which he opposed the Accademia della Crusca's "canonization" of Boccaccio and Dante as linguistic models; the following year he published a commentary on Aristotle's *Poetics*; and in 1616 Beni published his commentary on Tasso's *Gerusalemme Liberata*. On these works, see Diffley, *Paolo Beni*, pp. 121–205. During the last twenty years of his life, moreover, Beni seemed to have intensified the scholarly collaboration with Galileo Galilei. In fact, Anna de Pace argued that Galileo's engagement with Plato's *Timaeus* in the context of the more philosophical implications of Copernicanism was fostered by the discussions between Galileo and Beni; see her "Galileo interprete del *Timeo*," in Guido Canziani, ed., *Storia della scienza, storia della filosofia: interferenze*, Milan: Franco Angeli, 2005, pp. 39–76. Moreover, if

we believe Giovanni Battista Manso (a Neapolitan nobleman who was a personal friend of Galileo's and the patron of, among others, Torquato Tasso), Galileo and Beni had observed together Jupiter's satellites and the moon's spots through the telescope. On Beni's role in the astronomical observations, see the letter from Manso to Beni, 18 March 1610, published by Antonio Favaro in *Galileo Galilei e lo Studio di Padova*, 2 vols., Firenze: Le Monnier, 1883, vol. II, pp. 313–319. On the relationship between Galileo and Beni in the context of their respective problems with the Roman Inquisition, see also Lino Conti, "Galilei e Paolo Beni: astrologia, determinismo e Inquisizione," in Patrizia Castelli and Giancarlo Pellegrini, eds., *Storici, filosofi e cultura umanistica a Gubbio tra Cinque e Seicento*, Spoleto: Centro italiano di studi sull'alto medioevo, 1998, pp. 307–329.

80. Paolo Beni, *Comparatione di Torquato Tasso con Homero e Virgilio*. The initial version of this work, printed in Padua in 1607, included seven sections. Soon after, however, Beni added three more sections and published the complete version of the *Comparatione* in 1612, again in Padua. Traditional scholars have studied this work as an example of Beni's Baroque and "modern" preferences, even though, more recently, Diffley has revised this assessment by showing that Beni's judgment had less to do with Beni's Baroque taste and more with a Humanistic-infused interpretation of Aristotle's *Poetics*: see Diffley, *Paolo Beni*, pp. 121ff.

81. Beni, "Discorso Nono," pp. 65–99, entitled "Che differente e varia debba formarsi l'Attion Heroica dall'Historica: & in che consista tal differenza e varietà: e che in ciò ancora il Tasso resti ad Homero di gran lunga, a Virgilio in qualche parte, superiore."

82. Dunque per avventura la verità e falsità fia quella che li farà differenti?. . . et invero mentre il Filofoso va ricercando la verità delle divine & humane cose (siasi che la ricerchi sol per intenderle, o pur'anco, come avvien nell'humane, per operare) ne si ferma ne' particolari, questi vengon poi dall'Historico raccolti e tessuti con recarci sopratutto avanti e proporci gli avvenimenti humani. E pertanto il Poeta, s'ei non voglia arrogarsi l'altrui uffitio, vien'astretto ad inventar' e fingere nuovi avvenimenti, ne dee a guisa d'Historico spiegar e rappresentar' i veri. Ibid., pp. 69–70.

83. Posciache mentre commanda che il Poeta attenda al verisimile, non ha per inconveniente alcuno ch'ei canti ancora le cose vere pur ch'habbiano sembianza di verisimili. . . Opinione invero alquanto difficile a potersi credere, anzi almeno in sembianza assai lontana dal vero. Posciache qualhor il Poeta s'incontri a cantar cose vere, come senza dubbio in alcune cose avvien talhora, non potrà distinguersi dall'historico si come all'incontro l'historico si scoprirebbe similissimo al Poeta qualhor'al verisimile, come sovente suole, si appigliasse. Gia che mentr'egli non può esser agevolmente sicuro e certo del vero, vien astretto a scriver quello ch'egli ha, o per giuditio altrui tiene, per verisimile. . . posciache la certezza e sicurezza nelle cose humane (massime riguardosi alle cagioni & a consigli, & insomma all'altre circostanze de' fatti) difficilmente può haversi e molto di rado. Laonde Tucidide, Livio, & altri assai narrano frequentemente fatti & altre cose, confessandole e proponendole per verisimili e probabili anzi che certe. Ibid., p. 71.

84. Parmi dunque che molto si possa dubitar se Aristotele in questo luogo, nel qual distingue il Poeta dall'historico, conceda il falso per materia al Poeta massime Heroico: poscia che da una parte ei pare, che in tutto lo ritenga dentro a' cancelli del falso, poiche non commanda ch'ei narri o canti il verisimile o necessario, ma secondo il verisimile e necessario, che vuol dir ad imitatione del verisimile, ma non il verisimile istesso. Ibid., p. 73.

85. Onde aviene che il vero ancora possa cantarsi qualhor porti sembianza di verisimile, e non tanto come vero, quanto come verisimile si riguardi & attenda. Ibid., p. 77.

86. Laonde sia ben vero che il Dialettico e l'Oratore, il qual narra, prova e conclude il verisimile, non venga di necessità ristretto in modo alcuno dentro a' confini del falso; poiche mentre probabilmente ragiona, il suo parlare sta come in bilancia del vero o falso, potendo riuscir talhor vero, e talhor falso. Ma il poeta, il qual, come ho detto, non narra l'istesso verisimile, che è quello che si presenta nelle cose, ma narra ad imagine di quel verisimile, il quale in dette cose si rappresenta. . . e questo è imitare, cioè dir falso, benche tenga imagine e somiglianza di vero. & in questa guisa il falso del poeta sarebbe mezzano tra'l verisimile dell'Oratore, & il falso d'huomo mendace, che fuor d'ogni verisimile mentisse. Ibid., p. 73.

87. Ibid., pp. 81ff.

88. Claudio Scarpati and Eraldo Bellini, *Il vero e il falso dei poeti*, pp. 42–44.

89. Diffley, *Paolo Beni*, pp. 121–135, quot. at 125 and 130. For a different and still useful perspective on the *querelle*, see Hans Baron, "The *Querelle* of the Ancients and Moderns as a problem for Renaissance scholarship," *Journal of the history of Ideas* 20 (1959), pp. 3–22.

90. Paolo Beni, *In Aristotelis libros Rhetoricorum... Commentarii*, 2 vols., Venice 1624–25.

91. The orations included in this second volume are either reprints of orations that Beni delivered and published before (e.g., Beni's *Disputatio... in qua quaeritur an sive actori, sive reo, & in universum Oratori ingenuo, liceat in Iudiciis & concionibus affectus concitare*, Rome, 1594, which became the first of the disputations included in the second volume of the *Commentarii*), or enlargements and revisions of previous works (e.g., parts on the enthymeme that appear in both volumes of the *Commentarii* repeat, sometimes verbatim, what Beni had already said in the 1594 "Digressio" on Aristotle's definition of enthymeme). Beni's personal notes and drafts on the question of enthymeme can be found in ASV, Beni II 85.

92. "Digressio in Aristotelis locum de Materia Enthymematis. Habita in Patavino Gymnasio cum ornatissimi triumviri ac Gymansii Moderatores ad Authorem audiendum accessissent," ASV, Beni II 71, fos. 1r–3v.

93. Quo sane in loco secum ille enthymema vel potius enthymematis propositionem tam multis ac variis rationibus, tam iteratis approbationibus confirmavit, ut multas nobis ac varias creaverit dubitationes. Inter quas non postrema illa est, fortasse etiam omnium maxima, quam subiiciam. Etenim docebat Oratoris industriam in iis versari quae agitantur in iudiciis, quaeve consultatione indigent ac deliberatione. Haec vero addebat non una tantum ratione effici posse, sed varias in partes cadere. Quibus positis concludebat res quae plerunque accidunt, sive aliter atque aliter contingere possunt, non necessariis sed probabilibus rationibus tantum, contra vero necessarias necessariis solum, concludi. Atque hoc est quod in praesentia dubitationem habet: neque enim videtur cum ratione consentire, ut quae consultatione indigent ac deliberatione, ac proinde varias in partes cadere solent, non interdum perspicuis ac necessariis argumentis evinci possint ac demonstrari. "Digressio," f. 1v.

94. See vol. I, pp. 78ff., and vol. II, pp. 59ff.

95. Itaque Franciscus Patricius in suis Dialogis de Rhetorica, qui vere pulcherrimi sunt, Platonis vestigiis insistens Aristotelem Socratico more eludit atque refellit.... Haec volui cursim attingere in proposita controversia, non quidem ut Aristotelem refellerem, sed ut significarem Academicorum Principem longe aliter docere, atque illius decreta interim breviter saltem referrem: etenim Aristotelis interpretes Quintiliani & M. Tullii praecepta recolunt illi quidem, de antiquioribus autem ac praesertim de Academicis, quorum Principem idem Aristoteles habuit praeceptorem, ac quocum praecipue pugnat, merum apud hos silentium. Ut propterea hac etiam de causa statuerim Aristotelem in Rhetoricis quoque praeceptis (id quod in Dialogis nostris faciam) cum Platone conferre. Tametsi enim rem hanc breviter saltem attingerim ubi Rhetoricae definitionem & Aristotelis sententiam explicarem, quemadmodum animadvertere licet ubi decimo responderem argumento, attamen ut res uberius ac Platone in primis & M. Tullio audito disceptetur, in Disputationibus ero prolixior. Beni, *Commentarii*, vol. I, pp. 81–82 (but see the entire section on this, pp. 44–84).

96. Beni, "Disputatio seu Controversia quarta... in qua Aristoteleae Rhetoricae initia & fundamenta... oppugnantur primum, mox variae defensionis rationes tentantur ac viae," pp. 52–80, and "Disputatio seu Controversia quinta," pp. 81–109.

97. Aristotle: ... ut me semel explicem sic statuo, verissime affirmari posse, nullam certam ac propriam materiam Oratori praestituendam omnino esse ac definiendam, sed omnino concedendum ut quaecunque verisimilibus probari argumentis possunt aut suaderi, peragret omnia. Ibid., p. 70.

98. dum... haec scribis, videris totam Rhetoris facultatem ad πιθανόν referre ac necessaria praecludere argumenta. Contra vero dum ais, Oratoris esse demostrare rem factam, vel non factam esse, sive id ita, vel aliter se habere, eiusdem esse facultatis & verum & verisimile intelligere... pauca esse necessaria, ex quibus oratoriae ratiocinationes conflentur: enthymemata alia verisimilia, alia licet pauca, esse necessaria: non solum ex iis quae sunt necessaria, verum etiam ex his quae plerunque evenire solent argumentandum, signis necessario concludi quaedam, nec posse ullo modo dissolvi, denique his controversiam omnem dirimi, videris necessaria argumenta Oratori concedere. Ibid., p. 64.

99. An non tu, Aristoteles, inde probas verum cernere & simile vero eiusdem esse facultatis, quod πρὸς τὰ ἔνδοξα στοχαστικῶς ἔχειν eius fit qui eodem modo se habeat ad veritatem [see Aristotle's *Rhetoric,* 1.1.11]? At cum hoc pronunciaveris, ut Rhetoricae vim ac munus declarares, minus opportune, ne dicam inepte id pronunciasses, nisi ἔνδοξον ad Rhetoricam quoque pertineret. Ibid., p. 72.

100. Plato's appearance closes the first part of the dialogue, at p. 80. The second part, devoted to Plato's point of view, can be found at pp. 81–109.

101. Tu vero Plato, ut Sophistas varios profligabas, non unas, sed varias diffidentesque opiniones ac definitiones in medium attuleris, ad extremum tamen vix aut ne vix quidem dissidium inter vos [i.e., Plato and Aristotle] ullum deprehenditur. Ibid., p. 108.

102. See, e.g., the first *disputatio* of the second volume and pp. 83–84 of the first volume.

103. For a more detailed account of these features of Beni's commentaries on Aristotle's *Rhetoric,* see Diffley, *Paolo Beni,* pp. 223–243.

104. Ibid., p. 240.

105. On the place of this text within the tradition of ecclesiastical historiography in post-Tridentine Italy, see Ditchfield, *Liturgy, Sanctity and History,* pp. 291–327, esp. 308–310.

106. Ginzburg, "Description and citation," pp. 13ff.

107. Ita quidem germanae historiae nequaquam adhuc meretur nomen: sed aenigma (ut dicebam) aut symbolum vel imago quaedam aut umbra tutius dicetur Historiae: praesertim vero quia consilia, causae, dictae & huiusmodi alia multa quae plane ad rem gestam pertinent, narratione (ut docui) aperiri quidem possunt, pictura nullo modo possunt. Beni, *De historia libri quatuor,* Venice, 1611 pp. 57–58.

108. Quod si ad coniecturas interdum confugere libeat quas proprio ingenio hinc inde ex rebus ducas, non reprehenderim: ita tamen ut singularem rerum gestarum momenta fidemque indices, ut quae sive coniectura, sive fama, sive auditione testium, sive Annalibus ac veteribus monumentis, sive spectatione ipsa aut tractatione nituntur, non difficile intelligantur. Ibid., pp. 27–28. See also another passage, pp. 93–94: "Tum publicos Annales & consimilia monumenta in secundis ponat amplectaturque non invitus. Inde laudatos testes audiat & sectetur. Proxime non obscuram famam admittat. Ad extremum veritati indagandae coniecturas quoque adhibeat: quas sane cum aliunde pro sua industria ac solertia ducat, tum maxime ex iconibus, lapidibus, picturis quae vetustatem referant, & rerum gestarum notas contineant ac symbola. Et huc etiam contulerit priscorum thermas, pontes, moenia, publicae aedificia, ruinas ipsas spectasse: etsi percaute ad coniecturas inde iudiciumque descendendum. Quod si priscorum item bellicas machinas atque arma, insigna, vestes, & id genus alia observet, interdum hinc quoque coniectare aliquid liceat non temere. Illud tamen interim cavebit diligenter, ut quoniam propositi cognitionis gradus veritati non aeque serviunt, eorum quae narrantur vim ac momenta indicet oratio ita scilicet ut intelligere liceat quid compertum sit habendum in certisve ponendum: quid fere constans, quid verisimile, quid subobscurum."

109. Iam vero conciones obliquae minus suspiciosae videri possunt, cum non tam verba quam dictorum summam sequantur. Nam minus abest a verisimili ut historicus resciverit eorum quae concione continentur summam & capita, quam ut verba ipsi & rescire, & memoriae mandare, & literis consignare potuerit. Sed tamen ne istae quidem aliqua suspicione carent; tum quod interdum difficile quoque sit ut historicus concionum summam & capita resciat (fluxa enim est quaeque aures animumque facile praetervolat oratio) tum quia verendum est ne author ipse quae sibi probabiliter dici potuisse videantur, Imperatori verbi gratia seu legato affingat, quod alioquin ieiuna videri possit historia. Ibid., pp. 37–38.

110. Nam dum aliqui historiam nescio quo pacto quadripartito distribuunt, nimirum in Divinam, Ecclesiasticam, Naturalem, Humanam, ii mihi tum naturalem inconsulte huc videntur intrudere, tum Ecclesiasticam a Divina non necessario dissociare. Denique cum Ecclesiastica, praesertim si a Divina distinguatur, humana censenda sit, humana aliqua e contrario Ecclesiastica, imperitam plane & confusam esse partitionem istam nemo non fateatur. Ibid., p. 145.

111. Nam qui rursus historiam tribus coercent generibus, divino scilicet, naturali, humano, ac divini nomine Deum resque expertes interitus; naturalis animantium plantarum &, ut ipsi loquuntur, naturales causas & progressiones, humano humanas actiones & praecepta intelligunt; interdum etiam quartum addunt genus quo Mathematicas comprehendant,

vereor ne omnium absurdissimi videantur nam quid est hoc aliud nisi divinam humanamque Philosophiam cum historia confundere, ac rei, de qua agitur, notionem penitus ignorare? Ibid.

112. Mea quidem sententia, illa & commodior & brevior sit historiae non dicam partitio sed tractandae ratio, ut qui universam rerum gestarum atque adeo germanae historiae cognitionem expetat, his veluti gradibus ad eam contendat. Ac primus sit latinae linguae cognitio.... Alter ille [gradus] sit, terreni huius Orbis descriptio seu Geographica cognitio.... Postremus gradus ad Chrononologiam pertinet temporumque rationem, sine qua in historiae campo minus foeliciter verseris ne dicam temere. Ibid., pp. 146–147.

113. Sacram vero appello quae sacris primum litteris tum Ecclesiasticis monumentis continetur: cuiusmodi sunt Pontificum successiones, Concilia, acta Martyrum, Pontificiae sanctiones, fidelium divinique cultus propagatio, quaeque sive ab haereticis, sive a Schismaticis, sive a Catholicis ipsis passa sit res Christiana ac summatim eorum oeconomia quibus orta adoleverit peregeritque ad hanc usque aetatem ac diem. Qua in re ut me iis liberem dumetis aut salebris in quibus rem versari docui ab initio, dum nullam quae mihi satisfaceret partitionem invenirem, nihil huc ex profanis vel gentibus vel factis revocari vetem quae sacris rebus gestis & Ecclesiasticis intelligendis conferre possint: quemadmodum ad profanam quoque historiam ea patiat transferri quibus iuvari queat eius cognitio. Alioquin nihil est cur sacra cum profanis misceantur, aut profana sacris adhibeantur. Ibid., pp. 149–150.

114. In posteriore vero praeter sacros novi Testamenti libros & Eusebium & Ecclesiasticos ferme scriptores caeteros... & qui ferme instar omnium esse potuisset si opus absoluisset, Caesarem Baronium. De quo sane quoniam in propria quam de Baronii Cardinalis Annalibus tandiu edidimus disputatione, verba fecimus, nihil attinet dicere hoc tempore. Illud tamen unum monebo Ecclesiasticos Baronii Annales cum reliquos huius ordinis historicos diligentia & copia superare, tum (nisi te longitudo deterrat ac prolixitas, atque inprimis liberiores infinitimos campos excursiones, rerumque varietate ac multitudine interpellata series, retardet ac torqueat, aut interdum suspiciosae tibi ac lubricae illius coniecturae videantur) longe ac late nos instituere posse & erudire. Ibid., pp. 150–151.

115. Ego vero de Theologo sic sentio; huic primum in divinorum librorum Oraculis haerendum: ac propterea vel quia sacrae litterae Mundi incunabula & antiquitates offerunt statim, vel quia mortalium procreationem & propagationem, quaeque per Reges inprimis & Sacerdotes ducitur, Christi genealogiam continent, vel quia Prophetarum meditatio accuratam temporum & antiquitatum requirit cognitionem, vel demum quia Hebraei populi bella, victorias, clades, uno verbo dicta factaque persequuntur, ego quidem Theologum ab Historico nunquam dissociarim: sed eum qui divinos hosce libros evolvat ac tractet, non minus historicum quam Theologum haberi iubeam tantum abest ut eos audiendos putem qui, nescio quo pacto, iactant historiae studium ad Theologum non pertinere. Ibid., p. 235.

116. ut vera germanaque divinarum literarum oracula, haereticorum interpretationibus imposturisque reiectis, illibata prorsus inviolataque servarentur: vel certe ad pristinum candorem, quoad eius fieri posset, integritatemque restituerentur... ut historia ab Ecclesiae incunabulis, hoc est ab ipso Liberatoris nostri adventu, ad haec usque tempora, conderetur, qua tum Christi & Apostolorum, tum Petri reliquorumque summorum Pontificum, Traditiones, Concilia, Canones, immo vero, quantum iniuria temporum pateretur, Martyrum, sanctissimorumque Ecclesiae Antistitum ac Procerum, facta dictaque omnia perpetuae memoriae traderentur: atque in cospectu fidelium, certo annorum ordine, perspicuoque stylo, sed inprimis Christiana fidelitate & integritate, digesta, tanquam in publico hominum theatro collocarentur. Beni, *De Ecclesiasticis Baronii Cardinalis Annalibus Disputatio*, pp. 17–18.

117. Melchioris Cani liber, in quo Theologici explicantur Loci, in promptu est omnibus: commendavit enim illum posteritati tum elegantia & stylus qui longe spendidior est quam in Theologo magnopere cerni soleat, tum vero eruditio atque doctrina qua perfectum Theologum describit ac fingit. Porro hunc ego Cani Theologum minus parabilem iudicaveram aliquando... Haec inquam omnia in Theologo requirit Canus: atque ex his quasi fontibus argumenta deducere posse iubet qui Theologi partes sustineat. Quae sane cum mecum ipse reputarem, vix ac ne vix quidem adduci poteram ut crederem, posse haec omnia ab homine comparari: praesertim vero quia cum in eos animum diligenter intenderem qui Theologorum Coryphaei hactenus haberentur, neminem his instructum omnibus deprehenderem, sed potius

animadverterem ab hac laude abesse omnes. Ita demum cum mihi quidem talis tantusque Theologus optandus magis quam sperandus videretur, interdum non sine moerore aliquo Theologica studia prosequebar. Sed ecce tibi, cum Baronium lectitare coepissem, sententiam facile deposui, & cum meliore (ut spero) commutavi. Intelligebam enim Theologum Baronii lectione Ecclesiasticis historiis ad miraculum excoli posse: ad profanas etiam si non uberius, mediocriter certe, & ad rerum divinarum studia opportune admodum informari. Ad haec Apostolicis traditionibus, Ecclesiaeque ritibus & institutis, adde etiam Conciliorum decretis, excellenter imbui: denique ad divinarum literarum sanctorumque Patrum ac totius Pontificii iuris intelligentiam non vulgariter iuvari, cum ex iis pro re nata explicet multa: in reliquis regiam nobis viam ostendat & patefaciat. Quid igitur prohibeat solers ingenium & navum (neque enim homines ad Theologiam ficti sunt omnes, sed solertissimi quique & strenui) linguarum Philosophiaeque cognitione, florente aetate (id enim multis usu venire cernimus) comparata, tum Scholastico Theologorum pulvere accurato quinquenii labore protrito, ad reliqua prope omnia Baronio Duce aggredi: atque ita demum omnes Christianae sapientiae partes (de Caesareo nanque iure Cano haud assentior: nisi tamen illius initia Theologo explorata esse velit, ut ad ius Pontificium faciliorem sibi aditum patefaciat) perdiscere & comparare? id quod eo minorem habet difficultatem, quod istarum studia doctrinarum, ut mutuo se iuvant, & pleraque uno eodemque tempore in eandem contemplationem cadunt, optime iungi possunt, atque altius semper in animo consignari. Haec itaque sunt, mea quidem sententia, quibus Theologiam ditavit ornavitque Baronius, atque e summis angustiis & egestate ad magnam rerum omnium copiam ubertatemque traduxit. Ibid., pp. 33–35. On the historical aspects of Cano's *De locis theologicis*, see the still relevant considerations of Albano Biondi, *L'autorità della storia profana (De humanae historiae auctoritate) di Melchor Cano*, Torino: Edizioni Giappichelli, 1973.

118. Haec inquam omnia tractanda essent & decernenda: quorum tamen disceptatio & diiudicatio tum bene longam ac variam disputationem requireret, tum (ut ingenue fatear) meas vires quam longissime superaret. Beni, *De Ecclesiasticis Baronii Cardinalis Annalibus Disputatio*, p. 41. But see the entire section devoted to discussing the style of the *Annales*, pp. 40–44, in which Beni anticipates the same criticism he later repeated in *De historia*.

119. We have several drafts of this work, all contained in ASV Beni II 123. Part A of this folder contains the full version of Beni's proposal, and my quotations come from it. On this work, see Maurizio Sangalli, "Di Paolo Beni e di una riforma dello studio di Padova (1619)," *Studi veneziani* 42 (2001), pp. 57–134.

120. On Beni's proposal in the context of the history of Padua University and, more generally, the history and structure of early modern Italian universities, see Paul F. Grendler, *The Universities of the Italian Renaissance*, Baltimore: Johns Hopkins University Press, 2002, esp. pp. 387–496 passim.

121. Non si vede a che uso poi serva l'haver atteso a disputar così astratte et intricate materie o sottigliezze se non forse alla Theologia Scholastica, porgendo nuovo campo di venir a nuove contese Metafisice [sic] etiandio in Theologia (poiché non è dubbio che la Theologia Scholastica per buona parte ridotta a digressioni o questioni metafisice). . . queste letture di Metafisica vengon lette da Dottori i quali iurarunt in verba Magistri, non permettono poi che sia in tutto libero il valersi di detta Metafisica senza obligarsi o di seguir poi in Theologia affatto Scoto o San Thomaso: e pur converrebbe che chi spende tanta fatica e tempo in tal Metafisica, almeno ristasse libero per valersene in Theologia (poiché ad altro non par che serva) con riservarsi il giuditio libero come nelle cose problematiche è concesso a qualunque altro non habbia giurato in verba Magistri. Che perciò al presente la Metafisica viene a guisa d'un'ampia fucina ove qualunque scola, siasi o di San Thomaso o di Scoto, o d'altri celebri e privati Dottori Scholastici, ciascuno fabrica armi a difesa della sua scola o Dottore. ASV, Beni II 123 A, fos. 79v–80r.

122. E per questo chi si risolvesse a metter' in cambio della Metafisica una buona concorrenza di due valenti scritturisti (che questa sarebbe vera Metafisica, o più tosto divina filosofia) con far che questi facesero buon progresso, si trarrebbono. . . grandissimi commodi. Ibid., f. 81r.

123. Io non loderei che alcuno, siasi o lettore o scolaro, si obligasse a seguir in tutto Scoto: anzi. . . a difender la sua dottrina: la quale è ben sottile e porge largo campo a dispute e contese, ma però non vien quasi mai ad uso né a Predicatori, né a Casisti, né a Confessori, restando quasi infeconda e sterile nel servigio Ecclesiastico. Ibid., f. 97v.

124. Ne perciò loderei all'incontro che alcuno si obligasse tanto alla sentenza [erased: "dottrina"] di S. Thomaso, che nel Theologare [added: "non curando di essaminar bene le ragioni, ma"] contentandosi [erased: "etiandio"] della semplice autorità, deponesse affatto il proprio sentimento e giuditio. Se ben non saprei se non lodare ch'altri dopo diligente essame, qualhor non venisse da viva o assai probabile ragione guidato a contrario parere, prontamente abbraciasse l'opinione e dottrina di S. Thomaso. Ibid., fos. 97v–98r. The corrections made by Beni in this draft are a further proof of Beni's distate for those who considered Aquinas's "opinion" a "doctrine" and "failed to examine all the reasons well."

125. Resta che per compimento di quanto appartiene alle letture, si ragioni della Theologia Scolastica. . . Con tutto ciò voglio io esser breve: percioché havendo io con una mia Disputa latina intitolata "De Ecclesiasticis Baronii Cardinalis Annalibus," fatto prova di formar anco un perfetto Theologo, son quivi andato accennando molte cose le quali appartengono alla Theologia Scolastica. Ibid., f. 97r.

126. Necesse est ibi per Memorias intelligi Martyrum Ecclesias, in quibus, et in honorem eorundem Martyrum altaria erigerentur: sed demonstremus insuper non ex verbis tantum, sed ex rebus, Memoriam esse nominatam Ecclesiam. . . . Id ipsum dicimus de memoria S. Stephani Prothomartyris, quam Anconae fuisse, idem Augustinus sequenti sermone [sermon 323, text in PL vol. XXXVIII] testatur, cum ait, Memoria antiqua ibi erat, et ipsa est ibi. . . . Vides ergo, Ecclesias etiam dictas esse Memorias, quomodo et parietes indicant, et lapides ipsi clamant. Plura his adderem, nisi scirem plus satis te ipsum persuasum. Manuscript copies of the letter from Baronio to Rullensis, dated 23 January 1595, can be found in VAL Q 23, fos. 27v–28v, and VAL Q 44, fos. 46–48. The letter is also printed in Albericius, *Epistolae et Opuscula*, vol. I Epistola LXXII. See also *Annales*, vol. I, ad annum Christi 57, ¶129.

127. Beni's treatise is entitled "Trattato della Memoria locale: in cui si spiega il modo facile per acquistarla" and can be found in ASV, Beni II 129, fos. 66r–79v. This folder also contains Beni's "Avvisi per ben comporre in prosa et in rima" (fos. 1r–65v), whose importance in the context of the seventeenth-century debates over the Italian language has been noted by P. B. Diffley in "Paolo Beni e la lingua italiana: la prospettiva di un umanista di Gubbio," in Patrizia Castelli and Giancarlo Pellegrini, eds., *Storici, filosofi e cultura umanistica a Gubbio tra Cinque e Seicento*, pp. 331–373.

128. On this topic, see at least Frances A. Yates, *The Art of Memory*, Chicago: University of Chicago Press, 2001, and Lina Bolzoni, *The Gallery of Memory. Literary and Iconographic Models in the Age of the Printing Press*, Toronto: University of Toronto Press, 2001.

129. Ma posto che pur si voglia usar per concetti la Memoria locale, e con figure rappresentative disporli in luoghi, fia ben di sapere o supporre che quest'artificio è composto d'Immobile e Mobile. Immobile è il luogo ove per opra dell'intelletto o imaginativa si locano le figure rappresentanti i concetti. Mobile è la figura rappresentante: perché servito ch'habbia a spiegar il concetto nell'occorrenza presente, non più si adopra, ma si lascia sviar di mente e porre in oblio. ASV, Beni II 129, f. 68v.

130. Ma di gratia prima che passiamo più oltre, rechisi essempio dell'Immobile. Io entrando nella chiesa di S.ta Giustina di Padova per la porta sinistra soleva servirmi di tutta quella tela di muro e di capelle in giro ritornando fino alla destra porta, e vi stabiliva un luogo immobile per cento [erased: "venti," "quaranta"] settantatre luoghi o parti del detto luogo immobile. Ibid., f. 70v.

131. Ma di gratia rechiamo essempio per dichiarar tutto ciò che appartiene a questa parte mobile, sicome pur con essempio habbiam dichiarato quant'appartiene all'immobile. Siasi dunque che tu voglia far invettiva contro di Aristotele mentre definisce la Rhetorica dicendo che è facoltà per ritrovare quello che si offerisce per probabile in qualunque cosa, che apunto scrisse che la Rhetorica (riferirò con latine voci la proposta definitione) est facultas videndi quid in unaquaque re sit probabile, o vaglia a persuadere; e pertanto volendo tu oppugnar questa sentenza o definitione, et oppor nel primo luogo che malamente l'habbia chiamata facoltà per esser il nome di facoltà ambiguo. . . locherai nel primo luogho che apunto sarà il primo e ben ampio pilastro della capella che prima troverai a man manca, locherai dico un huomo in habito di Filosofo e palliato, il qual vibri più lingue. E questo simulacro, qualunque si sia, devrà servir a te per argumento dell'ambiguità e dei varii significati di questa voce facoltà, posta in principio di tal definitione, perciochè venendo tal figura da te inventata

e posta in questo primo luogo per opporre ad Aristotele l'ambiguità e moltiplicità di questa voce, tal simulacro assai ti ridurrà a memoria l'argomento dell'ambiguità o multiplicità da esser opposto. Ibid., fos. 72r–v.

132. Ibid., fos. 72v–75v.

133. Ma eccoci in laberinto maggiore: poiché tal definitione Aristotelica cade nella Dialettica, essendo che la Dialettica disputa per l'un e l'altra parte probabilmente. E chi non s'accorge che quella Pedia di cui tien ragionamento Aristotele ne' libri degl'Animali cade sotto questa istessa definitione? Certamente l'huomo erudito vien descritto in guisa che solo probabilmente ragiona di qualunque cosa. Ibid., f. 75v. Beni is here referencing the beginning of Aristotle's *De partibus animalium*, 639a 1–12, in which Aristotle draws the distinction between παιδεία and ἐπιστήμη in the terms Beni has reported here.

134. Ma come locherò io (dirà alcuno) questa Pedia per ricordarmi dell'argomento detto? che agl'altri argomenti ultimamente proposti non mancheranno imagini. Già ti ho detto che per locar si possa e debba valer alcuno di cose laide o ridicolose. E però havend'io veduto un mio amico il qual haveva un grande e mostruoso piede, intorno al quale fu per risa composta un'opra intitolata la Scarpide, io porrei in questo luogo 16.o il detto mio amico, il qual stendesse quel mostruoso piede, e di qui mi ricorderei della Pedia, e dell'argomento meditato in tal soggetto. Ibid., f. 75v.

135. Finalmente che la definition proposta non può liberarsi da repugnantia, poiché il vero è tanto congiunto col verisimile che bene spesso sono inseparabilmente congiunti: il che avvien anco del falso e della menzogna la qual prende sembianza di vero. Si che il voler investigar solo il probabile non è possibile senza incontrarsi nel vero o nel falso. Per lasciar che l'investigar in ciascuna cosa quel tanto ch'ei sia atto a far fede e probabilità è cosa infinita e cosa da desiderar piuttosto che sperare. Ibid., f. 76r.

136. For a stimulating discussion on the relationship between the "essentialist" and the "relativist" view of Church history, see Euan Cameron, *Interpreting Christian history. The challenge of the churches' past*, Oxford: Wiley-Blackwell, 2005.

Chapter 4

1. See, in addition to *L'Âge*, Fumaroli's "The Fertility and Shortcomings of Renaissance Rhetoric," and Fumaroli's preface and postface to the *Histoire de la rhétorique dans l'Europe moderne (1450–1950)*, Paris: Presses Universitaires de France, 1999. For a recent overview of the place occupied by the Jesuits within the history of Renaissance rhetoric, see Peter Mack, *A History of Renaissance Rhetoric*, pp. 164–185. On the debate over the significance of rhetoric in early modern culture, see at least Jerrold E. Seigel, *Rhetoric and Philosophy in Renaissance Humanism*, Princeton, NJ: Princeton University Press, 1968; Nancy S. Struever's *The Language of History in the Renaissance*, Princeton, NJ: Princeton University Press, 1970, *Theory as Practice. Ethical inquiry in the Renaissance*, Chicago: University of Chicago Press, 1992, and, with Brian Vickers, *Rhetoric and the Pursuit of Truth: Language Change in the Seventeenth and Eighteenth Centuries*, Seminar Paper Series: William Andrews Clark Memorial Library, Los Angeles, 1985; Ernesto Grassi, *Rhetoric as Philosophy. The Humanist Tradition*, University Park: Pennsylvania State University Press, 1980; Victoria Kahn, *Rhetoric, Prudence, and Skepticism in the Renaissance*. Ithaca, NY: Cornell University Press, 1985; Brian Vickers, *In defence of rhetoric*, Oxford: Clarendon Press, 1988. Insightful considerations on the philosophical and epistemological role of rhetoric in the development of Humanist and Renaissance skepticism and relativism can be found in Zachary Sayre Schiffman, *On the Threshold of Modernity*, pp. 9–52. On the importance of language in the early modern process of identity formation, see also Peter Burke, *Languages and Communities*.

2. On the collaboration between the professors of rhetoric at the university and those at the Jesuit College in this early phase of the second Renaissance, see McGinness, "The Collegio Romano, the University of Roma, and the decline and rise of rhetoric in the late Cinquecento," *Roma moderna e contemporanea* 3 (1995), pp. 601–624.

3. Fumaroli's interpretation of the second-Renaissance Ciceronianism can be found in *L'Âge*, pp. 162–230, and in "Cicero Pontifex Romanus."

4. Fumaroli's general thesis is still at the core of much scholarship on early modern Roman rhetoric and esp. on the Jesuit devout Ciceronianism: for a recent assessment, see, e.g., Christian Mouchel, *Cicéron et Sénèque*.
5. I will be quoting from the Pamplona 1589 edition of this work.
6. Perpiñán revised and corrected Soares's treatise in 1565. On the numerous early modern reprints and editions of both the original and the revised version of *De arte rhetorica* see Lawrence J. Flynn, "The *De arte rhetorica* (1568) by Cyprian Soarez S.J: A Translation with Introduction and Notes." Ph.D. Thesis, 2 vols., University of Florida 1955; on the significance of this text in the context of early modern Jesuit rhetoric see Mack, *A History of Renaissance Rhetoric*, pp. 177ff. On the role of Perpiñán in the development of the Jesuit curriculum and in particular in the revival of Renaissance Humanism within Jesuit education, see O'Malley, *The first Jesuits*, Cambridge, MA: Harvard University Press, 1993, pp. 253–264; Allan P. Farrell, *The Jesuit code of liberal education. Development and scope of the "Ratio Studiorum"*, Milwaukee: Bruce, 1938, pp. 92ff. passim; Fumaroli, *L'Âge*, pp. 172–175. Two useful overviews on the Jesuits' curriculum are François de Dainville, *L'éducation des Jésuites (XVe–XVIIIe siècles)*, Paris: Les Éditions de Minuit, 1978, and Luce Giard, ed., *Les Jésuites à la Renaissance. Sistème éducatif et production du savoir*. Paris: Presses Universitaires de France, 1995. For a reconsideration of the role of the liberal arts curriculum in the Jesuits' moral theology, see Robert A. Maryks, *Saint Cicero and the Jesuits. The Influence of the Liberal Arts on the Adoption of Moral Probabilism*, Farnham: Ashgate, 2008. For a general overview of the influence of Aristotle's *Rhetoric* on the Jesuits, see Françoise Douay-Soublin, "Les Jésuites et l'autorité de la *Rhétorique* d'Aristote," in Gilbert Dahan and Irène Rosier-Catach, eds., *La "Rhétorique" d'Aristote. Traditions et Commentaires de l'Antiquité au XVIIe Siècle*, Paris: Vrin, 1998, pp. 331–346.
7. See Fumaroli, "Cicero Pontifex Romanus."
8. The relatively consistent manuscript collection of Perpiñán's works (in large part in Perpiñán's own handwriting) can be found in the Fondo Curia [hereafter FC] and in the Fondo APUG [hereafter APUG] of the Archivio della Pontificia Università Gregoriana, in Rome. As a whole, the collection comprises a number of different works, including letters, poems, and orations, some of which were published by Petrus Lazeri in *Perpiniani Opera*, Rome, 1749 (for a full description of the APUG manuscripts containing Perpiñán's works, see Darío Martínez Montesinos, "Pedro Juan Perpiñán en el *Archivio Storico della Università Pontificia Gregoriana di Roma* (APUG)," which is part of the APUG collection and is available through the APUG archive. I would like to thank Professor Martín Morales SJ, the director of the APUG, for giving me access to Montesinos's work and to Perpiñán's entire collection during my research visits at the archive). Concerning Perpiñán's *De oratore*, nineteenth-century scholars such as Sommervogel (*Bibliothèque de la Compagnie de Jésus*, vol. VI), Augustin de Backer (*Bibliothèque des écrivains de la Compagnie de Jésus*, 7 vols. Liège: L. Grandmont-Donders, 1883, vol. III), and Bernard Gaudeau (*De Petri Ioannis Perpiniani vita et operibus*, Paris: Retaux-Bray, 1891) attest that Perpiñán wrote it during his tenure as professor at the Roman College, more specifically between 1562 and 1564. Sommervogel adds that the treatise remained in manuscript and that a copy of it, partially written in Perpiñán's own hand, could be found in a private library in France (see Sommervogel, p. 553). There seems to be no trace of that French manuscript today, but Montesinos, based on his extensive collation of all of Perpiñán's manuscripts in APUG, has argued that substantial fragments of this work can be found in two APUG manuscripts, FC 1563 and APUG 1179, which, if taken together, give a good sense of the scope and main arguments of Perpiñán's treatise. After examining the content of these manuscripts, I fully agree with Montesinos, but I should mention that the nature of these manuscripts is somewhat contested. One of them, FC 1563, has been briefly analyzed by Jean Dietz Moss in "The rhetoric course at the Collegio Romano in the latter half of the sixteenth century," *Rhetorica* 4, no. 2 (1986), pp. 137–151, at 143–145. Moss, mistakenly reading a note (in a different hand from the rest of the manuscript) at f. 1v that says "opus ineditum" as "opus medium" (p. 143), identified its content as lecture notes for an "intermediate course" on rhetoric. Aside from the (mistaken) reading of the initial note, Moss's opinion that the manuscript contains just lecture notes seems partially justified by the fact that in a few parts of the text Perpiñán makes references to supposed "auditors," and responds to objections made by supposed "students," as if

the text did indeed report the content of a classroom lecture. However, if one examines carefully the content of both manuscripts APUG 1179 and FC 1563, one sees that even though some sections of FC 1563 do seem written in a lecture notes type of format, other parts of FC 1563 and virtually the entire APUG 1179 are not written as lecture notes, but they are arranged as chapters, or individual sections, of a scholarly treatise. Finally, I should add that no relevant difference, in terms of content, can be discerned between the material present in both manuscripts, and indeed Perpiñán would often repeat the same exact arguments in a lecture format and in a treatise format. All these elements, taken together, make me conclude that those two manuscripts do indeed contain parts of Perpiñán's own *De oratore*, which, as was often the case in the early modern world and is still often the case, Perpiñán must have elaborated while teaching his course on rhetoric. Since teaching and research were not two completely separate activities but indeed Jesuit professors routinely taught doctrines that they later reviewed and systematized for publication, I think that the amphibious nature of those manuscripts, in part lecture notes and in part scholarly treatise, is itself indicative of the intellectual atmosphere of the college and of the development of Perpiñán's and his colleagues' intellectual trajectories. Therefore in the following pages I will not make any effort to identify the format (i.e., lecture note vs. scholarly treatise) of the parts of the manuscripts that I analyze, unless the particular format is relevant with respect to the argument that Perpiñán makes. Also, some sections of Perpiñán's works appear identical in both manuscripts, and in this case I have given references to both. Some other sections are more fully developed or less fragmentary in one manuscript than the other, and in this case I have quoted from the manuscript containing the fuller version.

9. My analysis in the following pages is based on Strada's unpublished material which is to be found in three manuscript folders, two in APUG and one in ARSI. The first one, APUG 1188, contains some lecture notes from a course on Aristotle's *Poetics* that Strada taught in 1608. The second, APUG 1163, is in Strada's own handwriting and contains numerous works, viz., a part of Strada's own commentary on Aristotle's *Poetics* (fos. 1r–59v), which covers a much ampler set of topics than the lectures of the 1608 course; fragments of a commentary on Aristotle's *Rhetoric* (fos. 61r–97v); a treatise entitled *De affectibus* (fos. 101r–155r); and a treatise entitled *De elocutione* (fos. 157r–220v). The third manuscript, ARSI Opp. Nn. 13, contains a treatise entitled *De contexenda oratione Libri Duo* (fos. 1r–195r), as well as a few unpublished orations by Strada and by Tarquinio Galluzzi.

10. For a fundamental overview on this topic, see Lawrence D. Green, "The Reception of Aristotle's *Rhetoric* in the Renaissance," in William W. Fortenbaugh and David C. Mirhady, *Peripatetic Rhetoric after Aristotle*, New Brunswick, NJ: Transaction, 1994, pp. 320–348, as well as Dahan and Rosier-Catach, *La "Rhétorique" d'Aristote. Traditions et Commentaires*. An important work touching on the role of Aristotle's *Rhetoric* in the Western Latin cultural world is John Monfasani's *George of Trebizond. A biography and a study of his rhetoric and logic*, Leiden: Brill, 1976. On the influence of Aristotle on early modern education and on the Jesuits' curriculum, see Paul R. Blum, *Studies on Early Modern Aristotelianism*, Leiden: Brill, 2012.

11. *Ratio Studiorum*, 1599, rule no. 1. The critical edition of the *Ratio* can be found in *Monumenta Pedagogica Societatis Iesu*, vol. 129, Rome, 1986. For an English translation, see *The Jesuit Ratio Studiorum of 1599*, trans. Allan P. Farrell, Washington, DC, 1970.

12. Illa res abditas investigat, investigatas comprehendit, comprehensas digerit & componit, dissipata colligit, collecta dividit, praeterita recordatur, cernit instantia, futura coniectat, & extrema conferens primis, omnium rerum cursum & eventorum consequentiam notat: sed haec omnia veluti quibusdam obruta tenebris latent, inclusa penitus in pectoribus & animis nostris: quae ubi lumen orationis accessit, tum demum ab omnibus patefacta & illustrata cernuntur. Perpiñán, *Orationes duodeviginti*, Pamplona, 1589, "Oratio VI, De arte rhetorica discenda," p. 102r.

13. rationem autem ne fallatur atque erret disserendi vis, quam Logicam vocamus, informat: at orationem, quo sit aptior ad persuadendum bene dicendi facultas quam eloquentiam dicimus, verbis sententiisque locupletat. Ibid.

14. Perpiñán's definition of rhetoric in this oration resonates with Soares's definition of rhetoric in *De arte rhetorica*: "Rhetorica est vel ars, vel doctrina dicendi," *De arte rhetorica libri tres ex*

Aristotele, Cicerone, & Quintiliano praecipue deprompti, p. 1 (I am quoting from the Paris 1584 ed.). On the implications of the debate between Quintilian's definition of rhetoric as the art of fine speaking and the Aristotelian-Ciceronian definition of rhetoric as the art of persuasion among Renaissance intellectuals, see John Monfasani, "Episodes of anti-Quintilianism in the Italian Renaissance: quarrels on the orator as a *vir bonus* and rhetoric as the *scientia bene dicendi*," *Rhetorica* 10, no. 2 (1992), pp. 119–138, now in id., *Language and Learning in Renaissance Italy*, Farnham: Ashgate, 1994.

15. habet enim eloquentia vim talem, ut eadem de re duas contrarias rationes explicare possit. Perpiñán, "Oratio VI," pp. 104r–v.

16. Nam quod nonnulli nobilissimi Rhetores eloquentiam virtutem esse contendunt, neque posse nisi in bono viro reperiri, optandum quidem illud est, sed parum verum. Ibid., p. 104v.

17. Quid igitur est, quod in tantis malis. . . facere debeamus, veritatis & religionis amatores? Hoc unum opinor: arma impiis & perfidiosis extorqueamus e manibus, ut eiusdem ipsi petantur telis, quibus nos oppugnant: & quoniam in utramque partem valet copia dicendi, ut eam haeretici transferunt ad Ecclesiam opprimendam, sic nos ad eandem fortiter defendendam convertamus. Ibid., p. 105r.

18. In his oration "De arte rhetorica discenda" Perpiñán explicitly elaborates on the role of the orator as a "culture hero," as McGinness put it, of the new *respublica Christiana*, at pp. 103v–104r (for McGinness's definition of the Christian orator as a "culture hero," see *Right Thinking and Sacred Oratory*, pp. 16–17).

19. On this, see at least O'Malley, *Praise and Blame*, and McGinness, *Right Thinking and Sacred Oratory*, together with Fumaroli, *L'Âge*.

20. Rhetorica est vis, aut facultas in unaqueque re videndi quod sit accommodatum ad persuadendum. FC 1563, f. 6r.

21. Ricoeur, *The rule of the metaphor. Multi-disciplinary studies of the creation of meaning in language*, English trans., Toronto: University of Toronto Press, 1977, p. 11. On this issue, see also William M. A. Grimaldi, *Studies in the philosophy of Aristotle's "Rhetoric"*, Wiesbaden: Franz Steiner Verlag GMBH, 1972.

22. This is articulated clearly in Carlo Reggio, *Orator Christianus*, Rome, 1612, book IV, ch. 1.

23. On Muret's attitude toward Aristotelian rhetoric and philosophy, see Christian Mouchel, "Les rhétoriques post-tridentines (1570–1600): La fabrique d'une société chrétienne," in Fumaroli, ed., *Historie de la rhétorique*, pp. 431–497, esp. 464–467.

24. For Perpiñán's arguments concerning the substantial agreement between Cicero and Aristotle as opposed to Quintilian, see FC 1563, fos. 6r–v and fos. 48v–54r.

25. Existimavi aliquando persuadere quidem finem esse oratoris, rhetoricae autem bene dicere, cum ad hunc finem omnia eius precepta videantur referri ut bene dicamus. Quae sententia si vera esset facile dirimeret illam controversiam quae Quint.est cum Arist. et Cic. de fine. . . sed nunc et scripta rhetorum diligenter evoluenti et rhetoricae naturam accuratius intuenti, longe aliter videtur. Cum enim artis percepta referantur ad bene dicendum, bene dicere autem in eadem arte pertineat ad persuadendum, profecto fieri non potest ut bene dicere sit artis extremum. Ibid., fos. 8r–v (see also the corresponding passage in APUG 1179, f. 34r, where Perpiñán repeats the same argument virtually verbatim, albeit in a slightly different structure).

26. See FC 1563, fos. 12vff., and again fos. 46r–49v, where Perpiñán substituted the example of the head of state with that of a general of an army. Also, see the corresponding passages in APUG 1179, fos. 8vff.

27. tum multorum animos vehementer conturbavit eloquentia namque saepe falsis utitur sermonibus. FC 1563, f. 19v.

28. Ibid., fos. 19r–v.

29. Haec Quint. ita confutat, ut confiteatur sermonibus falsis uti oratores ipsos non falli contendat. . . hanc Quint.i refutationem ideo non probo, quare etiam si oratorem non falli fatemur, tum sermones falsos esse confitemur interdum. Ibid., f. 19v.

30. Eloquentia non secus ac logica spectari potest duobus modis, vel avulsa et seiuncta ab omnibus causis quam plurimi vocant docentem, ut cum praecipitur ad conciliandos animos significandam esse lenitatem et mansuetudinem; vel coniuncta et copulata cum re certa, ut quo loco Cic. in Catilina significavit clementiam suam ad conciliandum. Ibid., fos. 19v–20r.

31. Hoc idem sensisse Platonem de eloquentia adiuncta cum causis perspicuum est; nam in Gorgia ex duo fecisset genera persuasionis. . . eloquentiam statuit esse persuasionis effectricem non illis quae scientiam pariat sed. . . quae opinione, et fide contineatur, oratorem autem ipsum non uti oratione ad res perdocendas apta, veramque scientiam gignente in animis auditorum, sed probabilia et apposita ad fidem faciendam; non enim inquit oratores tantam tam brevi tempore multitudinem docere posse: ex qua disputatione apparet, quae ab oratoribus tractentur in causis, ea opinione, non scientia, contineri, cum opinio quaedam sit fides, neque ab illis ita homines doceri, ut rem. . . percipiant et comprehendat, sed. . . ut credant. . . . A Platone nihil Aristoteles dissentit. Ibid., fos. 20v–21r.

32. Socrates quoque apud Plat. in Phaedro probat ei qui sit bene dicturus nota et perspecta esse debere de quibus dicat. FC 1563, f. 56r.

33. Adde quod qui veritatis est expers et ignarus non potest animo videre quod sit simile vero, ut idem Socrates paulo infra confirmat. Vere enim scripsit Arist. in lib.1 de arte rhet. videre quod sit verisimile eius esse hominis qui possit videre quod sit verum, et illum esse probe affectum ad coniiciendum quod sit in unaquaque re probabile, quod eodem modo sit affectus ad cognoscendam ipsam veritatem. Ibid.

34. Quare non recte M. T. colligit oratores ea dicere quae ipsi nesciant. . . hoc ex ambiguitate scientiae facillime refutatur, nam primo huius verbi significare potest illud accidere ut orator de eo quod sciat, id est certo cognoscat et intelligat, ut si ipse viderit alias aliud dicat. Sed et contrariae duorum oratorum defensiones, et eiusdem diversa eadem de re diversis temporibus oratio demonstrat non esse eiusmodi suapte natura, ut et vera et falsa esse possit. Quae autem sunt eiusmodi ea vera illa germanaque scientia nequeunt comprehendi, quae non modo verarum certarumque rerum est, sed etiam earum quae nullo modo queant aliter evenire. Ibid., f. 21v.

35. ut scientia illa tum dicitur ab antiquis Aristoteleis quae tota refertur ad cognoscendum, sic. . . quae ratiocinatio est verae scientiae conficiens illa sola nominatur ab iisdem, cuius finis extremus est cognitio veritatis. Quare cum omnia quae in dialecticis et rhetoricis praeceptis sunt ratione conclusa, non ad cognitionem pertineant sed ad usum, quae fuit omnium veterum et Platonicorum et Aristoteleorum sententia, namque quae fiunt in his artibus veras esse demonstrationes confitebar quod eo dico constantius, quare demonstratio ratiocinatio esse dicitur quae efficit, ut sciamus. Aristoteles autem in primo de arte rhet. quem locum supra descripsimus neque a dialecticis aut rhetoricis praeceptis fieri quemquem in ullo genere scientem et intelligentem. Ibid., f. 25v.

36. scientia dicitur rhetorica non illa exquisita et subtili philosophorum definitione sed vulgari quodam opinione. Ibid., f. 6v.

37. scientias esse rerum; rhetoricam aut et dialectitam non rerum esse sed rationum et argumentorum. Ibid, f. 25r.

38. Quocirca cum neque dialectica, neque rhetorica aut ipsa per se verum de rebus enuntiet aut rationem nostram perficiat neutram illis quanquam generibus contineri necesse est. Est enim utraque comes tum et administra aliarum virtutum quae ipsae per se perficiant hominum cogitationem atque rationem. Ibid., f. 25v. Perpiñán stated the same concept in another part of his work, when he attacked Quintilian's opinion that an orator and a philosopher could treat the same subject but in a different style: "a philosopho tenui quodam et subtili dicendi genere, ab oratore copiose et ornate." Perpiñán, by contrast, argued: "Existimo verius ita rem explicari posse, eloquentiam et dialecticam, quasi instrumenta quaedam esse sapientium: dialecticam quidem ad res cognoscendas et in certum ordinem redigendas, eloquentiam ad eas illustrandas et populariter dicendas" (FC 1563, f. 38r, and APUG 1179, f. 3v).

39. Sed nonnulli recentes dialectici qui iidem se dicendi magistros esse profitentur has rursus artes partim necessarias ad orationem et disputationem esse tradunt, sine quibus illa constare non possit, partim non necessarias, quae voluptatis tantum et ornatus ea adhibeantur. Necessarias esse . . . dialectiam quae docet tractationem rerum, postremo grammaticam qua verborum tractatio continetur. . . . non necessariam esse rhetoricam, sed tantum ministram quandam voluptatis in orationem . . . haec ut verum fatebar, mihi magis concinne distributa videntur quam vere. FC 1563, f. 26r.

40. Just to give a sense of how much of Perpiñán's manuscripts concerned these same issues, it will be worth noting that in his manuscripts Perpiñán devoted a separate section (FC 1563,

fos. 31v–42v, and APUG 1179, fos. 37v–38v) to the difference between rhetoric and dialectic, another long section on the nature of rhetorical persuasion (FC 1563, fos. 49v–52v), a third shorter section on the relationship between truth and rhetorical probable (FC 1563, fos. 56r–v), a very long discussion of Aristotle's claim that rhetoric was the ἀντίστροφος of dialectic (FC 1563, fos. 67v–73r, and APUG 1179, fos. 16r–24v), and a separate section on the difference between the probable and the verisimilar (FC 1563, fos. 90r–91r, and APUG 1179, fos. 53r–v).

41. Persuasionis autem duo genera fiunt a Platone in Gorgia. Alia est persuasio διδασκαλική, hoc est disciplinae, ac scientiae, quae veram perfectamque scientiam eius quod persuadetur conficit in animo auditoris, ut cum geometra demonstrat in omnibus triangulis duo latera esse longiora tertio. Alia est persuasio πιστευτική, hoc est fidei et opinionis, quae ad scientiam quidem perfectam non pervenit, fidem tantum et opinionem eius quod persuadetur ingenerat in animo auditoris, ut cum philosophi probant rem totam non esse diversam a partibus omnibus coniunctis, aut contra esse diversam. Prior ille persuasio propria est earum artium quae vere sunt germanarumque scientiae, ut geometriae et arithmeticae. Posterior est oratoris. Omnes enim artifices omnium artium id profecto persuadent quod docent, sed ita ut pariant perfectam rei scientiam. Orator autem fidem tum excitat, et opinionem. At ne haec quidem persuasio propria videtur oratoris, nam dialecticus, hoc est qui probabiliter disputat de quocunque re proposita, id profecto etiam persuadet, neque gignit veram rei scientiam, sed fidem tantum quandam et opinionem, non possumus negare. Ibid., f. 50r.

42. Probabile ut Arist. definit in primo cap. lib. primi Top. est quod probatus aut omnibus ut quod appetendum sit idem esse bonum. . . aut plerisque ut prudentiam divitiis anteponendam esse. . . aut sapientibus et ipsi quidem aut omnibus. . . aut plerique. . . aut certe iis suis quorum est spectata maxime et perspecta sapientia. APUG 1179, f. 53r. This whole section, which in APUG 1179 is in Perpiñán's handwriting and appears as a stand-alone section, is repeated also in FC 1563, fos. 90r–91v, where it forms a chapter of a larger work entitled "Quibus rebus comparetur eloquentia P. P. Perpiniani liber" (the title of this work appears in a different hand than the rest of the ms., and, according to the already quoted analysis by Montesinos, it was a subsection of Perpiñán's lost *De oratore* rather than a separate work).

43. nam si semper de rebus euiusmodi sermo esset quae vulgo essent cognitae ex opinione vulgi perpetuo spectari oporteret probabilitatem rerum, verum cum ea saepe incidant in disputationem quae ne in mentem quidem veniant plebi, in his quod probabile sit ex animo et opinione sapientium quibus vulgus credit ponderandum est. APUG 1179, f. 53r.

44. Probabile autem non quia probabile est continuo verum est aut falsum, sed utrumque potest esse, neque vero illud necesse est, ut quod probabile sit idem modo verum esse possit modo falsum, sed satis est non omnia probabilia vera esse aut falsa, sed partim vera partim falsa. Ibid.

45. quare probabile non differt a vero falsitate, sed a probationis ratione et modo quem ἐπίκρισις Alexander appellat. Nam veritas ex re ipsa ponderatur si ea consentiat cum eo quod dicitur, at probabilitas non ex re sed ex auditorum animis et opinionibus ponderanda est, quibus omnia quae conveniunt probabilia dicuntur etiam si non ita sint ut homines opinantur. APUG 1179, f. 53r (see also FC 1563, f. 90v).

46. See Johannes M. Van Ophuijsen, *Alexander of Aphrodisias, On Aristotle's "Topics 1"*, Ithaca, NY: Cornell University Press, 2001, §§1.1.6–1.1.8.

47. Perpiñán's own manuscript version of this section contained nothing on sophistical syllogisms, and it was all devoted to discussing the difference between the probable, the credible, and the verisimilar, as we will see in a moment. But since Perpiñán did not ignore that the text from Alexander concerned sophistical syllogisms, he must have thought that he should have offered a few words on this topic. This is why he added a marginal note in his manuscript, which reads: "The *probabile* is also that which has a certain similitude with generally accepted opinions, whether it be true or false. Even though in this last sense, i.e., the *probabile* having a certain similitude with what usually happens or with what is held in people's opinion, it is not properly a probable thing but simply looks like a probable thing, nevertheless this kind of *probabile* is of great importance in popular orations, and orators make use of it. For this reason therefore Aristotle in the first book of *Rhetoric* teaches that eloquence borders on sophistry" (Probabile autem est id quod habet in se ad hoc quandam similitudinem,

sive id falsum sit sive verum. Quamquam hoc postremum quod similitudinem habet tum ad ea quae plerumque fiunt aut in opinione posita sunt, non est res ipsa probabile sed videtur esse, habet tum in oratione populari saepe plurimum momenti eoque utantur etiam oratores ideoque Aris. in primo rhet. sophisticae finitimam esse docet eloquentiam [see Aristotle's *Rhetoric*, 1.1.12-14]). APUG 1179, fos. 53r–v.

48. This is the translation of George A. Kennedy, *Aristotle on Rhetoric. A theory of civic discourse*, Oxford: Oxford University Press, 2007. On this, see also Grimaldi, *Studies in the philosophy*.

49. See supra, p. 122 and note no. 33.

50. Porro verisimile sic ab Aristotele definitur in Analyticis Prioribus fere extremis, verisimile est propositio probabilis quod enim plerunque ita fit aut non fit aut est vel non est.... Ex quo apparet, omnia verisimilia in probabilibus esse Aristotelis iudicio et sententia, sed probabilia tamen latius parere quod idem Ciceronis verba declarant posita in primo libro de inventione.... Cicero verisimile vocat id quod Arist.est εἰκόν, quod Cicero dicit probabile, id Aristoteles appellat ἔνδοξον; quare perspicuum est magno in errore versari eos qui probabilia a verisimilibus perinde distinguunt, quasi essent omnino diversa, et oratori quidem verisimilia tantum, dialectico probabilia attribuunt.... Nihil enim esse posse ad persuadendum accomodatum nisi idem sit probabile, et quicquid probabile sit, id esse aptum ad persuadendum. APUG 1179, fos. 53r–v.

51. See, e.g., A. A. Long and D. N. Sedley, *The Hellenistic Philosophers*, 2 vols., Cambridge: Cambridge University Press, 1987, vol. I, pp. 438ff.; but also Alain Michel, *Les rapports de la rhétorique et de la philosophie dans l'oeuvre de Cicéron. Recherches sur les fondements philosophiques de l'art de persuader*, Louvain: Peeters, 2003.

52. See O'Malley, *The first Jesuits*, pp. 136–152; Jonsen and Toulmin, *The Abuse of Casuistry*, pp. 87–88 and 164–175; José R. Maia Neto, "Academic Skepticism in Early Modern Philosophy," *Journal of the History of Ideas* 58, no. 2 (1997), pp. 199–220; Robert A. Maryks, *Saint Cicero and the Jesuits*, pp. 83ff.; Fumaroli, *L'Âge*, pp. 37–46. On the impact of Cicero's Academic skepticism on Humanist rhetoric and dialectic, see at least Jerrold E. Seigel, *Rhetoric and Philosophy*; Victoria Kahn, *Rhetoric, Prudence, and Skepticism*; and Lisa Jardine, "Lorenzo Valla: Academic Skepticism and the New Humanist Dialectic," in Myles Burnyeat, ed., *The Skeptical Tradition*, Berkeley: University of California Press, 1983, pp. 253–286.

53. The section entitled "Similitudines et dissimilitudines logicae atque Rhetoricae" can be found in both FC 1563, fos. 31v–32v, and APUG 1179, fos. 37v–38v. However, many of the arguments presented in this section are repeated almost verbatim in several other places throughout both manuscripts.

54. FC 1563, fos. 64v–73v, and APUG 1179, fos. 16r–24v. I will be quoting from the former.

55. On the exegesis of this expression and, in particular, on the significance of the Renaissance debates on it, see Lawrence D. Green, "Aristotelian Rhetoric, Dialectic, and the Traditions of ἀντίστροφος," *Rhetorica* 8, no. 1 (1990), pp. 5–27.

56. Neque dubium esse potest quin Aristotelis haec fuerit sententia; nam ex tribus lib. de arte rhet. duos priores in aperienda inveniendi ratione consumpsit... et in lib. 1 eloquentiam dixit esse quasi quoddam symulachrum dialecticae. FC 1563, f. 64v.

57. Nam quod novi rhetores ex hoc ipso loco sententiam suam demonstrare conantur, dictumque putant eloquentiam dialecticae symulachrum quod ab ea inventionem omnem et dispositionem mutuetur, valde mihi videntur errare. Si enim in eloquentia nulla est inventio, nulla dispositio, cum his duabus partibus tota dialecticorum ars contineatur, ut ipsi volunt, nihil erit in eloquentia simile dialecticae. Quare hoc sensisse arbitror Aristotelem, cum dialectica habeat inventionem et dispositionem suam, item eloquentia inveniat et disponat simillimam esse eloquentiam dialecticae. Ibid.

58. See Green, "Aristotelian Rhetoric," pp. 10ff.

59. ἰσόστροφος quod Alex. Aphrod. in prohemio lib.1 top. et ita interpetantur ut dicant significare id quod in eodem versantur... quidem in eadem re tractanda occupatum est. Verum non mihi multum probatur eorum interpretation.... Existimo igitur antistrophon [sic] nonnunquam idem valere quod isostrophon [sic] et similitudinem declarare, ut illi tradunt, sed eam similitudinem aliter esse accipiendam... in comparationibus proportionum dicitur analogon [sic] id quod alteri proportione respondit ut cum dicimus eandem esse proportionem duodecim ad octo et sex ad quatuor, duodecim sunt analoga sex, octum sunt

analoga quatuor. FC 1563, fos. 65r–v. On the popular *Lexicon Graeco-Latinum*, published by Claude Baduel in 1554 allegedly out of the manuscript notes of Guillaume Budé, see John Considine, *Dictionaries in Early Modern Europe. Lexicography and the Making of Heritage.* Cambridge: Cambridge University Press, 2008, esp. pp. 31–38.

60. Deinde cum Plato in Gorgia duas partes fecisset eius curae, quae corpori adhibetur, ut sit probe affectum totidem ait esse partes eius artis quae est in animo excolendo occupata progymnastica quidem legalem ἀντίστροφος autem medicinae iustitiam, cum analogiam et similitudinem proportionis inter eas artes significare velit. Rursus cum quatuor constituisset partes adulationis, mangonium, rationem condiendi cibos, sophysticam et rhetoricam utitur hac geometrica proportionum comparatione. Quod mangonium gymnasticae idem sophistica arti legali et quod ratio condiendi cibos medicinae idem rhetorica iustitiae proportione reddit, et paulo post suam de rhetorica sententiam comprehendens colligit eam esse ἀντίστροφος rationi condiendi cibos. Ex quo perspicuum est quod in comparatione proportionum alteri respondat, id ἀντίστροφος vocari, in omni autem comparatione proportionum similitudo inest earum rerum quae comparantur, nam si rhetorica eandem habet proportionem ad iustitiam, quam ad medicinam habet ratio condiendi cibos, oportet rhetoricam ei rationi similem esse iustitiam aut medicinae. FC 1563, fos. 65v–66r.

61. See Green, "Aristotelian Rhetoric," pp. 25–26.

62. Quare cum ἀντίστροφος similitudinem declarat non id significat quod versatur in iisdem rebus. . . sed contra quod in dissimili genere rerum, simili tamen et eodem prope modo versatur, FC 1563, f. 66r.

63. See Green, "Aristotelian Rhetoric," pp. 15–17, for a survey of the positions taken by the main Renaissance commentators on this point.

64. Sunt haec quidem a Cic. scripta, et multorum eruditorum animos vehementer conturbant. Sed si totam Ciceronis sententiam diligenter inspiciamus, longe illud altero sentisse reperiemus. FC 1563, f. 67v.

65. Erat enim ei propositum in oratore demonstrare non solum eloquentiam sed etiam dialecticam assumendam esse oratori, ad hoc autem probandum ineptum est dissimilitudinem eloquentia ac dialecticae declarare. Indicare autem coniunctionem earum facultatum, valde utile atque firmum. Quocirca M. T. dialecticam finitimam et vicinam eloquentiae dicit esse, et incumbit quantum potest ad hanc affinitatem confirmadam, utiturque et Zenonis et Aristotelis testimonio ad hoc efficiendum. . . verbis autem illis ex altera parte responditur dialecticae non differentiam sed cognationem eloquentiae ac dialecticae demonstrari docebimus, cum Aristotelis sententiam aperiemus. Ibid., fos. 67v–68r.

66. Ibid., fos. 68r–v.

67. Ibid., fos. 68v–70v.

68. Verum vim verbi graeci parum subtiliter bonus interpres mihi videtur explicasse; non enim ἀντίστροφον est quod in iisdem rebus est occupatum, sed quod in diversis idem proportione reddit et alio nomine dicitur ἀνάλογον a graecis. Ibid., f. 70r.

69. in diversis generibus eloquentia et dialectica versant, sed earum modo cum utraque rationem habeat disserendi. . . . Namque disserere, quod Graece dici διαλέγεσθαι, nihil est aliud nisi sermone uti, quod Plato in Alcibiade primo docet [*Alcibiades I*, 129b–c] . . . . Falsus enim fuit Marsilius Ficinus ambiguitate verbi. . . Plato autem in eodem lib. facile declarat . . . non rationem, verum sermonem designare voluisse. . . . Nam et apud graecos illa verba διάλογος et διαλογισμός ab hoc verbo facta colloquia personarum significant, διάλεξις refertur ad sermonem, et apud Latinos disserere translatione venusta est spargere et quasi disseminare sermonem. . . . Haec non sentientes isti novi rhetores atque dialectici qui multo se plus quam omnes rhetores vidisse gloriantur interpretatione Marsilii decepti in eundem errorem imprudentes inciderant; hoc enim intelligendum est etsi rationis usus maxime cernatur in sermone, tamen his verbis omnibus et graecis et latinis sermonis usum designari, non rationis, in ratione autem disserendi (hoc est utendi sermone) tradendi versantur duae facultates, hoc est dialectica et eloquentia. Ibid., fos. 71r–v. Cf. the different opinion that Perpiñán expressed on the *vis disserendi* in his published oration "De arte rhetorica discenda," p. 102r (see also supra, p. 117 and note no.13).

70. Dialecticus enim quod in re ipsa sit, probabilis inquirit, sive id hominibus sit credibile futurum, sive incredibile, neque tam laborat ut his hominibus persuadeat, quam ut rem ipsam

probet, neque accomodat ad animos hominum disputationem sed ad naturam rerum, ut quando ad perfectam scientiam pervenire non potest, ad id certe quod scientiae proximum est perveniat. At orator non tam quod sit in natura rei quaerit, quam quod sit aptum ad animos auditorum, in quibus tractandis diximus illum esse occupatum. Quare duo sunt genera persuasionis conficientis solam opinionem, unum accomodatum ad naturam rerum, quod in maximarum artium disputationibus versatur, alterum populare accomodatum ad animos multitudinis magis quam ad naturas rerum: illud dialectiorum est, hoc oratorum. FC 1563, f. 50r. On the Ramists' understanding of *disserere* as the essential action of dialectic rather than rhetoric, see Peter Mack, *Renaissance Argument. Valla and Agricola in the traditions of rhetoric and dialectic*, Leiden: Brill, 1993, pp. 344–349, and id., *A History of Renaissance Rhetoric*, pp.136ff. On Valla's interpretation of Cicero's *ratio disserendi*, see Jardine, "Lorenzo Valla," pp. 263ff.

71. FC 1563, fos. 31v–32r, and also fos. 63v–64.
72. Porro in animis hominum quemadmodum docet Plato in 4 lib. de rep. . . duae dicitur esse partes. . . una mentis rationis particeps, quae propria est hominum. Altera expers rationis, agrestis, fera, et immanis, quae nobis est communis cum bestiis, in qua sunt sensus, et omnes animorum motus atque impetus. Illa prior ratione et consilio tota gubernantur, posterior sine ratione, sine consilio, impetu quodam fertur et rapitur. Ibid., f. 52r.
73. Ac posterioris quidem duae rursus fiunt partes a philosophis. Una concupiscens, quae voluptate alitur, et ea quae delectant appetit, ac persequitur. Altera irascens, in qua irarum existit ardor, quae impetu quodam refugit id quod naturae repugnat et nocet. Ibid. See also Aquinas's *Summa, Ia* 81, 1–3, and *De anima*. René-Antoine Gauthier, who was the editor of the Leonine edition of Aquinas's *De anima*, mentions often William of Moerbeke's translations of Aristotle's *Rhetoric* and *De anima* as possible sources for Aquinas's own thinking on passions.
74. Ac dialectici quidem quare non accomodant ad animos hominum tractandos disputationes suas, sed ad rem ipsam docendam, illa tantum adhibeant ad persuadendum quae ad rationem et mentes admoventur, oratores autem qui non tam quaerunt quod in re sit, quam ut id quod propositum est persuadeant auditoribus, duobus ad persuadendum utuntur instrumentis, quorum unum ad rationem admovetur alterum ad alteram animi partem agrestem, atque feram. Ad rationem admoventur argumenta et caetera, quae valent ad docendum. Ad animi vero partem feram et immanem admoventur motus. FC 1563, f. 52r.
75. On Giles of Rome's reflections on the relationship between rhetoric and dialectic, see James J. Murphy, "The scholastic condemnation of rhetoric in the commentary of Giles of Rome on the *Rhetoric* of Aristotle," now in id., *Latin Rhetoric and Education in the Middle Ages and Renaissance*, Farnham: Ashgate, 2005, ch. V.
76. Primum enim quod afferunt de sententia stoicorum omnes motus animorum esse vitiosos falsum esse probant gravissimi authores, Aristoteles. . . D. Augustinus in lib. 9 de civitate dei, c. 4 et in lib. 14 c. 9. Ibid., f. 53v. We should note that Augustine, in the parts of *De civitate Dei* quoted by Perpiñán, had not defended the passions as positive, but had simply attacked the Stoic idea of ἀπάθεια as something that only unjustifiably proud individuals could think they could attain, since living completely free of passion would be tantamount to living completely free of sin, which is something humans just cannot do.
77. verum etsi perniciosum est mentem iudicis ab officio deducere motu animorum, non video cur utile non sit si quando iudices sua sponte fuerint quasi inflexi, et ab aequitate alieni. . . permotione ad aliquem aequitatis partem. . . adducere, ideo responderi potest iis qui concitationibus gravioribus a luce veritatis averti vociferantur animos auditorum. Ibid., fos. 53v–54r. On the hermeneutical significance of Aristotle's ἐπιείκεια (equity), see Gadamer, *Truth and Method*, pp. 310–321, and also Kathy Eden, *Hermeneutics and the rhetorical tradition. Chapters in the ancient legacy and its Humanist reception*, New Haven, CT: Yale University Press, 1997, pp. 7–19, and id., *Poetic and legal fiction in the Aristotelian tradition*, Princeton, NJ: Princeton University Press, 1986. For a different view on the relationship between rhetoric and hermeneutics in antiquity, see Glenn W. Most, "Rhetorik und Hermeneutik: Zur Konstitution der Neuzeitlichkeit," *Antike und Abendland* 30 (1984), pp. 62–79 On the philosophical importance of the Aristotelian notion of the relationship between passions and judgment, see at least Eugene Garver, *Aristotle's Rhetoric: An art of character*, Chicago: University of Chicago Press, 1994, pp. 104–138.

78. Green, "Aristotelian Rhetoric," p. 21.
79. On this point, see, among others, Cesare Vasoli, *La Dialettica e la Retorica dell'Umanesimo. "Invenzione" e "metodo" nella cultura del XV e XVI secolo*, Milan: Feltrinelli, 1968; Jerrold E. Seigel, *Rhetoric and Philosophy*; Peter Mack, *Renaissance argument*; and Lisa Jardine, "Lorenzo Valla." For an overview of the Renaissance Latin commentaries to Aristotle's *Rhetoric*, see the inventory published by Charles H. Lohr in *Studies in the Renaissance* 21 (1974), pp. 228–289; and *Renaissance Quarterly* 28 (1975), pp. 689–741; 29 (1976), pp. 714–745; 30 (1977), pp. 681–741; 31 (1978), pp. 532–603; 32 (1979), pp. 529–580; 33 (1980), pp. 623–735; 35 (1982), pp. 164–256.
80. Here I disagree with Robert Maryks, who in my view has dulled the Aristotelian edge of Perpiñán's reflections on the relationship between rhetoric and dialectic, which he merely interprets as the expression of "the influence of Ciceronian probability on the Jesuit way of reasoning" (Maryks's relatively short analysis of Perpiñán's manuscripts can be found in *Saint Cicero*, pp. 101–105, quot. at 105).
81. Indeed, in APUG 1179 there are two small sections that attest to Perpiñán's Ciceronianism: the first, entitled "Themata pro componendis orationibus per M. Tulium tradita Romae" (fos. 45r–52r), is a collection of sketches for sacred orations to be constructed according to the Ciceronian model (topics range from the perfection of the monastic life to an encomium for St. Catherine to a condemnation of gluttony). The second is a fragment (the beginning of the fragment is at fos. 140r–146r, and then the fragment continues at fos. 126r–132r) of a chapter entitled "De elocutione," modeled as a commentary of Cicero's considerations on *elocutio*. At the beginning of this section Perpiñán argued that from his reading of Cicero's various considerations on *elocutio* he had identified eight fundamental characteristics of *elocutio*: "prima est ut eleganter loquamur, secunda ut ornate, tertia ut plane dicamus, quarta ut sit illustris, quinta ut sit brevis, sexta ut sit probabilis, septima ut sit suavis, octava ut sit apta rebus et congruens" (f. 141v). The manuscript only reports the chapter on the first of these characteristics, i.e., the *elegantia loquendi*.
82. vehementer vigilandum est iis, qui sapientiae flagrant studio, enitendumque omni cura, ac diligentia, ut Rhetoricae, dialecticaeque praeceptis optime cognitis, ad reliquarum artium fastigium contendant. Quam viam iucundam, facilem, brevem, & quasi compendiariam, non modo non asperam, atque arduam, aut longam esse comperient. Quod ut facilius consequantur, hi tres libri artificium dicendi a veteribus traditum breviter explicabunt. Soares, *De arte rhetorica*, "Proemium," unfol. On Soares's work in this context, see Mack, *A History of Renaissance Rhetoric*, pp. 177–182.
83. Sed quo maior utilitas ex eloquentia percipi possit, Christianis praeceptis diligenter ea purganda est. Ut enim bonus agricola vitem, quae sylvescit, & in omnes partes nimia funditur, ferro coercens, tum fructu laetiorem, tum aspectu pulchriorem reddit: sic eloquentia si amputetur errorum inanitas, in quos dilapsa est vitio hominum divinas leges ignorantium, suam admirabilem speciem recuperabit. Excidatur igitur mentiendi licentia, quam severe divinis praeceptis interdictam, oratori Quint. & antiqui Rhetores concedunt: amputetur procacitas, & vitium illud teterrimum lacerandi alios probris, contumeliis, maledictis, cui utinam ne Demosthenes & Cicero tantopere indulsissent: resecetur arrogantia, & inanis laudis appetitus, qui aciem animi perstringit: intelligatur iniquum esse tenebras auditoribus offundere, ne verum perspiciant, & suffragium, atque sententiam dicendo corrumpere, quod a Graecis & Romanis oratoribus est facilitatum. Hic tot tantisque deletis maculis, continuo existet illa divina, & coelestis Christianae eloquentiae pulchritudo, quae tanto erit praeclara magis & eximia, quanto diligentius ad omnium hominum utilitatem conferetur, & ad laudes celebrandas Dei Opt. Max. qui sermonem homini dedit ad societatem & coniunctionem cum hominibus tuendam. Soares, *De arte rhetorica*, "Proemium," unfol.
84. Nihil tamen a nobis dicitur de christianis oratoribus, quos concionatores appellamus. Nam alia quaedam est eorum ratio. Sunt enim vitae magistri, cuique rei vel tenuissimam suspitionem oratores antiqui fugiebant. Oportet autem magistrum non in eo ipso peccare quod profitetur. Atque ut paucis dicam, cum hoc sit propositum chrisitanis oratoribus ut homines impellant ad bene vivendum, quod antiquis oratoribus non erat propositum, necesse est eos honestissime vivere, homines namque ad honestam vitam magis excitantur exemplis quam verbis. FC 1653, f. 36v, and APUG 1179, f. 3r.

85. Gadamer, *Truth and Method*, pp. 418ff. (quot. at 427).
86. Fumaroli, *L'Âge*, pp. 190–202, and "Cicero Pontifex Romanus."
87. Fumaroli, "Cicero Pontifex Romanus," pp. 821ff. (quot. at 824).
88. ARSI, Opp. Nn. 13, fos. 1r–195r.
89. See Mouchel, *Cicéron et Sénèque*, pp. 271–296.
90. Mouchel, *Cicéron et Sénèque*, p. 281. Fumaroli defined Strada's *Prolusiones* and Reggio's *Orator* as a "beau diptyque," which represented the fullest development of Ciceronianism in, respectively, the profane and the sacred eloquence (*L'Âge*, p. 186). On the importance of Reggio's work in the context of post-Tridentine preaching, see Maria Luisa Doglio and Carlo Delcorno, eds., *La predicazione nel Seicento*, Bologna: Il Mulino, 2009.
91. The treatise is organized as an exposition of the four parts in which a speech is composed (following the division that can be found in Cicero's *Partitiones oratoriae*). The first book (fos. 4r–114v) is devoted to explaining the *exordium* and the *narratio*, and the second (fos. 114v–195r) to explaining *confirmatio* and *peroratio*. Mouchel, who has analyzed this text in his above-quoted book, has noted the similarity between the content of the *Prolusiones* and the content of this manuscript, which he defined as "la versione scolaire des *Prolusiones*" (*Cicéron et Sénèque*, p. 472, note no. 152).
92. Falluntur qui Oratorem concludunt ea tanquam regione, septumque continent iis terminis, ut eleganter & ornate dicat.... Sed invenire quid apte dicat, quae fundamenta jaciat orationis, quam rerum molem attollat, quibus argumentorum praesidiis omnia communiat, hoc adeo Artis hujus est, ut addictus huic parti Aristoteles Rhetoricam ex inventione definiat, eumque perfecti Oratoris appellatione spoliare non dubitet, qui inveniendo minus excellat: cumque persuasionem fide ac motu comparari dicat, inter ea quae fidem faciunt, atque ideo persua-dere possunt, elocutionem non enumeret, nisi tanquam comitem, quae inventioni ad fidem famuletur. Strada, *Prolusiones academicae*, p. 10.
93. See ibid., pp. 14–19, and supra, ch. 2, pp. 62–63.
94. Probabilitas seu verisimilitudo secunda est in narratione conditio, sed plane princeps; cum enim narratio fiat propter fidem, sicut peroratio propter motum, constat quanta cum proba-bilitate narrandum sit. Hinc initio diximus narrationem esse fundamentum constituendae fidei quod sine veritate, aut similitudine veritatis, fieri nequit. Strada, *De contexenda oratione*, ARSI, Opp. Nn. 13, fos. 28v–29r.
95. APUG 1163, fos. 157r–220v (this, like all of the other works to be found in this manuscript, is in Strada's own handwriting).
96. Ibid., f. 189r.
97. Quibus de virtutibus a Cic. hic assignatis ita agimus ut more nostro quae ex Aristotele ac Demetrio hunc spectant inseramus. Ibid.
98. Ibid., fos. 157r–v.
99. Ibid., f. 158v.
100. The part on metaphor can be found at fos. 159v–172r. On the importance and specificity of metaphor for Aristotle, as opposed to the Latin tradition (especially that of Quintilian), and on the consequences of this for Renaissance rhetoric, see Lawrence D. Green, "Aristotelian lexis and Renaissance *elocutio*," in Alan G. Gross and Arthur E. Walzer, eds., *Rereading Aristotle's "Rhetoric"*, Carbondale: Southern Illinois University Press, 2000, pp. 149–165.
101. APUG 1163, fos. 160v–161r.
102. Alterum vero quod si pertranslata discamus modo tum faciliori, celeriorique tum effica-ciori... et quasi tunc se perfecte didicisse putat dum rei causam intellexit hoc enim esse perfecte scire, nempe rem per causam cogitare Arist. docuit homines naturae accomodationi sic confici potest. Et quoad facilitatem et celeritatem attinet, magis dilectari homines in iis quae celerius faciliusque addiscunt quam contra docet Arist. in probl. Sect. 18 probl. 3 quae-rit enim cur homines... exemplis et facilius potius gaudeant quam entymematibus... quia et discunt et celeri discant atque per exempla inquit et fabulas facilius discitur.... Constat igitur ex hoc Arist. loco celeriter faciledque discire delectabilius esse, at vero hanc facilem celeremque rerum scientiam a translatis effici testatur loco supra allato in 3 rhet. Arist. ubi postquam dixisset iucundum esse... facile discire eaque... esse suaviora quae hoc magis effi-cerent... translatio autem hoc maxime facit. Et sane cum in unico translationis modo integra similitudo contineatur qui translatum verbum audit ac percipit, semel... ea omnia discit

quae in similitudine per plura verba cognoscenda erant quare celerius discit. Ibid., f. 161r. On the complexity of the role of metaphor as a vehicle for understanding in Aristotle's *Rhetoric* see Richard Moran, 'Artifice and Persuasion: the work of metaphor in the *Rhetoric*', in *Essays on Aristotle's Rhetoric*, pp. 385-398.

103. Superest ut ostendamus qua ratione per translationem modo hominis naturae maxime convenienti discamus. Hic autem modus est ratiocinatio, cum enim ratio propria sit hominis cuius natura in eo tota consistat animal rationis particeps sit, hinc est ut uti hac ratione seu ratiocinari, actio sit quaedam hominis naturae accomodatissima. APUG 1163, f. 161v.

104. Hoc autem opus ratiocinandi in translatione potissimum apparet dum animadvertitur similitudo connexusque duarum rerum. . . itaque unum comparatur cum altero quidque in utroque sit simile deprehenditur. Ibid.

105. Haec enim ratiocinatio tunc exercitur quando ex re aliam deducit ingenium et ita prior res cognita gradus est ad posteriorem ut multa simul conferendo mens tandem quod indagat sagaci tanquam nexu comprehendat. Ibid.

106. ita explicat Arist. loco citato. Videndum est inquit ne longe ducantur translationes sed ex propinquis atque eiusdem generis sic enim vertit Maior. [marginal note: "At Car. Sigon. non longe transferre oportet sed ab iis quae cognata et conformia sunt"] Hermolaus damnantur et qui a remotis et longinquis translationes ducunt nam a propinquis et unigenis mutuari translationes oportet. . . Victorinus enim non e longinquo transferre dicit sed ex iis quae sunt sub eodem genere eiusdem speciei. Ibid., f. 168v. On these commentators' interpretations of this Aristotelian passage, see also Green, "Aristotelian *lexis*," pp. 160–161.

107. Arist. sententia. . . non probari illa argumenta quae in promptu sunt (sunt autem in promptu quae nemini ignorantur nulla disquisitione ad ea percipienda opus est) neque illa. . . quae cum prolata sunt adhuc tam non percipiuntur, sed probari illa quae sive ac statim aedita sunt nos in sui cog.em ducunt etiam si prius nihil sciremus, sive parvo intervallo animus noster posterior est, eaque quae iam dicta sunt intelligentia comprehendit, hoc enim modo. . . scientia ac perceptio rerum non contingi ubi res aut obscuriores quam intelligi possint aut tritae adeo atque obviae nihil ut novi in illi addiscamus. Ideo autem sentire Arist. intelligendus est cum translationem reiicit alienam et in promptu existentem quod ibi nihil perciperetur, hic nihil novi percipietur. . . est enim solertis acutique hominis sicut etiam in p.lia arcere quid in rebus multum inter se distantibus simile sit, qua ingenii laude commendatur Archytas. Ibid., fos. 168v–169r.

108. Ricoeur, *The rule of the metaphor*, p. 7. On the cognitive role of metaphors in historical research, see also Collingwood, *The Idea of History*, pp. 95–96.

109. See Ricoeur, *The rule of the metaphor*, ch. 1, and also id., "Between Rhetoric and Poetic," in Amélie Oksenberg Rorty, ed., *Essays on Aristotle's "Rhetoric"*. Berkeley: University of California Press, 1996, pp. 324–384.

110. Gadamer, *Truth and Method*, pp. 427–436 (quot. at 428).

111. Ibid., pp. 436–484.

112. See supra, ch. 2, pp. 54–55.

113. See ibid, pp. 62–63.

114. Strada's lecture notes for this course can be found in APUG 1188, fos. 1r–68v.

115. This second version of book 1 and the draft of book 2 can be found in APUG 1163, fos. 1r–59v.

116. Caeteri, si in his litteris occupantur, aut de Deo ac natura disquirunt, quod teologorum ac philosophorum munus est, aut hominum facta posteris tradunt, aut quid agendum fugiendumque sit, in publicis congressionibus privatisque suadent, quae res ad Historicos, et Oratores pertinent, atque hi omnes non proferunt in lucem aliquid novi, sed accipiunt materiam iam praeexistentem, quam ut explicent, evoluanturque connitentur, si vero in rerum opificio destinentur res illi quidem non progignant, sed modum nescio quem addunt, atque ita plura componunt, ut novum quid ex illis existere videatur, quarum cum hi non tam nova cudant, quam vetera resarciant, potius variare, mutareque ea, quae facta sunt, quam facere dicendi sunt. Solus Poeta hoc habet, ut faciat dum suo ex ingenio promit ea, quae nunquam antea fuerunt, eruntque in posterum. APUG 1163, f. 1v (most of this passage was added later and did not appear in the lecture notes; cf. APUG 1188, fos. 1v–2r).

117. Atque hinc Poetae non modo nobilitatem cognoscite, quippe qui, dum novas rerum species ex nihilo format, Deo proximum aemulumque in mundi molitione se gerat, sed eiusdem naturam. Ibid.

118. On the importance of the concept of imitation in linking oratory and poetry in Plato's *Sophist*, I found useful Noburu Notomi, *The Unity of Plato's "Sophist" between the Sophist and the Philosopher*, Cambridge: Cambridge University Press, 1999.

119. Iam cum quod attinet ad alterum initio propositum agendum nunc est, quae sit imitatio, in qua poeseos natura consistit. Et quoniam huius rei definitionem disco magna parte ex Platone eius in Sophista verba recitanda sunt. Visum est, inquit, quam primum artem imaginariam simulacrorum videlicet effectricem dividere oportere, cuius duas species distinguo; unam quidem assimulandi artem video cuius opus est secundum exemplaris commensurationes quoad longitudinem, latitudinem, profunditatem, convenientesque colores aemulam imaginem fabricare. APUG 1188, fos. 16r–v (see also APUG 1163, fos. 9v–10r).

120. Igitur species altera assimulatix cum videatur vocari non debet partem igitur alteram assimulatricem, ut supra diximus, appellabimus, quid porro quod apparet quidem pulcro simile cum non sit pulcrum et si quis penitus inspicere queat nec simile cui simile videtur, quo illud nomine nuncupabimus? . . . has quidem duas imaginariae facultatis species supra ponebam, unam quae similitudines efficit, alteram quae fantasmata conformat. Ibid.

121. Haec Plato, ex quibus apud hunc authorem positis verbis sic naturam Poeseos investigo. Poetica, ut paulo ante confecimus, imitatio est, igitur in assimilando versatur, imitari enim est aliquid exprimere atque assimilare, praeterea si in assimilando versatur igitur aliquod exemplar perpetuo respicit haec ars, quod assimilet, ac exprimat, hoc vero dum respicit, aut ita exprimit, ut cum illo poeta conformet omnino imitamentum suum, aut exemplar hoc plane negligit, seque ab illo seiungit dum poeta poema condit, aut denique partim accedit ad exemplar dum illud exprimit, partim ab eo recedit, dum idem despicit. Ex quibus hisce modis primus esse non potest, nam licet ille modus imitandi sit, non tamen est aptus poetae, quasi in ea imitatione natura poeseos sita sit, sed est aptus historico, qui rem uti gesta est cum fide narrat, cum tamen poeta (sicut paulo post cum Aristot. dicemus) rem uti geri debuerit exponat, neque secundus modus satis est, cum illa imitatio non sit, nan si imitari ut diximus est ad alicuius exemplar conformare opus suum, poeta, qui nihil habet cum exemplari commune, sed ab eius norma longissime recedit, quo modo imitari dicendus est? Ibid., fos. 16v–17r.

122. Superest ergo ut imitatio illa in qua poeta propositum sibi exemplar habet, et ad quod partim se conformat, partim ab exemplari discrepat poetica, quam quaerimus, imitatio sit: haec autem est fantastica imitatio, in qua aliquid simile exemplari, aliquid vero dissimile reperitur. Ibid, f. 17r.

123. Aio igitur huiusmodi poesim dum partim exemplar ad exprimendum sibi proponit nec totum exprimit non posse historicam dici, quia non servat historiae leges quae iubent rem exponi uti est scitum enim illud bonum ex integra causa, malum vero ex singulis defectibus. APUG 1188, f. 18r (see also APUG 1163, f. 10v).

124. Sit ergo verisimile. . . id quod poeta imitatur, id est fingat ille quidem plurimaque pro ingenio suo commentetur, meminerit tamen figmenta ut ea sint, quae probari possint in vulgus verique opinionem ingenerare, quod non faciet si inter se commenta discrepabunt. . . . Qui ergo hoc imitando materiamque sibi propositam quamvis veri fines excedentium, veri similitudine vestiunt. . . ad veri speciem composito proponunt. Hi demum verisimili seu imitari, seu fantasma verisimile tractari dicendi sunt. Atqui hoc definiens Aristoteles dicebat poetae officium esse non ea exponere quae facta sunt, sed qualia fieri debuerunt, sic enim ait "Perspicuum est ex dictis non ea, quae facta sunt dicere hoc poetae opus est, sed qualia utque fieri debuerunt, et ea quae effici possunt secundum verisimile, vel necessarium". . . *sensus autem illorum verborum (quae effici possunt secundum verisimile vel necessarium) non est ita accipiendus, quasi Aristoteles velit materiam poeseos esse verisimilem, vel necessariam, sic enim non differret ab historia, cuius materia necessaria est, cum vera necessario sit, sed. . . eas actiones exprimere poeta debet, quae. . . posita una sequatur alia necessario, sive ut plurimum, verbi gratia si Achillem iracundum fingit. . . contemptumque ab Agamemnone commemorat, necessitate nescio qua cogitur poeta ut eundem ultionis appetentem describat, et verisimilitudine inducitur, ut inexorabile eundem faciat; necessitas ergo non ad res naturales, sed ad earum nexum, nodumque*

referenda est atque hoc est apud Aristotelem narratum ea quae effici possunt secundum verisimile vel necessarium. APUG 1188, fos. 19r–v. I have written in italics the parts of this passage that were added by Strada later in his own revision to the lecture notes (cf. APUG 1163, fos. 11v–12r.)

125. Ricoeur, *The rule of the metaphor*, p. 42, but see the entire section on poetic imitation, pp. 35–43.

126. *Additum denique qua ratione sint hominum mentes ad hasce affectiones sive inertes. . . concitandae sive perfervidae ac temerariae reprimendae. Quod ut in rebus humanis primum est posse nimirum hominem in hominis animum in dicendo delabi ut (quod Dei imperium solum est) eius arbitria quamcumque velit in partem moderetur sic etiam nos Rhetorum principem inter alias hanc affectuum scientiam. . . concludimus habere dicit.* Strada, *De Affectibus*, APUG 1163, fos. 101r–155r, quot. at 155r.

127. Gadamer, *Truth and Method*, p. 449.

128. On this, see Bertelli, *Ribelli, Libertini e Ortodossi*, pp. 23ff.

Chapter 5

1. The quote comes from his *Mythe et épopée*, 3 vols., Paris: Gallimard, 1968-1973, vol. III, p. 14. Among the classic studies on the origin and significance of oaths in the ancient Western civilizations, see at least Émile Benveniste, "L'expression du serment dans la Grèce ancienne," in *Revue de l'Histoire des Religions* (1948), pp. 81–94; id., *Indo-European Language and Society*, trans. Elizabeth Palmer, London: Faber & Faber, 1973; id., *Problems in General Linguistics*, trans. Mary Elizabeth Meek, Coral Gables, FL: University of Miami Press, 1971; Louis Gernet, *The Anthropology of Ancient Greece*, trans. George Hamilton and Blaise Nagy, Baltimore: Johns Hopkins University Press, 1981; G. Glotz, "Iusiurandum," in C. Daremberg and E. Saglio, eds., *Dictionnaire des antiquités grecques et romaines*, Paris: Hachette, 1887–1919; Rudolf Hirzel, *Der Eid, ein beitrag zu seiner Geschichte*, Leipzig: S. Hirzel, 1902; as well as the already quoted Dumézil (in addition to *Mythe et épopée*, see *Archaic Roman Religion*, 2 vols., English trans. by Philip Krapp, Baltimore: Johns Hopkins University Press, 1996).

2. Giorgio Agamben, in *The Sacrament of Language*, gives a synthetic and useful overview of the main traditional scholarly trends on oaths (see pp. 1–19 in particular).

3. Paolo Prodi, *Il Sacramento del Potere*, p. 22.

4. Ibid., pp. 289–291.

5. See ibid., pp. 403ff., and also David Martin Jones, *Conscience and Allegiance in Seventeenth-Century England. The political significance of oaths and engagements*, Rochester, NY: University of Rochester Press, 1999.

6. Prodi, *Il Sacramento del Potere*, pp. 420–426.

7. Agamben, *The Sacrament of Language*, p. 2.

8. Ibid., p. 21.

9. Ibid., p. 50.

10. Ibid., p. 33.

11. Ibid., p. 11.

12. I borrow the expression "società giurata," or "sworn society," from Prodi; see *Il Sacramento del Potere*, pp. 161ff.

13. Lorenzo Valla, *De professione religiosorum*, in *Opera Omnia*, 2 vols., Turin: Bottega d'Erasmo, 1962, vol. II, pp. 99–149 at 116–117.

14. *Quid illud iusiurandum, quod plus quam ullius testimonii locum obtinet, quo milites obligantur, quo promissa servantur, quo foedera custodiuntur? Nonne ea ratione institutum est, quod fidem si fallas, deos verearis iratos, qui si non irascuntur, nulla est ratio iuramenti? De voluptate*, in *Opera omnia*, vol. I, pp. 896–999 at 961. Valla is here forcefully responding to the point Cicero had made in *De officiis*: "sed in iure iurando non qui metus, sed quae vis sit, debet intelligi. . . iam enim non ad ira deorum, quae nulla est, sed ad iustitiam et ad fidem pertinet" (3.104). Interesting reflections on this point can be found in David Wootton, "The fear of God in early modern political theory," in *Historical Papers / Communications historiques* 18, no. 1 (1983), pp. 56–80. Valla's hostility to oaths was later taken up by some radical Protestant sects, which refused the oath as an expression of both one's religious faith and

one's political allegiance and as such were marginalized and in many cases persecuted by both the territorial states and the confessionalized churches. On this, see Prodi and his bibliography, *Il Sacramento del Potere*, pp. 339–386.

15. The first edition of both the Spanish and the Latin version, entitled *De cavendo iuramentorum abusu*, appeared in Salamanca. My quotations come from the Madrid 1770 Spanish edition.

16. que con la fuerza del juramento de su nombre esforcemos nuestra autoridad que por razon del pecado estaba flaca y enferma. Ibid., pp. 29–30.

17. la licencia del jurar por el grande amor que nos tiene, y cuidado de nosotros... para quitarnos de pleytos, y para que apaciguadas nuestras discordias, viviesemos en paz y en tranquilidad. Ibid., p. 22.

18. el supremo principio y primera fuente de la verdad. Ibid., p. 23.

19. See ibid., pp. 67ff.

20. Ibid., pp. 176ff.

21. Iuramentum est dictio per divinam attestationem confirmata. Soto, *De iustitia et iure*, p. 253r.

22. habet enim ius quaecunque publica potestas, tam civilis quam spiritualis iure & more exigendi a cive, & a quocunque sibi subdito iuramentum ad detegenda coercendaque mala, quae sive in reipublicae pernicie oriuntur, sive in iniuriam proximi. Et qui tunc non iuraret contra praeceptum ageret non solum obedientiae, verum & religionis. Ibid. p. 255r.

23. si ratio iurandi per se in omnibus consideretur eiusdem esse omnia speciei: Deum enim in testem implorare sive in assertionibus sive in promissionibus fiat sive in execrationibus eadem est iurandi speciei, quia idem est testis & testimonium. Differunt tamen accidentarie hoc est ratione materiei, quae per se alio genere differunt: ut pollicitatio & assertio si enim animal per album dividas & nigrum, licet per se duae sunt differentiae coloris sunt tamen genere animalis accidentariae. Ibid., p. 254r.

24. On Soto's elaboration on the *vulnus incredulitatis*, see ibid., pp. 255r and 257r–v.

25. quoanim licet qui iurat veneretur diligatque Deum, non tamen in hunc finem ordinat iuramentum, sed in necessitatem manifestandae veritatis: quocirca non est nisi ob talem necessitatem, optandum. Circa has solutiones intricat hic Caietanus nescio quam metaphysicam, forsan non tam necessariam utrum iuramentum sit finis manifestationis veritatis, an e converso manifestatio sit finis iuramenti. Nam profecto res est: & secundum Sanctum Thomam & in se ipsa patentissima. Forma enim iuramenti est Deum in testem adducere: & hoc non tam proprie dicitur referri in reverentiam Dei, quam esse ipsissimam reverentiae exhibitionem, nam est testimonium fidei qua Deum confitemur supremum rerum testem, utilitas autem & effectus eiusdem attestationis est manifestatio veritatis.... Quod si cui absurdum appareat id quod praestantius est in id referri quod inferius est, intelligat nihil absurditatis habere: quando inferius vicissim in superius refertur. Mortuus enim Deus est ob nostram salutem: eo quod eadem salus in gloriam refertur.... Quapropter non solum manifestatio veritatis est iurandi finis: ob id quod iurans in ipsam illud refert, verum quod Deus illud ad illam proxime ordinavit, licet rursus manifestatio ipsa in eius gloriam redundet. Ibid., f. 257v.

26. Iuravit enim Deus per semetipsum Abrahae (ut habetur in Genesi) quod ex eius semine missurus esset super omnes gentes benedictionem. Veruntamen Deus non ea ratione iurat qua homines: nempe quod indigeat veritatem suam iuramento confirmare. Tam firma quippe est simplex eius assertio, quam iuratio: iurat enim per semetipsum. Ibid., f. 254v.

27. This is canon 9, *causa XXII*, question IV (text in *Corpus iuris canonici*, eds. Aemilius L. Richter and Emil A. Friedberg, 2 vols., Graz: Akademische Druck und Verlagsanstalt, 1959, vol. I, col. 877). On the importance of the councils held in Toledo in the sixth and the seventh centuries for the establishment of the religious legitimacy of political oaths in sixteenth- and seventeenth-century Europe, see Luciano Pereña et al., *"De iuramento fidelitatis." Estudio Preliminar*, Madrid: Consejo Superior de Investigaciones Científicas, Escuela Española de la Paz, 1979, pp. 447–490, and P. Prodi, *Il Sacramento del Potere*, pp. 90–96.

28. Sed ut concilio Toletano habetur quod vigesimasecunda quaest.4 canon. immutabilis refertur iurare Dei est a se ipso ordinata nullatenus convellere, sicut poenitere, eadem ordinata cum voluerit immutare. Sic enim per Heremiam dicit: Loquar adversum gentem, ut erradicem & destruam & disperdam, si poenitentiam egerit gens illa a malo suo, agam & ego poenitentiam a malo quod cogitavi, ut facerem eis [Jeremiah 18:7–8]. Itaque quod Deus sine iuramento affirmat, nonnunquam ceu comminatorium immutat: quod vero iuramento

asserit immutabile firmat. Et ideo mysterium filii sui tanquam immutabile iuramento firmavit Abrahae. Unde in Psal.109 e regione [sic] iuramento Dei eius opponitur poenitentia. Iuravit enim, inquit, Dominus, & non poenitebit eum: id est quia iuravit non poenitebit. Tu es sacerdos in aeternum, & c. [this reference is to Psalm 109:4 in the *Vulgata*, and Psalm 110:4 in the King James Bible]. Et ad Hebrae. 6 Paul. volens, inquit, Deus abundantius ostendere immobilitatem consilii sui, interposuit iusiurandum, ut per duas res immobiles (scilicet pollicitationem & iusiurandum) quibus impossibile est mentiri Deum fortissimum solatium habeamus [Hebrews 6:17–18]. Soto, *De iustitia et iure*, p. 254v.

29. Grotius, *De iure belli ac pacis*, Paris, 1625, book II, ch. XIII, §II (trans. by A. C. Campbell, Washington, DC, 1901).

30. For a discussion of the implications of the theological debates over God's absolute and ordained power in medieval and early modern Europe, see Francis Oakley, *Omnipotence, Covenant & Order. An excursion in the history of ideas from Abelard to Leibniz*, Ithaca, NY: Cornell University Press, 1984, and id., "The Absolute and Ordained Power of God in Sixteenth- and Seventeenth-Century Theology," *Journal of the History of Ideas* 59, no. 3 (1998), pp. 437–461.

31. Divus Thomas. . . respondet. . . obligatio non videtur iuramentum respicere assertorium, quod est de praesenti vel de praeterito. Neque vero illud quod non est in potestate iurantis implere, ut si quis crastinam pluviam iuraret futuram: sed de his duntaxat quae per eum qui iurat facienda sunt.... Tam assertorio quam promissorio sua innata est obligatio. Diversimode tamen quoniam obligatio assertorii de praesenti vel praeterito non fertur in rem iuratam, sed ad actiones iurandi refertur. Hoc est nemo iurat, id verum efficere quod asserens iurat. Sed tamen obligatur id praecise iurare quod verum est. Et ideo in prima conclusione non simpliciter negavit obligationem ad iuramentum assertorium respicere, sed dixit videtur: alias sibi hanc tertiam contradiceret, qua asserit quodammodo obligationem in ipsum cadere. Attemen in iuramento eorum, quae per iurantem exequenda sunt obligatio cadit e converso super rem iuramento firmatam. Tenetur enim quisque id verum efficere, quod sub iusiurando pollicetur. Itaque differentia est haec, quod in iuramento assertorio obligatio non nascitur ex iuramento, sed ipsum antecedit: tenetur enim quisque iurare verum. In promissorium vero e converso obligatio est effectus iuramenti: ex eo enim quod quis iurat manet obligatur iuramentum implere. Soto, *De iustitia et iure*, p. 258v.

32. See ibid., pp. 262r ff.

33. Humanae aures talia verba nostra iudicant, qualia foris sonant. Divina vero iudicia talia foris audiunt, qualia ex intimis proferuntur. Apud homines cor ex verbis: apud Deum vero verba pensantur ex corde. The text of the canon can be found in *Corpus iuris canonici*, vol. I, col. 885.

34. Quacumque arte verborum quis iuret, Deus tamen, qui conscientiae testis est, ita hoc accipit, sicut ille, cui iuratur, intelligit. The text of the canon can be found in ibid.

35. Quid ergo si quis exterius iuret proferendo verba & tangendo Evangelia, intus tamen non habeat iurandi animum? Respondetur in illo casu non esse verum, sed fictum iuramentum, & tunc habere locum verba Grego. quod Deus non habet illud pro iuramento. Ipse enim mentium scrutator videt iuramentum non nasci ex corde. In foro autem exteriori omnino ab ecclesia quae per externa verba iudicat, reputatur iuramentum: parique modo in praetorio civili. Sed numquid in conscientia qui sic iurat, tenebitur id implere. Respondetur minime quidem, ex vi iuramenti, utpote quod nullum est, atque adeo neque contra illi veniens periurii reus fiet. Teneri autem potest aliis legibus verbi gratia. Si quis ut puella frueretur quae sui copiam illi facere renuerat, antequam sponsalia illi iuraret, profecto si verbis iurat, tenebitur lege iustitiae fidem promissi servare. Et pariter in quibuscunque aliis contractibus ubi intervenerit 'Do ut des'. Deinde gratia cavendi scandali, si quis solemniter iuravit, quamvis ficte in re alicuius momenti, proculdubio si non posset plane persuadere se non vere iurasse, teneretur ficto iuramento sub reatu mortali stare, ne scandalum daret, haberetur que in opinione aliorum periurus. Soto, *De iustitia et iure*, p. 262v.

36. Intentio iurandi semper in externa iuratione includitur, dummodo & advertenter fiat & qui iurat non illam peculiariter & expresse mente removeat. Quare qui non habet animum se obligandi mentitur quidem circa materiam iuramenti quae est promissio, non tamen circa ipsam iurationem: imo vere iurat. Ibid.

37. cum ille tunc respondet 'sic iuro', non solum est assertio in actu signato (ut dicunt logici) id est non solum asserit se iurare: tunc enim solum esset simplex mendacium: sicut si nollens rem aliquam dicere, 'sic volo', sed est iuratio in actu exercito. Etenim sicut cum dicis 'ego loquor', non solum significas te loqui, sed vere illud exerces. Pari modo cum ais 'sic iuro', perinde est ac si dicas 'Deus est mihi testis, me pecunam exhibiturum', aut 'per Deum pecuniam dabo'. Ibid., p. 263r.

38. Austin, *How to do things with words*, pp. 1–24 (quot. at 11; Austin's emphasis).

39. On the this dualism, see also the insightful consideration of Adriano Prosperi in "Fede, giuramento, inquisizione," now in id., *America e Apocalisse e altri saggi*, Pisa: Istituti Editoriali Poligrafici Internazionali, 1999, pp. 233–247.

40. At vero duplici hic distinctione opus est. Quoniam aut externa verba relata ad mentem iurantis plane falsa sunt aut aequivoca, scilicet in uno sensu vera, & in altero falsa, aut denique ea arte prolata, ut alter cui iuramentum exhibetur ipse callere nequeat. Secunda distinctio est ex parte iurantis. Aut enim ab eo exigitur iuramentum, quod iure facere tenetur, videlicet a suo praelato iuridice aut a privata persona, cui ratione contractus iurare tenetur; aut exigitur per vim aut per iniuriam, ut illi contingit, qui in nemore incidit in latrones, vel si iudex contra ius illud vult extorquere. Soto, *De iustitia et iure*, p. 263r.

41. His suppositis prima statuitur generalis regula, si verba exterius prolata respectu intentionis iurantis, plane falsa sunt, id est menti eius dissona, universim & absque ulla exceptione est peccatum mortale. Id quod praesenti exemplo mostratur, ubi extra sine restrictione iuratur & in mente non habetur absoluta intentio, neque iurans excusatur per illam mentalem restrictionem, 'dabo si debeo' aut 'iuro dare si debeo'. Nam postquam illam verbis non explicatur extra. Ibid.

42. Quando autem simulatio sit in verbis, quae vel sub aequivoco, vel artificiose proferuntur, ita ut sensum possint recipere, quem iurans intendit, licet eum alter non percipiat, tunc si iuramentum iure petitur, non licet tale amphibologia uti propter iniuriam quae fit illi qui ius habet petendi. Quando vero vi illata petitur, licitum est ea fraude petentem deludere. Verbi gratia: si iniurius ille nequam sic rogaret.... 'Iuras mihi numerare pecuniam?' Alter responderet: 'Tibi iuro numerare', non ut esset sensus: 'Numerare tibi, hoc est solvere aut tradere'; sed 'tibi iuro apud me pecuniam recensere': quandoquidem, numerare utrumque significat. Quare tale iuramentum esset verum, iustum, & prudens atque adeo consonum documento Hieron. in canone citato, utilem. Quoniam tunc simulatio (quoniam absque falsitate fieret) utilis esset. Quamobrem sententia Isidori, quacunque arte verborum, &c. non esset eiusmodi iuramentis contraria: quoniam intelligitur, quando iuramentum est, aut falsum, aut alteri contra ius praeiudiciale. Ibid., pp. 263r–v.

43. See supra, ch. 1, pp. 15–19.

44. For instance, the alleged "novelties" of Suárez's theology (coupled with the luxurious privileges that supposedly Suárez had managed to acquire by taking advantage of his academic credentials) were at the center of a high-profile controversy between Suárez and Gabriel Vázquez, arguably the most famous and influential Spanish Jesuit theologians at that time, which started in the second half of the 1580s and lasted all through the 1590s; a detailed account of the controversy can be found in Raoul de Scorraille, *François Suarez de la Compagnie de Jésus*, 2 vols., Paris: P. Lethielleux, 1912, vol. I, pp. 283–314.

45. Just to mention a few examples, Suárez participated in the controversy over the *Interdetto* in Venice with a treatise entitled *De immunitate ecclesiastica contra Venetos*, which was written in 1607 but was never published because Robert Bellarmine, among others, deemed it doctrinally problematic (see the exchange between Bellarmine and Suárez over this book in ARSI, Fondo Gesuitico 652, fos. 209r–211v). Also, Suárez's position on grace and free will was very controversial both inside and outside the Society of Jesus (see ARSI, Fondo Gesuitico 660, fos. 47rff., for internal censures over Suárez's treatise *De divina gratia*, 3 vols., which Suárez wrote between 1606 and 1609 but was published only starting in 1619). On all these instances and more, see Scorraille, *François Suarez*, passim.

46. Until very recently, scholars have mostly ignored the historical, theological, and philosophical implications of Suárez's thought. The reader who might want to consult a biography of Suárez, e.g., will still have to recur to the already quoted 1912 work of Scorraille, *François Suarez*, which, albeit full of rather interesting documentary appendices, is marred by

a generally apologetic approach that dulls the edges of Suárez's thought in order to present it as perfectly in line with the Jesuit hierarchy (equally apologetical in tone and far less interesting in terms of documentary apparatus is Joseph Fisher's *Man of Spain: Francis Suarez*, New York: Macmillan, 1940). Only very recently has modern scholarship started to explore more fully the radical originality of certain aspects of Suárez's thought. As far as Suárez's political philosophy is concerned, its originality with respect to other Jesuit positions is hinted at by Quentin Skinner, *The Foundations of Modern Political Thought*, 2 vols., Cambridge: Cambridge University Press, 1978, vol. II, and is explored fully by Harro Höpfl, *Jesuit political thought*. Suárez's metaphysical and theological positions are also currently the object of a profound historical and philosophical reevaluation. The seeds of this reevaluation have been planted by Martin Heidegger, for whom Suárez was a fundamental thinker insofar as he ushered the medieval Scholastic way of understanding metaphysics into the modern world (see Heidegger's *The fundamental concepts of metaphysics*, English trans., Bloomington: Indiana University Press, 1995, pp. 51–55, and *The basic problem of phenomenology*, English trans., Bloomington: Indiana University Press, 1975, pp. 77–99). Among the recent works providing a reconsideration of Suárez's philosophy, see José Pereira, *Suárez between Scholasticism and modernity*, Milwaukee: Marquette University Press, 2006; Benjamin Hill and Henrik Lagerlund, eds., *The philosophy of Francisco Suárez*, Oxford: Oxford University Press, 2012; Daniel Schwartz, ed., *Interpreting Suárez*, Cambridge: Cambridge University Press, 2012.

47. For more details on this story, quite possibly apocryphal, see Scorraille, *François Suarez*, vol. I, pp. 169–171.

48. A note of the catalogue reporting the professors of the college for the year 1584 described Suárez as a man *"mediocri ingenio,"* albeit *"in theologicis optime versatus"* and *"ad omnia aptus, praecipue ad docendam scholasticam,"* quot. in Scorraille, *François Suarez*, vol. I, p. 173.

49. *De vita et moribus R. P. Leonardi Lessii e Societate Iesu Theologi Liber*, Brussels, 1640, dedicatory epistle "reverendis in Christo patribus, caeterisque Societatis Iesu religiosis per Belgium," unfol.

50. The censures, five in total, can be found in ACDF, Index, Protocolli FF, fos. 6r–20r. They are all anonymous and undated (although it seems fairly reasonable to date them shortly before 1640). The censure that appears first in the folder (fos. 6r–15r) is much longer than the others and quotes in full the condemned parts of the original manuscript that were deleted from the printed version, thus allowing us to compare the printed version with what the original manuscript might have been. One of the other anonymous censors seemed to imply that in addition to reading and censoring the book himself, he had spoken about the book with Cardinal de Lugo, who had suggested some ways to further correct it; see f. 17r.

51. ACDF, Index, Protocolli FF, fos. 7r–8r, 18r, 20r. On Bellarmine's relationship with Lessius's soteriology, see Tutino, *Empire of Souls*, ch. 2.

52. Unaque revulsit radicitus eum qui continuo stimulabat et haesitationem iniiciebat scrupulus, quasi veterum doctorum prope iurandum esset in verba, neque fas foret a maiorum aut plurimum sententia discedere, imo. . . plus auctoritati tribuere quam rationi. ACDF, Index, Protocolli FF, f. 6r.

53. Ad quam prudenter Suarez nullius esse sacrilegii in rebus quae nec ad fidem nec ad bonos mores pertinent, a gravium doctorum opinone desciscere, quandoque enim (ut Poeta venusinus notavit) etiam bonum dormitare Homerum, et veniam facile dari quod longo in opere quis somnus obrepserit [Horace, *Ars Poetica*, 359–360]. Nam nullum aliquem tam perspicacem esse, ut omnia pervideat vel pervidere satis possit, neque sic obviam esse veritatem ut in multis saepe non lateat aut fugiat quam sagacissimos. Itaque quemadmodum corporeis oculis familiare est ut plures plura cernant idem quoque hominum mentibus accidere. Ibid., fos. 6r–v.

54. In terrae visceribus complures adhuc abditas auri argentique venas delitescunt, in conchyliis margaritas, in montibus gemmas, ad quas et si nemo hactenus pervenerit, aliquando tamen perventuri sint aliqui. Non aliter in scientiis evenire. Ibid.

55. Inde plerumque contingere aiebat ut absque ulla veritatis indagatione alter alterum sequatur tamquam ovis ovem. Quare aciem mentis suae audaciter Lessius in omnia intenderet, neque id statim ratum haberet quod ab aliis quos probaret iudicatum videret. . . ac proinde

cum nulla illum vincula impedirent. . . confidenter ex omnibus quodcumque maxime specie veritatis moveret, imo et si quod non contemplando assecutus foret, libere expromeret. Et inde Leonardi animus nimio angore laxatus, ac quasi vinculis et carceribus emissus. . . ampla scientiarum spatia coepit decurrere. Ibid., f. 7r.

56. The first censor commented positively on the fact that in the revised version of the text (the one that went into print), Suárez's words "deleta sunt" (f. 6r), and another censor agreed that as a condition for allowing the printing of the manuscript Suárez's words "videntur omittenda" (f. 18r).

57. sacrilegium non esse, in quibusdam sententiis, quae neque fidem neque mores concernunt, a magnorum quorundam placito discedere. *De vita et moribus*, p. 26. Notice some small but significant variations with respect to the corresponding phrase in the manuscript: the *gravium doctorum* has now become *magnorum quorundam*, and the *sententiae* have become *placitum*.

58. The first and second volume of *De religione* appeared, respectively, in 1608 and 1609. The third and fourth appeared only posthumously, mainly because of the controversial treatment of the relationship between grace and free will that Suárez offered in the third volume and because of the strong defense of the originality of the Society of Jesus with respect to other religious orders that constituted most of the fourth volume. I will be quoting from the complete edition of this work published in Lyon in 1630. The treatise *De iuramento & adiuratione* is the fifth one of the second volume and can be found at 296–511. It was divided into four sections, dealing respectively with the assertory oath, the promissory oath, perjury, and blasphemy. Suárez justified having included the treatise on oaths in a work on the Catholic religion by claiming that the oath was a special act by which we could speak with God, akin to prayer and vows (which were the topics, respectively, of the fourth and sixth treatises of the same volume II); for the general frame of Suárez's treatise, see *De iuramento*, p. 297.

59. Iurare. . . oportere esse enunciationem in qua Deus testis afferatur. . . [finis] est confirmare veritatem. Suárez, *De iuramento*, p. 298.

60. Ad hoc autem magis explicandum, considero iuramentum prius esse spectandum, prout est quaedam actio apta ad confirmandam veritatem, praescindendo ab hoc, quod cedat, vel non cedat in honorem eius qui in testem invocatur, sed praecise intuendo ad utilitatem & fructum illius actionis in ordine ad veritatem confirmandam: deinde vero spectandum est iuramentum, ut in se continens divinum cultum, supposita priori eius utilitate, vel necessitate. Ibid., p. 317, but see the entire section 314–317.

61. ex iure humano ibi solum requiri verba, ut iuramentum fidem faciat, vel obligationem inducat, ubi constiterit legem humanam talem formam iurandi postulare ad hos effectus. Ibid., p. 323.

62. Nam iuramentum proprie significat actionem humanam, nemo enim dicet hominem dormientem iurare, etiamsi verba ad iurandum sufficientia proferat, & idem est de amente et similibus. Ibid., p. 299.

63. Neque etiam invenitur ibi aliquis effectus, quem Deus facturus sit, qui ex intentione iurantis pendeat, nam ut diximus, iuramentum non debet fieri eo animo, ut Deus exhibeat aliquod extraordinarium signum, quo ostendat veritatem. Effectus ergo iuramenti totus videtur positus in opinione audientium videlicet ut inde moveantur ad credendum verum esse, quod dicitur, hic autem effectus aequaliter sequitur, sive proferens talia verba habeat intentionem iurandi, sive non. Ibid., p. 300. See also p. 301: "sine intentione iurandi, ut dixi neque posse definiri, an verba ad iurandum proferantur, nec ne, neque distingui iuramentum a non iuramento. Haec autem intentio exterius declaranda est, vel sufficienter exprimenda, ut de iuramento possit hominibus constare, hoc autem duobus modis fieri potest, scilicet, aut vere, aut dolose, & circa hoc maxime versatur difficultas tacta, an scilicet sufficiat dolosa intentio, vel si non sufficit, quid magis operetur ad rationem, vel effectum iuramenti, intentio vera, quam ficta, quando in prolatione verborum eadem est species, seu forma iurandi, etiam apud homines? Ad quod in primis dicendum est esse magnam differentiam apud Deum, nam qui habet veram intentionem iurandi, quantum est in se Deum inducit ad testificandum, quod non facit is, qui apparenter tantum iurare intendit, seu ita proferre verba ac si iuraret. Unde fit, ut si fortasse assertio falsa sit, minor iniuria fiat Deo per fictum, quam per verum iuramentum, quia est diversa malitia, nam iuramentum vera intentione factum erit periurium, cum dolosa autem intentione, erit mendacium perniciosum & scandalosum. Et posterior potest declarari

ex poenis, nam si lata esset excommunicatio propter periurium, incurreret illam, qui verba proferret ex vera intentione iurandi, non autem qui ficta, sicut non incurrit poenas haeretici qui ficta intentione adorat idolum. Denique in aliis effectibus, quos iuramentum habere potest, invenitur magna differentia, quia iuramentum fictum per se non inducit obligationem, sicut verum, ut infra videbimus. Est ergo unum iuramentum verum, utique veritate in essendo, aliud tantum apparens, & haec differentia ex intentione provenit."

64. Ad inconveniens autem illatum respondemus certitudinem, quae ex iuramento resultat, non esse talem, aut tantam, ut non sit dolis hominum, & deceptionibus exposita. Sicut ergo potest homo mentiri etiamsi iuret, ita potest dolose, & ficte iurare, etiam si aliud exterius profiteatur. Neque propterea inutile est iuramentum. . . quia satis est, quod homo teneatur peculiari obligatione dicere verum, quando Deum in testem adducit. Ibid., p. 300.

65. Nihilominus dico, iuramentum non esse ex his, quae necessario supponunt peccatum, vel effectus eius in humana natura. Probatur, quia licet humana natura esset integra, & innocens, ignoraret negative multa, praesertim contingentia, praeterita, & futura, & presentia etiam quoad tempus, sed distantia quoad locum, vel occulta quoad internos actos: posset ergo in illo statu unus homo ad alterum loqui de rebus sibi notis, & alteri ignotis, & alter possit illi credere propter testimonium eius. Deinde testimonium illud etiam in illo statu non esset infallibile, quia homo etiam in illo statu non erat impeccabilis, posset ergo mentiri, quia non erat magis confirmatus in bono in illa materia quam in aliis, sed haec fallibilitas testimonii humani, & moralis necessitas credendi illud, est de se sufficiens ad capacitatem, & ad usum iuramenti, ergo haec capacitas esset in statu innocentiae. . . illa fallibilitas, & necessitas non pertinent ad effectus peccati originalis, sed per se sunt coniunctae, cum conditione humanae naturae. Ibid., p. 336.

66. quia sicut Deus revelavit homini lapso promissionem incarnationis, ita potuisset illam sub iuramento promittere Adamo, vel alicui posterorum eius, etiam si in innocentia perseverassent, nam congruitas illius iuramenti non sumitur tantum ex infirmitate & ignorantia hominis lapsi, sed etiam ex aptitudine mysterii ad illud commendandum, & ad ostendendum propositum Dei absolutum, & per modum cuiusdam extrinseci auxilii, ad confortandum hominem in fide, seu ad credendum. Ibid., p. 337.

67. Item verba non habent vim obligandi, nisi ratione consensus, ut constat in matrimonio & in omnibus contractibus, & in professione ac votis. Et ratio est, quia interior voluntas est quasi anima verborum, nec verba habent efficaciam nisi ut sunt signa mentis. Est autem haec assertio intelligenda est de obligatione per se, & ex vi iuramenti: nam ex rationibus extrinsecis poterir oriri obligatio ex iuramento exteriori, etiamsi animus defuerit. Ibid., p. 356.

68. Contra vero. . . obiicitur. . . hoc modo enervatur fructus & finis iuramenti. Nam finis iuramenti est confirmare veritatem, & firmare pacta inter homines, cum autem homines non intueantur cor, si totum hoc pendet ex intentione loquentis, & non ex significatione verborum, frustra adhibetur iuramentum, quia tam incerta & obscura manet obligatio, ac si non adhiberetur. Ibid., p. 362.

69. Propter haec aliqui limitationem adhibent huic assertioni, nimirum, ut locum habeat, quando intentio dolosa iurantis vel potest commode adaptari verbis secundum aliquem proprium sensum eorum, vel quando de tali intentione iurantis potest ex aliis circunstantiis, vel coniecturis, aut probationibus sufficienter constare.... Imo etiam adhibenda erit eadem limitatio, quando omnino deest intentio iurandi modo omnino interno, & per se occulto, quod etiam est contra omnes, utraque sequela patet, quia tunc etiam frustrari videtur finis & effectus iuramenti. Nulla est ergo necessaria limitatio, quantum ad forum conscientiae spectat: si in eodem foro constet, iurantem solum voluisse iurare iuxta mentem suam & sensum. Ibid.

70. Ad tertium superiori libro capit. 2 declaratum est, quomodo non sit contra fructum iuramenti, quod eius propria obligatio pendeat ex intentione iurantis. Argumentum enim illud aeque probat de intentione iurandi simpliciter, & de intentione iurandi in tali vel tali sensu, eadem enim est ratio, ut ostensum est. Non obstat ergo, quod intentio sit necessaria, quia satis est quod homo teneatur habere rectam & debitam intentionem, si iurat, nam certitudo iuramenti necessario pendet ex conscientia iurantis, non enim iuramentum interponitur expectando a Deo speciale signum veritatis, sed solum quia propter reverentiam divini nominis creditur observanda veritas, tam in re iurata quam in modo & intentione iurandi. Addimus praeterea, quod licet iuramentum dolosum in conscientia non obliget ex vi iuramenti, potest

obligare ratione iniustitiae, & detrimenti inde secuti, quo sensu videtur intelligenda communis distinctio doctorum allegatorum. Item ratione scandali vitandi, poterit etiam sic iurans
teneri, quia si hominibus constet de iuramento facto, & non de intentione occulta, & postea
videant non servari, inhonoratur Deus in conspectu hominum, quod etiam contra religio-
nem est. Hinc etiam tale iuramentum in foro exteriori censebitur obligare, quia homines non
iudicant de occultis, sed de his quae patent, neque in hoc creditur iuranti, quando dolose
egit, & inique ex parte sua, secus quando prudenti cautela iusta occasione usus est. Ibid.,
p. 363.

71. See supra, ch. 1, pp. 15ff.

72. Denique alias nullus esset sermo certus inter homines, sed quilibet posset loqui & scribere
quae vellet, concipiendo mente sensum quem verba secundum aliquam significationem non
faciunt: quod est contra omnem fidem humanam, nec minus nocet societati hominum quam
apertum mendacium. Suárez, *De iuramento*, p. 475.

73. Sed nihilominus probabilis est dicta ratio Navarri.... Denique potest aliter explicari ratio,
quia liberum est homini mentem suam exprimere, vel non exprimere, ergo est etiam liberum
inchoare expressionem & non finire. Ergo cum in mente totum hoc concipio, non feci hoc
hodie, possum inchoare expressionem huius conceptus, & non finire illam, ergo licet dicam
non feci hoc, & ibi sistam, animo non finiendi propositionem in rigore non mentior. Quia
nondum finivi sermonem meum, & non intendo per illa sola verba aliquid integre significare,
ergo licet iurem, non iurabo falsum, quia non intendo iurare quod exterius sonat absqe alio
quod mente concipio. Ibid., pp. 475–476; italics in the original.

74. Agamben, *The Sacrament of Language*, pp. 69–70.

75. Austin, *How to do things with words*, p. 10; Austin's italics.

76. On these models, see the seminal considerations by Prosperi, *Tribunali della coscienza*,
pp. 213ff. See also Miriam Turrini, *La coscienza e le leggi. Morale e diritto nei testi per la confessione nella prima età moderna*, Bologna: Il Mulino, 1991, pp. 189–241; and Paolo Prodi,
Una storia della giustizia. Dal pluralismo dei fori al moderno dualismo tra coscienza e diritto,
Bologna: Il Mulino, 2000, pp. 283–306.

77. Prosperi, *Tribunali della coscienza*, pp. 485–507.

78. Rutilio Benzoni, *Tractatus de fuga*, Venice, 1595, pp. 104r–109r. This episode is discussed in
Prosperi, *Tribunali della coscienza*, pp. 503–504.

79. Verum, ut dixi, etiam talium necessitati ita auxiliandum est, ut et actio illis poenitentiae, et
communionis gratia, si eam, etiam amisso vocis officio, per indicia integri sensus postulant,
non negetur. At si aliqua vi aegritudinis ita fuerint aggravati, ut quod paulo ante poscebant,
sub praesentia sacerdotis significare non valeant, testimonia eis fidelium circumstantium
prodesse debebunt, ut simul et poenitentiae et reconciliationis beneficium consequantur.
The text of Leo's letter to Theodore Bishop of Fréjus is in PL, vol. 54, cols. 1011–1014 (quot.
at cols. 1013–1014). This text became the canon 49 of the *Tractatus de penitencia*, which was
the question III, *causa* XXXIII of the second part of Gratian's *Decretum* (text in *Corpus iuris
canonici*, vol. I, col. 1170)

80. S.mus dominus noster. . . hanc propositionem, scilicet per literas seu internuntium confessario absenti peccata sacramentaliter confiteri & ab eodem absente absolutionem obtinere,
ad minus uti falsam temerariam & scandalosam damnavit & prohibuit. A copy of the original
decree can be found in ACDF, SO Censurae Librorum 1570–1606, fos. 512v–513r.

81. Suárez's *De poenitentia* was first published in the fourth volume of his *Commentariorum ac
disputationum in tertiam partem divi Thomae*, Coimbra, 1602. Suárez explored the question
of verbal and nonverbal confession and absolution especially in the third section of the
Disputatio XIX (at 457-462) and in the four sections in the *Disputatio XXI*. The first three
sections of this latter disputation can be found at 496–507. The fourth and last section can be
found in the edition of the work reproduced in *Opera omnia*, Paris: L. Vivès, 1856–66, 26 vols.,
vol. XXII, pp. 462–465, as well as in many other editions (see infra, note no. 90). Suárez
himself explained that "postquam autem hoc decretum [i.e., the 1602 decree by Clement
VIII] Romae promulgatum est, intra breve tempus, scilicet sexta die Septemb. ejusdem anni
1602, ad manus meas pervenit Coimbricae, ubi degebam. Quo eodem tempore quartum de
poenitentia tomum typis mandabam, jamque fere finitum habebam, librosque per Castellam
et Lusitaniam distribuere inceperam; et licet liber nondum esset aliis communicatus, eo

quod ejus initium non esset excusum, tamen intra triduum perficiendus et evulgandus erat. Recepto autem pontificis mandato, quamvis opinionem quam ipse damnabat ego etiam in meo libro reprobarem et quam ipse approbavit ego amplecterer, quia tamen necessarium fuit gradum certitudinis a sanctissimo declaratum nostris scriptis adjungere, id quanta potui fidelitate, obedientia ac celeritate praestiti in disp.19 sec.3 ejusdem tomi, ita ut liber ad nullius manus perveniret nisi juxta pontificium mandatum emendatus... Contigit autem, ut inferius eodem libro disp.21 sec.4 quaestionem aliam longe alienam tractarem...In qua quaestione sententia mea fuit absolvendum esse hujusmodi aegrotum a sacerdote praesente ex testimonio nuncii et circumstantium...ne ex hac parte decretum pontificium huic meae locutioni repugnaret." Suárez's text, together with other documents pertaining to this episode and other unpublished works, was published in Jean Baptiste Malou, *R. P. Francisci Suaresii... opuscula sex inedita*, Paris: P. Lethielleux, 1861, pp. 102–163 (quot. at 106). On this entire affair, see also Scorraille, *François Suarez*, vol. II, pp. 51–116.

82. Propter haec decreta, et propter usum Ecclesiae censui semper hanc opinionem esse veram, et piam, et conformem Christi institutioni, qui ex parte poenitentis solum postulavit, ut suam conscientiam aperiat sacerdoti quantum et quale potest, ut patet etiam de integritate, de qua infra dicetur. Et hoc etiam declarat praedictus usus Ecclesiae, qui de absolutione, nihil tale declaravit, et ideo non est de illa similis ratio, praesertim quia forma habet praescripta verba, non autem confessio. Denique et hoc consentaneum obligationi poenitentis, a quo non exigitur nisi ut satisfaciat quantum potest ergo nec ut confiteatur nisi quantum potest, timeri autem potest ne praedicta declaratio Pontificia huic opinioni in aliquo derogare videatur, quia damnat hanc propositionem, licere per litteras seu internuncium confessario absenti peccata sacramentali confiteri, et ab eodem absente obsolutionem obtinere, ubi utrumque membrum videtur damnare. Existimo tamen non fuisse mentem S.mi de hac opinione tractare, sed solum de illa, quae dicit sacramentum poenitentiae posse perfici, ac consumari inter absentes. Atque ita illam particulam 'et' non esse divisive sed complexive sumendam, et praecipue illud damnasse propter eos qui dicebant absolutionem posse dari in absentia. Moveor tum ex circumstantiis literae nam aliud si voluisset, potius id explicasset per particulam 'vel.' Item hoc clare indicat illud singulare signum demonstrativum (hanc propositionem) nam ex eo constat solam hypoteticam propositionem per modum unius damnari, tum praeterea quia illa erat contra verba de qua tractabatur tum denique quia sola illa opinio est aliena ab usu Ecclesiae, haec autem est illi, et decretis conformis. Nihilominus declarationem hanc, eiusdem Pontificis censurae subicio, sicut cetera omnia, quae tam in hoc, quam in caeteris operibus meis continentur. Suárez, *De poenitentia*, in *Opera omnia*, vol. XXII, p. 465.

83. At the beginning of May 1603 the pope personally selected the members of the committee entrusted with the task of reading Suárez's work: "Feria 5.a die 8.a Maii 1603 .... Pro censuranda doctrina Patris Suarez Jesuitae in materia confessionis sacramentalis et absolutionis per literas S.mus mandavit vocari ad congregationem R. Archiepiscopum Armacanum, Patrem Radam Procuratorem Ordinis Minorum Observantiorum, Procuratorem Ordinis Carmelitani ac Patrem de Monopulo Procuratorem Ordinis Cappuccinorum." ACDF, SO Decreta 1603, f. 102v.

84. Die ultima Julii 1603, in Generali congregatione habita coram S.mo. Relata doctrina P. Franc. Suarez Jesuitae contenta in 4.o tomo ab ipso aedito super 3.a parte sancti Thomae in materia confessionis sacramentalis disp.21 sec.4 ubi de sensu decreti a S.D.N. super dicta materia emanati die 20 mense Junii anno 1602 tractat; relata etiam censura super eadem doctrina in Cong.ne patrum theologorum de mandato S.tis Suae facta, auditis votis, etc. S.mus decrevit ut liber suspendatur donec emendetur ac corrigatur, et correctio ac emendatio a Cong. S. Romanae et Universalis Inquisitionis approbetur. Libri vero hact. sevulgati, ut moris est, colligantur et serventur in hoc stylus S.ae Inq.nis. Inhibeatur eidem P.ri Franc. Suarez ne amplius possit scribere vel edere libros ad sacram theologiam pertinentes nisi prius eosque libros quos edere voluerit ad hanc urbem et Sacram Congregationem S.tae Inquisitionis miserit et ab ea approbati fuerint. Moneatur idem P. Franciscus Suarez ut consulat suae conscientiae ratione excommunicationis in dicto decreto contenta. ACDF, SO Censurae Librorum 1570–1606, f. 572r and SO Decreta 1603, fos. 176r–v.

85. Between 1601 and 1603 Suárez manifested his desire to leave Coimbra because the teaching duties he had as the chair of *Prima* seemed too burdensome for him, but Philip III refused

to accept Suárez's resignation and successfully retained him at Coimbra. For more details on this affair, see Scorraille, *François Suarez*, vol. II, pp. 47–49.

86. Havendo la S.tà N. ordinato che dal libro de penitentia che scrisse il P. Fran. Suarez della compagnia di Giesù si levasse la dechiaratione che diede al decreto di V.S. de confessione per litteras fu per la più breve essequutione di questo ordine levato da esso libro non solamente la dechiaratione sudetta ma anco tutta quella parte di esso libro dove detta dechiaratione fu messa e per che. . . cognoscendo la M.tà Cat.ca che di questo non solo perde riputatione questo dottore che è delli piu gravi et essemplarii et di bon nome che habbia la suddetta compagnia in lettere, religione, modestia, e virtù ma anco è nota dell'istessa religione et dell'approbatione che di questo libro fecero si suoi consigli Regii essendo anco detta maestà chiarita per relatione di persone molto gravi e di scienza e cuscienza che d. P. Suarez ha proceduto in questo con sincerità grande e senza malitia. . ..supplica però a V.S. se degni di considerare che nei libri di Spagna non si faccia in questo novità alcuna e che nelle future impressioni la dottrina della sess. 4 resti intiera poiché essa non dispiace a V.S. se non la dechiaratione del detto decreto quale si potrà levare overo accommodare come più piacerà a V.B. ACDF, SO Censurae Librorum 1570–1606, fos. 572v–573r.

87. On 7 August 1603 the inquisitors read Acquaviva's memo but reiterated that the condemned sections of the work needed to be eliminated from both the already printed copies and from all future editions: See ACDF, SO Decreta 1603, f. 180v.

88. A copy of Suárez's defense can be found in ACDF, SO Censurae Librorum 1570–1606, fos. 522r–534r.

89. On 12 February 1604 the Congregation decided that "Scripturae Patris Francisci Suarez Jesuitae. . . videantur etiam a Patribus theologis qui intervenerunt in Congregationi alias facta super eius scriptis, deinde deliberabitur" (ACDF, SO Decreta 1604–1605, f. 29v), and on 7 April 1604 "Memoriale exhibitum ab oratore Regis Hispaniarum pro Patre Francisco Suarez Jesuita fuit lectum, ac dictum ut fiat Congregatio Theologorum" (ibid., f. 64v).

90. The various meetings and judgments of the Inquisition over Suárez's case between 1604 and 1605 can be found in ACDF, SO Censurae Librorum 1570–1606, fos. 580r–581v, and also in ACDF, SO Decreta 1604–1605, fos. 25v–367v passim, and ACDF, SO Decreta 1605, fos. 76v–150v passim. I should also note that while Suárez's case was officially closed in 1605, the question of how to regulate the confession given to a moribund and, more specifically, the question of how much leniency should be applied in this specific case with respect to the rigidity of the rule concerning oral confession and absolution did not end in 1605. In 1614 Paul V published the Roman Ritual, in which it was prescribed that whenever a moribund happened to lose her voice just as she was confessing her sin and was therefore unable to finish her confession, if the confessor could identify the penitent's sins by her gesture or by the testimony of other people, he should absolve her. This reopened the debate within the Catholic camp between those who believed Suárez and the Jesuits had been right all along and those who had always opposed them, and this battle continued throughout the seventeenth century. The ACDF contains an interesting account of the seventeenth-century afterlife of the Suárez debate (SO Censurae Librorum 1570–1606, fos. 574r–577v), and the ARSI contains a folder in which the theologians of the Roman College responded to various questions concerning Suárez's opinion on verbal and written confession throughout the seventeenth century (Fondo Gesuitico 657, fos. 269–277v). Also, the 1655 Lyon edition of Suárez's *Tractatus de vera intelligentia auxilii efficacis* included a defense of Suárez's opinion on the legitimacy of a written confession in extreme necessity, entitled *Dissertatio pro Francisco Suaresio de gratia aegro oppresso collata per absolutionem a Sacerdote praesente impensam praevia peccatorum expositione epistolari* and composed by the French Jesuit Théophile Raynaud. The fact that Raynaud and an important section of the French Jesuits decided to reiterate Suárez's opinion on grace and free will and on the written confession in the context of the battle between Jesuits and Jansenists is a testament to the great popularity of Suárez in the seventeenth century, which might explain the fact that, despite the final and official condemnation of the Inquisition, the incriminated passages of *De poenitentia* continued to appear in several editions of Suárez's works in the seventeenth century as well as in the Venice 1740–1 and the Paris 1856–66 editions of Suárez's *opera omnia* (on this, see Scorraille, *François Suarez*, vol. II, p. 101).

91. Quia certum est, quod licet forma huius sacramenti sit essentialiter determinata ad talia verba voce humana prolata, quae ex vi sua postulant praesentiam, nihilominus materia eius, quae est confessio, non habet essentialiter talem determinationem ad certa verba, imo nec ad verba, sed potest quolibet sensibili signo fieri, et quocumque modo possibili, scilicet per interpretem vel per testes si aliter fieri non possit. ACDF, SO Censurae Librorum 1570–1606, f. 532r.

92. Item licet per se debeat integra confessio, si tamen non potest fieri, sufficit dimidiata, et minima si occasio aliud non offerat. Ibid. The question of the legitimacy of a confession *dimidiata* or *minima* was a thorny one in post-Tridentine Catholicism. Suárez and all his Catholic contemporaries were aware that regardless of whether one saw confession as a juridical act or as an act of spiritual medicine, post-Tridentine Catholicism was compact in its emphasis on the need to confess thoroughly and regularly. However, this newly stressed need created much demand, which could not be easily satisfied. For instance, during Easter festivities (the time traditionally prescribed for annual confessions) prospective penitents flooded the churches while the confessors, faced with an immense crowd to deal with, could not afford long individual confessions. There were other occasions in which confessors could not devote much time to performing their duties; e.g., when sailors were at sea and their ship was about to sink, it was pivotal that all sailors received the comfort of confession in their extreme hour, but of course the confessor needed to maximize his time in order to make sure that all sailors received their confession before the ship sank. All these cases were widely debated by early modern Catholic theologians; Suárez himself discussed them in *De poenitentia, Disputatio XXIII*. Adriano Prosperi, in *Tribunali della coscienza*, offers an insightful examination of this issue (pp. 491ff.). Eventually the Catholic Church decided to assume a more rigid position on this matter: among the 65 laxist propositions condemned by Innocent XI in 1679, we find the following proposition (no. 59): "Licet sacramentaliter absolvere dimidiate tantum confessos, ratione magni concursus poenitentium, qualis verbi gratia potest contingere in die magnae alicuius festivitatis aut indulgentiae."

93. Cur ergo non idem dicetur de praesentia, vel cur definiri crederem esse de essentia huius materiae per se spectatae ut poenitens illam exhibeat coram sacerdote, et quod non sufficiat alius modus quando necessita [sic] extrema cogit, dummodo tota confessio ad hoc ordinetur ut sacramentum in praesentia sacerdotis consumetur, et confessor certus fiat de dispositione poenitentis, quantum potuerit, et tunc eum in praesentia absolvat. ACDF, SO Censurae Librorum 1570–1606, fos. 532r–v.

94. See Prosperi, *Tribunali della coscienza*, pp. 543–548. On the iconographic and literary significance of the image of the "window into the heart" in early modern culture, see also Bolzoni, *The Gallery of Memory*, pp. 151–173.

95. Tandem non vidi quid incommodi aut moralis nocumenti timeri posset ecclesia ex hac doctrina ut fuerit authoritate pontificia damnanda et prohibenda. Nec enim hinc datur occasio abutendi confessione in absentia, quia si homines intelligant illam confessionem esse inutilem, quando in praesentia possunt loqui, quia necessarium est ut confessor praesens adveniat, et per se examinet poenitentem, et ab illo obtineat confessionem si potest illam facere, nullum est periculum quod velint homines absenti confiteri, nisi in eo casu in quo timent periculum amittendi sensui priusquam confiteri valeant. ACDF, SO Censurae Librorum 1570–1606, f. 532v.

96. Agamben, *The Sacrament of Language*, p. 70.

97. Suárez devoted two entire parts of his treatise to discussing specifically perjury and blasphemy; see *De iuramento*, pp. 473ff.

98. See, e.g., the numerous sections Suárez devoted to discussing the exact nature of the public obligations arising from the oath and to discussing how both the pope and the secular princes can, in specific circumstances, invalidate the oath; pp. 431ff. For Prodi's discussion of the originality and importance of these aspects of Suárez's reflections on the oath as the sacrament of power, see *Il Sacramento del Potere*, pp. 420–423.

99. See Suárez's *Defensio Fidei*, Coimbra, 1613, esp. book VI, *De iuramento fidelitatis*. On the background and significance of Suárez's position in the controversy over the Oath, see, among the others, L. Pereña et al., *"De iuramento fidelitatis." Estudio Preliminar*; W. B. Patterson, *King James VI and I and the Reunion of Christendom*, Cambridge: Cambridge University Press, 2000, ch. 3; H. Höpfl, *Jesuit political thought*, pp. 332ff.

100. On this, see Tutino, *Empire of Souls*, ch. 2.
101. The censures to Lessius's *De iustitia et iure* can be found in ARSI, Fondo Gesuitico 654, fos. 1r–74v passim. In addition to the judgment over the treatise, the censures contained also extensive comments and/or suggestions on how to modify specific passages. They all came from either Rome or Louvain/Antwerp, and they were done mostly in 1603 and 1604. The folder contains also some later documents; especially interesting are those concerning the development of the debate over Lessius's doctrine of grace and free will in the 1620s (see fos. 56rff. passim).
102. Those elements were especially praised, e.g., in the censures written by Carolus Scribanus from Antwerp (fos. 39Cr–v) and by Cornelius a Lapide from Louvain (fos. 41r–42v).
103. de parte illa operis P. Leonardi Lessii de iustitia et iure in qua de contractibus, de iudiciis, deque iustitiae distributivae... agit... admodum mihi placet tota illa tractatio ob claritatem, brevitatem, & methodum. Antwerp, June 1, 1603, ibid., f. 39A.
104. haec sunt quae... occurrunt [in Lessius's work]. In primis ut possit edi ratio est, quod copiose, breviter, ac dilucide maiore ex parte tractat res morales. In contrarium vero est, quod interdum propter brevitatem maxime in rebus difficilibus se non satis explicat, deinde quoniam non raro sequitur opiniones magis largas. Praeterea frequenter solet dicere opiniones quas non sequitur esse probabiles, quarum tamen usus in praxi minime est consulendus. Non raro etiam in difficilioribus opinionibus et quae dubium ingerunt lectori, non adhibet autores. 22 December 1603, ARSI, Fondo Gesuitico 654, f. 1r.
105. Dicit quod iurare falsum animo non iurandi non esse peccatum... si falsitas sit penitus ignota et per iniuriam cogitur iurare. Expedit non dicere, saltem sine autoribus. Ibid., f. 13v.
106. Sic in regno Lusitaniae irriti redduntur per legem omnes contractus, obligationes, conventiones, promissiones, remissiones & distractus iuramento confirmati, si alioquin ad forum saeculare eorum cognitio pertinebat, nisi cum regis facultate iuramentum appositum fuerit. Simili fere modo in regno Castellae: exceptis quibusdam contractibus, ut refert Molina disp.149. Quod ideo factum est, ne lites super huiusmodi contractibus traherentur ad forum ecclesiasticum, iuramentum enim facit ut causa quae alias mere est civilis, fiat fori mixti, ut patet ex cap. fin. de foro competenti in 6 [this reference is to canon 3, *titulus* II, book II of the *Liber Sextus*, which can be found in *Corpus iuris canonici*, vol. II col. 997]. Lessius, *De iustitia et iure*, Louvain, 1605, p. 559.
107. Dicit in regno Lusitaniae irritos esse omnes contractus iuratos et iuramenta ipsis apposita, si absque Regis facultate fuerint apposita. Videat auctor quo pacto intelligendum sit id quod ait Molina, quem pro hac re citat, et de quibus contractibus loquatur. Nam hoc quod ait non est universim verum. ARSI, Fondo Gesuitico 654, f. 13v.
108. Haec nobis se offerint R. P. N. Generali proponenda, ut ipse de libri editione deliberet. Inter nos autem ita convenit: P. Antonius Maria Menù et P. Joannes de Salas censent librum edi posse, dummodo serventur quae in censura sunt notata. Ad quos cum aliquo tamen dubio accedit P. Christophorus Gillius. P. autem Joannes Lorinus exigit praeterea ut emendatum ac recognitum remittat iterum videndum. 22 December 1603, ARSI, Fondo Gesuitico 654, f. 1r.
109. Intorno all'opera del P. Leonardo Lesio mi pare di dovere in particolare per scarico di conscientia rappresentare a V.P. le cose seguenti: primo quanto l'autore è di maggior credito, et l'opera più aspettata, e è per haver maggior spaccio insieme per esser breve, tanto corre maggior pericolo se non è qual deve... 2. Nella censura commune non si è detto quanto io penso che sia la larghezza dell'auctore nella opinione la quale pare ch'egli vadi affettando. Dubito, per quel mi vien detto, che il plauso che ha fra mercanti e negotianti et altri nasca da questa causa, et che tutta via crescerà più, con danno di lui et della Compagnia. Lorin to Acquaviva, Rome, 21 December 1603, ibid., fos. 3r–4v, at f. 3r.
110. Io coram Domino dico quello che giudico spediente per il ben comune della Chiesa, Compagnia et dell'auctore et credo che lo posso dire più liberamente, toccandomi più presto a promuovere li nostri tramontani... è da notare che soli tre hanno letto il libro et che da Fiandra non è venuto niuna censura se non encomii. Ibid., f. 4r.
111. On how Lessius specifically applied this feature of the Jesuit thought in his political theory, see Höpfl, *Jesuit political thought*, ch. 7.

112. Est autem Iuramentum nihil aliud quam attestatio divini Numinis vel invocatio divini testimonii ad fidem faciendam vel promissionem firmandam. Lessius, *De iustitia et iure*, Louvain 1605, p. 546 (this definition is identical in Lyon 1622 at p. 614, and in Lyon 1653 at p. 505).

113. See the *Dubitatio VIII*.

114. etiamsi iuramentum non obliget per se & vi sua nisi secundum mentem iurantis, ut dictum est: tamen ratione damni, vel scandali secuturi, potest obligare iuxta mentem exigentis; & hoc solum probat argumentum allatum. Reverentia enim divina etiam obligat ad vitandum scandalum in materia religionis; & non solum ut nihil agas quod contra honorem divinum vere sit; sed neque quod videatur esse. Deus etiam accipit sicut alter intelligit; quia censet te ad hoc obligatum non praecise vi iuramenti, sed quia teneris alterum non decipere, causam damni & scandali non dare, seposito tamen periculo damni & scadali, nulla obligatio gravis nascitur in foro conscientiae: nam deceptio illa per se non est mortifera. In foro tamen externo cogendus est implere quod secundum verborum legitimam interpretationem visus est promisisse.…. Quandocunque aliquis iniuste cogitur ad iuramentum, vel alias habet iustam causam celandi mentem suam oratione ambigua, vel tacita restrictione; non peccat, etiamsi alieno sensu iuret. Quod intellige, si necessitas vel utilitas iuramentum exigat. *De iustitia et iure*, Louvain 1605, pp. 556–557. On the repercussions of Lessius's elasticity in matters of equivocation and mental reservation, see supra, ch. 1, pp. 32–35.

115. Prodi highlights the pivotal importance of Lessius's elaboration on this topic in *Il Sacramento del Potere*, pp. 423ff.

116. Sed difficultas est, quomodo potestas humana hoc possit, cum obligatio naturaliter & necessario resultet ex iuramento, iure enim naturae tenemur cavere ne Deum faciamus testem falsi. Lessius, *De iustitia et iure*, Dubitatio XII, "Quibus modis tollatur obligatio in iuramento & cuius auctoritate," Louvain 1605, pp. 559–562 (quot. at 559).

117. Respondeo, dupliciter intelligi posse id fieri. Primo, eum in cuius favorem fit, reddendo inhabilem ad acceptandum, cum enim iuramentum promissorium non obliget, nisi promissio acceptetur ab eo in cuius favorem factum est, si hic sit inhabilis ad acceptandum, nulla potest nasci obligatio. Quod autem talis inhabilitas etiam lege civili induci possit, non videtur dubitandum, quia lex civilis potest reddere inhabilem ad officia, ad contractus, ad alienationes, ad acquisitionem bonorum & similia, cur non etiam ad valide acceptandum alterius promissionem? Ibid.

118. Verum hic modus non videtur sufficiens, quia etiamsi acceptatio sit invalida, & contractus irritus, iuramentum tamen non revocandi talem contractum potest esse validum, ut patet in contractu minoris quo alienat rem immobilem sine auctoritate iudicis, adhibito iureiurando de non contraveniendo: & in contractu pupilli qui pubertati proximus. This passage was added in *De iustitia et iure*, Lyon, 1622, p. 629.

119. Cf. Louvain 1605, p. 559: "Obligatio iam inducta tolli potest quinque modis. Primo, mutatione materiae, ut si res iurata fiat impossibilis iuranti aut illicita, superiore vetante"; and Lyon, 1622, p. 629: "Obligatio iam inducta tolli potest quinque modis. Primo, mutatione materiae, ut si res iurata fiat impossibilis iuranti aut illicita, superiore vetante: *quo modo etiam potestas saecularis subinde uti potest*"; my italics.

120. Cf. Louvain 1605, pp. 559-560: "Secundo, condonatione, ut si is in cuius favorem factum est, remittat obligationem: quivis enim potest condonare promissionem factam in suum favorem, etiamsi facta sit in modum voti, ut si voveas Deo, & iures te ducturum Catharinam pauperem, vel daturum illi dotem ut melius nubat. Contrarium tenet Sotus lib.8 de iustitia q.1 art.9 et quidam alii. Sed probatur, quia qui facit tale votum vel iuramentum non intendit se obligare nisi sub tacita conditione, si ille, de cuius commodo agitur velit acceptare. Non enim intendit initium ad beneficium acceptandum cogere, vel nolenti obtrudere, ergo si ille nolit vel condonet, non obligatur, cessat enim conditio sub qua obligatio inducta est"; and Lyon, 1622, p. 629: "Secundo, condonatione, ut si is in cuius favorem factum est, remittat obligationem: quivis enim potest condonare promissionem factam in suum favorem, etiamsi facta sit in modum voti, ut si voveas Deo, & iures te ducturum Catharinam pauperem, vel daturum illi dotem ut melius nubat. Contrarium tenet Sotus lib.8 de iustitia q.1 art.9 et quidam alii. Sed probatur, quia qui facit tale votum vel iuramentum non intendit se obligare nisi sub tacita conditione, si ille, de cuius commodo agitur velit acceptare. Non enim intendit initium ad beneficium acceptandum cogere, vel nolenti obtrudere, ergo si ille nolit vel

condonet, non obligatur, cessat enim conditio sub qua obligatio inducta est, *eodem ex iusta causa uti potest civilis potestas"*; my italics.
121. Lessius, *De iustitia et iure,* Louvain 1605, p. 561.
122. Ibid.
123. Cf. Louvain 1605, p. 561: "Quinto, dispensatione, seu absolutione. Haec fit auctoritate superioris"; and Lyon, 1622, p. 631: "Quinto, dispensatione, seu absolutione. Haec fit auctoritate *solius* superioris"; my italics.
124. *De iustitia et iure,* Louvain 1605, p. 561.
125. In poenam quoque relaxatur iuramentum subditorum, quo obstricti sunt principi, vel alteri superiori, quando ille privatur per summum pontificem vel alium superiorem officio, vel dignitate, ratione cuius ei praestitum erat iuramentum. *De iustitia et iure,* Louvain 1605, p. 562.
126. Denique interdum ratione boni communis relaxari potest, ut quando quis cum iuramento promisit alicui sponte vel coacte non accusare, non denuntiare, non contra testari, & similia. Nisi enim talia relaxari possent, crimina detegi & puniri, iudicia exerceri, innocentia defendi, iniquitas opprimi non posset, quae omnia sunt contra bonum publicum. Itaque huiusmodi relaxare potest Summus Pontifex, Episcopus, & authoritatem quasi episcopalem habens, & etiam princeps secularis, quia ratio officii ipsius postulat ut possit tollere obligationes, quae ipsius rectam administrationem impedirent. Ibid.
127. Ex dictis patet, etiamsi iuramenti cognitio quando agitur utrum obliget in conscientia, an non obliget, utrum possit relaxari, an non possit, ad forum ecclesiasticum tantum pertineat, ut patet cap. final. de foro competenti in 6 [this reference is once again to canon 3, *titulus* II, book II of the *Liber Sextus,* which can be found in *Corpus iuris canonici,* vol. II col. 997], tamen quando manifeste constat de iniuria vel iniustitia exactoris vel quando constat tale iuramentum bono publico noxium esse, posse etiam principem secularem, & aliquando iudicem inferiorem, non solum praecipere ut ille remittat, sed etiam sua authoritate remittere & relaxare, quia haec potestas non est per se spiritualis, sed generatim fundata est in potestate gubernandi. Sine enim hac potestate, gubernatio civilis prorsus imperfecta esset ac manca & plurimis incommodis occurrere nequiret. Ibid.
128. Ex quibus patet, duobus modis posse tolli obligationem iuramenti, nimirum mediate & immediate. Mediate tollitur, quando condonatur ipsa promissio seu eius executio, tunc enim ex consequenti simul evanescit obligatio iuramenti. Immediate, quando condonatur ipsa obligatio orta ex iuramento erga promissarium ad exequendam promissionem. *De iustitia et iure,* Lyon, 1622, pp. 631-632.
129. His positis tanquam certis & perspicuis, facile intelligi potest quomodo superior possit relaxare iuramentum. Sicut enim is in cuius favorem & commodum praestitum est, potest illud relaxare, ita etiam eius superior, cui vel ille pleno iure subest, sicut pupillus tutori, vel religiosus praelato, vel saltem cui materia promissa subest, ita ut possit eam prohibere, vel de ea disponere, sicut filius familias in quibusdam subest patri, & subditus suo principi.... Unde cum Christus Dominus omnium sit superior, potest ipse omnem talem obligationem condonare. Et consequenter idem potest Summus Pontifex, Christi vicarius, in omnibus Christianis, quando iusta causa subest, quia Deus omnem illi potestatem concessit, quae erat necessaria ad rite gubernandam ecclesiam, & ad obviandam periculis animarum quae ex obligationibus iuramentorum & votorum solent inter homines incidere. Nisi enim talis potestas ecclesiae data esset, gravissima sequerentur incommoda, & multae animae ratione huiusmodi vinculorum perirent. Itaque Summus Pontifex, ut Christi Vicarius, & omnium Christianorum superior, potest immediate tollere & condonare omnem obligationem ex iuramento promissorio ortam erga aliquem, quando iusta causa subest. Ibid., p. 632. Among those just reasons and just as he had already done in the Louvain 1605 edition, Lessius explicitly mentioned the case of subjects absolved from their oath of alleagiance to a prince whom the pope deposed (cf. Louvain 1605 p. 562, and Lyon, 1622, p. 632).
130. Denique interdum ratione boni communis relaxari potest, ut cum quis promisit alteri cum iuramento non accusare, non denuntiare, non contra testari, & similia, nisi enim talia relaxari possent, crimina detegi & puniri, iudicia exerceri, innocentia defendi, iniquitas opprimi non posset: quae omnia sunt contra bonum commune.... Circa praedicta notandum est, non omnem relaxationem iuramenti esse dispensationem proprie in iuramento. Cum enim is, in cuius commodum factum est, illud condonat, non est dispensatio, nec

actus spiritualis potestatis, sed nuda condonatio. Similier cum fit per superiorem illius posita legitima causa: ut si iudex ad puniendum usurarium qui absque principis permissu usuras fecisset, condonaret seu irritaret obligationem iuramenti praestiti usurario a mutuatariis de solvendis usuris. Verum tunc est proprie dispensatio, quando praelatus ecclesiasticus, vel alia persona ecclesiastica ab illo auctoritatem habens, tamquam Dei vicarius & nomine Dei obligationem condonat, & vinculum iuramento inductum dissolvit. Unde patet, dispensationem iuramenti esse solius potestatis ecclesiasticae. *De iustitia et iure*, Lyon, 1622, p. 632.

131. Ill. DD. mandarunt. . . moneri suaviter R.mum Patrem Generalem Jesuitarum ut moneat d. Lessium ad amovendum a suo opere de iustitia et iure verbum illum utilitas. . . c.42 disputatione 9a. . . ut etiam amoveat a d.o opere quod alibi habet Principes temporales absolvere posse a iuramento. ACDF, Index, Diarii III, "Congregatio habita 17 Julii 1624," fos. 125r–v. See also supra, ch. 1, p. 35 for the significance of the censors' comments on *utilitas* in the context of the debate over equivocation and mental reservation.

132. *Dubitatio XII* can be found at pp. 517–521 of the Lyon 1653 edition.

133. Prodi, *Il Sacramento del Potere*, pp. 11–12.

134. Agamben, *The Sacrament of Language*, pp. 70–71.

SELECT BIBLIOGRAPHY

Manuscript Sources

ACDF

Index, Diarii III (minutes of the meetings of the Congregation of the Index, early 1620s).

Index, Protocolli FF (miscellaneous documents from the Congregation of the Index).

Index, Protocolli KK (miscellaneous documents from the Congregation of the Index).

Index, Protocolli RR (miscellaneous documents from the Congregation of the Index).

SO Censurae Librorum 1570–1606 (documents concerning the condemnation of books on the part of the Congregation of the Inquisition).

SO Decreta 1603 (minutes of the proceedings of the Congregation of the Inquisition, 1603).

SO Decreta 1604–1605 (minutes of the proceedings of the Congregation of the Inquisition, 1604 and 1605).

SO Decreta 1605 (minutes of the proceedings of the Congregation of the Inquisition, 1605).

SO Decreta 1679 (minutes of the proceedings of the Congregation of the Inquisition, 1679).

St. St. O 1-n (folder on Beni's trial).

St. St. UV 45 (miscellaneous documents on probabilism, including the discussion over the 65 laxist propositions condemned by Innocent XI in 1679).

APUG

APUG 1163 (miscellaneous works by Famiano Strada, autograph).

APUG 1179 (miscellaneous drafts and fragments of Pedro Juan Perpiñán's rhetorical works, autograph).

APUG 1188 (lecture notes for a course on Aristotle's *Poetics* that Famiano Strada taught at the Roman College in 1608, autograph).

APUG 1292 (Giovanni Antonio Viperano's *De Bello Turcico Historia*).

FC 899 (lecture notes from the courses taught by Carlo Reggio and Stefano Tucci at the Roman College).

FC 1563 (miscellaneous drafts and fragments of Pedro Juan Perpiñán's rhetorical works, autograph).

FC 2056E (miscellaneous manuscripts of José Alfaro, some autograph).

ARSI

Fondo Gesuitico 650b (Epistolae Selectae).

Fondo Gesuitico 652 (Censurae Librorum).

Fondo Gesuitico 654 (Censurae Librorum).

Fondo Gesuitico 657 (Censurae Opinionum).

Fondo Gesuitico 660 (Censurae Librorum).

Fondo Gesuitico 662 (Censurae Librorum).
Fondo Gesuitico 664 (Censurae Librorum).
Hist. Soc. 54 (catalogue of the *Dismissi* from the Society of Jesus, sixteenth and seventeenth centuries).
Instit.186e (miscellaneous documents pertaining to the structure and doctrines of the Society).
Ital. 107 (correspondence, Italian province, middle of the 16th century).
Ital. 108 (correspondence, Italian province, middle of the 16th century).
Ital. 135 (correspondence, Italian province, second half of the 16th century).
Opp. Nn. 13 (Famiano Strada's unpublished *De contexenda oratione Libri Duo* and some orations by Strada and Tarquinio Galluzzi).
Rom. 132 (miscellaneous documents pertaining to the Roman Province).

ASV

Beni II 71 (unpublished orations and digressions by Paolo Beni, autograph).
Beni II 85 (miscellaneous notes and fragments on Aristotle's *Rhetoric* by Paolo Beni, autograph).
Beni II 117 (various manuscript parts of the *Qua tandem* by Paolo Beni, autograph).
Beni II 123 (various drafts of Paolo Beni's *Discorso intorno alla riforma dello Studio di Padova*, autograph).
Beni II 129 (various unpublished works by Paolo Beni, autograph).
Beni II 137 (miscellaneous letters, notes, and drafts by Paolo Beni, autograph).

BAV

Manoscritti Vaticani Latini 5684–5695 (manuscript version of Baronio's *Annales Ecclesiastici*, autograph).

BOD

MS. Seld. Supra 81 (Degory Wheare's epistles, some autograph).

VAL

N 76 (Draft of Tommaso Bozio's work on the Donation of Constantine).
N 100 (Bozio's autograph draft of his work on the Donation of Constantine).
Q 23 (Baronio's epistles, some autograph).
Q 44 (Baronio's epistles, some autograph).

Printed Primary Sources

Abbot, George. *Quaestiones sex.* Oxford: ex officina Iosephi Barnesii, 1598.
[Anon.] *De vita et moribus R. P. Leonardi Lessii e Societate Iesu Theologi Liber.* Ed. by Thomas Courtois. Brussels: apud Godefredum Shovartium, 1640.
Agricola, Rudolph. *De inventione dialectica.* Cologne: Gymnich, 1539.
Bañez, Domingo. *Decisiones de iure & iustitia.* Venice: apud Societatem Minimam, 1595.
Barbaro, Daniele. *In tres libros Rhetoricorum Aristotelis commentaria.* Lyon: apud S. Gryphium, 1544.
—. *Della eloquenza.* Venice: Vincenzo Valgrisio, 1557.
—, and Ermolao Barbaro. *Aristotelis Rhetoricorum libri III Hermolao Barbaro interprete.* Basel: Westhemer, 1545.
Barbaro, Ermolao. *Epistolae, orationes et carmina.* Florence: Bibliopolis, 1943.
Barnes, John. *Dissertatio contra aequivocatores.* Paris: R. Baragne, 1625. (French ed.: *Traicté et dispute contre les equivoques,* Paris: R. Baragne, 1625)
Baronio, Cesare. *Annales Ecclesiastici.* 12 vols. Rome: ex Typographia Vaticana, 1588–1607.
—. *Paraenesis ad rempublicam venetam.* Rome: Ferrariae 1606.
—. *Essortazione dell'Illustrissimo et reverendissimo Signor Card. Baronio.* Rome: Zannetti, 1606.

——. *Venerabilis Caesaris Baronii. . . Epistolae et Opuscula.* Ed. Raymundus Albericius. 3 vols. Rome: ex Typographia Komarek, 1759–1770.

——. *A Cesare Baronio. Scritti Vari.* Sora: M. Pisani, 1963.

——. *Le Testimonianze Baroniane dell'Oratorio di Napoli.* Ed. Mario Borrelli. Naples: Lithorapid, 1965.

Baudouin, François. *De institutione historiae universae.* Paris: apud A. Wechelum, 1561.

Bayle, Pierre. *Dictionnaire historique et critique.* 2 vols. Rotterdam: Reinier Leers, 1697.

Bellarmine, Robert. *Ven. Cardinalis Roberti Bellarmini Politiani SJ Opera Omnia.* Ed. Justin Fèvre. 12 vols. Paris: L. Vivès, 1870–1876.

Benci, Francesco. *Orationes et Carmina.* Ingolstadt: Sartorius, 1592.

Beni, Paolo. *In Platonis Timaeum. . . decades tres.* Rome: ex Typographia Gabiana, 1594.

——. *Disputatio. . . in qua quaeritur an. . . liceat in Iudiciis & concionibus affectus concitare.* Rome: ex Typographia Gabiana, 1594.

——. *Oratio habita in sacro Clementis IIX Pont. Max. . . . consessu.* Rome: ex Typographia Gabiana, 1594.

——. *De Ecclesiasticis Baronii Cardinalis Annalibus Disputatio.* Rome: Impressores Camerales, 1596.

——. *Discorsi sopra l'inondation del Tevere.* Rome: Facciotto, 1599.

——. *Qua tandem ratione dirimi possit Controversia quae inpresens de efficaci Dei auxilio & libero arbitrio inter nonnullos Catholicos agitatur.* Padua: L. Pasquati, 1603.

——. *Comparatione di Torquato Tasso con Homero e Virgilio.* Padua: L. Pasquati, 1607.

——. *De historia libri quatuor.* Venice: apud I. Vincentium, 1611.

——. *Comparatione di Torquato Tasso con Homero e Virgilio.* Padua: Martini, 1612.

——. *L'anticrusca.* Padua: Martini, 1612.

——. *In Aristotelis Poeticam Commentarii.* Padua: Martini, 1613; Venice: apud I. Guerilium, 1622, 1623, 1624.

——. *Orationes quinquaginta.* Padua: per F. Bolzettam, 1613.

——. *Il Goffredo.* Padua: per F. Bolzettam, 1616.

——. *In Aristotelis libros Rhetoricorum. . . Commentarii.* 2 vols. Venice: apud I. Guerilium, 1624–1625.

——. *Oratoriae disputationes.* Venice: apud I. Guerilium, 1624.

Benzoni, Rutilio. *Tractatus de fuga.* Venice: apud Societatem Minimam, 1595.

Bodin, Jean. *Methodus ad facilem historiarum cognitionem.* Paris: apud M. Iuvenem, 1566 (2nd ed. Paris: apud M. Iuvenem, 1572).

[Budé, Guillaume], ed. Claude Baduel. *Lexicon Graeco-Latinum.* Geneva: apud I. Crispinum et N. Barbirium, 1554.

Calvin, Jean. *Traité des reliques.* Ed. Irena Backus. Geneva: Labor et Fides, 2000.

Cano, Melchor. *De locis theologicis libri duodecim.* Salamanca: M. Gastius 1563.

Casaubon, Isaac. *De rebus sacris et ecclesiasticis Exercitationes XVI.* London: Norton, 1614.

Castelvetro, Lodovico. *Poetica d'Aristotele.* Basel: Perna, 1576.

——. *Esaminatione sopra la retorica a Caio Herennio.* Modena: Andrea and Girolamo Cassiani, 1653.

Corpus iuris canonici. Eds. Aemilius L. Richter and Emil A. Friedberg. 2 vols. Graz: Akademische Druck und Verlagsanstalt, 1959.

Ducci, Lorenzo. *Ars historica.* Ferrara: Baldinus, 1604.

Enchiridion Symbolorum. Eds. Heinrich Denzinger et al. Freiburg: Herder, 2001.

Frugoni, Francesco Fulvio. *De' ritratti critici abbozzati e contornati da Francesco Fulvio Frugoni. Ripartimento primo.* Venice: Combi & La Noù, 1669.

Flacius Illyricus. *De ratione cognoscendi sacras literas.* Düsseldorf: Stern-Verlag-Janssen, 1968.

—— et al., eds. *Ecclesiastica Historia.* 7 vols. Basel: Oporinus, 1561–74.

Galileo Galilei. *Le Opere.* Edizione Nazionale. 20 vols. Florence: Barbera, 1929–39.

Galluzzi, Tarquinio. *Orationum tomi I–II.* Rome: Zanetti, 1617.

——. *Orationum tomi I–III* Milan: Bidellius, 1630.

——. *Carminum libri tres.* Rome: Mascardus, 1611.

——. *Carminum libri tres. Altera editione plurimum aucti.* Rome: Zanetti, 1616.

——. *Virgilianae Vindicationes.* Rome: Zanetti, 1621.

——. *Rinovazione dell'antica tragedia.* Rome: Stamperia Vaticana, 1633.

——. *In Aristotelis libros quinque priores Moralium ad Nicomachum.* Paris: S. Cramoisy, 1632–1645.

Garnet, Henry. *A treatise of equivocation.* Ed. David Jardine. London: Longman, Brown, Green, and Longmans, 1851.

George of Trebizond. *Rhetoricorum libri quinque.* Lyon: apud S. Gryphium, 1547.

Gregory of Valencia. *Commentariorum Theologicorum.* 4 vols. Ingolstadt: Sartorius, 1591–7.

——. *De rebus fidei.* Lyon: apud Heredes G. Rovillii, 1591.

Grotius, Hugo. *De iure belli ac pacis.* Paris: apud N. Buon, 1625.

—— et al. *Dissertationes de studiis instituendis.* Amsterdam: apud L. Elzevirium, 1645.

Kessler, Eckhard, ed. *Theoretiker humanistischer Geschichtsschreibung.* Munich: Fink, 1971.

Lessius, Leonardus. *De iustitia et iure.* Louvain: Masius, 1605.

——. *De iustitia et iure.* Lyon: Larjot, 1622.

——. *De iustitia et iure.* Lyon: P. Borde, L. Arnaud, and C. Rigaud, 1653.

——. *Opuscula.* Antwerp: Moretus, 1625.

Maioragio, Marcantonio. *Decisiones XXV.* Lyon: apud S. Gryphium, 1544.

——. *Antiparadoxon.* Lyon: apud S. Gryphium, 1546.

——. *Epistolicarum quaestionum libri II.* Milan: Moscheni, 1563.

——. *In tres Aristotelis libros, De arte Rhetorica... explicationes.* Venice: De Franceschi 1571.

——. *Commentarius... in librum primum De Oratore.* Venice: De Franceschi, 1587.

——. *Commentarius in dialogum De Partitione Oratoria.* Venice: De Franceschi, 1587.

Mascardi, Agostino. *Silvarum libri IV.* Antwerp: Moretus, 1622.

——. *Prose vulgari.* Venice: Fontana, 1626 (1st ed., 1625).

——. *Discorsi morali su la Tavola di Cebete Tebano.* Venice: Pelagallo, 1627.

——. *La Congiura del Conte Gio: Luigi de' Fieschi.* Venice: Scaglia, 1629.

——. *Oppositioni e difesa alla "Congiura del conte Gio. Luigi de' Fieschi" descritta da Agostino Mascardi.* Venice: Ventura, 1630.

——, ed. *Saggi accademici.* Venice: Fontana, 1630.

——. *Dell'arte historica.* Rome: Facciotti, 1636.

——. *Dell'arte historica.* Ed. Adolfo Bartoli. Florence: Le Monnier, 1859.

Molina, Luis de. *Concordia liberi arbitrii cum gratiae donis.* Lisbon: apud A. Riberium, 1588.

——. *De iustitia et iure.* Venice: Sessa, 1611–1614 (1593–1609).

Monumenta Pedagogica Societatis Iesu, vol. 129. Rome: Institutum Historicum Societatis Iesu, 1986.

Morton, Thomas. *A full satisfaction concerning a double Romish iniquitie.* London: Weaver, 1606.

Muret, Marc-Antoine. *Alexandri Aphrodisiensis in octo libros Topicorum Aristotelis explicatio.* Venice: apud I. Gryphium, 1554.

——. *Aristotelis Ethicorum ad Nicomachum liber quintus.* s.l. [1565].

——. *Hymnorum sacrorum liber.* Paris: apud M. Patissonium 1576.

——. *C. Cornelii Taciti Annalium... liber primus.* Rome: apud Heredes A. Bladii 1580.

——. *Aristotelis Rhetoricorum Libri Duo.* Rome: apud B. Grassum, 1585.

——. *Epistolarum... liber.* Cologne: P. Horst, 1585.

——. *Orationes.* Lyon: apud A. Gryphium, 1591.

——. *Opera Omnia.* 3 vols. Leipzig: Luchtmans, 1834–41.

Navarrus (Martín de Azpilcueta). *Enchiridion sive manuale confessariorum et poenitentium.* Rome: apud Victorinum Romanum, 1573 (1st Portuguese ed. Coimbra: por I. de Barreyra & I. Alvares, 1549; 1st Spanish ed. Coimbra: por I. de Barreyra & I. Alvares, 1553)

——. *Commentaria.* 3 vols. Venice: ex officina D. Zenarii, 1588.

Panvinio, Onofrio. *Epitome pontificum romanorum.* Venice: Strada, 1557.

——. *Historia de vitis pontificum romanorum.* Venice: apud M. Tramezinum, 1562.

——. *Opus de vitis ac gestis summorum pontificum.* Cologne: apud M. Cholinum, 1562.

——. *Chronicon ecclesiasticum.* Louvain: Bogard, 1573.

Pascal, Blaise. *Lettres écrites à un provincial.* [Cologne: Pierre de la Vallée], 1657.

——. *Litterae Provinciales.* Cologne: apud N. Schouten, 1658.

Patrizi, Francesco. *Della Historia diece dialoghi.* Venice: Arrivabene, 1560.

——. *Della Retorica dieci dialoghi.* Venice: De Franceschi, 1562.

Patrologia Latina. 221 vols. Ed. J. P. Migne. Paris, 1844–65.

Perpiñán, Pedro Juan. *Orationes duodeviginti.* Pamplona: T. Porralius, 1589 (Rome: Zanetti, 1587).

——. *Perpiniani Opera,* ed. Petrus Lazeri. Rome: typis Nicolai et Marci Palearini, 1749.

Persons, Robert. *A treatise tending to mitigation.* [Saint Omer: F. Bellet], 1607.

Possevino, Antonio. *Bibliotheca selecta*. Rome: ex Typographia Vaticana, 1593.

——. *Apparatus ad omnium gentium historiam*. Venice: Ciottus, 1597.

Ramus, Petrus. *Aristotelicae animadversiones*. Paris: Bogardus, 1543.

——. *Dialecticae institutiones*. Paris: Bogardus, 1543.

Raynaud, Théophile. *Theologia naturalis*. Lyon: Landri, 1622.

——. *Splendor veritatis*. Lyon: apud A. Berterium, 1627.

——. *De martyrio per pestem*. Lyon: Cardon, 1630.

——. *Discussio erroris popularis de communione pro mortuis*. Lyon: Boissat, 1637.

——. *Erotemata de malis ac bonis libris*. Lyon: Ravaud, 1653.

——. *Splendor veritatis*. Appendix of Lessius's *De iustitia et iure*. Lyon: P. Borde, L. Arnaud, and C. Rigaud, 1653.

——. *Dissertatio pro Francisco Suaresio*. Appendix of Suárez's *Tractatus de vera intelligentia auxilii efficacis*. Lyon: P. Borde, L. Arnaud, and C. Rigaud, 1655.

——. *Opera Omnia*. 19 vols. Lyon: Boissat and Remeus, 1665.

Reggio, Carlo. *Orator Christianus*. Rome: Zanetti, 1612.

Riccoboni, Antonio. *De historia commentarius*. Venice: apud I. Barilettum, 1568.

——. *Aristotelis Ars Rhetorica*. Venice: apud P. Meiettum, 1579.

——. *Aristotelis Liber De Poetica*. Venice: apud F. Valgrisium, 1584.

——. *Aristotelis Ethicorum ad Nicomachum*. Padua: apud L. Pasquatum, 1593.

Robortello, Francesco. *De historica facultate Disputatio*. Florence: L. Torrentinus, 1548.

——. *In librum Aristotelis De Arte Poetica Explicationes*. Florence: L. Torrentinus, 1548.

——. *De arte sive ratione corrigendi antiquorum libros Disputatio*. Naples: L. Loffredo, 1975.

Scaliger, Joseph. *Poetices libri septem*. Geneva: apud I. Crispinum, 1561.

Sigonio, Carlo. *Pro eloquentia orationes IIII*. Venice: Paolo Manuzio, 1555.

——. *De antiquo iure civium Romanorum*. Venice: Ziletti, 1559.

——. *Fragmenta Ciceronis*. Venice: Ziletti, 1559.

——. *Orationes septem*. Venice: Paolo Manuzio, 1560.

——. *Aristotelis de arte rhetorica*. Venice: Ziletti, 1566.

——. *Historiarum de Regno Italiae*. Basel: Perna, 1575.

——. *Historiarum de Occidentali Imperio*. Bologna: Societas Typographiae Bononiensis, 1578.

——. *De republica Hebraeorum*. Bologna: apud I. Rossium, 1582.

——. *Opera omnia edita et inedita*. Milan: Società Palatina, 1732–7.

Soares, Cipriano. *De arte rhetorica*. Paris: apud T. Brumennium, 1584 (1st ed. Coimbra: apud I. Barrerium 1562).

Soto, Domingo de. *De ratione tegendi et detegendi secretum*. Salamanca: apud P. De Castro, 1541.

——. *De cómo se ha da evitar el abuso de los juramentos [De cavendo iuramentorum abusu]*. Madrid: Roman, 1770 (first Latin and Spanish ed. Salamanca: Andreas à Portonariis, 1551).

——. *De iustitia et iure*. Salamanca: Andreas à Portonariis, 1553.

——. *De iustitia et iure*. Salamanca: Andreas à Portonariis, 1556.

——. *De iustitia et iure*. Lyon: apud Heredes I. Iuntae, 1569.

Strada, Famiano. *Prolusiones academicae*. Rome: Mascardus, 1617.

——. *De Bello Belgico*. 2 vols. Rome: Corbeletti, 1632 (vol. I), 1647 (vol. II).

Suárez, Francisco. *Commentariorum ac disputationum in tertiam partem Divi Thomae Tomus Primus*. Alcalá de Henares: in Collegio Societatis Iesu, ex Officina Typographica Petri Madrigalis, 1590.

——. *Commentariorum ac disputationum in tertiam partem Divi Thomae Tomus Secundus*. Alcalá de Henares: in Collegio Societatis Iesu ex Officina Typographica Petri Madrigalis, 1592.

——. *Commentariorum ac disputationum in tertiam partem Divi Thomae Tomus Tertius*. Salamanca: apud Ioannem et Andream Renaut, 1595.

——. *Metaphysicarum Disputationum*. Salamanca: apud Ioannem et Andream Renaut, 1597.

——. *Varia Opuscula Theologica*. Madrid: ex Typographia Regia, 1599.

——. *Commentariorum ac disputationum in tertiam partem Divi Thomae Tomus Quartus*. Coimbra: ex Officina Antonii à Mariz, 1602.

——. *Disputationum de censuris*. Coimbra: ex Officina Antonii à Mariz, 1603.

——. *Opus de virtute et statu religionis [De religione]*. 4 vols. Lyon: Cardon, 1630 (1st ed. of 1st vol., Coimbra: P. Crasbeck, 1608; 1st ed. of 2nd vol., Coimbra: P. Crasbeck, 1609; 1st ed. of 3rd vol., Lyon: Cardon, 1623; 1st ed. of 4th vol., Lyon: Cardon, 1625).

——. *Tractatus de legibus ac Deo legislatore*. Coimbra: D. Gomez de Loureyro, 1612.

——. *Defensio Fidei Catholicae*. Coimbra: D. Gomez de Loureyro, 1613.

——. *De divina gratia*. (1st ed. parts I and III Coimbra: D. Gomez de Loureyro, 1619; 1st ed. part II Lyon: P. Borde, L. Arnaud, and C. Rigaud, 1651).

——. *Tractatus de vera intelligentia auxilii efficacis*. Lyon: P. Borde, L. Arnaud, and C. Rigaud, 1655.

——. *Opera Omnia*. 26 vols. Paris: L. Vivès, 1856–66.

——. *R. P. Francisci Suaresii. . . opuscula sex inedita*. Ed. Jean Baptiste Malou. Paris: P. Lethielleux, 1861.

Talon, Omer. *Institutiones oratoriae*. Paris: Bogardus, 1545.

——. *Rhetorica*. Paris: ex Typographia M. Davidis, 1548.

——. *Rhetorica, Petri Rami praelectionibus illustrata*. Paris: apud A. Wechelum, 1567.

Valla, Lorenzo. *Opera Omnia*. 2 vols. Turin: Bottega d'Erasmo, 1962.

Van Ophuijsen, Johannes M., ed. *Alexander of Aphrodisias. On Aristotle's "Topics 1"*. Ithaca, NY: Cornell University Press, 2001

Vettori, Pietro. *Castigationes*. Lyon: apud S. Gryphium, 1541.

——. *Commentarii. . . in tres libros Aristotelis*. Basel: Oporinus, 1549.

——. *Commentarii in librum Demetrei Phalerei*. Florence: Iunta, 1562.

——. *Epistolarum libri X*. Florence: Iunta, 1586.

[Victorinus, Gaius Marius]. *Rhetoricorum libri recente castigati*. Venice: Pincius, 1509.

——. *Rhetorica Marci Tullii Ciceronis cum commento*. Lyon: I. Crepin, 1531.

——. *Commentarii in Rhetoricos M. Tullii Ciceronis*. Paris: ex Officina Roberti Stephani, 1537.

——. *Ars grammatica*. Florence: Le Monnier, 1967.

Viperano, Giovanni Antonio. *De scribenda historia liber*. Antwerp: Plantin, 1569.

——. *De summo bono*. Naples: ex Officina H. Salviani, 1575.

——. *Laudatio funebris Caroli V Imperatoris*. Messina: apud P. Spiram, 1558.

——. *Opera omnia*, 3 vols. Naples: ex Typographia I. Iacobi Carlini, 1607.

Wheare, Degory. *De ratione et methodo*. London: I. Haviland, 1623.

——. *De ratione et methodo*. Oxford: Lichfield & Turner, 1625

——. *Relectiones hyemales de ratione et methodo*. Oxford: Lichfield, 1637.

Wolf, Johann, ed. *Artis historicae penus*. 2 vols. Basel: Perna, 1579.

Secondary Literature

Agamben, Giorgio. *The Sacrament of Language: An Archaeology of the Oath*, English trans. by Adam Kotsko. Stanford, CA: Stanford University Press, 2011.

Alemanno, Laura. "La politica culturale di Maurizio di Savoia," in Michele Merolla, ed., *L'Accademia dei Desiosi. Storia e Testo*. Rome: Carocci, 2008, pp. 123–129.

Andreu, Francesco. *Pellegrino alle sorgenti. San Giuseppe Maria Tomasi*. Rome: Curia Generalizia dei Chierici Regolari, 1987.

Antonazzi, Giovanni. *Lorenzo Valla e la polemica sulla donazione di Costantino*. Rome: Edizioni di Storia e Letteratura, 1985.

Appleby Joyce, Lynn Hunt and Margaret Jacob. *Telling the Truth about History*. New York: Norton, 1994.

Astrain, Antonio. *Historia de la Compañia de Jesús en la asistencia de España*. 7 vols. Madrid: Razón y Fe, 1912–1925.

Austin, John L. *How to do things with words*. Cambridge, MA: Harvard University Press, 1975.

Backer, Augustin de. *Bibliothèque des écrivains de la Compagnie de Jésus*. 7 vols. Liège: L. Grandmont-Donders, 1883.

Backus, Irena Dorota. *Historical Method and Confessional Identity in the Era of the Reformation (1378–1615)*. Leiden: Brill, 2003.

Baron, Hans. "The *Querelle* of the Ancients and Moderns as a problem for Renaissance scholarship." *Journal of the history of Ideas* 20 (1959), pp. 3–22.

Barthes, Roland. *The Rustle of Language*. English trans. Berkeley: University of California Press, 1989.

——. *The Semiotic Challenge*. English trans. Berkeley: University of California Press, 1994.

Bellini, Eraldo. *Agostino Mascardi tra "ars poetica" e "ars historica"*. Milan: Vita e Pensiero, 2002.

Bellini, Piero. *"Denunciatio evangelica" e "Denunciatio iudicialis." Un capitolo di storia disciplinare della Chiesa*. Milan: Giuffrè, 1986.

Benveniste, Émile. "L'expression du serment dans la Grèce ancienne," in *Revue de l'Histoire des Religions*, 134 (1948), pp. 81–94.

——. *Problems in General Linguistics*, trans. Mary Elizabeth Meek. Coral Gables, FL: University of Miami Press, 1971.

——. *Indo-European Language and Society*. trans. Elizabeth Palmer. London: Faber & Faber, 1973.

Bertelli, Sergio. *Ribelli, Libertini e Ortodossi nella storiografia barocca*. Florence: La Nuova Italia, 1973.

——. *The King's Body: Sacred rituals of power in medieval and early modern Europe*. University Park: Pennsylvania State University Press, 2001.

Biagioli, Mario. *Galileo courtier. The practice of science in the culture of absolutism*. Chicago: University of Chicago Press, 1993.

Biondi, Albano. *L'autorità della storia profana (De humanae historiae auctoritate) di Melchor Cano*. Torino: Edizioni Giappichelli, 1973.

Black, Robert. "The new laws of history." *Renaissance Studies* 1 (1987), pp. 126–156.

Bloch, Marc. *The Historian's Craft*. English trans. Manchester: Manchester University Press, 1992.

Blum, Paul R. *Studies on Early Modern Aristotelianism*. Leiden: Brill, 2012.

Bok, Sissela. *Lying. Moral choice in public and private life*. New York: Vintage, 1978.

Bolzoni, Lina. *The Gallery of Memory. Literary and Iconographic Models in the Age of the Printing Press*. Toronto: University of Toronto Press, 2001 (first Italian ed., 1995).

Bonnell, Victoria E., and Lynn Hunt, eds. *Beyond the cultural turn*. Berkeley: University of California Press, 1999.

Bourdieu, Pierre. *Language and symbolic power*. English trans. Cambridge, MA: Harvard University Press, 1999.

Bowersock, Glen W. "Peter and Constantine." In William Tronzo, ed., *St. Peter's in the Vatican*. Cambridge: Cambridge University Press, 2005, pp. 5–15.

Braun, Harald E., and Edward Vallance, eds. *Contexts of Conscience in Early Modern Europe*. Basingstoke: Palgrave Macmillan, 2004.

Brinton, Alan. "St. Augustine and the problem of deception in religious persuasion." *Religious Studies* 19 (1983), pp. 437–450.

Burckhardt, Jacob. *Judgments on History and Historians*. English trans. by Harry Zohn, Indianapolis: Liberty Fund, 1999.

Burke, Peter. *Languages and Communities in early modern Europe*. Cambridge: Cambridge University Press, 2004.

——. "The Jesuits and the art of translation in Early Modern Europe." In John W. O'Malley, ed., *The Jesuits: Cultures, sciences, and the arts, 1540–1773*, vol. II. Toronto: University of Toronto Press, 2006, pp. 24–32.

——, and Ronnie Po-chia Hsia, eds. *Cultural Translation in early modern Europe*. Cambridge: Cambridge University Press, 2007.

Burnyeat, Myles, ed. *The Skeptical Tradition*. Berkeley: University of California Press, 1983.

Bynum, Caroline. "Why all the fuss about the body? A medievalist's perspective." In Victoria E. Bonnell and Lynn Hunt, eds., *Beyond the cultural turn*. Berkeley: University of California Press, 1999, pp. 241–280.

Calenzio, Generoso. *La vita e gli scritti del cardinale Cesare Baronio*. Rome: Tipografia Vaticana, 1907.

Cameron, Euan. *Interpreting Christian history. The challenge of the churches' past*. Oxford: Wiley-Blackwell, 2005.

Canziani, Guido, ed. *Storia della scienza, storia della filosofia: Interferenze*. Milan: Franco Angeli, 2005.

Cao, Gian Mario. *Scepticism and Orthodoxy: Gianfrancesco Pico as a reader of Sextus Empiricus*. Pisa: Fabrizio Serra Editore, 2007.

Carr, David. *Time, Narrative, and History*. Bloomington: Indiana University Press, 1986.

Castelli, Patrizia, and Giancarlo Pellegrini, eds. *Storici, filosofi e cultura umanistica a Gubbio tra Cinque e Seicento*. Spoleto: Centro italiano di studi sull'alto medioevo, 1998.

Cavaillé, Jean-Pierre. *Dis/simulations. Jules-César Vanini, François La Mothe Le Vayer, Gabriel Naudé, Louis Machon et Torquato Accetto. Religion, morale et politique au XVIIe siècle*. Paris: Champion, 2002.

———. "L'art des équivoques: Hérésie, inquisition et casuistique. Questions sur la transmission d'une doctrine médiévale à l'époque moderne." *Médiévales* 43 (2002), pp. 119–146.

Certeau, Michel de. *L'absent de l'histoire*. Paris: Mame, 1973.

———. *Heterologies: Discourse on the Other*. English trans. Minneapolis: University of Minnesota Press, 1986.

———. *The writing of history*. English trans. New York: Columbia University Press, 1988.

Chartier, Roger. *On the Edge of the Cliff*. English trans. Baltimore: Johns Hopkins University Press, 1997.

Clark, Elizabeth A. *History, Theory, Text: Historians and the Linguistic Turn*. Cambridge, MA: Harvard University Press, 2004.

Cochrane, Eric. *Historians and Historiography in the Italian Renaissance*. Chicago: University of Chicago Press, 1981.

———. "The Transition from Renaissance to Baroque: the Case of Italian Historiography." *History and Theory* 19, no. 1 (1980), pp. 21–38.

Collingwood, R. G. *The Idea of History*. Oxford: Oxford University Press, 1994.

Considine, John. *Dictionaries in Early Modern Europe. Lexicography and the Making of Heritage*. Cambridge: Cambridge University Press, 2008.

Conti, Lino. "Galilei e Paolo Beni: Astrologia, determinismo e Inquisizione." In Patrizia Castelli and Giancarlo Pellegrini, eds., *Storici, filosofi e cultura umanistica a Gubbio tra Cinque e Seicento*. Spoleto: Centro italiano di studi sull'alto medioevo, 1998, pp. 307–329.

Cotroneo, Girolamo. *I Trattatisti dell'ars historica*. Naples: Giannini, 1971.

Dahan, Gilbert, and Irène Rosier-Catach, eds. *La "Rhétorique" d'Aristote. Traditions et Commentaires de l'Antiquité au XVIIe Siècle*. Paris: Vrin, 1998.

Dainville, François de. *L'éducation des Jésuites (XVe–XVIIIe siècles)*. Paris: Les Éditions de Minuit, 1978.

Daremberg, C., and E. Saglio, eds. *Dictionnaire des antiquités grecques et romaines*. Paris: Hachette, 1887–1919.

Dedieu, Jean-Pierre. *L'administration de la foi. L'Inquisition en Tolède XVIe–XVIIIe siècle*. Madrid: Casa de Velázquez, 1989.

Delph, Ronald K. "Valla Grammaticus, Agostino Steuco, and the Donation of Constantine." *Journal of the History of Ideas* 57, no. 1 (1996), 55–77.

De Maio, Romeo, Luigi Gulia, and Aldo Mazzacane, eds. *Baronio storico e la Controriforma*. Sora: Centro di Studi Sorani "Vincenzo Patriarca," 1982.

de Pace, Anna. "Galileo interprete del *Timeo*." In Guido Canziani, ed., *Storia della scienza, storia della filosofia: Interferenze*. Milan: Franco Angeli, 2005, pp. 39–76.

Derrida, Jacques. "Plato's Pharmacy." Now in *Dissemination*, trans. by Barbara Johnson. Chicago: University of Chicago Press, 1981, pp. 61–171.

———. *Writing and difference*. English trans. Chicago: University of Chicago Press 1998.

Devlin, Christopher. *The life of Robert Southwell, Poet and Martyr*. London: Longmans, Green, 1956.

Diffley, P. B. *Paolo Beni. A Biographical and Critical Study*. Oxford: Clarendon Press, 1988.

———. "Paolo Beni e la lingua italiana: La prospettiva di un umanista di Gubbio." In Patrizia Castelli and Giancarlo Pellegrini, eds., *Storici, filosofi e cultura umanistica a Gubbio tra Cinque e Seicento*. Spoleto: Centro italiano di studi sull'alto medioevo, 1998, pp. 331–373.

Ditchfield, Simon. *Liturgy, Sanctity, and History in Tridentine Italy. Pietro Maria Campi and the Preservation of the Particular*. Cambridge: Cambridge University Press, 1995.

———. "'Historia magistra sanctitatis'? The relationship between historiography and hagiography in Italy after the Council of Trent (1564–1743 ca.)." In Massimo Firpo, ed., *Nunc alia tempora, alii mores. Storici e storia in età postridentina*. Florence: Olschki, 2005, pp. 3–23.

———. "What was sacred history? (Mostly Roman) Catholic uses of the Christian past after Trent." In Katherine Van Liere, Simon Ditchfield, and Howard Louthan, eds., *Sacred History. Uses of the Christian Past in the Renaissance World*. Oxford: Oxford University Press, 2012, pp. 72–97.

Doglio, Maria Luisa, and Carlo Delcorno, eds. *La predicazione nel Seicento.* Bologna: Il Mulino, 2009.

Doni Garfagnini, Manuela. "'Dell'arte historica' di Agostino Mascardi. Saggio teorico di storiografia del primo Seicento." In id., *Il teatro della storia fra rappresentazione e realtà.* Rome: Edizioni di Storia e Letteratura, 2002, pp. 325–370.

Dooley, Brendan. *Social history of skepticism. Experience and doubt in early modern culture.* Baltimore: Johns Hopkins University Press, 1999.

——. "*Veritas filia temporis:* Experience and belief in early modern culture." *Journal of the History of Ideas* 6, no. 3 (1999), pp. 487–504.

Douay-Soublin, Françoise. "Les Jésuites et l'autorité de la *Rhétorique* d'Aristote." In Gilbert Dahan and Irène Rosier-Catach, eds., *La "Rhétorique" d'Aristote. Traditions et Commentaires de l'Antiquité au XVIIe Siècle.* Paris: Vrin, 1998, pp. 331–346.

Dumézil, Georges. *Mythe et épopée.* 3 vols. Paris: Gallimard, 1968–1973.

——. *Idées Romaines.* Paris: Gallimard, 1969.

——. *Archaic Roman Religion.* 2 vols. English transl. by Philip Krapp. Baltimore: Johns Hopkins University Press, 1996.

Eden, Kathy. *Poetic and legal fiction in the Aristotelian tradition.* Princeton, NJ: Princeton University Press, 1986.

——. *Hermeneutics and the rhetorical tradition. Chapters in the ancient legacy and its Humanist reception.* New Haven, CT: Yale University Press, 1997.

Farrell, Allan P. *The Jesuit code of liberal education. Development and scope of the "Ratio Studiorum".* Milwaukee: Bruce, 1938.

Fasolt, Constantin. *The Limits of History.* Chicago: University of Chicago Press, 2003.

Favaro, Antonio. *Galileo Galilei e lo Studio di Padova.* 2 vols. Firenze: Le Monnier, 1883.

Feehan, Thomas D. "Augustine on lying and deception." *Augustinian Studies* 19 (1988), pp. 131–139.

Fernández-Armesto, Felipe. *Truth: A History and a Guide for the Perplexed.* New York: St. Martin's Press, 2001.

Fernández Santamaría, J. A. *Juan Luis Vives. Escepticismo y prudencia en el Renacimiento.* Salamanca: Ediciones Universidad de Salamanca, 1990.

——. *Theater of Man: J. L. Vives on Society.* Philadelphia: Transactions of the American Philosophical Society, 1998.

Firpo, Massimo, ed. *Nunc alia tempora, alii mores. Storici e storia in età postridentina.* Florence: Olschki, 2005.

Fisher, Joseph. *Man of Spain: Francis Suarez.* New York: Macmillan, 1940.

Flynn, Lawrence J. "The *De arte rhetorica* (1568) by Cyprian Soarez S.J.: A Translation with Introduction and Notes." Ph.D. Thesis, 2 vols., University of Florida 1955.

Fortenbaugh, William W., and David C. Mirhady, eds. *Peripatetic Rhetoric after Aristotle.* New Brunswick, NJ: Transaction, 1994.

Foucault, Michel. *The order of things. An archaeology of the human sciences.* English trans. New York: Random House / Pantheon, 1971.

——. *The archaeology of knowledge and the discourse on language.* English trans. New York: Pantheon, 1972.

Franklin, James. *The Science of Conjecture. Evidence and Probability before Pascal.* Baltimore: Johns Hopkins University Press, 2001.

Franklin, Julian H. *Jean Bodin and the Sixteenth-Century Revolution in the Methodology of Law and History.* New York: Columbia University Press, 1963.

Friedlander, Saul, ed. *Probing the limits of representation. Nazism and the "Final Solution".* Cambridge, MA: Harvard University Press, 1992.

Frugoni, Arsenio. *Incontri nel Rinascimento.* Brescia: La Scuola, 1954.

Fubini, Riccardo. *Storiografia dell'Umanesimo in Italia da Leonardo Bruni ad Annio da Viterbo.* Rome: Edizioni di Storia e Letteratura, 2003.

Fumaroli, Marc. "Cicero Pontifex Romanus. La tradition rhétorique du Collège romain et les principes inspirateurs du mécénat de Barberini." *Mélanges de l'École Française de Rome, Moyen-Age, Temps modernes* 90, no. 2 (1978), pp. 797–835.

——. "Rhetoric, Politics, and Society: from Italian Ciceronianism to French Classicism." In James J. Murphy, ed. *Renaissance Eloquence. Studies in the Theory and Practice of Renaissance Rhetoric.* Berkeley: University of California Press, 1983, pp. 253–273.

——. *L'Âge de l'éloquence: Réthorique et res literaria de la Renaissance au seuil de l'époque classique.* Paris: Champion, 1994.

——. "The Fertility and Shortcomings of Renaissance Rhetoric: The Jesuit Case." In John W. O'Malley, ed., *The Jesuits: Cultures, sciences, and the arts, 1540–1773.* Toronto: University of Toronto Press, 1999, vol. I, pp. 90–106.

——, ed. *Histoire de la rhétorique dans l'Europe moderne (1450–1950).* Paris: Presses Universitaires de France, 1999.

Gadamer, Hans-Georg. *Truth and Method.* London: Continuum, 2006.

Gaddis, John Lewis. *The Landscape of History. How historians map the past.* Oxford: Oxford University Press, 2002.

Gallagher, Lowell. *Medusa's Gaze: Casuistry and Conscience in Early Modern Europe.* Stanford, CA: Stanford University Press, 1991.

Garver, Eugene. *Aristotle's Rhetoric: an art of character.* Chicago: University of Chicago Press, 1994.

Gaudeau, Bernard. *De Petri Ioannis Perpiniani vita et operibus.* Paris: Retaux-Bray, 1891.

Gay, Jean-Pascal. *Morales en conflit. Théologie et polémique au Grand Siècle (1640–1700).* Paris: CERF, 2001.

——. *Jesuit Civil Wars. Theology, Politics and Government under Tirso González (1687–1705).* Farnham: Ashgate, 2012.

Gernet, Louis. *The Anthropology of Ancient Greece.* trans. George Hamilton and Blaise Nagy. Baltimore: Johns Hopkins University Press, 1981.

Giard, Luce, ed. *Les Jésuites à la Renaissance. Sistème éducatif et production du savoir.* Paris: Presses Universitaires de France, 1995.

Ginzburg, Carlo. "Contributo ad un dizionario storico. In margine al motto 'veritas filia tempo-ris.'" *Rivista Storica Italiana* 78 (1966), pp. 969–973.

——. *Il Nicodemismo: Simulazione e dissimulazione religiosa nell'Europa del '500.* Turin: Einaudi, 1970.

——. *Clues, Myths, and the Historical Method.* Baltimore: Johns Hopkins University Press, 1989.

——. "Alien Voices: the Dialogic Element in Early Modern Jesuit Historiography." In id., *History, Rhetoric, and Proof.* Hanover, NH: University Press of New England, 1999, pp. 71–91.

——. "Aristotle and History, Once More." In id., *History, Rhetoric, and Proof,* Hanover, NH: University Press of New England, 1999, pp. 38–53.

——. *The Judge and the Historian.* New York: Verso, 1999.

——. "Lorenzo Valla on the 'Donation of Constantine.'" In id., *History, Rhetoric, and Proof,* Hanover, NH: University Press of New England, 1999, pp. 54–70.

——. "The European Discover (or Rediscover) the Shamans." In *Threads and Traces. True, False, Fictive,* trans. by Anne C. Tedeschi and John Tedeschi. Berkeley: University of California Press, 2011, pp. 83–95.

——. "Description and citation." In *Threads and Traces. True, False, Fictive,* trans. by Anne C. Tedeschi and John Tedeschi. Berkeley: University of California Press, 2011, pp. 7–24.

Giulia, Luigi, ed. *Baronio e le sue fonti.* Sora: Centro di Studi Sorani "Vincenzo Patriarca," 2009.

Grafton, Anthony. "Joseph Scaliger and Historical Chronology: the Rise and Fall of a Discipline." *History and Theory* 14 (1975), pp. 156–185.

——. "Traditions of Invention and Inventions of Tradition in Renaissance Italy: Annius of Viterbo." Now in id., *Defenders of the Text. The Traditions of Scholarship in an Age of Science, 1450–1800.* Cambridge, MA: Harvard University Press, 1991, pp. 76–103.

——. *Joseph Scaliger. A study in the history of classical scholarship,* vol. I, "Textual Criticism and Exegesis." Oxford: Oxford University Press, 1983; vol. II, "Historical Chronology." Oxford: Oxford University Press, 1994.

——. *The footnote. A curious history.* Cambridge, MA: Harvard University Press, 1997.

——. *What was History? The Art of History in Early Modern Europe.* Cambridge: Cambridge University Press, 2007.

——. *Worlds made by Words. Scholarship and Community in the Modern West.* Cambridge, MA: Harvard University Press, 2009.

——. "Church History in Early Modern Europe: Tradition and Innovation." In Katherine Van Liere, Simon Ditchfield and Howard Louthan, eds., *Sacred History. Uses of the Christian Past in the Renaissance World*. Oxford: Oxford University Press, 2012, pp. 3–26.

——, and Joanna Weinberg. *"I have always loved the holy tongue": Isaac Casaubon, the Jews, and a forgotten chapter in Renaissance scholarship*. Cambridge, MA: Harvard University Press, 2011.

Grassi, Ernesto. *Rhetoric as Philosophy. The Humanist Tradition*. University Park, PA: Pennsylvania State University Press, 1980.

Green, Lawrence D. *John Rainolds's Oxford lectures on Aristotle's "Rhetoric"*. Newark: University of Delaware Press, 1986.

——. "Aristotelian Rhetoric, Dialectic, and the Traditions of ἀντίστροφος." *Rhetorica* 8, no. 1 (1990), pp. 5–27.

——. "The Reception of Aristotle's *Rhetoric* in the Renaissance." In William W. Fortenbaugh and David C. Mirhady, *Peripatetic Rhetoric after Aristotle*. New Brunswick, NJ: Transaction, 1994, pp. 320–348.

——. "Aristotelian *lexis* and Renaissance *elocutio*." In Alan G. Gross and Arthur E. Walzer, eds., *Rereading Aristotle's "Rhetoric"*. Carbondale: Southern Illinois University Press, 2000, pp. 149–165.

——, and James J. Murphy. *Renaissance Rhetoric Short-Title Catalogue, 1460–1700*. Farnham: Ashgate, 2006.

Grendler, Paul F. *The Universities of the Italian Renaissance*. Baltimore: Johns Hopkins University Press, 2002.

Griffiths, Paul J. *Lying. An Augustinian theology of duplicity*. Grand Rapids, MI: Brazos Press, 2004.

Grimaldi, William M. A. *Studies in the philosophy of Aristotle's "Rhetoric"*. Wiesbaden: Franz Steiner Verlag, 1972.

Gross, Alan G., and Arthur E. Walzer, eds., *Rereading Aristotle's "Rhetoric"*. Carbondale: Southern Illinois University Press, 2000.

Guazzelli, Giuseppe Antonio. "Cesare Baronio e il *Martyrologium Romanum*: Problemi interpretativi e linee evolutive di un rapporto diacronico." In Firpo, Massimo, ed., *Nunc alia tempora, alii mores. Storici e storia in età postridentina*. Florence: Olschki, 2005, pp. 47–89.

——. "La documentazione numismatica negli *Annali ecclesiastici* di Cesare Baronio." In Luigi Gulia, ed., *Baronio e le sue fonti*. Sora: Centro di Studi Sorani "Vincenzo Patriarca", 2009, pp. 489–548.

Haliczer, Stephen. *Sexuality in the Confessional. A Sacrament Profaned*. Oxford: Oxford University Press, 1999.

Haskell, Francis. *History and its Images. Art and the Interpretation of the Past*. New Haven, CT: Yale University Press, 1993.

Heidegger, Martin. *The basic problem of phenomenology*, English trans. Bloomington: Indiana University Press, 1975.

——. *The fundamental concepts of metaphysics*. English trans. Bloomington: Indiana University Press, 1995.

——. *Being and Time*. English translation Albany: SUNY Press, 2010.

Hill, Benjamin, and Henrik Lagerlund, eds. *The philosophy of Francisco Suárez*. Oxford: Oxford University Press, 2012.

Hirzel, Rudolf. *Der Eid, ein beitrag zu seiner Geschichte*. Leipzig: S. Hirzel, 1902.

Holmes, Peter, ed. *Elizabethan Casuistry*. London: Catholic Record Society, vol. 67, 1981.

——. *Resistance and Compromise: the Political Thought of the Elizabethan Catholics*. Cambridge: Cambridge University Press, 1982.

Höpfl, Harro. *Jesuit political thought. The Society of Jesus and the State, c. 1540–1630*. Cambridge: Cambridge University Press, 2004.

Hunt, Lynn, ed. *The new cultural history*. Berkeley: University of California Press, 1989.

Hunter, David G. "Vigilantius of Calagurris and Victricius of Rouen: Ascetics, Relics, and Clerics in Late Roman Gaul." *Journal of Early Christian Studies* 7, no. 3 (1999), pp. 401–430.

Huppert, George. *The Idea of Perfect History: Historical Erudition and Historical Philosophy in Renaissance France*. Urbana: University of Illinois Press, 1970.

Ianziti, Gary. *Humanistic Historiography under the Sforzas: Politics and Propaganda in Fifteenth-Century Milan*. Oxford: Oxford University Press, 1988.

———. *Writing History in Renaissance Italy: Leonardo Bruni and the Uses of the Past.* Cambridge, MA: Harvard University Press, 2012.

Jacquette, Dale. "Wittgenstein on lying as a language-game." In Danièle Moyal-Sharrock, ed. *The Third Wittgenstein. The post-"Investigations" works.* Farnham: Ashgate, 2004, pp. 159–176.

Jardine, Lisa. "Lorenzo Valla: Academic Skepticism and the New Humanist Dialectic." In Myles Burnyeat, ed., *The Skeptical Tradition.* Berkeley: University of California Press, 1983, pp. 253–286.

Jones, David Martin. *Conscience and Allegiance in Seventeenth-Century England. The political significance of oaths and engagements.* Rochester, NY: University of Rochester Press, 1999.

Jonsen, Albert R., and Stephen Toulmin. *The abuse of casuistry. A history of moral reasoning.* Berkeley: University of California Press, 1988.

Kahn, Victoria. *Rhetoric, Prudence, and Skepticism in the Renaissance.* Ithaca, NY: Cornell University Press, 1985.

Kelley, Donald R. "Historia integra: François Baudouin and his conception of history." *Journal of the History of Ideas* 25 (1964), pp. 35–57.

———. *Foundations of Modern Historical Scholarship: Language, Law, and History in the French Renaissance.* New York: Columbia University Press, 1970.

———. "Between history and system." In Gianna Pomata and Nancy Siraisi, eds., *Historia: Empiricism and Erudition in early modern Europe.* Cambridge, MA: Harvard University Press, 2005, pp. 211–237.

———, and David Sacks, eds. *The Historical Imagination in early modern Britain: History, Rhetoric, and Fiction, 1500–1800.* Cambridge: Cambridge University Press, 1997.

Kennedy, George A. *Aristotle on Rhetoric. A theory of civic discourse.* Oxford: Oxford University Press, 2007.

Klibansky, Raymond, and H. J. Paton, eds. *Philosophy and History. Essays presented to Ernst Cassirer.* Oxford: Clarendon Press, 1936.

Koselleck, Reinhart. *Futures Past: On the Semantics of Historical Time.* English trans. by Keith Tribe. Cambridge, MA: MIT Press, 1985.

Kristeller, Paul Oskar. "Rhetoric in Medieval and Renaissance Culture." In James J. Murphy, ed. *Renaissance Eloquence. Studies in the Theory and Practice of Renaissance Rhetoric.* Berkeley: University of California Press, 1983, pp. 1–19.

LaCapra, Dominick. *Rethinking intellectual history: texts, contexts, language.* Ithaca, NY: Cornell University Press, 1983.

———. *History and Criticism.* Ithaca, NY: Cornell University Press, 1985.

———. *History and reading: Tocqueville, Foucault, French studies.* Toronto: University of Toronto Press, 2000.

Lake, Peter, and Michael C. Questier, eds. *Conformity and Orthodoxy in the English Church, c. 1560–1660.* Woodbridge: Boydell Press, 2000.

Lamberigts, Mathijs, and Leo Kenis, eds. *L'Augustinisme à l'ancienne faculté de théologie de Louvain.* Louvain: Leuven University Press, 1994.

Lauro, Agostino. "Baronio, De Luca e il potere temporale della chiesa." In R. De Maio, L. Gulia, A. Mazzacane, eds., *Baronio storico e la Controriforma.* Sora: Centro di Studi Sorani "Vincenzo Patriarca," 1982, pp. 361–418.

Lavenia, Vincenzo. *L'infamia e il perdono. Tributi, pene e confessione nella teologia morale della prima età moderna.* Bologna: Il Mulino, 2004.

Leites, Edmund, ed. *Conscience and casuistry in early modern Europe.* Cambridge: Cambridge University Press, 2002.

Levine, Joseph M. *Humanism and History: origins of modern English historiography.* Ithaca, NY: Cornell University Press, 1987.

———. *The autonomy of history: truth and method from Erasmus to Gibbon.* Chicago: University of Chicago Press, 1999.

Lohr, Charles H. "Renaissance Latin Aristotle Commentaries." *Studies in the Renaissance* 21 (1974), pp. 228–289; *Renaissance Quarterly* 28 (1975), pp. 689–741; 29 (1976), pp. 714–745; 30 (1977), pp. 681–741; 31 (1978), pp. 532–603; 32 (1979), pp. 529–580; 33 (1980), pp. 623–735; 35 (1982), pp. 164–256.

Long, A. A., and D. N. Sedley. *The Hellenistic Philosophers*. 2 vols. Cambridge: Cambridge University Press, 1987.

Lyon, Gregory B. "Baudouin, Flacius and the plan for the Magdeburg Centuries." *Journal of the History of Ideas* 64 (2003), pp. 253–272.

Lyotard, Jean-François. *The Postmodern Condition: A Report on Knowledge*. English trans. Minneapolis: University of Minnesota Press, 1974.

———. *Political writings*. English trans. Bill Readings and Kevin P. Geiman. Minneapolis: University of Minnesota Press, 1993.

Mack, Peter. *Renaissance Argument. Valla and Agricola in the traditions of rhetoric and dialectic*. Leiden: Brill, 1993.

———. *A History of Renaissance Rhetoric 1380–1620*. Oxford: Oxford University Press, 2011.

Maia Neto, José R. "Academic Skepticism in Early Modern Philosophy." *Journal of the History of Ideas* 58, no. 2 (1997), pp. 199–220.

Malloch, A. E. "Father Henry Garnet's *Treatise of equivocation*." *Recusant History* 15 (1981), pp. 387–395.

Mannucci, Francesco Luigi. *La vita e le opere di Agostino Mascardi*. Atti della Società Ligure di Storia Patria, vol. XLII. Genoa, 1908.

Maryks, Robert A. *Saint Cicero and the Jesuits. The Influence of the Liberal Arts on the Adoption of Moral Probabilism*. Farnham: Ashgate, 2008.

Mastellone, Salvo. "Tommaso Bozio l'intransigente amico del Baronio, teorico dell'ordine ecclesiastico." In R. De Maio, L. Gulia, A. Mazzacane, eds., *Baronio storico e la Controriforma*, Sora: Centro di Studi Sorani "Vincenzo Patriarca," 1982 pp. 219–230.

Maylender, Michele. *Storia delle Accademie d'Italia*. 5 vols. Bologna: Cappelli, 1926–30.

Megill, Allan, ed. *Rethinking Objectivity*. Durham: Duke University Press, 1994.

———. *Historical Knowledge, Historical Error: A Contemporary Guide to Practice*. Chicago: University of Chicago Press, 2007.

McCuaig, William. *Carlo Sigonio. The changing world of the late Renaissance*. Princeton, NJ: Princeton University Press, 1989.

McGinness, Frederick J. "The Collegio Romano, the University of Roma, and the decline and rise of rhetoric in the late Cinquecento." *Roma moderna e contemporanea* 3 (1995), pp. 601–624.

———. *Right Thinking and Sacred Oratory in Counter-Reformation Rome*. Princeton, NJ: Princeton University Press, 1995.

Merolla, Riccardo. "L'Accademia dei Desiosi." In id., ed., *L'Accademia dei Desiosi, Storia e Testo*. Rome: Carocci, 2008 pp. 5–43.

———, ed. *L'Accademia dei Desiosi. Storia e Testo*. Rome: Carocci, 2008.

Michel, Alain. *Les rapports de la rhétorique et de la philosophie dans l'oeuvre de Cicéron. Recherches sur les fondements philosophiques de l'art de persuader*. Louvain: Peeters, 2003.

Momigliano, Arnaldo. "Ancient history and the antiquarian." *Journal of the Warburg and Courtauld Institutes* 13 (1950), pp. 282–315, now in *Studies in Historiography*. London: Weidenfeld and Nicolson, 1966, pp. 1–39.

———. "Pagan and Christian historiography in the fourth century A.D." In id., *Terzo contributo alla storia degli studi classici e del mondo antico*. Rome: Edizioni di Storia e Letteratura, 1966, I, pp. 87–109 (originally published as "The conflict between Paganism and Christianity in the fourth century." Oxford: Clarendon Press, 1963, pp. 79–99).

———. "The Herodotean and the Thucydidean Tradition." In id., *The Classical Foundations of Modern Historiography*. Berkeley: University of California Press, 1990, pp. 29–53.

———. "The Origins of Ecclesiastical Historiography." In id., *The Classical Foundations of Modern Historiography*, Berkeley: University of California Press, 1990, pp. 132–152.

———. "The rise of antiquarian research." In id., *The Classical Foundations of Modern Historiography*, Berkeley: University of California Press, 1990, pp. 54–79.

Monfasani, John. *George of Trebizond. A biography and a study of his rhetoric and logic*. Leiden: Brill, 1976.

———. "Episodes of anti-Quintilianism in the Italian Renaissance: quarrels on the orator as a *vir bonus* and rhetoric as the *scientia bene dicendi*." *Rhetorica* 10, no. 2 (1992), pp. 119–138, now in id., *Language and Learning*, ch. 3.

———. *Language and Learning in Renaissance Italy*, Farnham: Ashgate, 1994.

Moran, Richard. 'Artifice and Persuasion: the work of metaphor in the *Rhetoric*.' In Amélie Oksenberg Rorty, ed., *Essays on Aristotle's "Rhetoric"*. Berkeley: University of California Press, 1996, pp. 385–398.

Moss, Jean Dietz. "The rhetoric course at the Collegio Romano in the latter half of the sixteenth century." *Rhetorica* 4, no. 2 (1986), pp. 137–151.

Most, Glenn W. "Rhetorik und Hermeneutik: Zur Konstitution der Neuzeitlichkeit." *Antike und Abendland* 30 (1984), pp. 62–79.

Mouchel, Christian. *Cicéron et Sénèque dans la rhétorique de la Renaissance*. Marburg: Hitzeroth, 1990.

——. "Les rhétoriques post-tridentines (1570–1600): La fabrique d'une société chrétienne." In Fumaroli, ed., *Histoire de la rhétorique dans l'Europe moderne (1450–1950)*. Paris: Presses Universitaires de France, 1999, pp. 431–497.

Murphy, James J. "The scholastic condemnation of rhetoric in the commentary of Giles of Rome on the *Rhetoric* of Aristotle." Now in id., *Latin Rhetoric and Education in the Middle Ages and Renaissance*. Farnham: Ashgate, 2005, chapter V.

——, ed. *Renaissance Eloquence. Studies in the Theory and Practice of Renaissance Rhetoric*. Berkeley: University of California Press, 1983.

——, and Lawrence D. Green. *Renaissance Rhetoric Short-Title Catalogue, 1460–1700*. Farnham: Ashgate, 2006.

Notomi, Noburu. *The Unity of Plato's "Sophist" between the Sophist and the Philosopher*. Cambridge: Cambridge University Press, 1999.

Oakley, Francis. *Omnipotence, Covenant, & Order. An excursion in the history of ideas from Abelard to Leibniz*. Ithaca, NY: Cornell University Press, 1984.

——. "The Absolute and Ordained Power of God in Sixteenth- and Seventeenth-Century Theology." *Journal of the History of Ideas* 59, no. 3 (1998), pp. 437–461.

O'Malley, John W. *Praise and Blame in Renaissance Rome: Rhetoric, Doctrine, and Reform in the Sacred Orators of the Papal Court, c. 1450–1521*. Durham, NC: Duke University Press, 1979.

——. "Content and Rhetorical Forms in Sixteenth-Century Treatises on Preaching." In James J. Murphy, ed. *Renaissance Eloquence. Studies in the Theory and Practice of Renaissance Rhetoric*. Berkeley: University of California Press, 1983, pp. 238–252.

——. *The first Jesuits*. Cambridge, MA: Harvard University Press, 1993.

——, ed. *The Jesuits: cultures, sciences, and the arts, 1540–1773*, vol. I. Toronto: University of Toronto Press, 1999. Vol. II, 2006.

Osmond, Patricia J. "*Princeps Historiae Romanae*: Sallust in Renaissance Political Thought." *Memoirs of the American Academy in Rome* XL (1995), pp. 101–143.

Panofsky, Erwin. *Studies in Iconology. Humanistic Themes in the art of the Renaissance*. Oxford: Oxford University Press, 1939.

Paravicini-Bagliani, Agostino. *The Pope's Body*. Chicago: University of Chicago Press, 2000.

Pastore, Stefania. "A proposito di *Matteo 18,15*. *Correctio fraterna* e Inquisitione nella Spagna del Cinquecento." *Rivista Storica Italiana* 113 (2001), pp. 323–368.

——. *Il Vangelo e la Spada. L'inquisizione di Castiglia e i suoi critici*. Rome: Edizioni di Storia e Letteratura, 2003.

Patterson, W. B. *King James VI and I and the Reunion of Christendom*. Cambridge: Cambridge University Press, 2000.

Pereira, José. *Suárez between Scholasticism and modernity*. Milwaukee: Marquette University Press, 2006.

Pereña Luciano, et al. *"De iuramento fidelitatis." Estudio Preliminar*. Madrid: Consejo Superior de Investigaciones Científicas, Escuela Española de la Paz, 1979.

Petrucci, Enzo. *Ecclesiologia e politica. Momenti di storia del papato medievale*. Rome: Carocci, 2001.

Pettegree, Andrew. "Nicodemism and the English Reformation." In id., *Marian Protestantism: Six Studies*. Farnham: Ashgate, 1996, pp. 86–117.

Phillips, Mark Salber. "Distance and Historical Representation." *History Workshop Journal,*. 57 (2004), pp. 123–141.

——. *On Historical Distance*. New Haven, CT: Yale University Press, 2013

Piergentili, Pier Paolo. *L'Archivio dei Conti Beni di Gubbio (note storiche e inventario)*. Vatican City: Archivio Segreto Vaticano, 2003.

Po-chia Hsia, Ronnie. "The Catholic mission and translations in China, 1583–1700." In Peter Burke and Ronnie Po-chia Hsia, eds., *Cultural Translation in early modern Europe*. Cambridge: Cambridge University Press, 2007, pp. 39–51.

Polman, Pontien. *L'élément historique dans la controverse religieuse du XVIe siècle*. Gembloux: Duculot, 1932.

Pomata, Gianna, and Nancy Siraisi, eds. *Historia: Empiricism and Erudition in early modern Europe*. Cambridge, MA: Harvard University Press, 2005.

Popkin, Richard H. *The History of Scepticism from Savonarola to Bayle*. Oxford: Oxford University Press, 2003.

Prodi, Paolo. *Il Sacramento del Potere: il Giuramento Politico nella Storia Costituzionale dell'Occidente*. Bologna: Il Mulino, 1992.

——. *Una storia della giustizia. Dal pluralismo dei fori al moderno dualismo tra coscienza e diritto*. Bologna: Il Mulino, 2000.

Prosperi, Adriano. *Tribunali della coscienza*. Turin: Einaudi, 1996.

——. *"America e Apocalisse" e altri saggi*. Pisa: Istituti Editoriali Poligrafici Internazionali, 1999.

Pullapilly, Cyriac K. *Caesar Baronius. Counter-Reformation Historian*. Notre Dame, IN: University of Notre Dame Press, 1975.

Quantin, Jean-Louis. "Reason and reasonableness in French ecclesiastical scholarship." *Huntington Library Quarterly* 74, no. 3 (2011), pp. 401–436.

Questier, Michael C. *Conversion, Politics and Religion in England, 1580–1625*. Cambridge: Cambridge University Press, 1996.

Raimondi, Ezio. *Anatomie Secentesche*. Pisa: Nistri-Lischi, 1966.

Revel, Jacques, and Lynn Hunt, eds. *Histories. French construction of the past*. New York: New Press, 1995.

Ricoeur, Paul. *The rule of the metaphor. Multi-disciplinary studies of the creation of meaning in language*. English trans. Toronto: University of Toronto Press, 1977.

——. *Time and Narrative*. 3 vols. English trans. Chicago: University of Chicago Press, 1984–5.

——. "Between Rhetoric and Poetic." In Amélie Oksenberg Rorty, ed., *Essays on Aristotle's "Rhetoric"*. Berkeley: University of California Press, 1996, pp. 324–384.

——. *Memory, History, Forgetting*. English trans. Chicago: University of Chicago Press, 2004.

——. *History and Truth*. English trans. Evanston, IL: Northwestern University Press, 2007.

Riondato, Ezio, ed. *Dall'Accademia dei Ricovrati all'Accademia Galileiana*. Padua: Accademia Galileiana di Scienze, Lettere ed Arti, 2001.

Rorty, Amélie Oksenberg, ed. *Essays on Aristotle's "Rhetoric"*. Berkeley: University of California Press, 1996.

Rose, Elliot. *Cases of Conscience. Alternatives open to Recusants and Puritans under Elizabeth I and James I*. Cambridge: Cambridge University Press, 1975.

Salmon, John H. M. "Precept, example, and truth: Degory Wheare and the *ars historica*." In Donald R. Kelley and David H. Sacks, eds., *The Historical Imagination*. Cambridge: Cambridge University Press, 1997, pp. 11–36.

Sangalli, Maurizio. "Di Paolo Beni e di una riforma dello studio di Padova (1619)." *Studi veneziani* 42 (2001), pp. 57–134.

——. "Paolo Beni: da gesuita a Ricovrato." In Ezio Riondato, ed., *Dall'Accademia dei Ricovrati all'Accademia Galileiana*. Padua: Accademia Galileiana di scienze, lettere ed arti, 2001, pp. 491–503.

Saxl, Fritz. "Veritas filia temporis." In R. Klibansky and H. J. Paton, eds., *Philosophy and History. Essays presented to Ernst Cassirer*. Oxford: Clarendon Press, 1936, pp. 197–222.

Scarpati, Claudio, and Eraldo Bellini. *Il vero e il falso dei poeti. Tasso Tesauro Pallavicino Muratori*. Milan: Vita e Pensiero, 1990.

Schiffman, Zachary Sayre. *On the Threshold of Modernity: Relativism in the French Renaissance*. Baltimore: Johns Hopkins University Press, 1991.

——. *The Birth of the Past*. Baltimore: Johns Hopkins University Press, 2011.

Schmitt, Charles B. *Gianfrancesco Pico della Mirandola (1469–1533) and his critique of Aristotle*. The Hague: Martinus Nijhoff, 1967.

Schreiner, Susan E. *Are you Alone Wise? The Search for Certainty in the Early modern Era*. Oxford: Oxford University Press, 2011.

Schwartz, Daniel, ed. *Interpreting Suárez*. Cambridge: Cambridge University Press, 2012.

Scorraille, Raoul de. *François Suarez de la Compagnie de Jésus*. 2 vols. Paris: P. Lethielleux, 1912.

Searle, John R. *Speech Acts. An essay in the philosophy of language*. Cambridge: Cambridge University Press, 1969.

——. *Expression and Meaning: Studies in the theory of speech acts*. Cambridge: Cambridge University Press, 1979.

Seaward, Paul. "Clarendon, Tacitism, and the Civil Wars of Europe." *Huntington Library Quarterly* 68 (2005), pp. 289–311.

Seigel, Jerrold E. *Rhetoric and Philosophy in Renaissance Humanism. The Union of Eloquence and Wisdom. Petrarch to Valla*. Princeton, NJ: Princeton University Press, 1968.

Shapin, Steven. *A Social History of Truth. Civility and Science in Seventeenth-Century England*. Chicago: University of Chicago Press, 1995.

Shapiro, Barbara J. *Probability and Certainty in Seventeenth-Century England*. Princeton, NJ: Princeton University Press, 1983.

——. *"Beyond reasonable doubt" and "probable cause." Historical Perspectives on the Anglo-American Law of Evidence*. Berkeley: University of California Press, 1991.

Shuger, Debora K. *Sacred Rhetoric. The Christian Grand Style in the English Renaissance*. Princeton, NJ: Princeton University Press, 1988.

——. *Censorship and Cultural Sensibility. The Regulation of Language in Tudor-Stuart England*. Philadelphia: University of Pennsylvania Press, 2006.

Skinner, Quentin. *The Foundations of Modern Political Thought*. 2 vols. Cambridge: Cambridge University Press, 1978.

Snyder, Jon R. *Dissimulation and the Culture of Secrecy in early modern Europe*. Berkeley: University of California Press, 2009.

Sommerville, Johann P. "The 'new art of lying': equivocation, mental reservation, and casuistry." In Edmund Leites, ed. *Conscience and casuistry in early modern Europe*. Cambridge: Cambridge University Press, 2002, pp. 159–184.

Sommervogel, Carlos. *Bibliothèque de la Compagnie de Jésus*. Brussels: Schepens; Paris: Pichard, 1890–1912.

Spiegel, Gabrielle M. *Romancing the Past: The Rise of Vernacular Prose Historiography in Thirteenth-Century France*. Berkeley: University of California Press, 1995.

——. *The Past as Text: The Theory and Practice of Medieval Historiography*. Baltimore: Johns Hopkins University Press, 1999.

Spini, Giorgio. "I trattatisti dell'arte storica della Controriforma Italiana." *Quaderni di Belfagor* 1 (1948), pp. 109–136. English trans. by Eric Cochrane as "Historiography: The art of history in the Italian Counter Reformation," in id., ed., *The Late Italian Renaissance, 1525–1630*. London: Macmillan, 1970, pp. 91–133.

Stella, Pietro. *Il Giansenismo in Italia*. 3 vols. Rome: Edizioni di Storia e Letteratura, 2006.

Struever, Nancy S. *The Language of History in the Renaissance*. Princeton, NJ: Princeton University Press, 1970.

——. *Theory as Practice. Ethical inquiry in the Renaissance*. Chicago: University of Chicago Press, 1992.

——. *The History of Rhetoric and the Rhetoric of History*. Farnham: Ashgate, 2009.

——. *Rhetoric, Modality, Modernity*. Chicago: University of Chicago Press, 2009.

——, and B. Vickers. "Rhetoric and the Pursuit of Truth: Language Change in the Seventeenth and Eighteenth Centuries." Seminar Paper Series, William Andrews Clark Memorial Library. Los Angeles, 1985.

Tejero, Eloy. "El Doctor Navarro en la historia de la doctrina canónica y moral." In *Estudios sobre el Doctor Navarro en el IV centenario de la muerte de Martín de Azpilcueta*. Pamplona: EUNSA, 1988, pp. 125–180.

Tellechea Idígoras, José Ignacio. *El Arzobispo Carranza y su tiempo*. 2 vols. Madrid: Ediciones Guadarrama, 1968.

——. *El Arzobispo Carranza: "Tiempos Recios"*. 4 vols. Salamanca: Universidad Pontificia de Salamanca, 2003-2007.

Tronzo, William, ed. *St. Peter's in the Vatican*. Cambridge: Cambridge University Press, 2005.

Turchetti, Mario. *Concordia o tolleranza? François Baudouin e i "moyenneurs"*. Geneva: Droz, 1984.

Turrini, Miriam. *La coscienza e le leggi. Morale e diritto nei testi per la confessione nella prima età moderna*. Bologna: Il Mulino, 1991.

Tutino, Stefania. "Between Nicodemism and 'Honest' Dissimulation: The Society of Jesus in England." *Historical Research* 79, no. 206 (2006), pp. 534–553.

——. *Empire of Souls. Bellarmine and the Christian commonwealth*. Oxford: Oxford University Press, 2010.

——. "'For the sake of the truth of history and of the Catholic doctrines': History, documents, and dogma in Cesare Baronio's *Annales Ecclesiastici*," *Journal of Early Modern History*, no. 17 (2013), pp. 125–159

Van Eijl, Edmond J. M. "La controverse louvaniste autour de la grâce et du libre arbitre à la fin du XVIe siècle." In Mathijs Lamberigts and Leo Kenis, eds., *L'Augustinisme à l'ancienne faculté de théologie de Louvain*. Louvain: Leuven University Press, 1994, pp. 208–282.

Van Liere, Katherine, Simon Ditchfield and Howard Louthan, eds., *Sacred History. Uses of the Christian Past in the Renaissance World*. Oxford: Oxford University Press, 2012.

van Sull, Charles. *Leonard Lessius, 1554–1623*. Louvain: Museum Lessianum, 1930.

Vasoli, Cesare. *La Dialettica e la Retorica dell'Umanesimo. "Invenzione" e "metodo" nella cultura del XV e XVI secolo*. Milan: Feltrinelli, 1968.

——. *Francesco Patrizi da Cherso*. Rome: Edizioni di Storia e Letteratura, 1989.

Vickers, Brian. *In defence of rhetoric*. Oxford: Clarendon Press, 1988.

Wabuda, Susan. "Equivocation and recantation during the English Reformation: The 'subtle shadow' of Dr. Edward Crome." *Journal of Ecclesiastical History* 44 (1993), pp. 224–242.

Walsham, Alexandra. *Church Papists: Catholicism, Conformity and Confessional Polemic in Early Modern England*. Woodbridge: Boydell Press, 1993.

——. "'Yielding to the Extremity of the Time': Conformity, Orthodoxy and the post-Reformation Catholic Community." In *Conformity and Orthodoxy in the English Church, c. 1560–1660*, eds., Peter Lake and Michael Questier. Woodbridge: Boydell Press, 2000, pp. 211–236.

——. "Ordeals of Conscience: Casuistry, Conformity and Confessional Identity in Post-Reformation England." In *Contexts of Conscience in Early Modern Europe*, eds. Harald E. Braun and Edward Vallance. Basingstoke: Palgrave Macmillan, 2004, pp. 32–48.

Watts, Derek A. *Cardinal de Retz: the ambiguities of a seventeenth-century mind*. Oxford: Oxford University Press, 1980.

White, Hayden. *Metahistory: The Historical Imagination in Nineteenth-Century Europe*. Baltimore: Johns Hopkins University Press, 1973.

——. *Figural Realism: studies in the mimesis effect*. Baltimore: Johns Hopkins University Press, 1999.

——. *The Fiction of Narrative: Essays on History, Literature and Theory, 1957–2007*, ed. Robert Doran. Baltimore: Johns Hopkins University Press, 2010.

Wickenden, Nicholas. *G. J. Vossius and the Humanist Concept of History*. Assen, Netherlands: Van Gorcum, 1993.

Wilcox, Donald J. *The Measure of Times Past. Pre-Newtonian Chronologies and the Rhetoric of Relative Time*. Chicago: University of Chicago Press, 1987.

Wittgenstein, Ludwig. *Philosophical Investigations*, trans. G. E. M. Anscombe. Upper Saddle River, NJ: Prentice Hall, 1958.

Woolf, Daniel R. *The Idea of History in early Stuart England: Erudition, Ideology and the "Light of Truth" from the Accession of James I to the Civil War*. Toronto: University of Toronto Press, 1990.

——. *Reading History in early modern England*. Cambridge: Cambridge University Press, 2000.

Wootton, David. "The fear of God in early modern political theory." *Historical Papers / Communications historiques* 18, no. 1 (1983), pp. 56–80.

Yates, Frances A. *The Art of Memory*. Chicago: University of Chicago Press, 2001.

Zagorin, Perez. *Ways of Lying. Dissimulation, Persecution and Conformity in early modern Europe*. Cambridge, MA: Harvard University Press, 1990.

Zen, Stefano. *Baronio storico. Controriforma e crisi del metodo umanistico*. Naples: Vivarium, 1994.

——. "Cesare Baronio sulla Donazione di Costantino tra critica storica e autocensura (1590–1607)." *Annali della Scuola Normale Superiore* 2, no. 1 (2010), pp. 179–219.

INDEX

Abbot, George: *Quaestiones sex* 28
absolve, -ution: from oaths 186–189; in a
  sacramental confession 14, 16, 19–20, 25,
  172–174, 176–178. *See also* confession
Accademia degli Umoristi 42
Accademia dei Desiosi 42–43
Acquaviva, Claudio 91–92, 95, 165, 175–176,
  180–182
Ad evitanda 91–92, 94
Ado of Vienne 104
adoration, act of: and language 12, 18; and the
  relics of martyrs 75, 78–79
adultery 17–19
Agamben, Giorgio 9, 151–152, 156, 172, 178,
  189–190
Alfaro, José: *Observationes* 37–39
Allen, Cardinal William 29
Alexander of Aphrodisias 126–132, 134–135
Alumbrados 20
ambiguity: and history 47, 60; and
  language 15–19, 21, 25–26, 34, 37,
  39, 149; and rhetoric 109, 123; and
  oaths 162–164, 168, 170–171, 183
amphibology 15, 163. *See also* equivocation
analogy: and language 12; and historical
  representation 72; and rhetoric/
  dialectic 129–130
anti-probabilist. *See* probabilist: anti-probabilist
antiquarian(s) 7, 40, 42, 58, 60, 68, 81, 85, 102
Aquinas, Thomas 13–14, 38, 91, 107, 154–156,
  159, 164, 174. *See also* Scholastic
Aragón, Pedro de 25
archives 45, 49–50, 59–60
Archytas 143
Arévalo, Bernardino de 14
Aristotle/Aristotelian 16, 21, 30, 42, 46, 52,
  54–55, 64–65, 68, 93, 96–102, 109–111,
  115–116, 119–123, 125–136, 139–146,

154; *De Partibus Animalium* 110;
  Poetics 54–55, 64–65, 97, 116, 144;
  Posterior Analytics 16; *Prior Analytics* 128;
  Problemata 141; *Rhetoric* 52, 99–101,
  109–110, 116, 119–123, 126–127,
  129, 133–134, 139–143; *Sophistical
  Refutations* 127; *Topics* 125–127, 129
ars historiae 7, 40, 46, 52, 55, 69, 71, 102
Augustine: and annals 89; and candles 78, 81;
  De Civitate Dei 108; on language 11–13,
  17, 20–21, 23; on passions 133;
  Retractationes 16
Austin, John L. 161–162, 172
authority: political and oaths 150–151, 162–
  163, 179, 184–188; public and historical
  records 59; public and oaths 150–151,
  156, 161, 163, 170–171, 178, 184, 188;
  religious/ecclesiastical 156, 185–188
Azor, Juan 25
Azpilcueta, Martín de. *See* Navarrus

Bañez, Domingo 27, 30–32, 39
Barberini, Cardinal Francesco 43, 49, 51
Barberini, Maffeo. *See* Urban VIII
Barbaro, Ermolao 142
Barnes, John: *Dissertatio contra
  aequivocatores* 33–36, 188
Baronio, Cesare: *Annales* 5–7, 68, 74–88
Baroque 55, 98–99, 147
Bede 104
being-in-time 2, 67. *See also* temporal/
  temporality *and* time
Bell, Thomas 29, 92
Bellamy, Anne 28
Bellarmine, Robert: *Controversia de ecclesia
  triumphante* 78–80; and *de auxiliis* 94,
  166. See also *de auxiliis*
Bellini, Eraldo 50, 98